Kingston upon Hull City Libraries
WITHDRAWN
FROM STOCK
FOR SALE

ISLANDS IN CHINA
STEPS TO THE BED OF GOD

**A journey that leads
to the meaning of life**

BOOK TWO

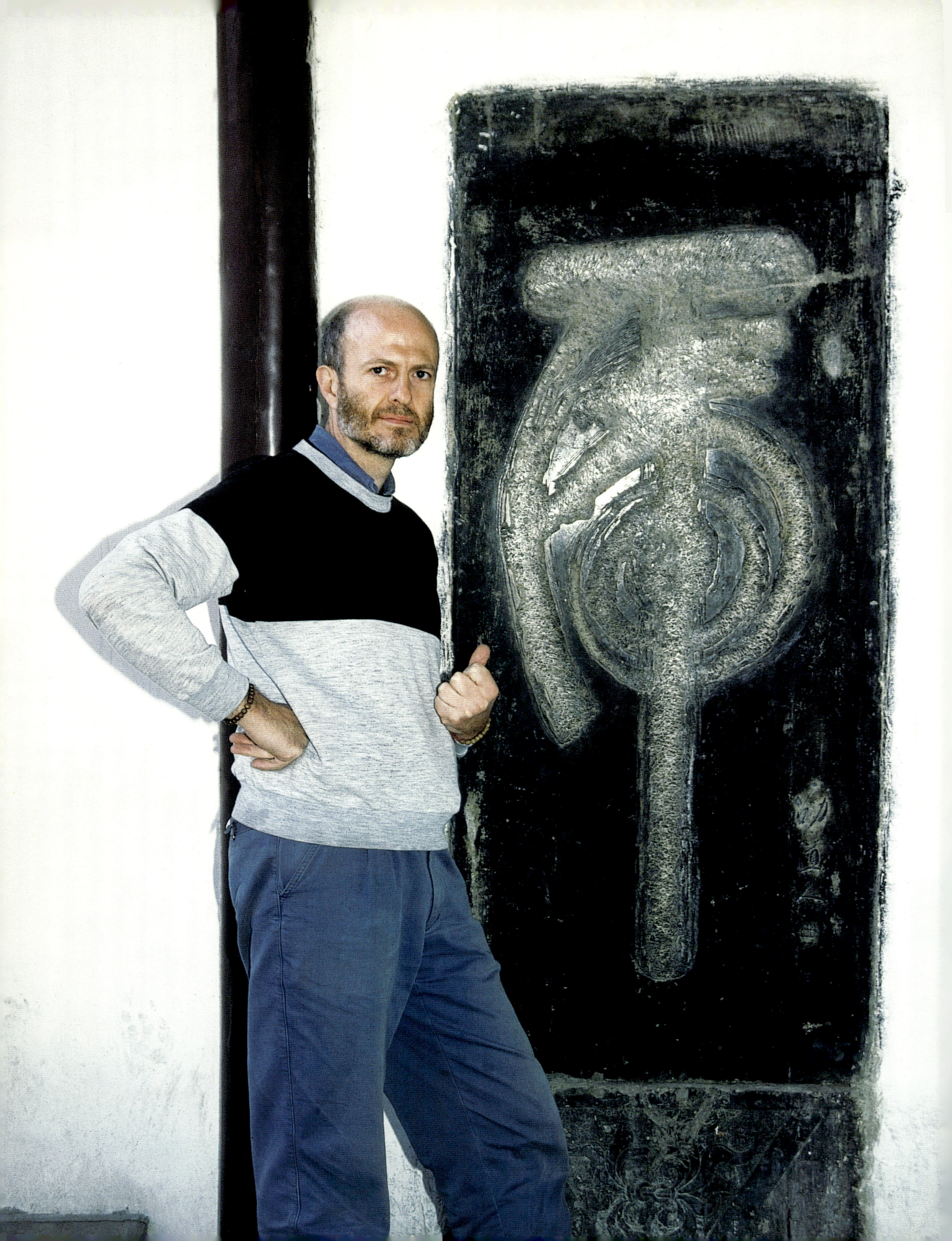

ISLANDS IN CHINA
STEPS TO THE BED OF GOD

BOOK TWO

PETER STANGER

PAGODA
PUBLISHING

Published 2003 by Pagoda Publishing
114A Rodmell Avenue, Saltdean, East Sussex BN2 8PJ, UK
ps@pagodapublishing.com   www.pagodapublishing.com

Copyright © Pagoda Publishing 2003
Copyright © Peter Stanger 2003
Photography © Peter Stanger 2003
CD © Pagoda Publishing 2003
All rights reserved. No part of this publication may be reproduced, stored in a retrieval system, or transmitted, in any form, or by any means, electronic, mechanical, photocopying, recording or otherwise, without prior written permission of the author or publisher.

British Library CIP (Cataloging in Publication) Data

Stanger, Peter
Islands in China: Steps to the Bed of God
Book Two
1. Stanger, Peter – Journeys – China
2. Spiritual biography
3. China – Description and travel
4. China – Civilization
1. Title
195.1.0459

ISBN number for this Book Two is 0 9539874 1 8
ISBN number for the set of Books One and Two is 0 9539874 2 6

Cover photograph shows the sunrise from the top of Huángshān. Frontispiece is of the author with the Chinese character for Tiger (hǔ), his shǔxiàng, the animal denoting the year of birth.
[photographed in Nánjīng Cháotiān Palace]

The translations of Chinese names and places are mainly the author's own. Eileen Aiping Gao assisted with some aspects of the Chinese language, particularly the tones of relatively obscure words.

Creative Director Christopher Impey
Design and layout Christopher Impey and Peter Stanger
Music track selection Peter Stanger
Text set in Bitstream Baskerville 10.25/12.25pt
Origination by DL Repro, London
Printed and bound in China

The publisher thanks David Horstead for his assistance with the printing of Book Two.

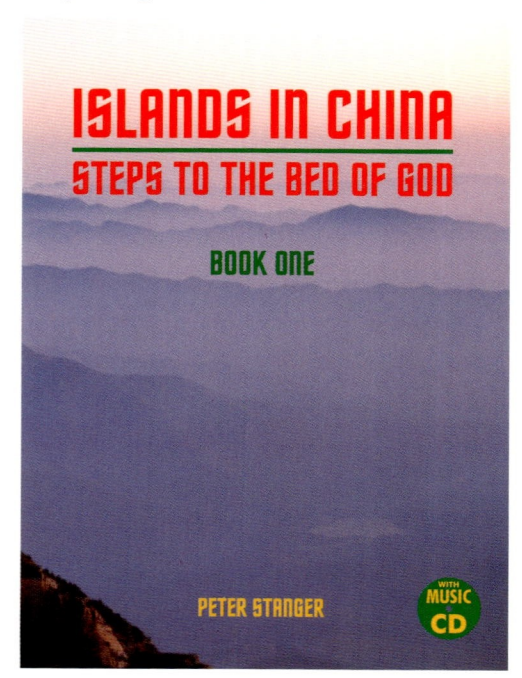

Book One was published in 2001.
ISBN number for Book One is 0 9539874 0 X

FOREWORD

This Book Two only makes sense if you read Book One beforehand. Being a journey and a story told equally through words and pictures, it is designed to be read in sequence. As glancing ahead spoils a thriller, leafing through the text and the author's photographs is best kept to a minimum.

Book Two completes the story.

With the 74-minute CD as an integral part of the experience, the music/photo sequences and moments of sound add a valuable depth and dimension in a way that has never previously been implemented in a book. Again, it is recommended that you curb your curiosity to sample the tracks prematurely. That done, the CD will continue afterwards to provide associated pleasure on its own. See page 10 for guidance on integrating the tracks with the book.

To the Korean fortune-teller who forecast about this book,
to God,
and
to Jong Seob

Changes will take place
when things come to a dead end,
and breakthroughs can be expected
when there is no way out.

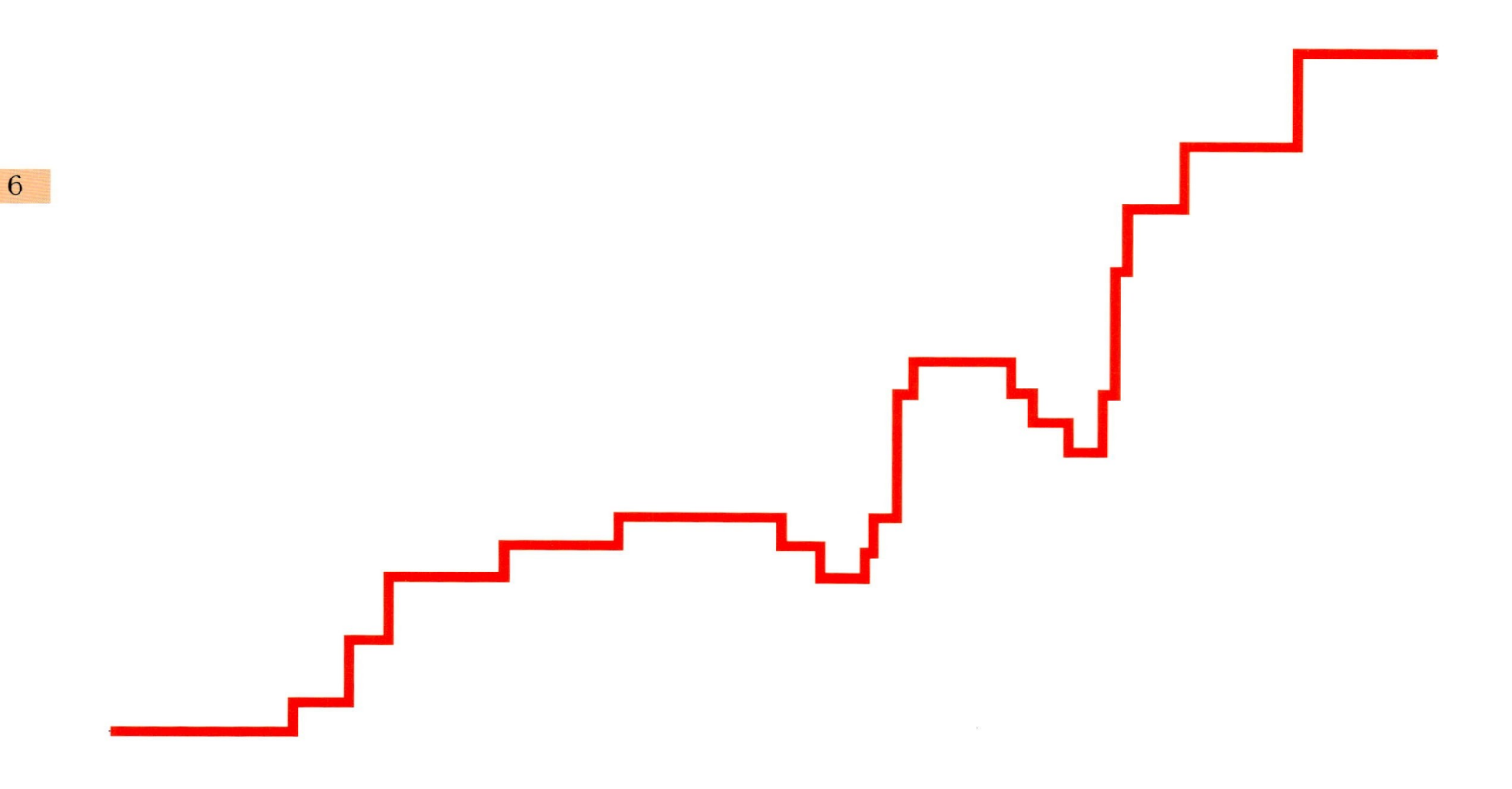

CONTENTS BOOK TWO

foreword	5
map of China and routes	8
preface	10
advice concerning the CD	10
pronunciation and tones	11
Chinese dynasties and dates	11

Part Two continued

map of route, chapters 12 and 13	12
chapter 12 **Huángshān**	13
Yíxìng	13
Jiǔhuáshān	15
Huángshān	18
chapter 13 **Pǔtuóshān**	64
two cities and a town	64
Pǔtuóshān	66
map detail of Pǔtuóshān	66

Part Three

map of route, chapters 14 to 22	78
chapter 14 **Yángshuò**	79
testing	98
chapter 15 **Guìzhōu Province**	103
map detail of route, Guìlín to Kǎilǐ	104
Zhàoxìng	106
Lángdé	111
Fēnpái	115
chapter 16 **Xīshuāngbǎnnà**	127
map detail of Xīshuāngbǎnnà	126
chapter 17 **Kūnmíng**	144
the Stone Forest	144
Why?	146
Kūnmíng	148
past, present and future	155
chapter 18 **Ruìlì and around**	159
chapter 19 **Dàlǐ**	167
Rift	174
anger	178
chapter 20 **Lìjiāng and Zhōngdiàn**	182
Lìjiāng	182
Zhōngdiàn	186
back to Lìjiāng	196
chapter 21 **Éméishān**	200
Lèshān	200
Éméishān	202
12 x 9	212
chapter 22 **Nánbù and end**	234
Chéngdū	234
Nánbù	235
Chóngqìng	240
the Three Gorges	244
Guǎngzhōu	247
Islands in China summary	250
chapter 23 **retrospective**	258
is and sunset	277

photos in the retrospective	294
supplemental	294
permissions	295
two inventions	296
photographic notes	296

music Part Two continued	297
music Part Three	298
index Book Two	300

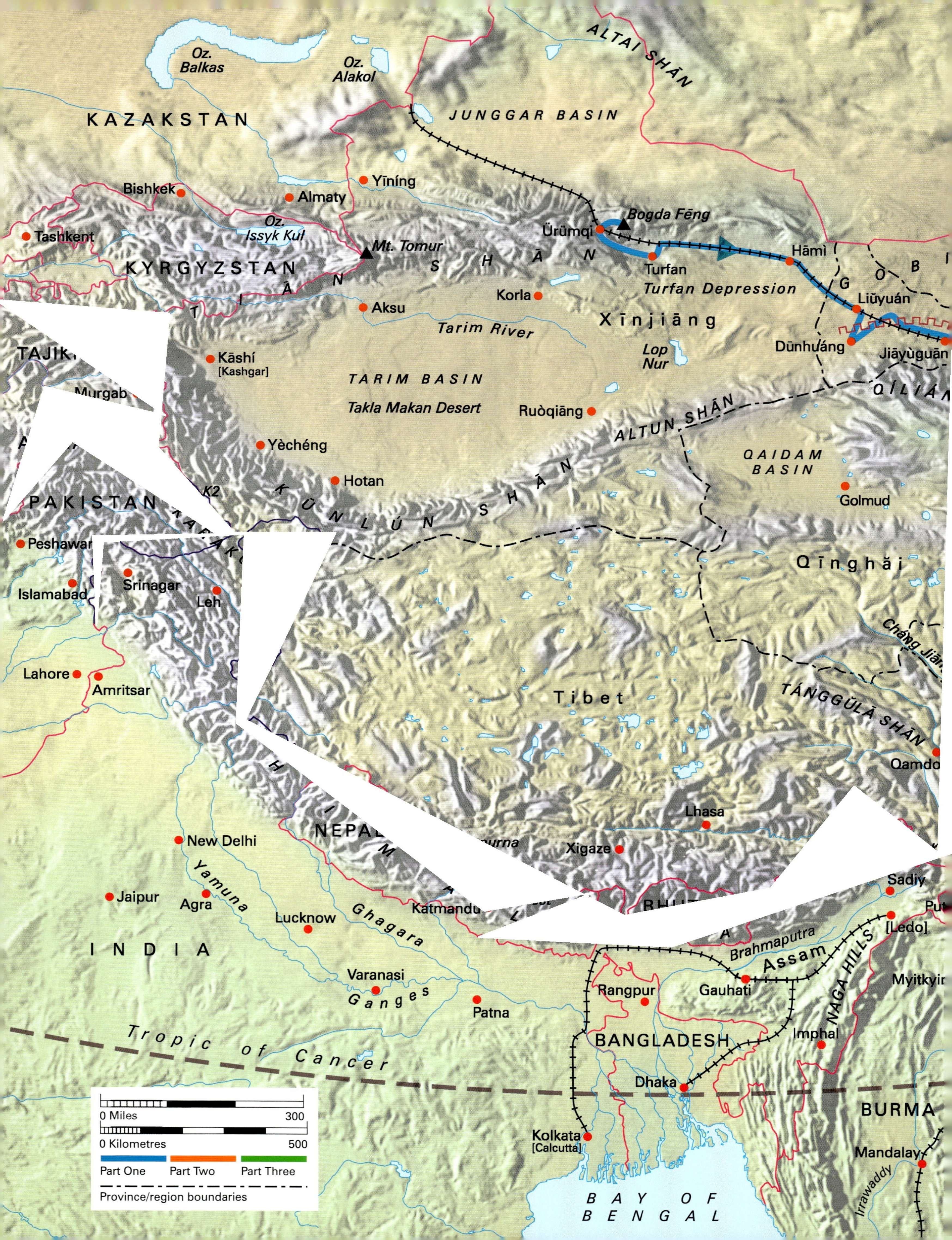

Oz. Balkas
Oz. Alakol
ALTAI SHĀN
JUNGGAR BASIN
KAZAKSTAN
Yīníng
Bishkek
Almaty
Oz. Issyk Kul
Tashkent
Mt. Tomur
Bogda Fēng
Ürümqi
Hāmì
GOBI
KYRGYZSTAN
TIĀN SHĀN
Turfan
Turfan Depression
Korla
Aksu
Liŭyuán
Tarim River
Xīnjiāng
Dūnhuáng
Jiāyùguān
Lop Nur
Kāshí [Kashgar]
TARIM BASIN
Takla Makan Desert
Murgab
Ruòqiāng
QILIAN
ALTUN SHĀN
Yèchéng
QAIDAM BASIN
Hotan
Golmud
PAKISTAN
K2
KŪNLÚN SHĀN
Peshawar
Qīnghǎi
Islamabad
Srinagar
Leh
Cháng Jiāng
Lahore
Amritsar
Tibet
TÁNGGŪLĀ SHĀN
Qamdo
Lhasa
NEPAL
Xigaze
New Delhi
Sadiy
Yamuna
Jaipur
Agra
Katmandu
[Ledo]
Lucknow
Ghagara
Brahmaputra
Assam
NAGA HILLS
Myitkyi
INDIA
Varanasi
Gauhati
Rangpur
Ganges
Patna
Imphal
BANGLADESH
Tropic of Cancer
Dhaka
BURMA
0 Miles 300
0 Kilometres 500
Kolkata [Calcutta]
Mandalay
Part One
Part Two
Part Three
Province/region boundaries
Irrawaddy
BAY OF BENGAL

MONGOLIA
DESERT
Inner Mongolia
Bāotóu
Huáng Hé
Great Wall
Yínchuān
Zhāngyè
Gānsù
Shaanxi
Qīnghǎi Lake
Xīníng
Lánzhōu
Tiānshuǐ
Màijīshān
Yellow River Huáng Hé
Wèi River
Yellow River
Yùnchéng
Hóng Dòng
Píngyáo
Tàiyuán
Dàtóng
Běijīng
Héngshān
Wǔtáishān
Chéngdé
Grand Canal
Tiānjīn
Shěnyáng
Liáoyáng
Yālù
NORTH KOREA
Sinŭiju
SEA OF JAPAN
P'yŏngyang
Korea Bay
Dàlián
Bó Hǎi
Wēihǎi
Inch'ŏn
Seoul
SOUTH KOREA
Kwangju
YELLOW SEA
Qīngdǎo
Jǐnán
Tàishān
Qūfù
Cheju Do
Zhèngzhōu
Yángzhōu
Nánjīng
Wúxī
Shànghǎi
Sūzhōu
Tàihú
Hángzhōu
Zhōushān I.
Shàoxīng
Tónglíng
Jiǔhuáshān
Huángshān
Yàndàngshān
EAST CHINA SEA
Wǔhàn
Yángzi River
Nánchāng
Sìchuān
Chéngdū
Éméishān
Gònggā Shān
Chángshā
Héngshān
Fúzhōu
Taipei [Táiběi]
TÁIWĀN
Xiàmén
Kaohsiung [Gāoxióng]
HÉNGDUÀN SHĀN
Zhōngdiàn
Lìjiāng
Dàlǐ
Salwe
Bǎoshān
AILAO MTS
Mekong
Kūnmíng
Yúnnán
Zhènyuǎn
Róngjiāng
Lóngshèng
Guìlín
Yángshuò
Guǎngzhōu
Macau
Hong Kong
Nánníng
SOUTH CHINA SEA
VIETNAM
Hanoi
Gulf of Tongkin
Hǎikǒu
Hǎinán I.
Jǐnghóng
LAOS
Louang Prabang
THAILAND

PREFACE

This book begins by continuing Part Two's journey from Book One, and in that sense the opening is not as normally encountered in a single volume. If you haven't read Book One for a while, it may reward you first to remind yourself of its episodes and ambience by flicking through the pages, since additionally several important references to those earlier incidents are made in Book Two.

The Cheju incident was described factually as it physically transpired, though unnecessary personal details were omitted, and it was as real a happening as eating a meal. In Book Two, portions of the subsequent personal events are portrayed as if on a different plane. They are just as genuine, but not in the common sense of our everyday lives. I do not tell the whole story in literal terms because that would distract the reader from the more important vision. Instead, I believe I distil what is the greater truth that applies to everyone. Given everything else in these books – the photographs, the essays, the music, the general attitude and approach of the author – the reader can decide whether to accept that is what is delivered.

So I urge the reader not to expect the private aspects to be explained, nor thereby to be disappointed or frustrated; rather to accept that they are omitted for a greater purpose and to concentrate on what that might be.

The journey continues to be related in the order that it occurred. Under the calculation that one picture is equivalent to a thousand words, Book Two features 364,000 words worth of colour photographs taken in China.

★ ★ ★

It has long been a frustrating aspect of the English language that it does not possess words that combine the third person pronouns, hence requiring interpolated phrases that interrupt the flow. I have devised the following, and recommend you quickly absorb them.

- *s/he* : she and/or he, pronounced 'sher-ee' – 's/he wore a coat'
- *h/his* : her and/or his, pronounced 'her-is' – 'h/his coat was grey'
- *h/him* : her and/or him, pronounced 'her-im' – 'led h/him to investigate'
- *h/himself* : herself and/or himself, pronounced 'her-imself' – 'seeing h/himself in the mirror'

They are used when the gender is immaterial, unknown, or refers to all sexes. They have been used sparingly; a sentence like 'S/he cleans the house while s/he goes to work' clearly does not add to the understanding of the human condition.

★ ★ ★

Approximate exchange rates at the time:
10 Chinese *yuán* (¥10) = £0.80, or US$1.30.

★ ★ ★

The utmost care has been taken to ensure that the text is sufficiently accurate without indulging in minute detail, and to choose words that convey relevant shades of meaning. In subjects as involved and wide-ranging as those discussed, there may be misleading choices of words, as well as false statements, despite facts being confirmed by different sources wherever possible. I humbly apologise for these.

ADVICE CONCERNING THE CD

The book can be read without playing the CD. However, as in movies or on television, the music adds a substantial dimension, well worth the arranging of a personal or portable player beside you, either with headphones or speakers. A main hi-fi system can also be winningly employed, particularly with remote control.

The advised place to listen to each track is given in the text. One of the tracks provides additional atmosphere as you continue to read. For a few it is suggested you cease reading and instead listen and reflect, perhaps looking back at some of the recent photographs and text. Others complement and add to a section of photographs without text, which are absorbed simultaneously ad lib. None of these require any expertise, musical knowledge, or preparation.

The greatest number are music/photo sequences, with the maximum effect achieved by listening to a set length of music while perusing one photograph, before continuing to the next. For these, basic instructions have been given before and during: most are easy and quick to assimilate. If they are not, I advise you ignore them and go by instinct the first time, without hurrying. After familiarisation with the instructions and the music, on a second run-through you will soon find you can turn the page precisely on the requisite cymbal crash, or whatever!

While beneficial, the synchronisation is not vital, so don't let it concern you: simply enjoy the music and the photographs together. During these music/photo sequences, if there are two or more photographs on a page, try and absorb only one at a time, which should lend a feeling of travel. Where deemed helpful, timings for the suggested start of photographs are given in parenthesis, as seen on the CD player's display screen.

You will soon learn to stop the machine before it proceeds to the next track – there are eight seconds in between for this purpose (up to track 12). If you wish to know what the music is after hearing it, see pages 297–299, which also contain related comments and information.

Musical terms used:
- *beat* the regular main pulse of a piece of music, as in *slow beats*
- *bar* a recurring pattern of beats, usually with a fixed number; so a waltz has 3 beats per bar
- *climax* the loudest or most exciting moment

In chapter 23 only:
- *tremolo* very fast multi-repetitions of a note, e.g. on a lute

PRONUNCIATION AND TONES

For Chinese words and places in the book, the modern *pīnyīn* ('spell sound') Roman alphabet equivalents are used, with some exceptions including *China* and *Confucius* that do not exist in the Chinese language. The tones of the vowels have been added to every Chinese word where appropriate and known – a first, of which I am aware, for any book covering China as a whole. For the little extra effort involved, it is well worthwhile imagining and hearing the sound of these as you read. On an *a* ('ah') vowel, the four main tones in *pǔtōnghuà* or simplified Mandarin are: *ā, á, ǎ* and *à*. They are all sung, and I mean sung not spoken. The first tone, *ā*, is like when the doctor asks you to say 'ah' while examining your throat – the pitch is fairly high, and remains horizontal or flat without varying. The second, *á*, commences at a lower pitch and slides back up. The third, *ǎ*, is more tricky – it begins lower still, sinks further down, then quickly slides up again! In practice, the third is often to my ears difficult to distinguish from the second. The fourth, *à*, returns to sanity by starting at a high pitch and promptly slides down.

When saying/singing Chinese words, slightly adapt the mouth to that of brushing your teeth – that will prevent you dropping your jaw too much, which is a tendency in Western speech. So the word *shān* (mountain), pronounced 'shahn', should not resonate at the bottom of the throat, but be pitched like a quiet shout, the pitch in this case remaining horizontal. You don't have to hold the note like Pavarotti – only momentarily.

As a guide, the following twelve words used in the books illustrate the basic principles of pronunciation.

the city Xī'ān, as 'Shee-'ahn'
tái (platform), as 'tie'
tiān (heaven), as 'tee-'ehn'
yuán (garden), as 'yü-'ehn'

the city Ürümqi, as 'Oo-'room-chee'
the city Luòyáng, as 'Loo/or-'yahng'
zhōu (island), as the name 'Jo'

the town Chéngdé, as 'Chung-der'
sì (temple), as 'ser'
the Yángzi River, as 'Yahng-tser'
Sìchuān Province, as "Tser-chooahn'
the city Guìlín, as 'Gway-leen'

x → sh, *i* often → ee, *a* → ah
ai → as 'eye'
usually *ian* → ee-ehn
after y and x, *ua* → üeh using German umlaut

u → oo as in 'choose', *q* → ch
o → as in 'or'
zh → j as in 'jug', *ou* → o as in 'slow'

eng → ung as in 'hung', *e* → er as in 'her'
after c, s, z and ch, sh, zh... *i* → er, as in 'her'
z (and *c*) → ts
sometimes *si* → tser
ui and *ei* → as in 'stay'

CHINESE DYNASTIES AND DATES

c.1600–c.1050 BC	**Shāng**	c.1300 BC Moses liberates Israelites from Egyptian slavery
c.1050–221 BC	**Zhōu (453–221 BC Warring States)**	776 BC first Olympian Games; 550–330 BC Persian Empire
221–206 BC	**Qín**	212 BC Archimedes dies
206 BC–AD 220	**Hàn**	27 BC Roman Empire established; 30 AD Jesus crucified
220–280	**Three Kingdoms**	c.250 Classic Period of the Maya begins (until 900)
265–420	**Jìn**	c.320 northern India united by the Guptas; 410 Rome sacked
420–581	**Southern and Northern States (386–534 Northern Wèi)**	c.500 legendary King Arthur; 538 Buddhism extends to Japan
581–618	**Suí**	597 Augustine made first Archbishop of Canterbury
618–907	**Táng**	622 Muhammad lives in Medina – Arab calendar begins
907–979	**Five Dynasties/Ten Kingdoms**	962 Otto made Emperor in Rome, restoring Holy Roman Empire
960–1279	**Sòng**	1095–1291 Crusades; 1167 University of Paris founded
1279–1368	**Yuán**	1347 Black Death comes to Italy from China
1368–1644	**Míng**	1453 Constantinople falls; 1516 Portuguese ships reach China
1644–1911	**Qīng**	1793 first British Embassy in China; 1848 Communist Manifesto
1911–1949	**Republic**	1914–1918 First World War; 1939–1945 Second World War
1949	**People's Republic**	1969 moon landing

PART TWO
continued

12

chapter 12

Huángshán

With seven eventful weeks having passed, Ritchie and I were seasoned Hàn China survivors. Packed, freezing buses with jackhammer suspension? To be expected. Trains with filthy floors sprouting like fungi? Par for the course. A television that changed channels when a human knelt on a bed, a bathroom door that locked only on the outside, men who barked "*lǎowài!*" in deadpan fashion as we passed, a receptionist who might give directions to a nearby bus stop by advising "Take a taxi"? All commonplace and natural. Nevertheless, the sense that further crazed incidents would flourish Svengali-like without warning kept the tingle of adventure forever buoyant.

In the last week of November 1995, we left behind the oasis island of Sūzhōu, and caught a bus via Wúxī around the north shore of Tàihú. We were embarking on a week's detour to climb two mountains in Ānhuī Province, calling initially at **Yíxīng** to buy some teapots.

Yixīng

It was three or four thousand years ago that tea was first partaken in China as a herbal medicine, with cultivation in the 2nd century BC mainly in Sìchuān Province. The practice did not reach Europe until 1610, where it remained a luxury for two and a half centuries until the clipper ships of the 1850s conveyed the leaves from Cathay to Britain in 99 days. India became the major grower later that century, relegating China to second place.

Tea drinking is an art to the Chinese, and a frame of mind. What other culture could have produced a *Book of Tea* (*Chá Jīng* by Lù Yǔ) in the 8th century? When Chán Buddhist monks of the time fasted or went without sleep, the brew peppered with spices and salt was drunk as a stimulant, with cups carried continuously. By the time the custom had transferred to monks in Japan, bushes had been planted throughout the Yángzi corridor and delta, while during the Southern Sòng (1127–1279) the practice spread to both the gentry and common populace. Bricks of steamed tea dust, leaves, and offshoots became accepted as currency: "I'll have half a brick's worth of rice, please".

Different processing leads to a variety of subtle flavours and final product names:

dark green tea	uses leaf tips straight from the bush; no fermentation	*Lóngjǐng, Biluochun*
yellow tea	stored until the leaves turn yellow; lightly fermented	*Foshan Huangya*
white tea	bleached naturally by the sun and wind; lightly fermented	*Shoumei*
light green tea	semi fermented	*wūlóng, Tiěguānyīn* (Iron Guān Yīn)
red tea	not as stimulating; entirely fermented	*Wuyishan gōngfū*
black tea	the type drunk in the West, uses withered and dried leaves; post fermented	*Liuan, Pu'er*

Tea can be infused with jasmine flower (*mòlì huā*), while *wūlóng* ('black dragon') uses the leaves of the chesima plant. Compared to its black counterpart, the standard Chinese green tea retains the colour of the leaf while containing 50% less caffeine, and causes less staining of your tea mug, teeth and innards. Connoisseurs, who can tell whether the leaves were picked in autumn or spring, prefer *Lóngjǐng* (Dragon Well) grown around Hángzhōu, *Máofēng* from Huángshān, and *Yǔhuā* (Rain Flower) from Nánjīng.

As crucial to the Chinese as the leaf, tea requires the finest tasting water. In a Nánjīng museum, I noted the following ancestors' consumer guide to spring water for tea.

4th the Hǔpǎo (Tiger Running) Spring, in Hángzhōu

3rd the Guān Yīn Spring of Hǔqiūshān (Tiger Hill), in Sūzhōu

2nd the Huì Spring of Huìshān (Benefit Mountain), in Wúxī

The winner

1st the spring next to Jīnshān (Gold Mountain) Temple, in Zhènjiāng (mentioned in chapter 10)

A further crucial ingredient is the type of teapot (*chá hú*), and Yíxīng (Suitably Exciting) County has been a major focal point of its creation for 400 years. The local clay exists in a dozen colours, including sesame, copper, and a shade the Chinese label 'pine tree flower', enabling a kaleidoscope of coloured pots to be fired. One clay is so rich in iron it is called *zǐshā* (purple sand). Bedded in hard rock or soft mud, the rougher outer mantle (*gangsha*) of this clay is turned into huge Ali Baba pots called 'dragon jars' used to store water, while the smoother, finely-grained inner layer is the raw material for teapots, the end product being more of a brown-red. The same museum recorded a number of advantages, and portrayed the Chinese philosophy of tea in a way I won't presume to improve.

> The purple tea sets, produced by colourful pottery clay of Yíxīng in the Míng dynasty, featured with good flavour preservation and were characteristic of non-break while temperature sharply changed and no sense of hot because of slowly conduction of heat.
>
> Drinking tea means 'tasting tea'. Tasting not only makes appraiseal *(sic)* of high grade tea and low grade tea, but also brings people into mental state and revery, and gives people some ideas of interest of diet. Several good friends drink together while talk. How enjoyable they are!

That is not all. Illustrating what makes the Chinese so inventive and endearing, the potters have a ball creating an assortment of weird, funky tea pots: shaped like bananas and melons, or logs with frogs – the trunks knotted and emblazoned with rings, or encrusted with moons and spindly-fingered ET aliens. Others are inscribed with ancient calligraphy, or smothered with snakelike and weird Nazca-line patterns, while many are gaudily festooned with flowers and fruits. Some also look like teapots! *(see 12-1)*

13

12-1

They come with a stern warning, underlined: 'Same teapot is only for same type of tea. Different type of tea must use different teapot.' We were about to test the claim that 'pouring tea from *zǐshā* teapot is really the art of the art'.

★ ★ ★

The new glass-fronted Yongxian Hotel was spacious and stylish, with uniformed pages enthusiastically transporting the well-heeled luggage of business people. With our mucky backpacks and general grubbiness we felt a touch out of place, but the correspondingly high room rate dropped smartly when we said we'd look elsewhere.

The main street had virtually disappeared under a welter of construction: is there anywhere in China that is not a building site? A meal in another hotel was worse than forgettable.

◆ ◆ ◆ ◆

The teapot stores purported to be in the neighbouring small town of Dīngshǔ (or Dīngshān), the centre of pottery production in China. A bellboy from the hotel, attired in a ritzy red-and-grey penguin suit with bell-bottoms, led us to the requisite bus stop along a street streaming with raggedly-dressed peasants dredging a poor living, his livery outfit bizarre in the context, though he didn't seem to notice. The minibus driver applied emergency brakes as a cyclist peddled out from a side street without looking. He shook his head: "The people have no experience of modern traffic".

In Dīngshǔ we wandered for miles without alighting on any pottery factories, and there seemed to be only one teapot store in the whole town. With silly prices marked, we tried bargaining but the stern owner wouldn't budge. The principal shopping street, with a supermarket that sold no chocolate, was smothered in emerging new concrete blocks and scaffolding. Fortunately, there was one compact shop surviving the development, and it was replete with pottery goodies at reasonable prices. The amiable middle-aged owner suggested taking our time and comparing elsewhere. A nearby store was selling cassettes of traditional music from southern China. "Can I listen *without* having to buy?" At long last sense prevailed, and the adolescent girl nodded sweetly. I bought two.

The town is close to some karst caves amid tea plantations. A motorbike taxi sufficed for twenty minutes along narrow country lanes to Líng'gǔ Dòng, where a long descent led into a bewildering array of caverns. More enjoyable was Zhāng'gōng Dòng, which required scrambling up a hill within a hill, the reward being a quiet Daoist hall with a view *(12-2)*. Behind and below were tea bushes bunched together in corrugated drills resembling a panoply of green umbrellas in rain-drenched Shànghǎi.

The friendly owner in town briefly took us around his Aladdin's cave of cups and miniature pots, but was more interested in brewing us different teas, dramatically pouring the amber liquid from some feet above the cups. He dismissed my enquiry concerning pottery prices with a "Pay what you like" reply, which caused momentary anguish on his wife's face. After we enjoyed tea made with "extra special leaves", he assembled a pile as a take-away gift. Graced by this hospitality, we decided on an assortment of goods, mine paraded in *12-1* (three of the pots were obtained later). One teaset came in that blue silk-covered box decorated with garden scenes. Inside was also the potter's photograph and signature – a charming, intimate gesture, which makes the usual purchasing of goods lamentably impersonal.

★ ★ ★

12-2

To reach Jiǔhuáshān, I had planned an adventurous cross-country route by bus reminiscent of the Hóng Dòng to Huáshān epic: south to Chángxìng, hours west to Xuānchéng, change to Nánlíng, and on to Qīngyáng. The CTS man in Sūzhōu, however, was adamant it was impossible, recommending instead an extended loop via Nánjīng. In retrospect, I would have preferred the direct way.

Thus we boarded a jam-packed bus heading away from our destination. With no room for shoulders, we felt like chickens in a coop for an uncomfortable six hours back to massacre city. Arriving late at an obscure bus station, the driver of the only taxi reported that local buses had ceased running for the night, and he then demanded an extortionate fare. He was lying of course and a bus eventually transferred us to the railway station. From there, according to the LP guidebook, 'a No 10 bus' was the one to catch to a convenient hotel near the Yángzi River Bridge, so we embarked on one – except it was a trolley bus that after a while turned off in a different direction. The conductress indicated the hotel was "over there", which had us tramping the streets of Nánjīng for two hours around midnight, with our heavy cumbersome packs, searching for the lodgings supposedly nearby. "Keep going" and "along there somewhere" were typical directions from oblivious locals.

When the hotel emerged off a pedestrian-unfriendly highway, it was "full." I looked at the receptionist incredulously. "There is no possibility of a room," he insisted. "All the hotels are full, and the taxis are busy." In desperation, we strode the streets once more, hoping for a taxi to convey us to our previous Normal University. One eventually halted, and the driver switched on the meter unprompted! Oh Glory be, an honest Chinese taxi man.

Picking our way through the grounds past the music school, this time silent of pianistic scales, was blissful *déjà vu*. The university was, after all, well named: back to normality. Even the unfazed receptionist dealt with the formalities promptly.

◆ ◆ ◆ ◆

A train heading southwards for 200 kilometres was the best we had encountered since Běijīng, its hard-seat compartment being half empty. Relaxedly following the Yángzi River into Ānhuī Province, it switched after Wúhú to a branch line, at the end of which was the copper-producing centre of Tónglíng. There we attracted innocent, curious crowds who advised taking a taxi to the bus station, even though it was around the corner. A bus climbing for three hours into the mountains completed this crass transfer from Yíxīng, one that had delivered a lottery of surprises.

Jiǔhuáshān

After the sheer weight of population in the cities of Wúxī and Nánjīng, stepping through the entrance gate of **Jiǔhuáshān** into dark, empty country stillness was as if crossing a barrier into a different world. Disappointingly, instead of the promised stay in an authentic mountain monastery, the monks of Qíyuán Monastery had deemed it fit to build a concrete block in their grounds no different from a myriad hotels. We were the only guests. At least the temple looked enticing inside. A man invited us to his café off the one narrow street, and diddled us on price. I sympathise when many espy a foreigner: all they see is $. Fruit sellers were still plying their trade late at night.

◆ ◆ ◆ ◆

The name of this mountain confuses most sources. Long ago it was *Jiǔ zǐ shān*, which does not mean 'Nine Mountains'. The Chinese characters reveal it to be 'Nine Sons (or Children) Mountain'. Enter one of the four greatest poets of the Táng – Lǐ Bái, also written Li Po, who lived 701–762. Renowned for his love of wine and drinking, he temporarily resided here writing a poem poetically mixing the similar sounding *huá* (splendid) and *huā* (flowers), in which he compared the 'nine splendid peaks' to 'nine lotus flowers' Some sources relate only the nine flowers part of the tale, while others claim the subsequent name translates as 'Nine Flower Mountain'. However, as written, Jiǔhuáshān means 'Nine Splendid Mountain'[1], which is a nonsensical name. Lǐ Bái was born and brought up over a 1,000 kilometres away, and was a perpetual traveller. It seems even the locals became confused by his slurred out-of-town accent!

---

[1] The alternative 'Mountains' is incorrect since the name refers to only one.

12-3

It is one of the four holy Buddhist mountains in China, and is particularly associated with anyone who has recently died, the bereaved family and friends journeying here to pray for h/his soul. They do so to the bodhisattva Kṣitigarbha, in Chinese Dì Zàng meaning Earth Depository, who oversees the passage of the *hún* part of souls through the usually ten Buddhist hells, which are judgement centres in Earth prisons prior to reincarnation. The bodhisattva's association with the mountain intensified in the 8th century when a Korean called Kim Kiao Kak, who meditated here most of his life, died aged 99. His body was miraculously unaltered on the mountain three years later, and since he resembled images of Dì Zàng as well, he came to be regarded as the bodhisattva reborn.

So it is not surprising that a local map claims the area has '99 peaks'. It suffered greatly at the hands of the Tàipíng rebels, the oldest current buildings being barely more than 99 years old. The number of temples has reduced too from 300 to less than 99, with thirteen major ones marked on the map, together with tens of abbeys, halls, pavilions, and grottos.

More important than this numbers game is that the place is enchanting, with mustard-yellow and whitewashed walls penetrating watercolour mists hovering over distant valleys (*12-3*, looking north). The atmosphere of the province was already living up to its name – the Emblem of Peace. Master artists have undoubtedly long drawn inspiration from this source, and we were walking through the very canvas. With brown-tiled roofs mildly swept upwards, contrasting white windows, multi-tinted autumnal trees, and the odd field, it could almost have been a village in Tuscany.

To the west of that view is *12-4*, showing the street about to curl its way further left to one of the peaks. There are various paths to Heaven, and ours commenced at the 'sombrero hat' of Zhǎntánlín Monastery, on the left of the photo.

12-5

12-4

After climbing south, the path descended steeply through a forest into a significant valley wherein lies Zhōng Mínyuán, a small settlement distinguished by a distinctive Magic Tree as sheltering as the lonesome pine at Tàishān. All paths converge here before the assault up the mountain, or you can take a cable car. Compared to others in China, it is a doddle: if this had been England of yore, the homely path passing between petite houses and halls would have been cobbled. A woman in an apron guarded a temple; a man casually shouldered room-long bamboo poles. A tiled roof, as corrugated as the previous tea bushes, was speckled with grey, orange and white mould. Complementing a black urn offsetting tan walls, bold black characters announced the 'Nation's Music Building'. Next came the tempting 'Dragon Phoenix Pub', while another sign by some steep steps greeted with a cheery 'Morning bright and sunny'.

As this domesticity yielded to the sparseness of grey slabs under grey weather, trees appeared out of nowhere, clinging to nothing except bare rock, hanging on to life where there should be none, fearlessly upright and proud *(12-6* overleaf*)*. A sympathetic monk greeted us by a bridge over a waterfall. Below the two highest peaks the path split, the correct way indicated by a beehive of builders creating a last staircase made of ornately balustraded marble reaching to Tiāntái – the Platform of Heaven. A bank of red calligraphy on a boulder signalled we had arrived, and inside a compact temple astride the summit people were praying in the dark. A platform did indeed afford an all-encompassing view of the route we had traversed *(12-5:* a figure in the top right-hand corner gives scale*)*. Out of shot to the left is the 1,400-metre Ten Kings Peak, a reminder of the Ten Hells. Heaven and Hell are side by side, and one can so easily take the other path, ending up at the unintended destination.

17

12-6

A prominent incense burner attracted a stream of devout people with private thoughts. Normally one to keep his emotions close to his heart, I could tell Ritchie was moved being here, and he followed the motions of others by lighting a candle, a simple gesture rocked with meaning. At his request, we restaged the quiet ritual for a snapshot souvenir *(12-7)* before descending back down.

In the terraced Zhăntánlín Sì (Chopped Sandalwood Grove Temple), a stout yellow-robed monk conversed with my friend, while I observed bells hanging from dragon mouths, young women stretching to light joss sticks on top of iron holders, lantern-bearing totem poles entwined with dragons, eaves sweeping skywards, and a couple of large multi-coloured beach umbrellas – the common and ordinary with the sacred.

We stumbled upon a substantial array of Yíxīng teapots. Flushed with enthusiasm fired by our Dīngshŭ husband and wife, we revelled in the profusion of imaginative shapes at rock-bottom prices in a store empty of other customers. I eyed a handcrafted 'designer' model, whereupon the assistant reduced the sticker price six-fold at a stroke! Two others cost a few dollars only. As we were leaving, an older boss reprimanded her for selling goods to foreigners at too low a price.

◆ ◆ ◆ ◆

12-7

Huángshān

No one was sure when a bus to the next mountain might depart, a problem settled early in the morning by a man selling tickets uttering the dreaded *méiyŏu* – there isn't one. However, a monk muttered a few words to the ticket staff on our behalf, and a suitable bus shortly and miraculously arrived! Hours later, we boarded a ferry across a mysterious lake – surely the Styx – after which we were ordered at Xianyuan to change buses promptly. Half a minute and a scramble later, a second bus sped through valleys taking us, we trusted, in the relevant direction.

To achieve the transfer in winter had always been uncertain, yet it turned out to be a smooth and pleasant eight hours – by the intercession of a monk!

The choice of accommodation in the bustling market town of Tāngkŏu at the foot of **Huángshān** was limited to two. We slept in one, whose restaurant was 'out of season', and couldn't resist the liberating sensation of eating at the other – the Free and Unfettered Hotel. There was certainly plenty of space in the cavernous dining room, where we were the only customers.

◆ ◆ ◆ ◆

Lĭ Bái was so overwhelmed by this mountain that he asserted it was almost 10,000 metres high – loftier than Everest. Its ridges and seventy-five peaks are spread over a wide area, the three highest being hardly over 1,800 metres. However, that is overly prosaic: in someone's estimation...

> It has the magnificence of Mount Tàishān, the precipitousness of Mount Huáshān, the mists and clouds of Mount Héngshān[1], the fantastic rocks of Mount Yàndàng[2], and the elegance of Mount Éméi.

The traditional evaluation is similar:

> Having seen the Five Holy Mountains in China, one becomes indifferent to viewing the other lesser mountains. Having seen Huángshān, one becomes indifferent to viewing the Five Holy Mountains. It is the most spectacular under Heaven.

A Táng emperor obviously agreed since he bestowed the current name meaning Yellow Mountain, that being the colour of the highest authority in the land (himself). UNESCO concurs: in 1990 it was included in the World's Top Ten Legacies of Nature. Its varying frigid, temperate, and subtropical climatic zones make it a natural botanic garden, with an estimated 3,000 plant species.

Not aware of these appraisals at the time, I still had driving within me that quest to discover a massif that closely represented the Chinese character for mountain, particularly Mĭ Fú's eagle-like rendition, as well as the classic Chinese scrolls of old. Would I find the three W-shaped peaks here?

★ ★ ★

[1] in Húnán Province
[2] in Zhèjiāng Province

12-8

Being the last day of November, it was stretching our luck weather-wise to stay a night or two on the summit. Having obtained bread and chocolate as reserves, we ignored both an advertising board picturing the merits of smoking in the crystalline air of the mountain's pines, and the beckoning of twenty out-of-work taxis, and walked along a river towards Huángshān Gate *(12-8)*. A woman there helped to negotiate a reasonable rate for a minibus to the lower cable car station, where a high-tech ticket resembling a credit card was issued allowing access onto the mountain. The cable car is one of the longest in Asia – indicative of the popularity of the mountain. Nevertheless, in sharp contrast to Tàishān, for the three hours climbing the Eastern Steps I cannot recall seeing anyone.

Except that is for this quartet of porters *(12-9 overleaf)*, and they were walking unlike anyone else I had seen in China. Previous ones usually had a spring in their step, a spark in their face, and sometimes a smile as one overtook. These four however were as slow as a sloth, every placement of a foot an achievement. And they were silent, as stone. The object of their torture was indeed a block of stone, covered in black cloth, strung on bamboo across their shoulders, the odd shoulder pad visible. The four groped for a safe landing for every step – one slip and someone could be crushed. With not enough room to pass for some time, and it would have been dangerous to try, we stayed in line as quiet as they, pitying their every agonised tread. It was a relentless snail-paced procession – the agony of the cross brought uncomfortably to my feet. Not a word was uttered.

Bizarrely they were well dressed, their trousers suitable for a party. The whole was one of the undying images that will remain to my grave. If I could have lifted the weight off their shoulders, I would have. At such times I wish I could harness the $qì$ of the universe and relieve their pain. While they are in this state, I feel they are better people than me.

It was evidence also for the strength and versatility of bamboo. Porterage is a tradition on this mountain as on others, maintained from father to son, and on some the whole water supply used to be hauled up on shoulders.

As we cautiously passed them, not a sigh or an acknowledgement of our presence did they emit, such was the concentration demanded.

Even without that load, the stacks of concrete steps were a debilitating effort. They are a deliberate choice. If you desire to reach the sacred summit, many will be painful. Or you can stay where you are – free will.

Ritchie and I continued quietly with our own thoughts. Was it by accident that hereafter mysterious rock shapes stealthily began to dominate? Some silhouettes resembled a mythical castle, with ramparts and battlements and odd pillars like sentinels. Was this an ascent into the haven of Heaven? There, unmistakably, a mosque. Behind it a large presence, a rock face… looming out of the blacks and shadowy greys. Like a romanticised oil painting, the entourage of rocks and vegetation coalesced into the elegance of drapes with the silkiness of lingerie, while on the opposite side pines appeared under a puff of clouds. This was scenery out of a fantasy, another world – yet it was real. I was about to comb a castle in Shangri-La.

Whose home was this castle?

Track 1 combines with the next two pages' photographs (1¾ minutes).

12-9

12-10

12-11

12-12

12-13

21

At the summit, the well-groomed paths of the gently curved wooded plateau led to a circular platform... overlooking what? At the eastern Seeing is Believing Peak, mists were swirling and clouding the scene. Capped by a smidgen of blue, at first they kept low *(12-14)*. Then dragon's breath, and something else, proceeded up the slabs of rock. Blue disappeared as the scene transmogrified, pinnacles arising as if generated by some eerie unearthly earthquake, bare but for an occasional lionhearted tree. In constant motion, the seas scuttled around as alive as your hand that's turning these pages *(see 12-15)*. This is a Lost and Hidden World, mists reshaping the images every ten seconds like hundreds of Chinese scroll paintings unfurling before one's eyes.

To the left – is that Immortal Person Peak, Xiānrén *(12-16)*? The local map declares it is around here somewhere. More than the hiding places of gods, mountains are where they dwell. Approaching closer, the clouds are a feather bed. Do I believe what I see? Oh, oh, oh....

12-17 is the classic Chinese scroll, in vertical format too, with black diluted to several shades of grey. It is the Bed of God: the delicate lotus flowers are protecting and presenting the feather Bed. Something is approaching the Bed, upper left. Is it Xiānrén? Yes it is the Immortal Person! The Maori consider mountains to be real gods. The Chinese have long viewed them as living entities, as well as paths to paradise. The written Chinese word for immortality *(xiān)* is the combination of the characters of 'mountain' *(shān)* and 'person' *(dīng)*. Even in their language, the Chinese know the connection between mountains and God – S/he is the Mountain Person.

As anyone's bed is, it is intimate, open, one hundred percent trusting, and thus open to abuse. The owner is exposed and raw.

"Look at me", S/he says.

The intonation is matter-of-fact: this is.

S/he has been crying. There is intense, inestimable sadness, as deep as inescapable black depression. Eternal tears.

The stage is reached where you kneel beside the Bed of God and ask:

"What is wrong with You? What is the matter?"

After 12 seconds of eternity, the answer comes hoarsely in a voice stunned with incredulity:

"I am falling into a black hole. There is no escape."

That voice. I have heard it before. One that is calmly coming to terms with the simply insoluble: facing in peace and calm the disaster of the Immortal not being Beneficent and Omnipotent.

"The void. And no one to turn to."

As before, it is a short conversation. What else can one say? S/he lies there immobile, vulnerable, bare. Beyond pain.

In a similar frame of mind, a female student of mine – dangerously despondent – had written some poetic falling phrases entitled 'Fall' (Autumn): leaves falling, herself falling.

I can't extricate myself from it; in fact, I might enjoy myself in it. When the cold wind touches me, a too clear sky gazes at me. I can't do anything, and I can't control myself. I watch movies alone, take a walk at night, and listen to Led Zeppelin's music at an ear-splitting volume. The return of Fall chilled me to the bones, but it made me feel again. Is Fall a season which makes one remember only memory?

She admitted 'enjoy'! The Paradox of Pain. One cannot be a Samaritan in such circumstances. All I could do was to scribble her a note:

Gina, remember this: you have talent, you have imagination, you are beautiful, you are sensitive. Don't throw this away by exploring only your darker side. See hope in a butterfly, find love in a smile; then see and find peace in yourself – it exists there!

Around a corner was a different perspective: the Bed protected within a fortress, its serrated edge under a patch of blue, a Cinderella castle in the sky. There, amazing Cathedrals – a City of Spires, the whole clasping and uplifting the elevated Bed in a Lotus Flower, a microcosm of Heaven *(12-18)*. The map indicates Shísǔn Bridge and Peak, meaning Stone Bamboo Shoots. The ramparts could well be baby bamboo shoots: the Designer's nursery.

Trace down the vertical wall, and view through a silvery black-and-white crack in the cover *(12-19* and *12-20)*. Dive into the Breath of God, the smoky mists evolving and dissipating, everything moving, everything still. Fine tall trees emerge on the rocks like teeth on a peaceful shark. Restless, majestic, the mood is private.

The ancient canvas changes again. Too much mist, a nebula of fog, I cannot see clearly... something is boiling up out of the vapour *(12-21)*. Reveal Yourself... more....

Pow! Almighty Power! From behind, a spread-eagled eagle flashes out of the cauldron. It is *the* Eagle: "*shān!*" "*Shān!*" "**Shān!**" *(12-22* and *12-23)*. It soars with a cohort of bodhisattvas to the left, the terracotta army guarding in compact formation.

A triptych of peaks tantalisingly materialise out of the ghostly cloak – three peaks in formation, the middle one the highest *(12-24)*. The mist is blanketing over with a wash of weak purple: "I'm losing You... please, come back".

The presence returns... like a pyramid. Re, the Sun God! Zoom in among the phallic pillars, the Egyptian heart of mystical creation. The foreground one is positioned between two mammaries *(12-25)*. The map reveals Shàngshén Peak – what else could that mean in a bed? – Rising Peak. O Hermaphrodite! Love and sex are part of Creation, part of God – from one to the other. The Creator understands Love and love from first principles. Everything is leading one in, everything pointing to.... Come forward. S/he does:

"This is My abode... This is Me."

12-26 The Eagle is complete with an eye, even a beak. It has terrific power. With the duvet of the Bed of God below, It is perched on high, seeing, observing every detail panoplied around, the head in the middle and two wings at the side. This was the character for mountain I had been searching for – and it was Mī Fú's version! Being here evoked the same feeling I had standing inside the crater of Krakatau, in the belly button of unimaginable power. Here, too, was the source of the 'eagle-talon' strokes in Chinese paintings of twisted, gnarled trees in bare, misty mountainscapes shorn of Time.

The Eagle has its wings raised, an intimate gesture: the wings of welcome, the cloak uncovering itself, inviting one to enter the abode. The posture conveys more – something tangibly significant. It is *wounded*, appealing for help, yet expressed without outward emotion: 'calm of mind, all passion spent'... Peace.

Behold the site of the Almighty's Heart on Earth, and the clouds are H/him breathing. When you look, can you not hear it? This *is* God: majesty, beauty... close, personal... suffering, peace. The symbols are animistic. The Creator is Everything.

A mountain of mist envelops the revelation, and the Amoeba dissipates back into the dark and light, hissing, whispering, fragmenting... *(12-27)*. It is hard to soar like an Eagle when one works with turkeys.

The following twelve pages of photographs are designed to be perused again, this time as a sequence with track 2, which is in three sections lasting 7½ minutes. The third section should intensify images 12-22 and 12-23, and dissipate on the last photograph (12-27).

12-14

12-15

12-16

12-17

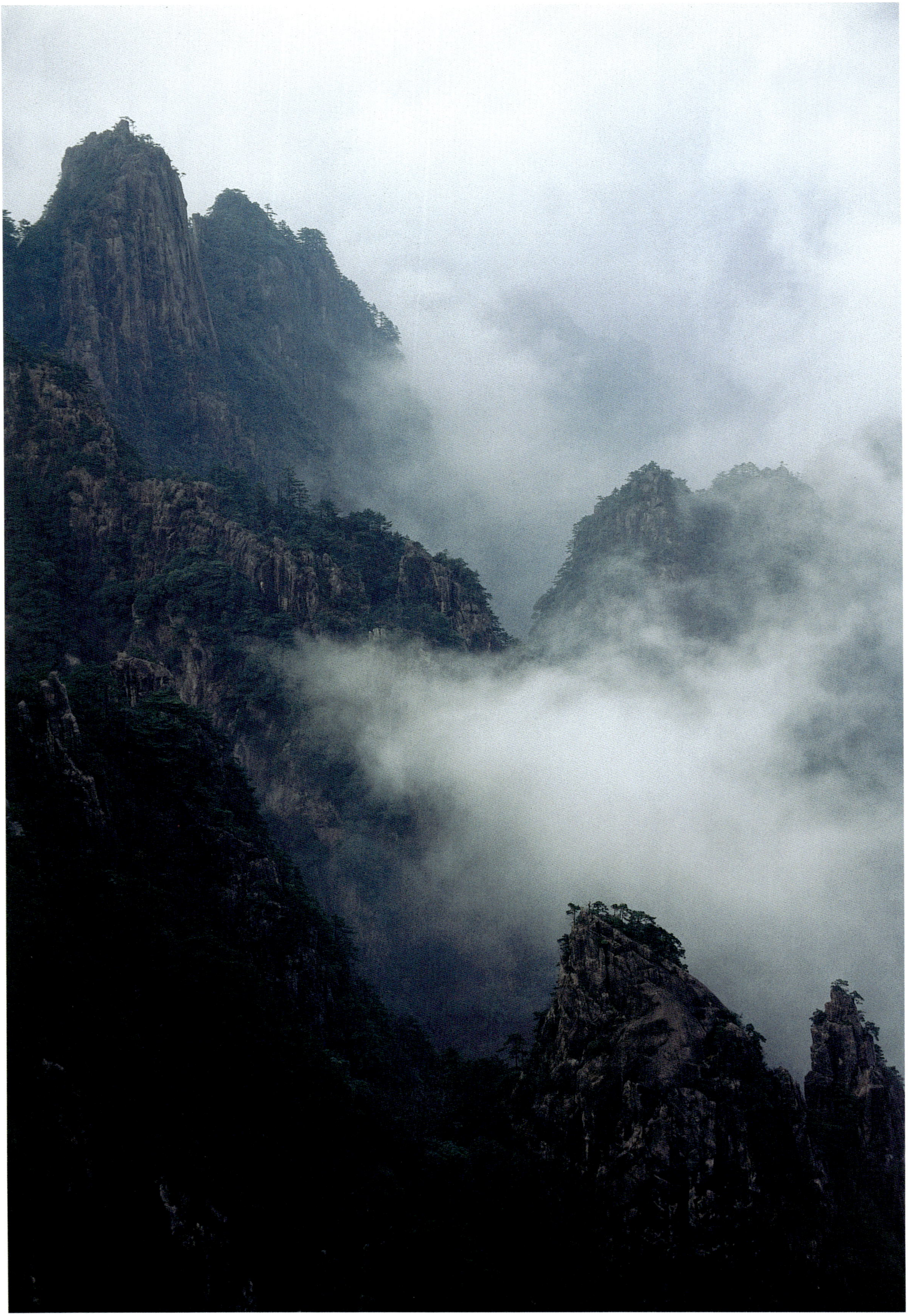

12-18

28

12-20

12-19

12-21

next page 12-22

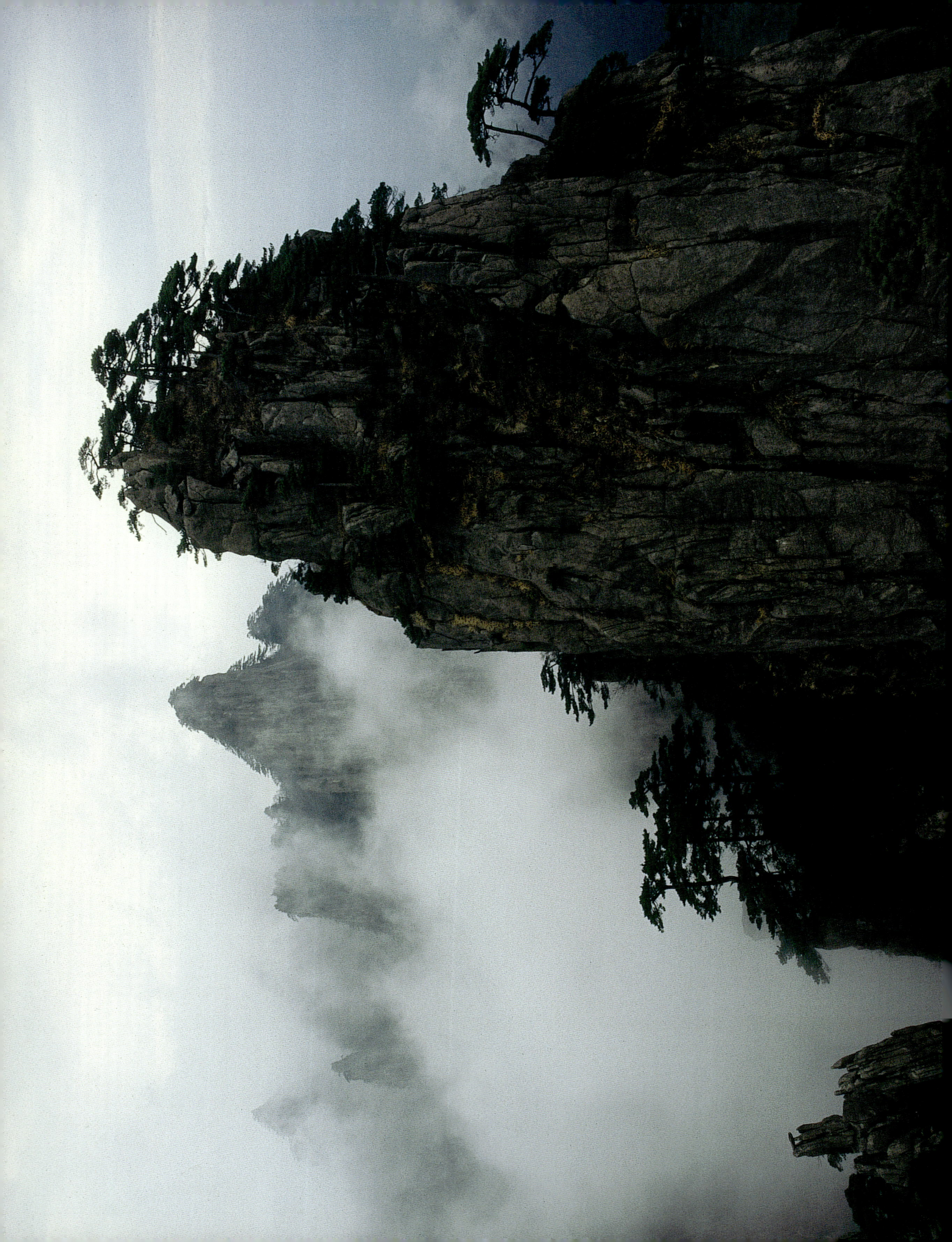

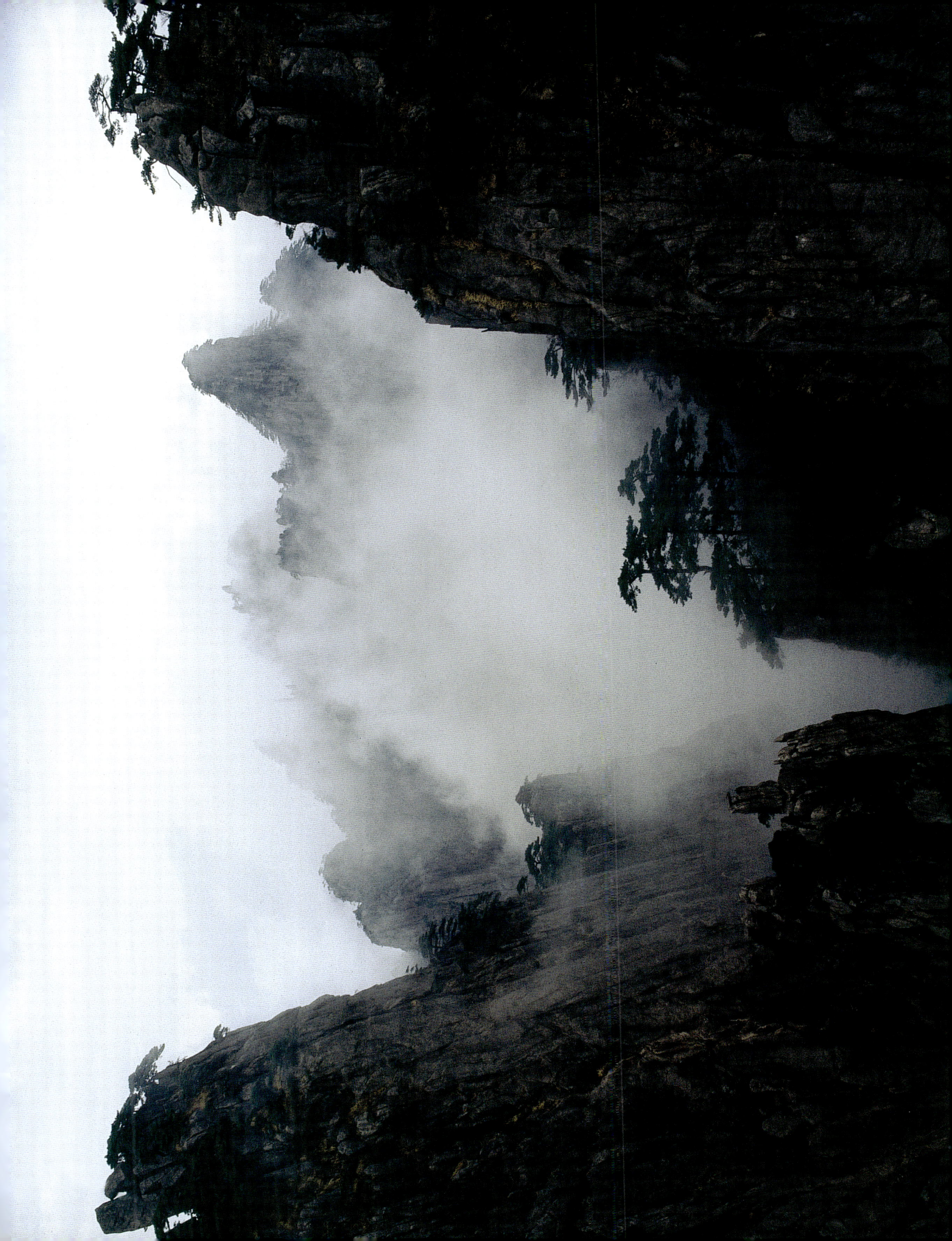

32

previous page 12-23

12-24

12-25

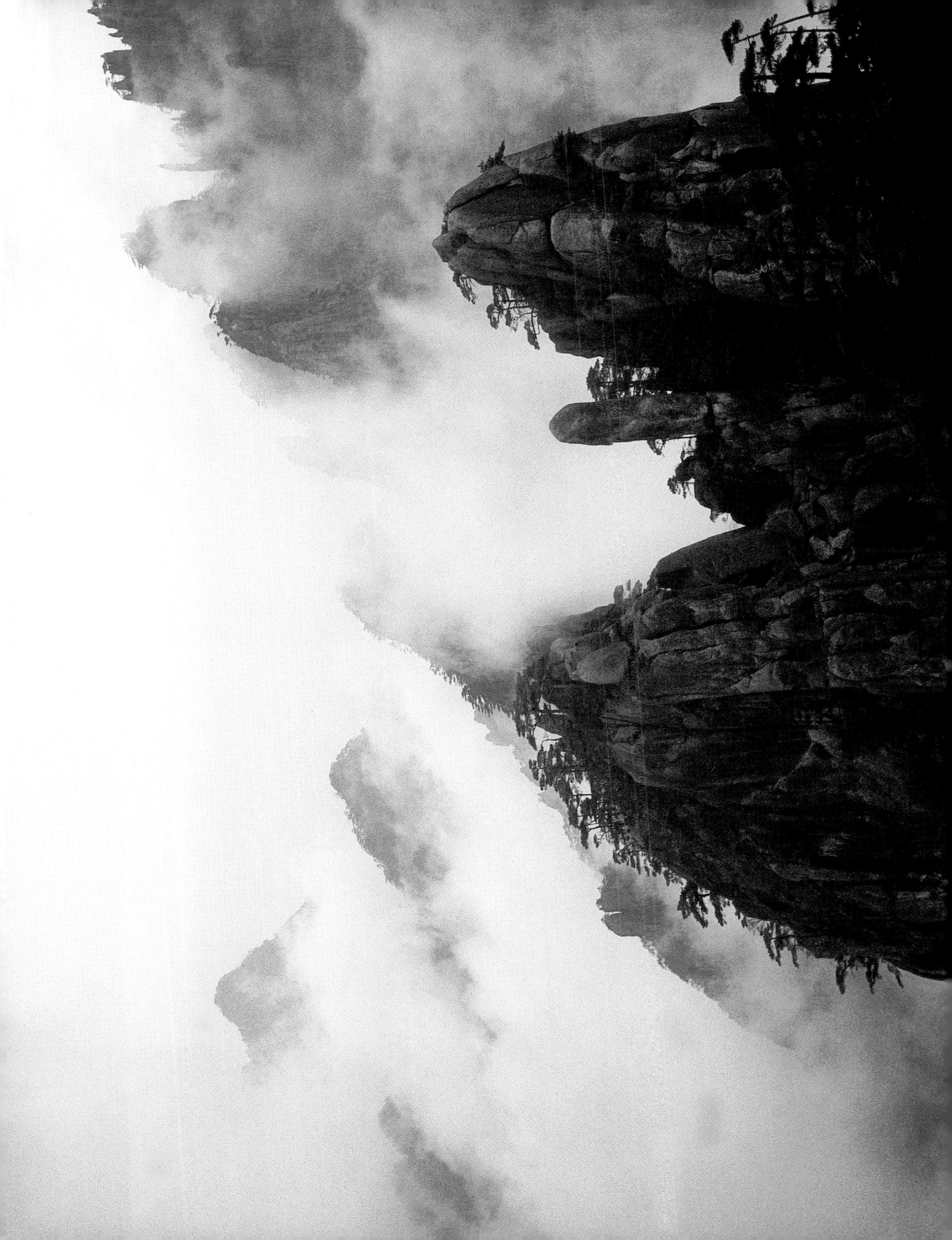

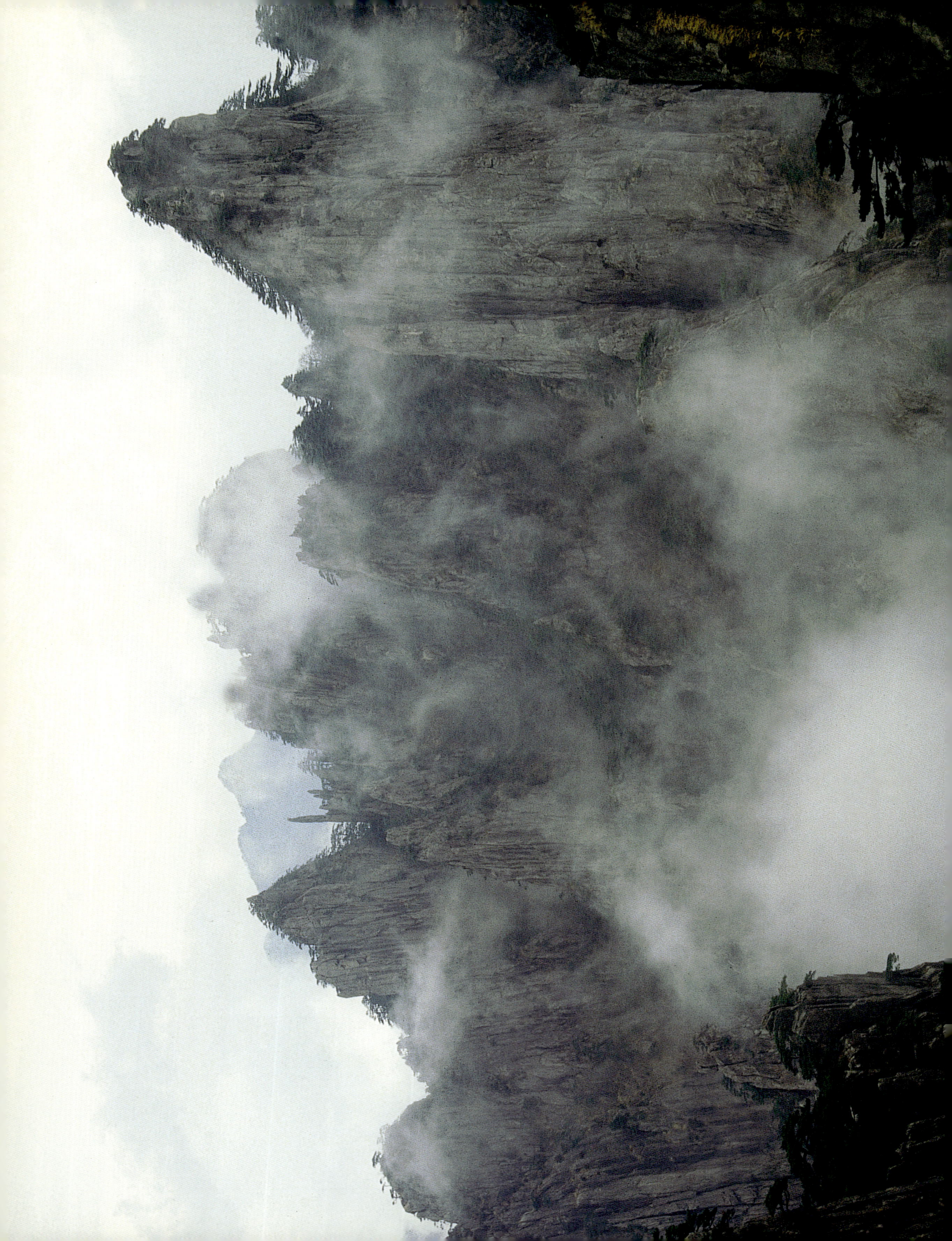

12-27

The summit's Běihǎi Hotel had reinvented itself into a spanking new block – hence the porters hoisting stone cubes – with a posh reception hall and even central heating. Alas, the young receptionists were disinterested, even rude to us and others. We resolved not to stay there, however cold the night might be. Beside a football pitch on which workmen were playing, the original accommodation of the hotel still existed – lines of old wooden shacks offering a cheap if depressing alternative. A short walk led to the Xīhǎi Hotel, its assumed pedigree confirmed by a concierge opening the door. What a tariff – even the rich might hesitate! Presumably the abundant guests had ascended by cable car. Cheap dormitories nearby were soul destroying, so it was back to Běihǎi's basic huts, which were cosy enough.

The guidebook revealed that most watchers of the sunrise throng the Qīngliáng Tái (Refreshing Terrace) overlooking Běihǎi, the North Sea of clouds. We dismissed it: there was room with a view only for a few. It was humbling though to see the hundreds of 'lockets of love': lovers had engraved their names onto padlocks and chained them to iron railings, clasping their love for ever. We decided to risk observing the sunrise from a modest platform near the Eagle, which was closer to the more apt Dōnghǎi, the East Sea. The light was failing fast as I captured these swirling rocks, a solid mirror of the swirling clouds *(12-28)*, before the sun took its temporary leave.

In the Xīhǎi Hotel, Yíxīng teapots were on sale! Prices commenced at $100, rising to $1,000 – ten to a hundred times the price we had paid at Jiǔhuáshān. They have won several international design awards, so they presumably sell at those prices. The absurd cost of dinner similarly raised a smile: was a bowl of tomato soup really worth ¥100? We declined and, after tucking into our survival provisions, dived under the dirty duvets on our beds.

◆ ◆ ◆ ◆

My mini alarm clock buzzed at 5.00, and soon after I was using a mini torch to erect the tripod in the dark clear stillness, our breath creating its own icy white mist. I didn't need a thermometer to gauge the degree of cold: after capturing the initial hint of light *(12-29)*, the camera's shutter stuck fast, a result of the batteries freezing. After unscrewing the camera, removing gloves, groping for a lightweight 20p British heptagonal coin to unscrew the cap, extricating the tiny batteries, warming up their replacements, reassembling everything, resuscitating my fingers, it was back in business! Exactly where on the horizon the sun would appear we couldn't pinpoint, and I hoped it wouldn't be blocked by a prominent rock in front.

There are 8 minutes of track 3 to incorporate ad lib with the next 20 pages, an average of half a minute per photograph. But timing is not important: an option is to repeat the track.

12-28

12-29

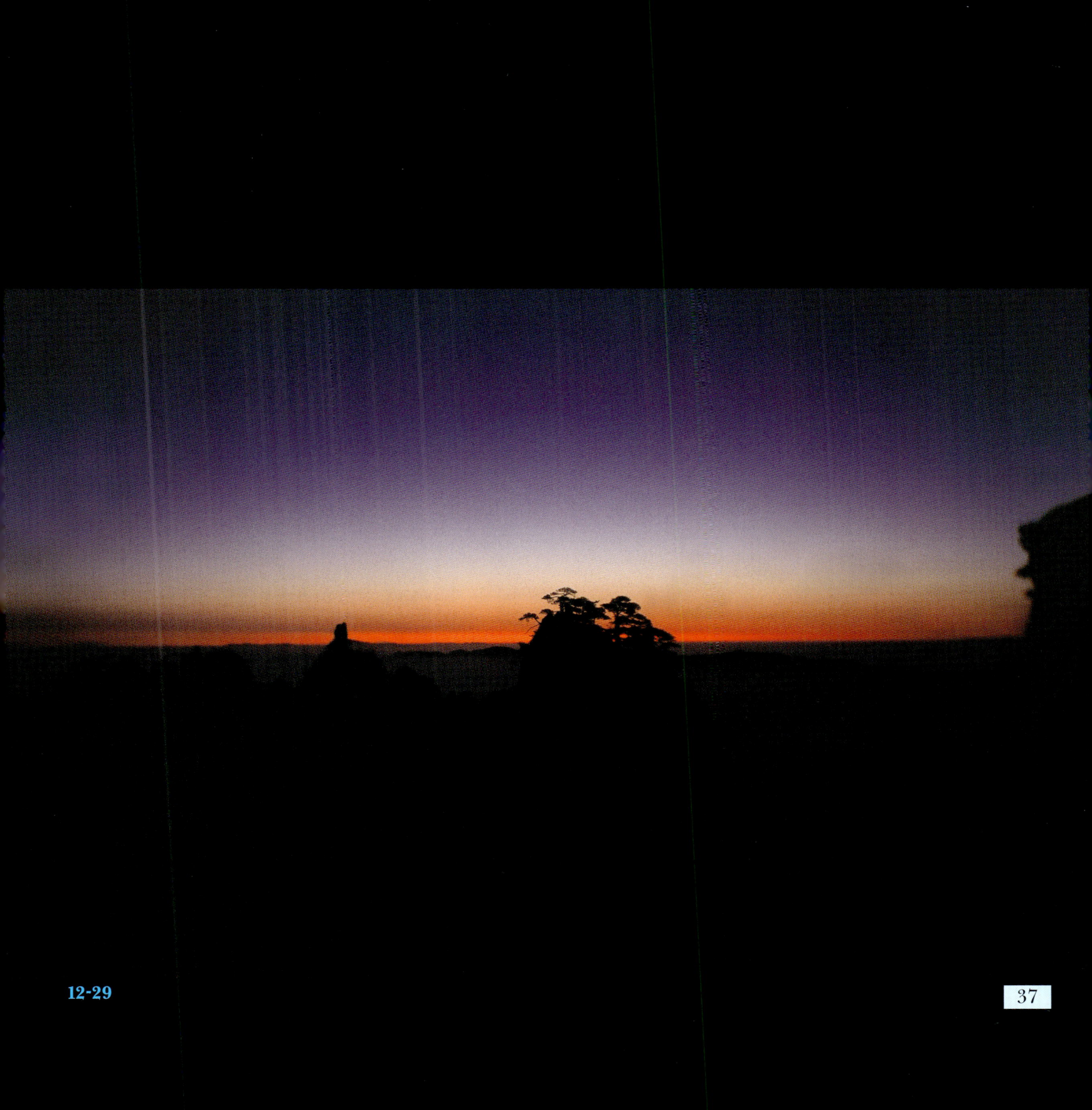

12-30

39

12-31

12-32

40

41

42 12-33

12-34

12-35

12-36

43

44

12-37

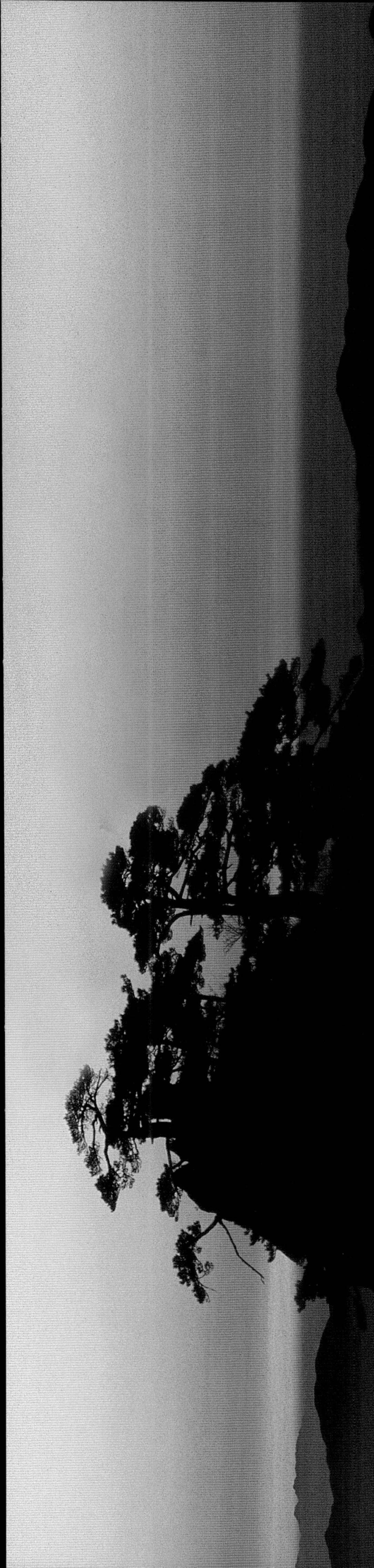

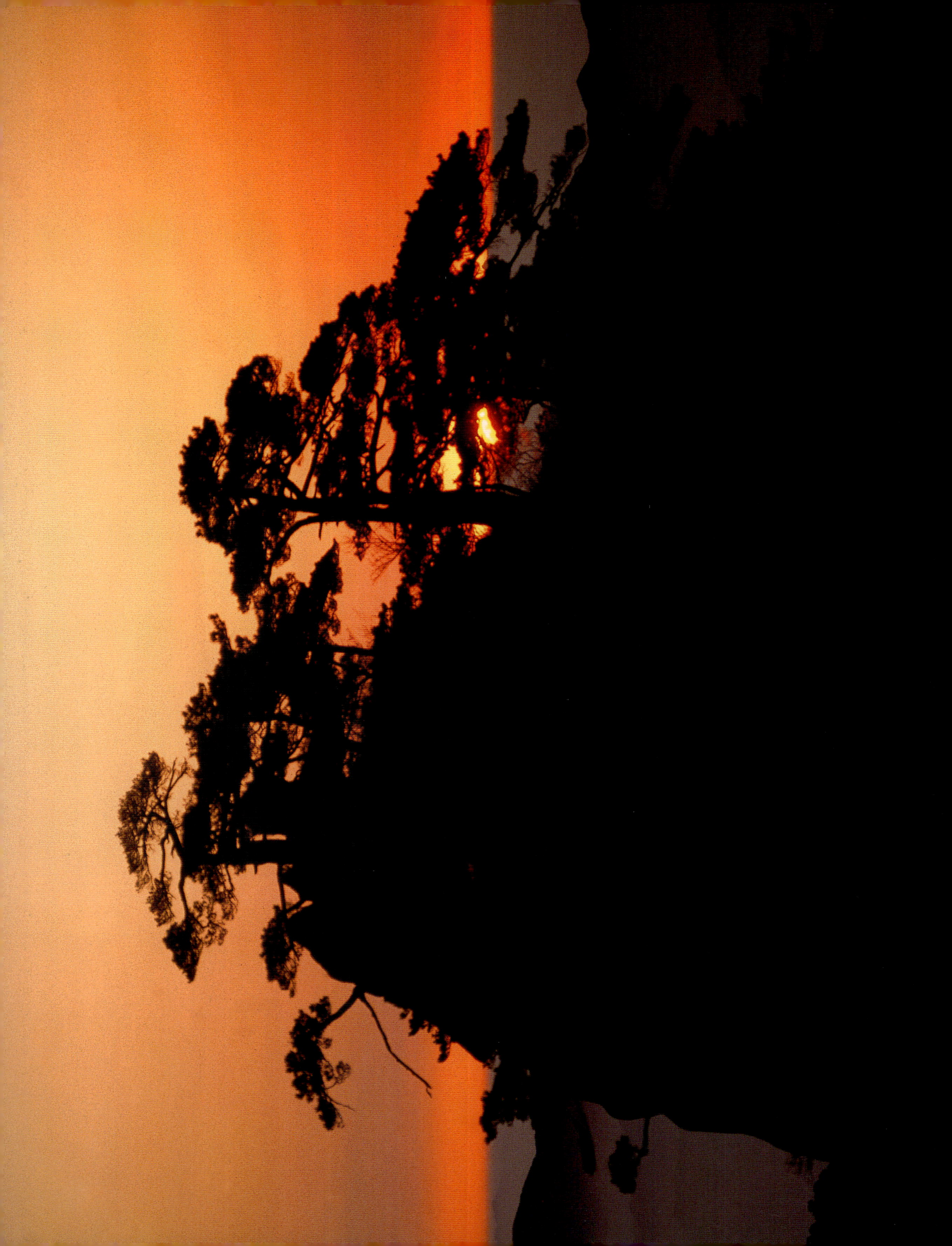

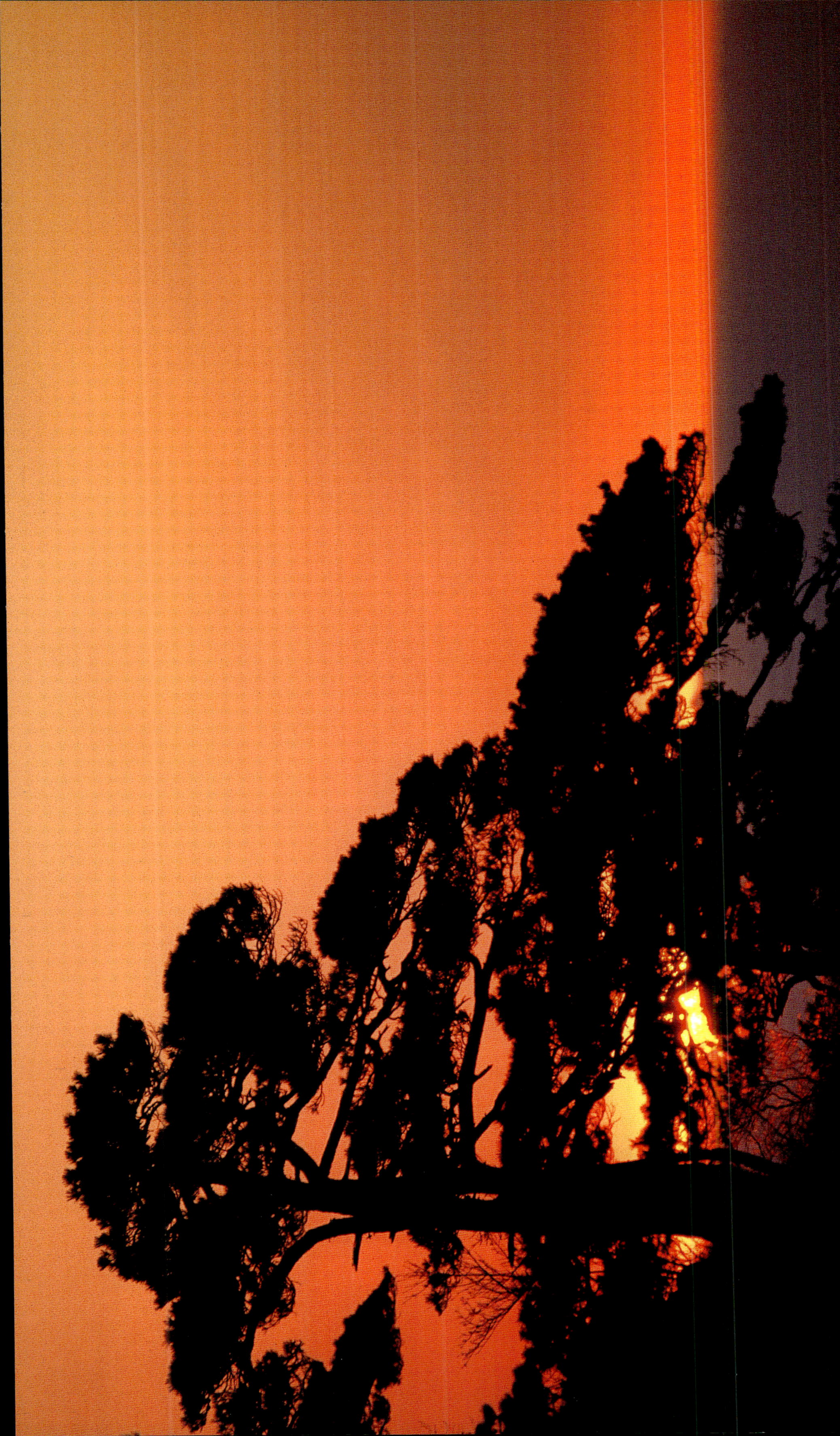

48   12-41   12-42

12-43

12-44

49

12-45

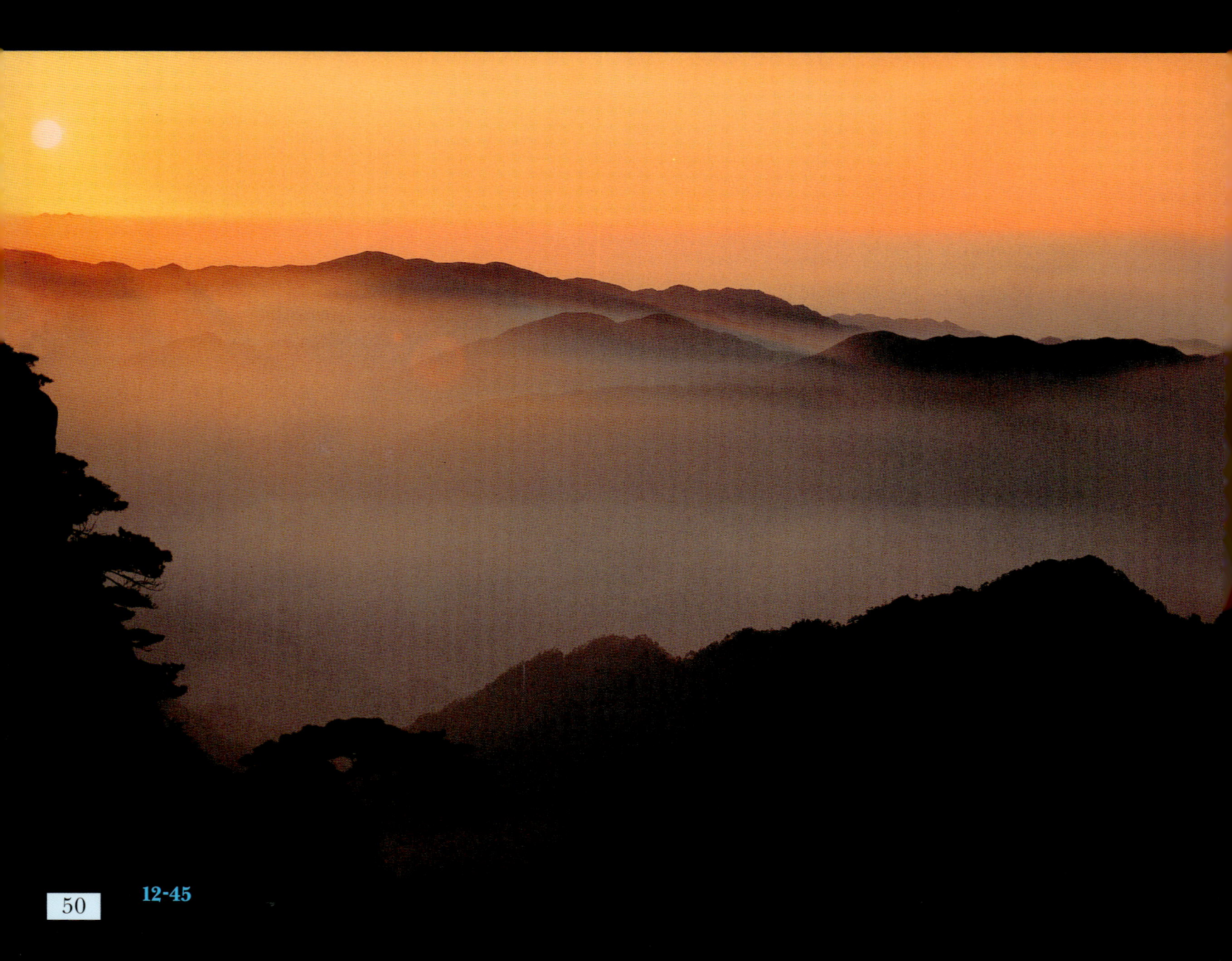

next double page 12-46

山

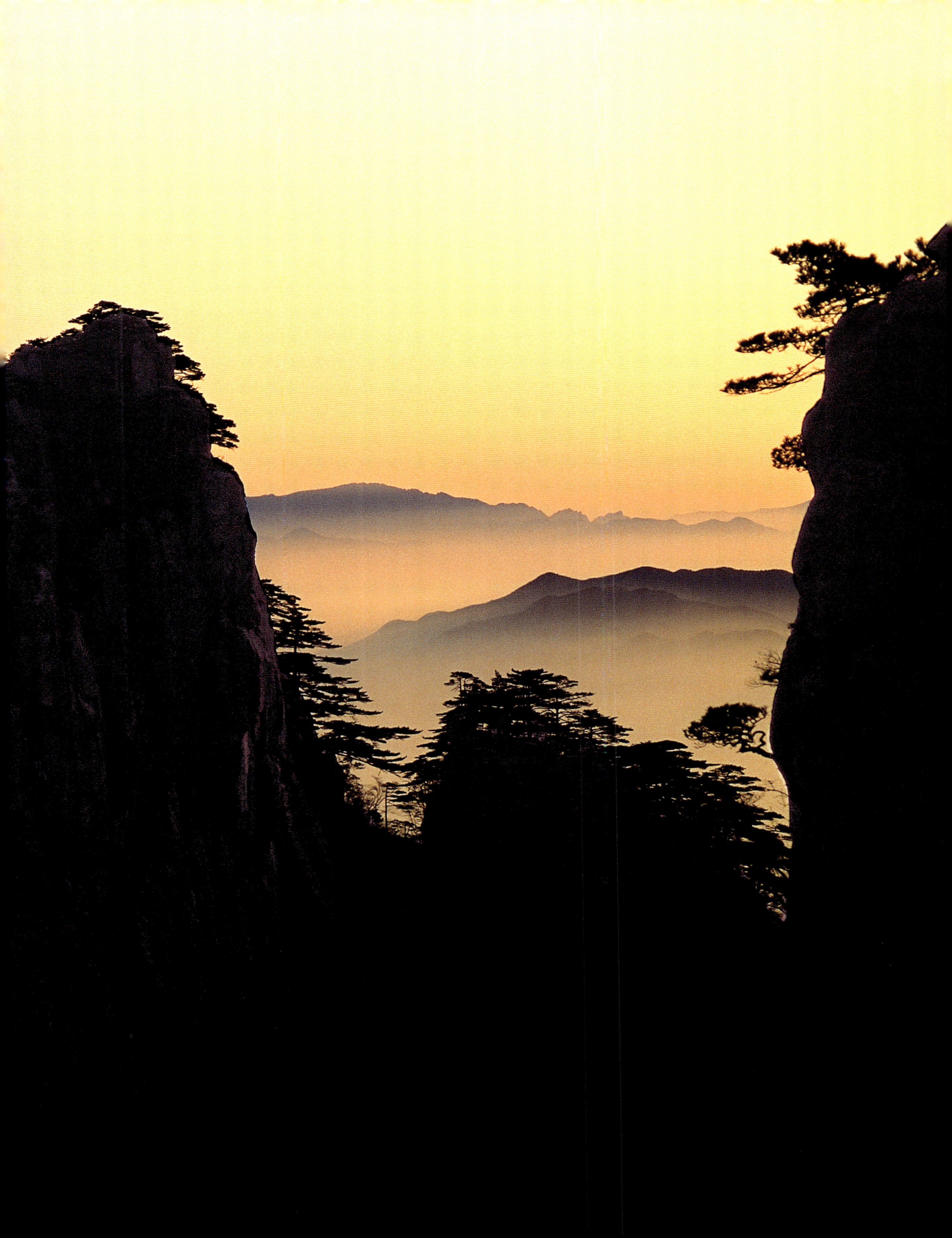

12-47

54

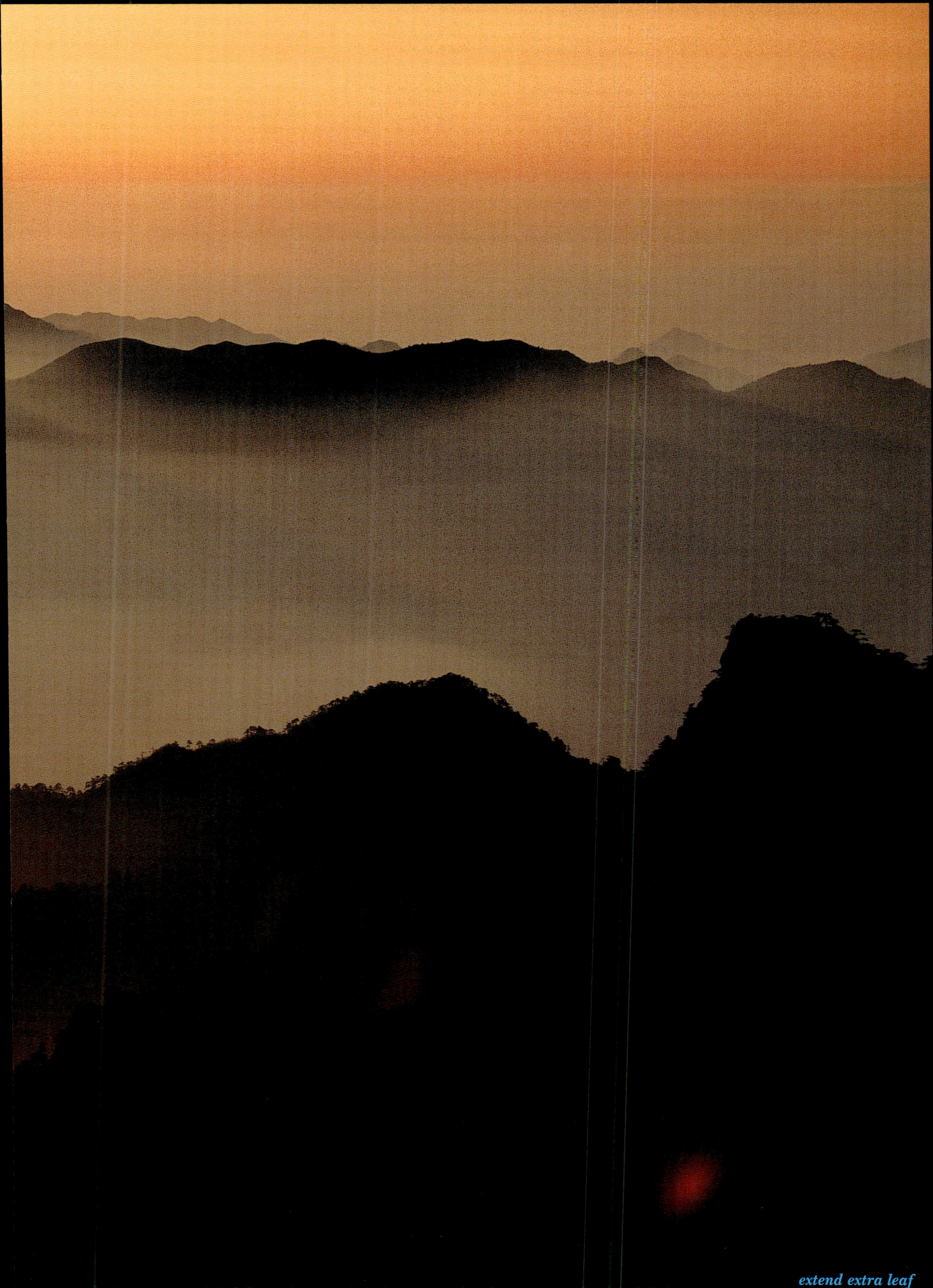

extend extra leaf

12-48

My central quest had been fulfilled! Mǐ Fú's black Chinese character for mountain had been found on this Immortal Peak, and caught on film. *12-46 is* Shān. The Eagle is the Shān. Like a painting, the silhouette matches the inkiness of Mǐ Fú's strokes, and the jagged edges of the bristles are reflected by the outline of the pines on the ridge, as if marching ants covered the body. The out-of-this-world colours, particularly the blue in the distance, were recorded naturally without filters. In Chinese Buddhist imagery, such as the cave paintings along the Silk Road, blue is the colour of mountains: it and they together represent Heaven. It was hard to recall that this was China, the colours so unlike the grey of the streets below.

There are various named pines, rocks, and stone pillars, as well as the five seas. In the Dōnghǎi is Guān Yīn Crossing the Sea, and elsewhere is a Celestial Pointing the Way. Is that a hint to follow?

One of the peaks is Shǐxìn, which translates as 'The Start of Faith'. It has a second meaning: 'The Beginning of a Message'.

Another message from God. How many more do we need?

★ ★ ★

We had been alone, apart from some traditional whoops of joy emanating from Refreshing Terrace as the sun broke through the sea. Having witnessed such a rewarding sunrise, it was unnecessary to stay a second night. The way to the Hòuhǎi (Rear Sea) was blocked, but on the western side of the mountain the Fēilái Shí, the Rock that Arrived by Flying, stood proud with its yellow calligraphy *(12-49)*. We perched silently and contemplatively on other rocks for the panoramas of Xīhǎi, the West Sea (overleaf *12-50, 12-51*).

Tramping up and down the grand staircases that constitute the Western Steps was an exhilarating slow-motion roller-coaster ride, a full seven hours of strenuous walking not to be underestimated. Memorable moments included cloudscapes *(12-52)*; weirdly-shaped rocks, including one apparently sculptured by Henry Moore *(12-53)*; seal-like crowds under the two highest peaks; a crevasse that is the Hundred Step Cloud Ladder *(12-54)*; a giant escalator of precipitous steps bypassing Liánlěi, Lotus Bud Peak – thank goodness we were not going *up* them; a solo tree commanding the Qiánhǎi, Front Sea *(12-55)*; and, always in one's immediate vision, steps and more steps to the Bed of God. Disappointing only was that the mysteriously inviting Capital of Heaven Peak was closed – even God has maintenance problems.

We were on Huángshān in the wintry 12th month, and had got away with it thanks to Grand Old Pa. We had been fortunate: mist in the afternoon, a clear bright dawn, and sunshine thereafter.

I have never come across a mountain like this in the whole world. 'Unique', as our Sūzhōu guide would have said. Perhaps Lǐ Bái was right after all.

12-49

60

59 12-50
12-51

61

12-52

12-54 12-55

12-53

chapter 13

Pǔtuóshān

two cities and a town

Renowned for its lotus blossoms in July, **Hángzhōu** (Navigation Island) is besieged by weekend trippers from Shànghǎi three hours away, and after our experience at Wúxī we had hoped not to arrive on a Saturday. Inevitably we did, after seven hours on a bus, but because of the time of year the hotels were not inundated. Ritchie's visa had expired, and with visions of a public execution if it wasn't renewed forthwith, searching for the PSB was an immediate priority. A receptionist gave one set of directions (inaccurate), and a local indicated another street (wrong), but the march gave us a feel for this famous city, the capital of Zhèjiāng (Zigzag River) Province. The ubiquitous demolition and construction in progress was a shock, while ancient dwellings remained in patches of rubble conferring a distinct Dickensian aura. Where was the celebrated beauty and greatness chronicled by visitors for 700 years? 'Along both sides of the main street', Marco Polo reported, '...are stately mansions with their gardens'[1]. No signs remain. We found the PSB office, which had shut for the weekend: Ritchie contemplated his imminent demise with guarded good humour.

◆ ◆ ◆ ◆

Further administration included obtaining flight tickets – his back to the UK, and mine for later in Yúnnán Province, which I had reserved from Korea months previously. Despite enquiring at the major Civil Aviation Administration of China (CAAC) building in this principal city, officials could neither confirm the reservations, nor issue tickets. CITS could not organise a tour to see outside villages, nor hire a car on our behalf, and it couldn't determine the boat times from Pǔtuóshān to Shànghǎi – information that would soon be of necessity. Strolling through the city provided opportunities for shopping, but little else.

◆ ◆ ◆ ◆

13-1

Far from proclaiming a guillotine sentence, the woman at the PSB was polite and civilised, the expired visa no problem, and a second extension granted instantly. Admin complete, a walk around West Lake was opportune, about which Polo was ecstatic.

> All round it are stately palaces and mansions, of such workmanship that nothing better or more splendid could be devised or executed.... Furthermore in the middle of the lake there are two islands, in each of which is a marvellous and magnificent palace, with so many rooms and apartments as to pass belief, and so sumptuously constructed and adorned.

It says something of this lake today, famed for being one of the most beautiful places in China, that the only photograph I deemed worth taking – indeed in the whole of Hángzhōu – was of these floral cabbages, the best scenery around *(13-1)*! The famed vistas were non-existent, with few trees, no magnificent hills, no magic. Other than the odd pavilion and midge-molested bridge, it was a large, pleasant goldfish bowl at best. Máo Zédōng was greatly enamoured of it. Fortunately, the Provincial Museum partly compensated with comely white jade, and remnants of the ancient local Liángzhū culture (c.3300–2300 BC).

Away from the lake, the Flying Peak beside Língyǐn Temple, the city's 'main attraction', was pleasant with mini-caves, rocks and paths, but the temple itself was overrun by the Chinese, and the entry fee was exorbitant. Despite the time, cost and energy to reach it, we decided not to enter. We were rapidly tiring of this mass-tourist type of China. Half-jokingly, I commented to my travel mate: "This is deteriorating into a shopping and eating trip for us!"

Dispirited by what we had seen, we decided to give a miss to the remaining sights – Precious Stone Hill, paddle boats on the lake, the mosque, Six Harmonies Pagoda, etc. Hángzhōu was the one severe disappointment for me in the whole of China. Even allowing for a touch of Rustichello hyperbole, how could it ever have been, as summarised by Polo, 'the finest and most splendid city in the world'? Even after the destruction caused by the Tàipíng Rebellion, some grand ground plan would have remained, and gardens and trees replanted. The Past is not Present here anymore.

◆ ◆ ◆ ◆

Our last week of travel together, in an area I knew nothing about, proved to be unexpected and enjoyable. The north coast of Zhèjiāng is blessed with a railway line constructed in the 1930s, the section to **Shàoxīng** being dispatched in an hour and a half. There was an instantly lighter atmosphere as we hiked along a canal, beside which a narrow residential lane was clean, open and welcoming. After checking in at the town's hotel, whose old-style restaurants are arranged around a charming pool, we were informed by CITS of a new attraction: an old canal area at Kěqiáo, twenty kilometres away. Glad of the advice, a minibus took us to a dusty town of concrete buildings resembling multi-storey car parks off a wide multi-lane highway, the surrounding area flat and featureless. There was no sign of an ancient canal village, and we returned amused and bemused to Shàoxīng.

---

[1] All Polo quotations are taken from *The Travels Of Marco Polo*, translated by Ronald Latham, the ones here from pages 182, 183/4, and 179.

The foremost north-south street contained two opera stores – I had never previously come across one in the world[1]! It indicates how popular the tradition was and is in this town. I had already purchased a double cassette of a Shàoxīng Opera (*The Dream of the Red Mansions*), and here were costume and make-up paraphernalia, musical instruments, and other realia beyond my ken. The gawky 'hats' were hilariously exaggerated, with glaringly coloured woollen pompoms and other baubles dangling on elongated springs, like the eyes of aliens on stalks. These peered over a crown of brass battlements as menacing as Dad's Army. To complement these were foot-long grey-and-white beards, secured like spectacles by wire around the ears.

Most tempting of all, on the walls were a few magnificent full-length opera costumes in full regalia. They were heavy, fully lined, thickly padded with white furry fringes, made of fine-quality crinkled materials in garish colours hand-detailed with gold wire, and studded with decorations tied onto the shoulders – including an ambiguous anthropomorphic creature staring fiercely. One garment caught my eye for the absurdly modest price of ¥250 – a mere £20. Wearing it made me feel like a Chinese emperor. But my already towering backpack could not conceivably accommodate it – unless I put the pack *in* it, perhaps!

I bought a beard as compensation.

A large store was selling musical instruments, and perambulating east into streets straight out of China's history, we strayed into an instrument maker's dark wooden workshop. Nearby, this AD 1204 bridge over a canal is supposedly in the shape of the Chinese character (*zì*) for eight (*bā*), hence the name Bāzì Qiáo (*13-2*). Note the 13th-century Scottish tartan.

To the south, entire areas were being demolished and rebuilt. An old, friendly caretaker welcomed us into the Qīngténg Study, which the Blue Guide describes as 'perhaps the most perfect example of domestic architecture surviving in China'. Frankly, my garden shed is more interesting – it's better to go to Korea for fine examples of ancient dwellings.

Tracing its origins to 2,400 years ago, Shàoxīng rice wine is famed throughout the nation, the most valued variety being *Huā Diāo* (Flower Engraving). I purchased a bottle of eight-year-old vintage to present to a family in Korea later. As well as sticky rice and yeast-fermented wheat, the ingredients include water from the local Jian Lake. This is so crucial to the taste that it has been hailed as the 'flesh', 'bone' and 'blood' of the wine, which makes me ponder what stagnates in the lake apart from H_2O.

◆ ◆ ◆ ◆

A three-hour train ride east through flat farming country provided a second railway classic, again courtesy of an official and to do with our luggage. The latter was tidily positioned on the racks above us, but minor strap ends hanging six inches through the bars perturbed the attendant. Most politely and without pomposity, he spent minutes fastidiously pushing all of them back through and tying them around the bars. There was no point to this exercise, other than fussy and meaningless housekeeping. Even with our experience of previous events, Ritchie and I could only gawp at such a performance. We smiled and thanked him.

Lonely Planet's apocalyptic vision of **Níngbō**'s railway station as a 'slithering mass of arms and legs', 'all pulling, pushing, punching, biting, scratching and perhaps killing' to obtain a ticket and one's wallet, was not on this occasion quite as terrifying.

Our expectation that it was to be a modest ancient town was belied by the significantly expanded population, now over five million: Níngbō (Calm Waves) is a fast-rising modern metropolis (*13-3* overleaf). An example of the business-like acumen is that in 1994 the Níngbō Zhōnghuá Paper Company, the largest in China, purchased two cardboard-making machines from a German consortium for $232 million, and was spending a further $168 million mostly on a new mill in the city.

Because of the city's position where the Yáo and Yǒng rivers meet twenty-five kilometres from the sea, thus sheltered from typhoon waves, its people have been foreign-business minded since the 5th century. Beginning when the Silk Road lost favour, silk products, salt, tea and pottery were exported from the city for 1,400 years, assisted by a system of canals, lakes, and rivers connecting with the Grand Canal which ended at Hángzhōu. Much was shipped to Korea and Japan, though a local porcelain made in the Táng Dynasty (618–907) has been found in East Africa.

The ancient town was enclosed within solid 10th-century walls, necessary to thwart attacks from determined pirates that continued into the 20th century. Fish were caught and salted, lumber milled, varnish formulated, bamboo harvested, ships built, and bankers proliferated. The Portuguese traded here in the 16th century, requiring major Chinese military action to quell their insolence and belligerence. That was a taste of the colonial arrogance to come, for the British forced the reopening of the port during the First Opium War (1841). Thereafter, Shànghǎi's booming port began to dominate, coinciding with people around Níngbō inventing the game of *má jiàng* (mah-jong).

In 1940, a Japanese military plane dumped over the town a cargo of plague-infected fleas, bred from mice and rats. It was more effective than dropping anthrax direct. Five hundred civilians perished.

Originally a library, there remains from the 16th century the Tiānyī Gé, an ornate, wooden, temple-like

---

[1] Apparently there's a superb one in Tiānjīn.

13-3

building with exaggeratedly curved southern-style eaves, offset by rich gold ornamentation. As well as fire-eating dragons, the ridges feature deer and protuberances resembling the sterns of boats – unique in China.

When we walked the principal east-west street, it was a carpet of reconstruction, punctuated by ghettos of deserted wooden slums in compressed alleys. Towering above them, new skyscrapers were reaching confidently to the sky, while a stylish walkway over a galactic intersection was a day away from opening. In narrow Kaiming Jiē, old dark shacks provided a last burst from the past. This is a mass knocking down of old China. I hope the people are able to retain the worthy aspects of that history, and wish them luck with their brave new world.

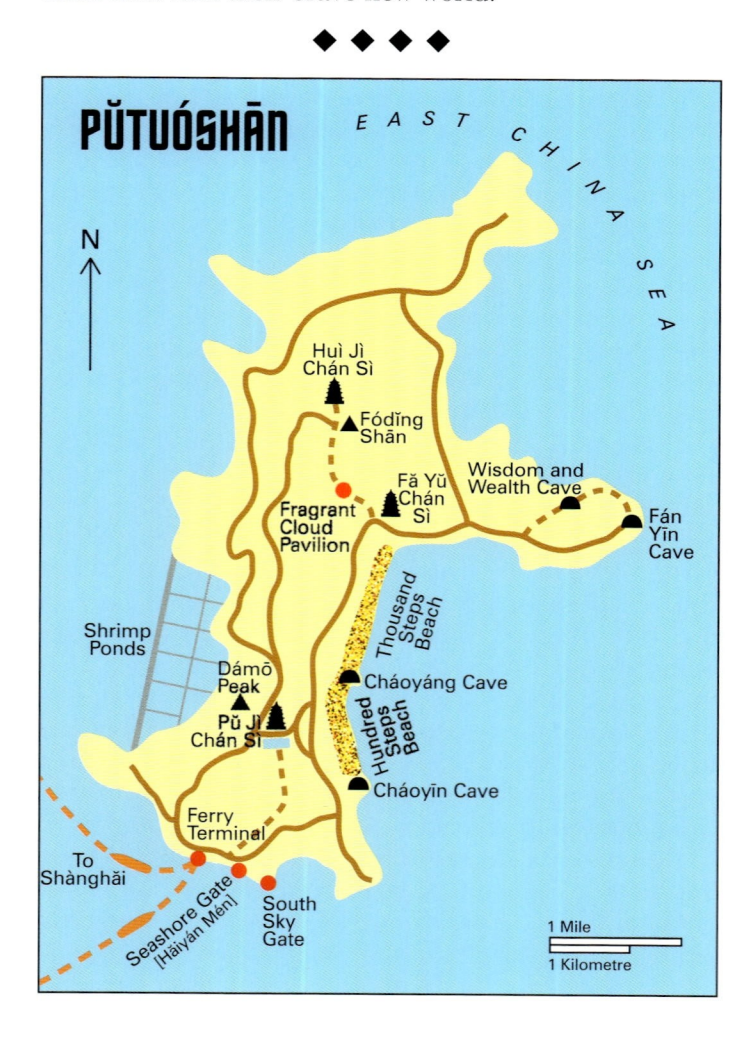

◆ ◆ ◆ ◆

Pǔtuóshān

Excluding the tiddlers, there are some 5,000 physical islands in China, the majority off the coast from Shànghǎi southwards – roughly half of the country's long 18,000 to 19,000-kilometre coastline. The cluster around Zhōushān Island, south-east from Shànghǎi, forms the largest archipelago. Off Zhōushān's east flank, easily missed on a map, is the island of **Pǔtuóshān**. *Pǔtuó* is the same corruption of *Potala* as in Pǔtuózōngshèng, the temple in Chéngdé [chapter 6]. Meaning 'White Flower', *Potala* is the Sanskrit name for the mountain on which Buddha met Avalokitesvara. In China the latter is Guān Yīn, the popular goddess whose statue is in most Chinese temples, and this island is her spiritual home. She can bring release from illness or life's sufferings, or respond to a woman's request to bear a child. Her full name, Guān Shì Yīn, declares no less that she 'Hears the Sounds of the World'. Such a sympathetic figure explains the island's popularity as a pilgrimage destination among people today, some of whom are desperate for help.

It has been so for a thousand years ever since she interceded miraculously when a boat off the island was in danger from a typhoon (from the Chinese *dà fēng*, meaning 'great wind'). Legends of this event grew, including that she walked on the sea, and the effect was dramatic. At one stage, there were 218 temples on the island, supporting two to four thousand monks – astonishing on a diminutive island eight kilometres long by an average two wide. Before the Japanese invaded China in the 1930s, there were still over a hundred temples and hermitages. The Cultural Revolution decimated them decades later.

The word *shān* in the name of the island is used in its alternative sense of 'hill', since its two peaks are of modest height – Fódǐng (Buddha Summit) Shān in the north half of the island (see map) being a lowly 291 metres.

Looking south from this peak, 13-4 shows the sweep of the two foremost beaches on the eastern side, with other islands in the distance. The Thousand Steps Beach is the first and longer one, after which a small pavilion marks the promontory that contains Cháoyáng (Facing the Sun) Cave. The headland at the end of the Hundred Steps Beach incorporates Cháoyīn (Sound of the Tide) Cave, which is where Guān Yīn has appeared most often to those who believe in her.

★ ★ ★

13-4

None of the above concerned us as we ran along the shorter beach as if liberated. After all the trials and hassles, the million minor but weighty decisions, the adjusting to a different culture and way of doing things, the juggling with bus and train timetables, avoiding being ripped-off at every turn, *et al*, we had succeeded in reaching our last destination in one piece, more or less in one mind. Being in such an unexpected spot was almost psychedelic. A clean, sandy, deserted, quiet, spacious, lazy beach – in China? After months of freezing buses and streets of concrete, it was exhilarating being on a real island. And it was balmy, almost tropical – in December, in the Republic of China! Visions of such beaches in the off-season in Hawaii, the Canary Islands or Sri Lanka are easy enough, but a Costa del China in winter – a double contradiction – we had never imagined could exist. The bizarreness sustained wide and disbelieving grins on our faces for days.

For the first time in two months, we relaxed – sitting for no other reason than for a rest, as if a pulled cork had vanquished the fizziness in a bottle. Below the pavilion over Cháoyáng Cave, time took a back seat as the sea lapping the shore rocked us into a lull of fazed contemplation *(13-5)*.

13-5

A ferry had taken five hours to reach this edge of the Central Nation, after which a twenty-minute walk – the limit now with my heavy pack – uphill from the south brought us to the residential centre, where a woman guided us to a back-alley guest house.

In an international-standard hotel, an exhibition of original paintings proved too tempting, and we both successfully bargained for one, mine that of a wise older Chinese philosopher with a young student, the effect simple and uncluttered. Another metre-long box was added to the pack.

The reverie on the beach was completed by this scene near the South Sky Gate *(13-6)*.

◆ ◆ ◆ ◆

The two principal monasteries in the northern section required a day's walking. While climbing the road on the west side overlooking substantial shrimp ponds delineated by a concrete causeway, I saw a bird. While it sang in a roadside tree, it dawned that I couldn't recall ever seeing one in the whole of Hàn China until then, with the sole exception of the bird of prey on Tàishān.

According to the subsequent photograph, something else was in the tree that still makes me ill at ease. This may not initially make sense, reader, but when later I studied all the slides, too many for comfort from this one on were slashed with lines of vivid red plus yellow *as part of* each photograph – they were not a developer's error. *13-7* is an example. As each ensued, I knew looking back what was about to happen (Part Three). It was and is a warning from the Amoeba: a *rift* in the photographs – a Rift in the universe. I mean exactly that. The first one in the tree makes it look like a burning bush. The rift is a portent of things to come, yet materialising afterwards to confirm that it was no accident – the future about to happen in the past.

The less significant explanation is that it was a light leak in the camera caused by ageing felt. Sometimes it appears as a small white splash. Yet it is not manifest on every shot – the majority are clear. It began in the middle of a roll, but I had already taken five pictures that morning and had not knocked the camera minutes before. Months later, I discovered that the six miniature screws that secure the top plate to the body were missing. I can understand one or two becoming loose, which I would have felt scraping against my fingers, but not all six, none of which I had noticed. It doesn't make sense, except in the non-worldly way of the previous paragraph.

The summit of Fódǐng Shān was encased in inevitable shops and takeaways. Along an extended corridor of ochre-yellow monastery walls, these words confirmed the location *(13-7)*: Fó Dǐng Dǐng Fó. The reversed repeat is a play on words: Buddha Summit – Supreme Buddha. The oily blobs of thick black characters, like liquid liquorice, shone as if alive. Note the tiled ridge's dragon mouths. Further along, a single character again in black brilliantine announced 'Buddha'! Steps zigzagging and undulating like a Chinese dragon led to the first courtyard of Huì Jì Chán Sì, Meditating on the Wisdom of Helping Temple *(13-8)*.

13-7

13-6

13-8

A tree-filtered fan-effect of the sun's rays filled the space in welcome. The eight words on the wall, read from right to left, are a chant formed around Guān Shì Yīn's name. As I took a close-up of the candles in their mini pavilion, the fanned rays fired directly at me, the burning candles seeming to mirror the colours of the burning *rift*.

With buildings up to 200 years old, the open main courtyard was a paean of colour, blue sky, relaxed business, and people watching people *(13-9)*.

13-9

13-10
13-11

Painters were at work on one of the roof-swallowing dragons, whose architectural term is *chī wén* – an acroterion *(13-10)*. To the left, its pair was next for the treatment *(13-11)*. What a transformation: the old colours reborn against a brushed blue backdrop!

The atmosphere was benevolent, a feeling enhanced a hundredfold when in a side corridor a pack of schoolchildren took an interest in me. It is always a pleasure to communicate with young people, their innocence and fun invigorating and ennobling, and after considerable laughter, I set the camera on the tripod, marshalled them in front, and let one of them take their own group portrait. Inevitably the timing was wrong, with some looking at me to one side, and the picture is not strictly a success *(13-12)*. But there is a glorious cohesiveness to them – twenty humans as one, so trusting, even suave and classy. There is a sacred purity too – humans who haven't yet had to face some of life's problems. It would be interesting to compare the picture with one of them thirty years hence.

A path descended past the Fragrant Cloud Pavilion to a clearing in the trees above Thousand Steps Beach, where I gave some bananas to a beggar with a missing leg, putting into practise my friend's example. According to him, "the smile on the crippled man's face was unbelievable." A similar yellow corridor preceded a walled courtyard haloed with tall, lime-coloured trees fronting the entrance arch to Fă Yŭ Chán Sì *(13-13)*.

To the right began the pilgrimage down the central path familiar to all temples in China. Barracks of monks' quarters line both sides, the path piercing arches of halls beckoning with bold calligraphy above and to the sides (here announcing the Sky King), while common women light candles of incense – candles of hope. With each step there is more beyond, the lines of perspective aiming for some distant point as one walks towards infinity. Then like a squid viewing a blue whale, you look up through the trees, whose gorgeous foliage here was in autumnal tints, at the colossus that is the main hall, and perambulate around incense burners as big as baby elephants *(13-14, 13-15)*.

13-12

13-13

71

First built in 1580, these intricate interlocking baleen plates of the supporting beams and brackets are as impressive as any in China – no wonder this is named the Nine Dragon Brackets Hall. The sign says 'The Passing Blessing is Boundless'. Inside, a substantial statue of Guān Yīn surveys all who enter. The grandly layered yellow roof tiles shine in the sun, while pavilions of candles echo the architecture with yellow tiles curving slowly palanquin-style to a central peak. Monks attend to the prominent *bōshānlú* (incense burner), the *shān* indicating its original Daoist purpose to represent the mountain of the Blessed Islands where Immortals live. In temples, there are usually three of them made of bronze dominating the open court in front of main halls, and are an art form in themselves. Up goes the smoke, up go your prayers, both leaving the earthly world and reaching for the Sky King.

A terraced garden behind includes a chamber out of which smoke pours through a window under an extraordinary roof of closely bunched acroterions (*13-16, 13-17*). The temple's ridges are full of them, their bulbous eyes, baubles on sticks, and cockatoo crests expressing a mean demeanour: "Behave, or else!" (*13-18, 13-19*). No wonder the temple is clean and quiet

The name of the monastery translates literally as 'Law Rain Meditation Temple' – *chán* being of the same

13-14

13-16

13-17

13-18

13-19

13-15

derivation as the Chán sect at Shàolín [chapter 8]. It is thus a place to Meditate on the Law of the Rain – that which gently but surely washes away malignancy and other undesirables, indicating they can always be overcome in such a manner. Such are my meditations anyway!

13-20

As we arrived, we overheard a Chinese guide extolling the exclusive virtues of the locale to an American woman on a reconnaissance trip for a future tour. If her group came, they "wouldn't find any other Westerners on the island".

"Well *they're* Westerners, aren't they?" she remarked disappointedly.

◆ ◆ ◆ ◆

A walk around the island took in the eastern peninsula, which is wilder and more remote. The primary draw is Fán Yīn (Brahma's Sound) Cave, approached by a narrowing ledge above the sea. The temple over the cave is as bizarrely positioned as the Monastery Hanging in the Sky near Dàtóng [chapter 7]. Perched in a V-shaped crevasse, one wonders what prevents it from sliding into the sea that slurps the pebbles below. An upper section is less precarious – sweetly compact, with a view of the East China Sea. The midday light was harsh, the heat forcing us to change into thinner trousers. I thought of my family preparing for Christmas in chilly, cloudy England!

73

A path over the peninsula took us to a tiny cave with an inconspicuous temple called Wisdom and Wealth, in which lies a miniature statue of Guān Yīn. It was deserted, apart from an old keeper who quietly welcomed us. With only the wind as companion, the unpretentiousness of the setting away from the madding crowd, its commonness, and its tranquil message made an impression on both of us – an exquisite jewel: wisdom and wealth in abundance where one least expects it.

Back at the residential centre, the old-style shops even sold those scrumptious chocolate Mylikes. At the nearby Pǔ Jì Chán Sì (Meditating on Universal Help Temple) with its 9 main halls, we acquired various Buddhist souvenirs including woodblocks and beaters. Across from the entrance, a large pool in late afternoon light created this farewell image *(13-20,* previous page).

◆ ◆ ◆ ◆

Departing every two days, a ship with iron bunk beds transported us overnight back to a different world. There was a warm smile of remembrance in my step as we strode along the Bund in Shànghǎi to the same Pǔjiāng Hotel of more than a year before. After obtaining tickets for the last ship to Hong Kong before Christmas, my colleague explored the city on his own (and was not impressed), while I made use of the 24-hour hot water in our baronial room to wash everything including packs and walking shoes.

The final day's shopping along Nánjīng Lù resulted in three substantial silk tablecloths being added to my pack, and new trainers – expensive by Chinese standards (£8). As we left the hotel, I ceremoniously dumped my previous Korean ones that had lasted twenty-six years *(13-21*: note the Kazak shoulder bag still in use). Light and airy, they were the most comfortable shoes for travel I have ever worn. The pack towered over my head threatening to topple me, if it didn't first buckle my knees. Fortunately the international wharf was only a short walk away.

The 'luxury liner' MV Shànghǎi was dowdy – the Chinese were not to spend money on a retiring ship – with toilets in some cabins dysfunctional, and our cupboard's lock inoperative. I stood on deck as the ship ventured down the Huángpǔ River, passing the dock's cranes, under the still-shining suspension bridge, both bringing back memories of the year before, instilling a sense of achievement concerning the journey so far. I thought of the manifold people who had made it memorable and enjoyable, and wondered what the next two months' travels would bring. There were diverse emotions and some tears: the end of anything successfully achieved being one of the sweetest tastes of life.

With the weather at sea dingy and cold, I spent much of the next two days in the ship's library, catching up on months of Chinese newspapers and taking notes. I returned Ritchie's compliment on the train to Chéngdé months before by grilling him with awkward questions about his approach to life. At meal times we waited until last to avoid the crush of the Chinese who dived in and grabbed what they could at the amiably served buffet – we were the only Westerners aboard.

I had last seen Hong Kong as well as Macau four years previously, travelling for two weeks among the islands, but along with Táiwān they are outside the scope of this book. This visit was an essential administrative six days, made comfortable by the virtue of staying with a cousin and family. The Tàishān sunrise film was developed (freeing the spare camera body), new film stocks replenished, later air tickets to Korea and the UK acquired, the Guìzhōu Overseas Travel Corporation visited, and my visa effortlessly renewed for another three months.

13-21

A visit to a doctor was almost an emergency. Apart from the gangrenous toe that had festered since Dàtóng, and the left thigh causing intermittent pain, I had noticed a possible hernia in the groin, and a boil had risen on my bum – not the best state to be in when commencing travels in south-west China! A riotously expensive doctor – thank goodness for insurance – suspected that a heavy pack (little did she know!) had been pinching the vertebrae in the back causing the leg problem, and issued pills that cleared the problem within two weeks. Antibiotics dealt with the streptococcal toe and boil, while, feeling around the groin area, she confirmed it was not a hernia.

The pack had to be lightened. Among the items ejected were reams of Chinese books, leaflets and maps acquired en route, the Lindqvist book, half of the LP guide and most of the Blue Guide, retaining torn-out sections. Plus 2 bulky rolled paintings, 3 large silk tablecloths, an embroidered silk cloth, 6 teapots and 4 cups, one Turkish-looking coffee pot and 6 brass cups, one *èrhú*, 12 cassette tapes, sets of postcards, a seal, ink-sticks, 5 fans and their stands, a litre bottle of rice wine, and the 49 rolls of film exposed so far. Much of that was sent to the UK, a total of 17 kilograms formerly on my back! The pack still weighed 13 kilos, with the daypack containing a further 6 kilos of photographic gear. In all, I had lately been carrying up to 40 kilograms in China – definitely not recommended.

Thirty hours before Christmas, Ritchie and I parted company at the airport after eighty days together. He had been an ideal travelling companion – someone not easy to find. We never disagreed about even one travel decision – amazing in itself. He was also scrupulous with money, which can otherwise cause friction when on the move. Above all, his dry humour, particularly in the zany surroundings we sometimes found ourselves, caused many a belly laugh replaying the situations days and months later at evening mealtimes, or in a room each night reliving the day's shenanigans. He made me see the humour in any episode – a great gift. If we occasionally grated on each other's nerves, he at least hid it well. Twelve weeks is not a short time constantly with someone, relationships never easy even in the course of normal living – then add the stresses and strains of travel. It was an achievement that we succeeded handsomely. We were incredibly favoured with the weather, the blue skies aiding the photography, although it was causing difficulty for the Chinese farmers. It had rained only three times in three months – including in Běijīng for a couple of hours, and in Dàtóng of course.

We had seen exactly sixty temples together, sustaining the interest virtually in all. *13-22* shows us at the Fragrant Cloud Pavilion on Pǔtuóshān, where we tasted some revelatory Chinese ice lollies with an unusual flavour – so good, we had seconds. We look relaxed, relatively clean and not too ragged, with I think a sense of relief on our faces at having survived. Plus a certain regret of a journey's conclusion – an end to memorably hewn events strewn throughout each day. Travel makes life a champagne privilege.

Six months later, he suggested we should repeat the precise journey in ten years time!

Near the ferry terminal on Pǔtuóshān is this Hǎiyán Mén, Seashore Gate – *13-23* taken as the sun was about to set. It marks a symbolic farewell to several phases, and is a gateway into a different dimension. I didn't know at the time the trials I was about to be subjected to, the next two months yielding a couple of nightmares.

13-22

13-23

77

PART THREE

chapter 14
Yángshuò

Setting up travel company on this leg of the journey could have resulted in a mixed party. Koreans cherish the concept of both sexes indulging in light-hearted frolics while travelling seriously. The candidates were former pupils eager both to sample a foreign land – the opportunities are rare for non-business Koreans – and to enhance their English in the concentrated practical environment that travel provides. One student wrote to me while studying English in Canada. 'This is why I learn English: it is to spend time talking to you and other Westerners.'

Being of greater age, which in Asia automatically evokes respect, I had been treated in Korea as a mentor, imparting advice about matters of life and philosophy. The close attention given was something I had only previously read about in tales of India – bards, teachers, and often bald wanderers being treated as wise sages. The Korean word for that type of person is *hunjang*, a 'teacher of Life'. A Korean maxim admonishes 'Do not step on the teacher's shadow', implying a respectful gulf of wisdom between you and those older.

For my part I had hoped to travel with folk of an Asian outlook. Inevitably difficulties arose: procuring leave from work and study, financing the project, and concerns of safety – business Koreans being attacked in certain areas of China for their money is a nagging reality. The possibilities dwindled to one – Tae Hun was to travel for a month, leaving the final four weeks on my own. Being in his twenties didn't concern me – I enjoy relating to any age: to a child aged five, to an old person aged eighty-five, and every permutation in between. There is as much to learn from a younger person as from an older one, reminding you not to lose those high, pioneering qualities of your own past. Besides, how often have I asked grannies and grandpas in their eighties how old they perceive themselves to be inside, the answer without fail being 'in my twenties'. One added she was astounded to perceive in a mirror the shrivelled form of her body cloaking her real soul. Young in heart – most of us are.

Koreans are educated in written Chinese characters, which was to prove helpful when I couldn't decipher them myself. However, since Koreans are not taught to speak the language, there was the distinct bonus that whenever the Chinese conversed with us over

14-2

14-1

the forthcoming weeks, they would invariably address the oriental-looking one, assuming he was Chinese. The look on their faces when it was the Englishman who replied in Chinese, while the 'Chinese' person couldn't utter a word, continually raised a smile.

So with a few days of 1995 remaining, with him having arrived from Seoul, the two of us boarded an evening flight in Hong Kong, and landed in Guìlín ('Gway-leen') in the north-east of Guǎngxī Province. With no bus available, I did not bargain as much as I should have done for the hour's taxi ride south, paying three times the going rate of ¥90, as I later discovered. The scenery along the straight road was mysterious and tantalising. Out of the darkness save for a milky moonlit tinge, massive mountainous shapes flashed by like ghosts on an assembly line. Imagining *14-1* at night would give an idea.

◆ ◆ ◆ ◆

Yángshuò is a few main streets of laid-back languidness. Lines of wheeled cigarette booths competing with those of wooden cafés advertising western menus were evidence of an international backpacker's haven, at this time of year hardly frequented. The *raison d'être* is the Lí River, and a road bridge overlooks the tourist, house and fishing boats, the eye unfailingly being drawn to the backdrop of bread-loaf pinnacles, like dragon's teeth scattered on a vast plain *(14-2/3/4)*.

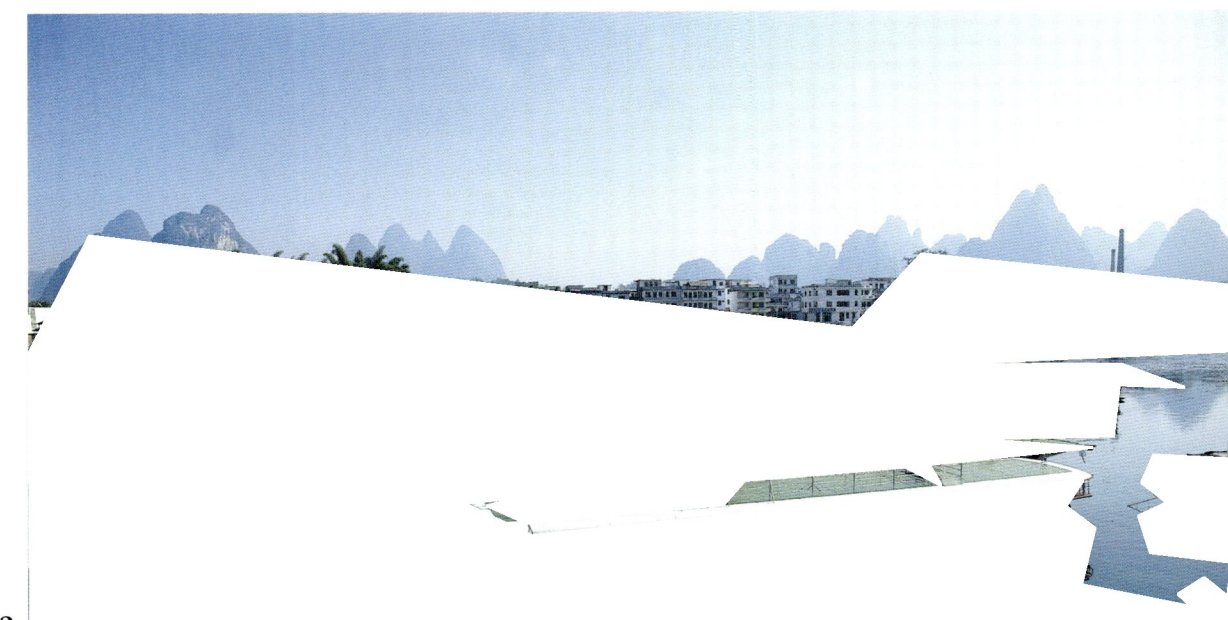

14-3

14-4

With the draw of market day at Xīngpíng four hours downriver to the north, bikes were parked on the roof of a barge, and we embarked with other Westerners on this world-famous ribbon of a river. The writer Hán Yù (768–824) in the Táng dynasty likened it to 'a green silk belt, the mountains like hairpins of turquoise jade'. The Chinese have allocated names to the variously-shaped limestone peaks along the valley, some of tilted plateaus mimicking miniature green versions of those in Utah canyons. On the west bank is Dragonhead Hill, Yellow Cloth in the Water, Pen Promontory, Carp and Snail Hills, Yearning for Husband Rock, Clean Vase, Nine Oxen Ridge, and Millstone and Cockfighting Hills. Opposite is Nine Horse Fresco Hill, Wave Crag, White Tiger Hill, Miller-at-Work Hill, Embroidery Hill, Helmet Crag, the nine peaks of Picture Hill, and Five Fingers Hill.

Much of the landscape's still, heady atmosphere derives from the local, distinctive Spiny Bamboo, *Bambusa arundinacea*, a species generously draped with arched, bushy fronds like frilly fingers fanning the air below the sentinel peaks. The graceful bends in the bamboo echo the curvatures in the river, which symbolise a map of the turns in our lives. In deeper water are suspended black fishing nets, while the shallows reveal shingles covered in yellows, browns and the greens of algae, and white stones complementing brown waterfowl and the tan beaks of white ducks. Thin rafts carry silky, black, fishing cormorants and their masters along satin waters, while a women in red washes whatnots at the edge. Cows luxuriate at leisure in this biblical Eden, under a concentrated radiant light. This boat ride strolls through a Chinese scrolled painting, and you become enmeshed in the landscape. "Whoever sees this, loses h/himself in eternity!"

With track 4 the synchronisation is not vital, and you may prefer to go with the mood. Short 15" introduction, then to next page.

14-5 ▲ *first 4 violin shimmers*

14-6 ▼ *solo cello (short); turn for the next shimmers*

14-7 ▲ *next 4 violin shimmers*

82

14-8 ▼ *solo cello*

14-9 ▲ *shimmers*

14-10 ▼ *(short); turn for next shimmers*

14-11 ▲ *shimmers*

14-12 ▼ *cello*

▲ *shimmers* ▼ *cello + few seconds silence* **14-14** 85

14-15 ▲ *high cello note, which drops*

14-16 ▼ *high sustained cello notes, unaccompanied*

14-17 *this page: long string crescendo; turn when volume resides...* 14-18

14-19

quieter this page; opposite page for final long crescendo

14-20

14-21

14-22

89

14-23

If you are wondering, reader, why this music of mystery and stealth, it is only partly a reflection of the river's aura as it seemed at the time. As the above photograph shows, I am wearing the new Chinese trainers for the first time, and look relaxed and content. Inside however, an evil was insidiously twisting and spreading unseen like a cancer. It had been implanted from the outside during the early hours of Christmas Day – a rude, unsubtle irony of which God was well aware. It was part of H/his plan. Despite the agony that event in Hong Kong had spouted, and was still doing, S/he willed it. Suffice to say it was intimately connected with the Cheju event.

My new travel companion, in shot in *14-12*, was unaware of it since it had been instigated before his arrival. I tried not to let it affect the travels, but the Amoeba was to pile on the pressure, and it was unbalancing me.

In that photograph, too, menacing like a pandemic plague about to burst, is the *rift*. The red and yellow slashes had returned, more vivid and insistent than ever. This and those to come have not been expunged from this book: each one is a portent ever advancing unbeckoned, about to unleash the Cane of Love. *14-21* (previous page) presents the mountains' looming presence, dwarfing life below. Plus the rift again, it's burning me up, the Universe is splitting. A burning bush approacheth – God manipulating our reality, and it is not a game. *14-22* is nothing, if not the Lord of the Universe.

★ ★ ★

14-24

14-25

The boat terminated at Xīngpíng *(14-24)*. Along this country village's narrow main street, off picture to the left, the market's activities were approaching their close. Seated women were selling dried produce, a man squatted smoking a cigarette, and an old man passed by bent double. Bicycles heaving with purchases were the prime transport, supplemented by tractors strolling the street carrying passengers. The four baskets in *14-25* each contain a pig – a common method of conveyance. Find the ears!

Back in Yángshuò, we boarded another boat as the night deepened, and noiselessly tagged a fisherman hunting the traditional way with trained, obedient cormorants, imported from a faraway coast *(14-26 overleaf)*. With their livery and beaks flecked with flashes of silver, the elongated necks of these graceful birds effortlessly gleaned through the water like silver arrows through ink. Memorable were the raft's narrow-bore tubes of bamboo like horizontal organ pipes, lashed side by side and curved at both ends to prevent water seepage. Distinctive too were the glints in the texture of the life-sustaining liquid on which the skiff was skimming, and the soundless unassuming fisherman with a characteristic straw hat. Suspended from a swan-neck pole reflected in the velvet fluid, a yellow lamp dangled deliciously just above the surface, drawing both our focus and fatally the prey. All this was in an ecosphere of silence, save for the lapping of the humble hunter's pole.

Gliding the punt onto a bank, and without uttering a word, the fisherman illustrated for us the ancient technique. As the birds dried their sheeny coats, wings spreadeagled in the still air, the yellow pouch and neck of each was bloated – barely visible bound string was restricting expansion of their throats further down. The man coaxed the catch into a basket by applying hand pressure on the throats. With the birds rewarded with a few of the fish, there was time for a quick snapshot souvenir *(14-27*: with the fisherman is another Korean tourist on the left).

◆ ◆ ◆ ◆

I exercised on the stone floor of the hostel's dormitory while everyone else slept: despite the challenging circumstances, I was sustaining the programme I had set every two days. Decent mountain bikes were more than sufficient for an hour's ride to Moon Hill, the road snaking between a proliferation of limestone mounds. Near the destination was an undeveloped cave system, which, guided by a friendly and gentle farmer, involved scrambling head bowed into an unlit cave-room with a squelchy mud floor, used locally for the occasional slippery madcap party.

92   14-26

14-27

14-28

As we climbed Moon Hill, the buildings of the farmer's small village seemed to nestle into the bosom of the pinnacles rising out of a plain *(14-28)*. The top of the hill was pierced by an almost perfectly spherical large hole, offering a ring of alluring blue *(14-29)*. It seemed an apposite moongate, through which on the other side you are confronted by one of the most famous views in the world *(14-30)*....

14-29

14-30

This never-to-be-forgotten scene is the product of two million years of erosion on towering carbonate rock that had accumulated beforehand below an immense shallow sea cloaking a sector of southern China. This extended from eastern Yúnnán and enveloped Guìzhōu and Guăngxī provinces. It took 400 million years for the limestone to form under the sea, which existed from early Cambrian times well into the Triassic Period, finally receding 200 million years ago as a result of continental uplift. There is no greater expanse of this karst on earth, which in total covers twelve percent of the planet's unfrozen land surface. Other examples are the karst plateau of former Yugoslavia, and a different 'dry' kind existing on the Nullarbor Plain in south-west Australia.

Scrambling over the arch of the moon hole, we turned and peered into the sun, the scenery stretching mesmerisingly into infinity *(14-31)*.

14-31

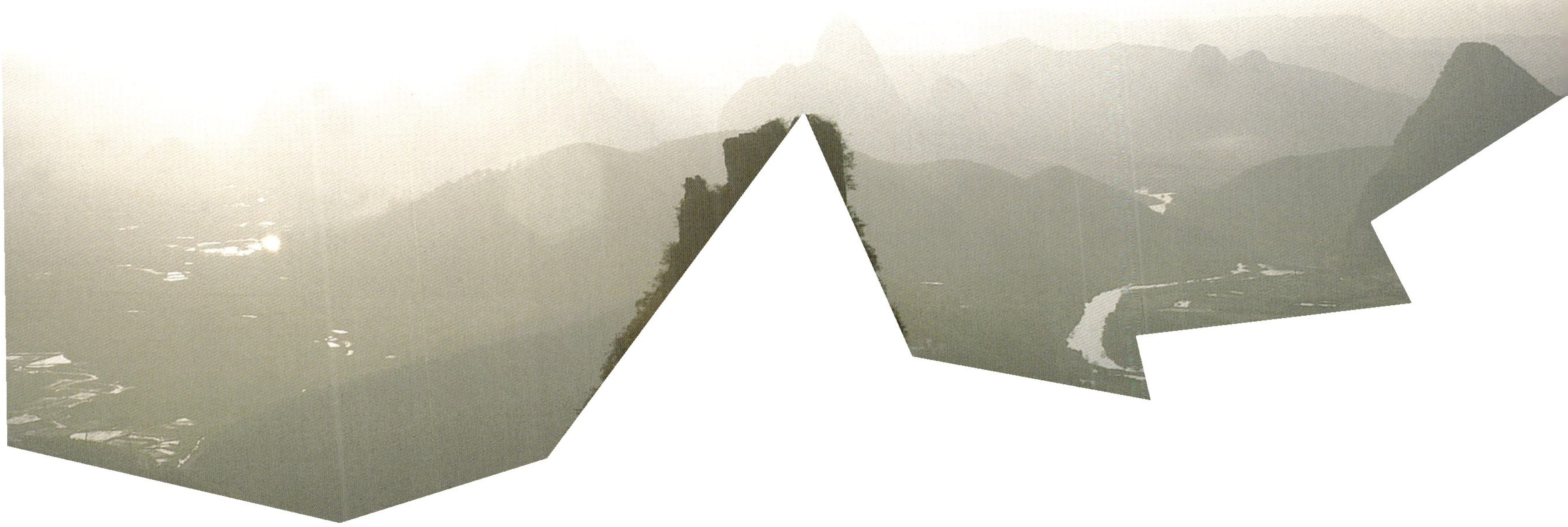

testing

> Then the Divine Vision like a silent Sun appeard above.
>
> William Blake, *Jerusalem*

We were alone up here. Except we were not. The Sun was closer than it had been, uncomfortably bright; it pierced the sky like 10,000 arrows, searing into my conscious mind as subtle as nuclear light. Yet with a placid silkiness, it was simply there, existing, invisibly pulsating – at the edge of one's life, but in the centre. The stillness in the atmosphere, the spiritual presence, was as palpable as the bulk of a supertanker emerging out of fog, passing mere metres in front.

In such luminosity, I was distinctly uneasy. The aggregate of circumstances had been set up, manipulated by the Sun itself over several lifetimes. The beaming message was singular and multiple, and I squirmed in its simple complexity.

> The Good are attracted by Mens perceptions
> And Think not for themselves
> Till Experience teaches them to catch
> And to cage the Fairies & Elves
>
> And then the Knave begins to snarl
> And the Hypocrite to howl
> And all his good Friends shew their private ends
> And the Eagle is known from the Owl
>
> *Motto to the Songs of Innocence & of Experience,*
> William Blake

Dear reader, how many times have you been *betrayed*? Not a minor event, by a secondary person, I mean a cataclysmic breaking of trust – by someone known all your life, or else close to you. I hope not often; it is the bitterest of poisons.

H. figuratively stabbed me in the back. He had a simple choice: embrace Good, or revel in his own evil. Rather than face himself, he chose the latter: ignorant dogma and arrogance, laced with a rash of racism and sexism, bursting forth out of its barely-contained box.

> "Peter, there's nothing about Life I can learn from you."

My reaction and anger was *justified*: and therein lay the problem, and the paradox.

He was a Western man, but betrayal had arisen twice previously, months before, both at the hands of Western women, one of whom I had known for fifteen years.

> ...downright lies
> and hurtful
> nonsense –
> often in the
> name of
> love.

Each time it occurred without warning, without a hint anything was wrong or out of place. The flip side of a woman loving you is often, in my experience, unhealthy possessiveness. Again, I was so angry about their inhumane illogic.

It is highly unlikely I will ever see those three again. That cataclysmic break-up of a relationship, in a quagmire of recriminations, had *never* happened to me before. This however was three times in four months! Trust broken on this third occasion was too much.

While the first two had been ameliorated by the Supreme Joy of the second Gift [chapter 7], and by the sheer excitement of the previous months travels in China, this Christmas one was different because of its association with the Cheju incident. H. had interfered blindly with the most significant event in my life, as if putting a knife into it, not realising what he was doing.

> People have their limitations; it is folly to try to force them to understand what is beyond their comprehension.
>
> Wáng Tíng Xiāng (1474-1544),
> *Shènyán (Cautious Words)*

It was my mistake, caused by ignorance and being too trustful. It was to have a knock-on effect on the remaining travels in China. Further, the Cheju words burned into my brain predicted a fourth break-up – one with God – and the 'time limit' for that was almost at hand. The final seconds were ticking like God's thunder drum. The symbol of the break – the Rift, the strange presence – was looming nearer.

★ ★ ★

14-34

Some are Born to Endless Night
Auguries of Innocence,
William Blake

O why was I born with a different face
Why was I not born like the rest of my race
William Blake,
letter to Thomas Butts, 1803

Another testing was in progress far away in Korea, at a far more gruelling level, entirely separate yet intricately related. I knew nothing of it at the time, although I later witnessed some of it and the resultant effects, after an indication of its content had been relayed to me. This page outlines it. Its horror was scorching and alarming – as is anything that involves the Almighty inflicting pain.

I've described, reader, what it is like to endure God bombarding the human mind with an external torrent of thoughts [chapter 9]. Mine was for a few nights. Can you imagine that same Deity doing so to a human for eighteen months, every night – during which period sleep is not permitted or possible? I swear to you this happened, and was happening. Each dawn when the grip was released, a modicum of sleep was allowed during the early hours.

As my meagre experience had resulted in scribbling on paper when each thought arrived, so in this case the hapless human wrote in journals every night. The scribbling, however, concerned deeper matters: the Creator's problems, the Creator's pain, truths about the Universe at large, as well as those on earth.

According to Dante's vision, Hell hath 9 Circles, the final descent being into the lake of icy nothingness after the previous passionate fires. Thereafter follows Purgatory, the place of cleansing. Earth, of course, *is* Hell – just look at so many people's lives. So this is how God purges one of human weakness (evil), by applying different intensities of pressure, thereby grinding down the passion to live, revealing a frigid indifference. Or is it purging H/himself? Oh, what a Divine Comedy, ha, ha, ha! Is Heaven – the *doppelgänger* of Hell – worth such a price?

"I am a little bit confused...."
I was not surprised, poor person. What is the outcome of being a child of God, as each of us is? This one withdrew into h/himself, attempting desperately to hold on to a semblance of balance, not comprehending the purpose of the tumultuous test, keeping it secret from everyone – even from close family and best friends. Not surprising that in melancholy mood s/he consoled h/himself in songs, over and over *im perpetuam*...

14-35

You have always been alone.
It's comfortable for you to be alone.
———
Actually you feel lonely because you betray yourself....
Come back to yourself who talks about your dreams with smiles,
even though it is hard.
Thermal Island, by Kim Jong Seo
(Korean singer/songwriter),
track 'Hey Man', translated

Why was the Amoeba executing this trial, and expecting a godlike reaction from a human?

Innocent unknowing goodness, whether actual or feigned, is a curse. That condition in a human has to be crushed. God *has* to destroy it. Otherwise becoming knowingly perfect cannot be achieved.

Of life's learning experiences, suffering is spasmodically the only way – the Great Teacher.

"If you wish to be the *best* person,
you must suffer the bitterest of the bitter."
the human's own words

What exactly was God relaying during the bombardment? Not being party to it, I can only guess by supposition:

> What are called vices in the natural world, are the highest sublimities in the spiritual world.
> William Blake
> (H. Crabb Robinson's diary)[1]

> If the sorrow of others is happiness for you, you can do anything.
> *Thermal Island* [ibid], 'Hey Man'

In similar words, I had told the human the following:

> Christ is the only God – And so am I and so are you.
> William Blake
> (H. Crabb Robinson's diary)[2]

> Each man has the essence of God, and all the wisdom and the power of the world within himself.
> Paracelsus (1493-1541),
> quoted in *Paracelsus*, by Hartmann

Some more than others – and that is a curse.

★ ★ ★

Up here in the spitting glare of the Sun, I was ashamed. I had won a blessing that was a lie – one expressly allowed by God in the 16 Cheju words, but for the time being. I was on the other side of the divide, and could not see myself.

> As if a man were Author of himself, And knew no other kin.
> Shakespeare,
> *Coriolanus*, V.iii. 36–7

God's nickname is Paradox. S/he was in the process of both personally and impersonally dispensing pain to that human.

The hyena clamping a wildebeest by its snout... if you were the wildebeest, would you enjoy that? This Sun's child *does* enjoy it! If the offspring enjoys it, does the Parent? Hyenas kill for meat – there is nothing personal about it. When God applies Pain, it also seems impersonal – the Cane of Love.

The next step has to be grasped:

"Do you like God?", I was once asked.

The answer for each of us has to be: plainly not all the time. The acerbic beauty of a desert is only likeable when you are not having to deal with its harshness.

The association of the human with me was that the eighteen-month bombardment had commenced soon after the Tarrega music incident in the Korean teahouse in Cheju [chapter 9]. Connections. No irrelevant coincidence. Someone had to suffer to put across the Message, and the Amoeba had chosen a scapegoat.

"One cannot gaze too long at the Sun." My words, my realisation! Yet at the same time, one has to remove the darkened visors:

> Don't look at me with sunglasses,
> Untie your necktie and see the world.
> The wall that surrounds you is too high.
> You can fly freely,
> waking yourself up from your long, long sleep.
> *Thermal Island*, 'Thermal Island'

The testing that really mattered for me was soon to be unleashed. God doesn't confront you with things you've learned before. That is a truism of how to teach.

"What is important is *you* – your ears, your mouth, your eyes...."

God will attack you, reader. That is going to happen – yesterday, tomorrow, in twenty years time, or in the next life.

When it does, will you be ready?

I wasn't.

---

[1] pp. 316/7 and [2] p. 310 of Blake Records, edited by G.E. Bentley jnr (Oxford, 1969)

We had to quit the moongate's magical mound scenery far too soon – there were pressing engagements ahead, and plans were tight. Concerned we hadn't done Yángshuò justice, I pressed Tae Hun for his opinion.

"We are pushed for time, but do you want to stay longer?"

"Can we stay for ever?"

"No!"

"Then, let's go!"

I creased with laughter. It was a typically Asian response to, and acceptance of the inevitability of Life. A travel companion had cheered me up in an instant.

Earlier, I had asked him what his last words were to his relations when departing for China.

"I said, 'I'm sorry'. I meant for my selfishness. I was sorry I couldn't help them on the family farm during the period away."

◆ ◆ ◆ ◆

The original 'Forest of Laurel Trees', which **Guìlín** means and where we stayed the night, no longer exists. Neither do the city's traditional buildings, destroyed in the Japanese aerial bombardment preceding WWII. There is little to detain even the tourist groups here: an amble up a narrow rocky passage to Solitary Beauty Peak was pleasant, but the view nothing special.

After cycling to Reed Flute Cave, we enjoyed mingling with bulging tourist parties, including a Korean one, for whom the iridescent, gay and gaudy cave lights were switched on, but not for individual sightseers! The dripping, calcified stalactites and counterparts were labelled 'Aurora over Lion Bridge', 'Waterfall splashing down from a high gorge', as well as 'melons and vegetables', 'peanuts', 'ginseng', and the pear-shaped 'Snowman'. A cathedral space deep within was worth seeing – the Crystal Palace of the Dragon King. This area of China has enormous potential to be a pure caving experience on a par with any in the world, the caves courtesy of the penetrating acidic groundwater after the Cambrian/Triassic sea receded. Unfortunately, tourism encourages damaging aspects more lurid than the lights: Americans and Japanese have paid $13,000 to 'own' organ-pipe stalagmites broken off from this cave.

Beforehand, I had attempted to confirm the three crucial forthcoming flights in Yúnnán, having failed previously in Hángzhōu. The spacious new CAAC office brought news of a worrying kind: my booking made in Korea was nowhere in the computer system, nor even on the long waiting lists, nor could CAAC make reservations let alone issue tickets. Why have a booking office if you cannot book flights was a classic Chinese conundrum.

Fortunately the Chinese have a solution to such problems. A young woman behind a desk revealed nonchalantly with a sweet smile that she had a 'friend' in the relevant local airline. After half an hour of discreet long-distance phone calls, I had the tickets in my hands. To secure them required a packet of cash on the counter, which emptied my money belt. The bank next door didn't exchange travellers' cheques – the only one in China in my experience. We were instantly in another Chinese-concocted crisis, and it was New Year's Eve as well! A dash on our bikes to the main bank in the city, ten minutes before it closed early for the celebrations, brought brow-stroking relief.

chapter 15

Guìzhōu Province

One of the ancient world's biggest national censuses was organised by the Hàn Dynasty in AD 2, the result suggesting there were 59 million taxpayers in China. In 1086 the country supported 108 million people, with pestilence preventing the 200 million mark being exceeded until 1762. Thereafter numbers exploded exponentially: a census less than seventy years later revealed a doubling to 395 million. The first one organised by the Communists was in 1953, divulging 583 million people; in 1995, the population officially reached 1.2 billion – it had doubled in forty-two years. Contributing to this was the resounding achievement of increasing life expectancy by over 50%. When the party came to power in 1949, 60% of babies died before they were one year old, and the average lifespan was between 35 and 45 years. Now it is 71.

Another communist success was that the birth rate halved in the same forty-two year period. Nevertheless, it is still three times the death rate. Sources are murky, but between fourteen and twenty-four million babies are currently born in China annually – the equivalent of reproducing one of the world's most populated capital cities year after year after year. People in cities until the 1960s had only an average two square metres of sheltered living area each – not much more than the space taken when sleeping, although this has since improved.

In China, the poor have been formally defined as those who earn under $35 a year. In 1993, there were twenty-seven million at this level; an additional fifty million managed only $50. It is not something most of us in the West could contemplate. Even so, that is immense progress compared to 1980 when, according to the World Bank, there were 220 million in China with less than adequate food, housing and clothing – the three litmus tests of abject poverty. Under such circumstances, it is salutary not to forget the words of the Chinese-American writer Lin Yutang in 1934:

> No one is entitled to condemn until he knows what famine means. Some of us have been forced in times of famine to eat babies.
>
> *My Country and My People* (p. 318)
> [William Heinemann]

In 1994, the average annual income for an urban dweller was officially ¥3,150 (£250), while those in the country secured ¥1,200 (£95). Most supplemented this through secondary jobs and moonlighting. Government workers in cities are paid double that, and in some state companies, earnings can reach ¥1,000 a month. Three-quarters of all Chinese people (900 million) do not pay income tax. Only a third of China's children reach high school. A 1990 census found that as many as 180 million adults are illiterate, 70% being women, although again that is a huge improvement on 1949 when perhaps 80% of the populous could not read.

If the above seems grim, there are remote ethnic regions of China where the reality was and is significantly worse than average. Meaning 'Noble Island', the province of Guìzhōu is one of the least visited by foreign travellers – open only since 1987. In 1998, its GDP per person was the worst in China – 60% less even than Tibet's. Poverty existed here not long ago to a degree most of us have never imagined. In the 1930s, people in Guìzhōu could reasonably expect to be dead in their twenties, having scarcely ever donned a dress or pair of trousers – extended families often possessed only one of each to share between them. Syphilis, leprosy, typhoid, smallpox and malaria were widespread, as was opium consumption.

Virtually all of the land in Guìzhōu is mountainous (87%) or hilly (10%), and even today 82% of the province's people live around these areas, not in the cities. A long-held Chinese adage is: 'In Guìzhōu, you will never see three consecutive days of sunshine, three taels of silver, or three *mǔ* of flat land'. It was through the convoluted mountains and those in Yúnnán that the Communists trundled on their Long March in 1934 away from the Guómíndǎng, eventually arriving in Yán'ān in the north after almost 10,000 kilometres of walking. Hiking from New York to San Francisco, back to Washington DC, and halfway to Los Angeles avoiding roads would give some sensation of that.

In his book *The Long March: The Untold Story*, Harrison E. Salisbury records some of the consequences of poverty in the hills at that time:

> They sold their children if anyone would buy them. They smothered or drowned baby girls. That was routine. The boys were killed too, if there was no market for them. The price for children fluctuated.... The infant mortality rate in Guizhou in 1934 was about 50 per cent. It was so high that a child's birth was not celebrated until it was at least a month old. Life expectancy was about thirty years.... Illiteracy was total.
>
> [Macmillan, 1985]

Aside from the 93% of the Chinese who are Hàn, sixteen of the sixty minorities nationwide have populations greater than a million. The largest are the Zhuang, numbering over 16 million, who live mainly in Guǎngxī Province. In all, the ethnic groups are spread over 60% of China's land – of more significance than their total numbers, 75 million, would indicate.

Being the same tribe as the Hmong in Thailand and Laos, the Miao have eked out a living in Guìzhōu's mountains for about 2,000 years. At over six million the most predominant of the thirty minorities in the province, they are fond of festivals at which up to 30,000 gather adorned in their best traditional costumes and weighty silver headgear. They dwell throughout the province but are most concentrated in the south-east, which is the only sector where the 2½ million Dong live. It was this area I chose to investigate for a week at the start of 1996.

★ ★ ★

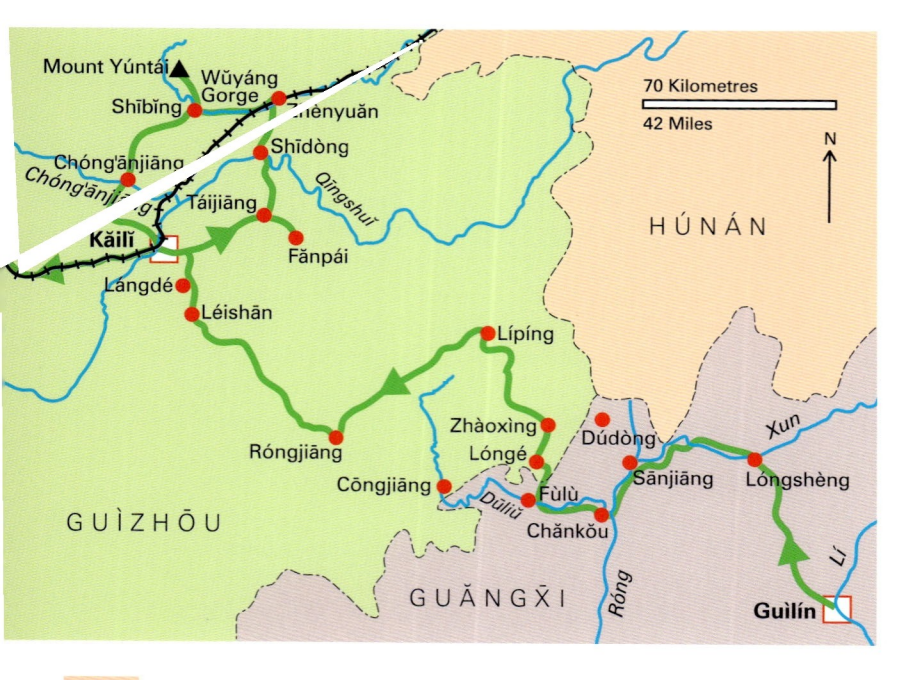

Reaching it from Guìlín was another matter. Lonely Planet's guidebook printed border towns on its map a hundred kilometres in the wrong direction[1], and stated that the route was 'only an option for travellers with time to kill' on buses that were 'very infrequent and travel at a snail's pace over roads that only barely qualify as such'. Gina Corrigan's book *Guizhou* didn't mention the route, but was otherwise vital for any traveller since it listed the exact days and whereabouts of many of the 400 annual festivals until the year 2003. It deemed there would be a Miao one in Léishān, south of Kăilĭ, on the 10th January, which promised to be a likely highlight of my travels. I had written letters to the Guìzhōu Overseas Travel Corporation in both Hong Kong and Guìyáng requesting confirmation of the date, information on the cross-border route, and that they arrange a four-day tour. Receiving no reply, I juggled with the planning of the entire previous three months itinerary so that we would arrive a week ahead, in case.

After a straightforward four hours northwards, the bus inched its way across a high bridge over a river into the main square of **Lóngshèng** (Dragon Victory), which was thronged with expectant people. Once more I experienced an adrenaline rush and involuntary intake of breath on being confronted with the sheer weight of Asian humanity. I didn't enquire too closely why the only hotel taking foreigners was a deserted barracks, with but a few Chinese guests. My Korean partner and I enjoyed a merry New Year's Eve in a restaurant in party mood, well cared for by local waitresses not too phased by a Westerner speaking Chinese, and a Chinese-looking one speaking only English.

◆ ◆ ◆ ◆

The regional hot spring a bus ride away was disappointing. No longer a natural outdoors encounter, it has been highly developed for tour groups, the waters channelled into individual baths indoors. Nearby, a river canyon featuring an enticing old-style pedestrian suspension bridge – a probable Chinese invention – was worth a wander. Walking back brought into view a plain example of those steep rice terraces that are one of Asia's greatest achievements *(15-1)*. Here they're given a name – the Dragon's Backbone (Lóngjī). The local people in the area include the Yao minority, and they manage to entice two crops annually from these dry terraces, sometimes reserving the steepest sections for easier-to-grow corn and sweet potato.

Next to a distinctive, spiritually charged flat rock projecting horizontally out of a hill, my companion communicated with an old woman *(15-2)*.

A couple of hours west by bus pitched us into the different world of **Sānjiāng** (Three Rivers), a dusty, desolate and poorer town. The Hostel of the Department Store was gut wrenching and the ancient shower inoperative – the second worse accommodation I encountered in China. The guidebook described the alternative hostel as 'a filthy rat-infested hole'. Despite asking for directions, we failed to locate the wooden Wind and Rain Bridge out of town that took Dong carvers eleven years to build, commencing in 1906.

---

[1] This was rectified in the 1998 edition.

From the only public telephone in town, Tae Hun phoned Korea in order to offer words of support to a former girlfriend who was undergoing a personal crisis.

◆ ◆ ◆ ◆

I had been informed that a travel agency existed in Sānjiāng called the Wind and Rain Bridge Travel Service. Sure enough at 2 Jianfeng Road near the bus station, two helpful bright women were a mine of information in English concerning the border crossing, and photocopied two detailed and accurate maps rendering the local names of places in *pīnyīn* and Chinese characters. It would be worth using their services[1] for a day or two exploring local minority areas, particularly the Yao, Miao and Dong villages on the sixty-kilometre road to Dúdòng ('Single Cave').

They advised hiring a 'taxi' into Guìzhōu, there being no buses. The three-hour journey west via Fùlù (Rich Emolument), along untarmacked roads that disintegrated into tracks and holes, indicated how richly fertile this region is. Deftly merging into an open plain planted with rice was a Wind and Rain Bridge surrounded by terraced hills *(15-3)*. As well as being meeting places, the name indicates that these ostentatious roofed bridges afford rest and shelter during turbulent weather. The plain featured giant barrel-shaped stacks of rice husks assembled off the ground around tall poles, resembling a formation of scarecrows. They are feed for oxen. Groups of houses were scattered like seed *(15-4)*.

We dived along the only street of a thriving village (Chǎnkǒu) whose entire occupants were engrossed in some outdoor event. The land beside the Dūliǔ (Willow City) River was initially flat, with primitive punts crossing the low water; then it deepened into a canyon *(15-5,* taken on the move crossing a bridge).

---

[1] telephone (86) 0772-861 3369; fax (86) 0772-861 2896

Note: photographs *15-3* to *15-10* were taken on a rogue roll of film that turned out to be prints, not slides.

15-2

15-3 *The nameplate translates as 'People Harmony Bridge'.*

15-4

15-5

The few other vehicles that plied the road were of the three-wheel, mechanised wheelbarrow-with-hood variety. Tantalising traditional houses appeared spasmodically around corners, sometimes two dozen clumped together for warmth and protection, their dark roofs coalescing into a giant armadillo. When within a grove of trees, they reminded me of longhouses in Borneo. Washing hung from slatted wooden balconies, while positioned over the edge of streams were tell-tale tiny shacks on stilts – the toilets. Alongside rivers crossed on low pedestrian bridges, larger villages possessed bamboo waterwheels whose buckets raised water into cheek-by-jowl rice fields commandeering every inch of available space.

A turn to the north took us imperceptibly into Guìzhōu. The one narrow street of the small Dong community at Lóngé (Dragon's Forehead) was a bottleneck of goods and people. It was market day, and the taxi could go no further. A bus at the other end took us over a stupendous pass dominated by a lone tree, like a Lord surveying his domain.

15-6

Zhàoxing

A lush agricultural valley fused into one of China's most spectacular minority towns. The largest Dong community in the country, **Zhàoxìng** ('The Start of Excitement') still only has one significant street, this time spaciously wide, lined both sides with traditional houses *(15-6)*. A variety of relaxed, communal activities were in progress in the mellow late afternoon light. Our presence seemed not to affect the people a whit, whether we kept our distance or came close. The ambience was warm and palpably of a strong, highly knit social society, each human knowing h/his purpose in the scheme of things.

The sense of a way of living handed down through the centuries was gleaned from scenes like a foot-powered threshing machine *(15-7)*, grain drying on rectangular reed mats, vegetables hanging from balconies, a two-wheeled barrow with javelin-length wooden handles, women carrying laden baskets dangling from a yoke, a man lounging on a low stool his feet stretched onto another, kids playing safely in this street of no vehicles, and dogs and chickens running free. The potential drabness of the brown houses was off-set by the reds, blacks, greens and blues of the people's clothing, while elder women were dressed in black pantaloons and jackets, only their socks and headgear conveying individuality.

A few contrasting buildings revealed brightly painted elements, such as in *15-8*, detail in *15-9*. The roof of the latter features sharply tilted curved eaves, as well as a cockerel and a small dragon dog – distinctly different from the animals on Hàn Chinese roofs. Built over a store, the building open to the elements is presumably the local theatre, with side panel paintings and a Chinese vista as backdrop. Each village has one for performing Dong opera in winter.

15-7

15-8

15-9

15-10

An outdoor snooker match was the major draw for the younger men and boys *(15-10)*. In the distance in that photograph can be seen one of the five drum towers in this town, each representing a different clan. Of a wooden architectural style unique to the Dong and constructed without nails or wooden pegs, they once housed a tree-trunk drum struck in times of fire, potential danger, or to assemble the populace. *15-11* shows another being renovated. Inspired traditionally by the look of Chinese fir trees, symbols of shelter, the tallest in town is 9 stories and twenty metres high, its square base kept aloft by sixteen slim fir tree pillars.

15-11

No other buildings are loftier.

The flying eaves adorn every level except the first two which feature painted dragon dogs, while at close range the more-than-four corners tilt upwards and coalesce as if the bow of a battleship. Above the supporting logs, a white horizontal board typically depicts a row of people holding hands and other scenes, while the sun glints off an array of round and oblong mirrors in the eaves. The towers are traditionally the focus for meetings and village business, as well as festivities, music and other social activities. A 'drum family' is defined as a number of Dong villages all within hearing range of any one drum.

A youthful crowd surrounded two men demonstrating an aluminium re-smelting process *(15-12)*. Old pots were melted in a makeshift bucket-sized oven – I think it *was* a modified bucket – the requisite temperature achieved by two blowpipes issuing from its base. The sizzling silver fluid was poured into a shiny metal box containing a pre-shaped mould, out of which emerged a new long-handled ladle. Judging by the tension and fascination in the faces of the children watching, this was high-tech stuff.

The realities of a basic life with minimal comforts were more obvious off the street, with clothes being washed in ponds a few inches deep. These areas seemed like slums to me – hell in Eden. My companion was more than usually subdued observing these scenes. At the end, the street bent sharply to the right, overseen by a house conspicuously inscribed with words in English wishing a good journey to those departing. Walking back along the street, the picture with two ducks taking an evening stroll *(15-13)* summarises one of the most pleasant communities it was my privilege to come across in China.

It was not only the street that created that impression. To one side, there was a new, substantial, traditional-style wooden building packed downstairs with Dong artefacts and souvenirs. Two floors above composed a clean hostel, and we were warmly greeted by the Dong manageress. The outside loo at the same level, a metre-square shack, was accessed along an elevated narrow ledge – akin to walking the plank. The whole couldn't have been more idyllic, and that was partly because of, not despite, the lack of facilities. Ever since witnessing the islanders of Bali taking an evening bathe in the streams of their balmy, tropical paradise, often under a speech-stopping sunset, and realising in comparison how Westerners are compacted into walled-in, cramped, sensationless shower cubicles with no view beyond their eyeballs, I have yearned to savour something similar whenever possible. I have washed under the stars in the rivers in the heart of Ecuador's and Borneo's rainforests, once unforgettably serenaded by a symphony of sound from invisible nocturnal insects.

15-12

15-13

The external experience offered here, while not as glamorous, was of unsurpassed luxury because the water was heated. The woman poured bucketfuls into a giant basin on an old-style wood-fuelled stove. With commensurably large ladles, she mixed hot and cold with studied care until the temperature was just so. Then she led me to an expansive courtyard bathed in post-sunset light, and deposited some burning candles for illumination. Nude and by myself, I gloried in the back-to-nature sensation of showering in the raw open gaze of the universe.

15-14

Give me that virtually anytime over a five-star hotel. My travel colleague was puzzled at my ecstasy.

"It was the first time I've bathed that way," I explained.

"Really?" Tae Hun was genuinely surprised. He had been through hard times as a child when his father's chicken-farming business collapsed, and he was brought up for three years by others, his parents not having the means to do so. To wash in that fashion was common for him.

We engaged in an affable discussion, helpful for his English, on the ethics of taking photographs while experiencing a different culture.

"It's selfish," he observed.

I rationalised why I didn't think it was in my case.

While not concurring, he remarked at the end, "People should be able to talk or disagree about most things without becoming irate."

Throughout this I was half aware of singing emanating from the floor below, and belatedly realised we were missing a rare performance of traditional Dong choral music. Taking the Walkman, we creaked down the unlit wooden staircase to be invited into a dark room glowing in the embers of a wood fire, around which four women and eight men sat on chairs, rehearsing intensely for an imminent concert.

It was a similar soprano, alto, tenor, bass split as in Western music, but with two differences: the men had less to do, often combining as a drone, and the soprano was solo. She was utterly captivating. About 26 years old, slightly plump with a round comely face, she sat cross-legged and simultaneously knitted (singing teachers in the West would have fainted). For nigh on four hours without a break she recited by memory the multitude of opening solo phrases that are her responsibility alone in Dong music, all with due modesty. Without her, nothing could start – the teenage girls delivered the refrains. Occasionally she faltered and was prompted by one of the tenors who, being older, was clearly steeped in the tradition. He knew every word and note, and led his section. The oldest man was the choirmaster who was as insistent on high standards as any of his counterparts in the West, yet was part of the circular group and one of the singers. In his late 40s, he would interrupt the rehearsal and indicate the traditional way, which often sparked a keen discussion as to what *was* the 'correct' way. It was a fascinating and instructive instance of how culture is passed down the ages and generations, and it was unfolding in front of me.

The music itself was memorably unlike any I have heard in the world. The microphone and machine were recording this, but unbeknown the batteries were fading, and the original tape on playback soon sounded like the chipmunks – the rare exquisite music ruined. I have resuscitated part of it in the studio by using special software to compensate for the increasing tempo and pitch. Despite the resultant poor quality, I hope it conveys some of the flavour.

Track 5

Singing is a dominant element of Dong traditions, as music is with the Miao. Without a written language until 1958, it has transmitted their history and culture over centuries. Alarmingly, their oral language has fifteen tones – the sound is like singing even when they speak! There are songs to say goodbye, to aid the management of crops, to begin a meeting, and to assist in keeping watch. An ancient Dong proverb declares: 'Here, only the dumb cannot sing'; another notes that 'Rice feeds the body, while singing feeds the soul'. In olden times, visitors were not allowed to enter a Dong village – the gate was actually barred – until they had responded *in kind* to the welcome offered to them in song by women at the barrier! I wonder if such a tradition has ever existed elsewhere in the world.

◆ ◆ ◆ ◆

豕

One of the Chinese characters that appeals to me is that for 'pig' (above) – full of bristling, black, scavenging fortitude. As Lindqvist suggests in her book, you have perhaps to turn it anticlockwise *(left)* to see it standing on legs, with tail curved and snout down. Having kept a lookout for its living counterpart for sometime, I was delighted to find a close match here *(15-14)*. The Chinese countryside usually lacks cattle, which would harm the precious land's food production. Pigs however are common: there are about 400 million – more than anywhere else in the world, the more so for providing a reliable source of equally cherished manure. The Chinese have domesticated pigs for 9,000 years; indeed the word for 'home', as written in Chinese, is represented by a pig with a roof over its head.

★ ★ ★

The daily late-morning bus was supposed to take us three hours north, but broke down. Fortuitously, we were by then on the highway from Cōngjiāng, and boarded another after only a few minutes. Sitting on the back seat – usually the last to be occupied in China – gave new meaning to the word dusty, with thick layers depositing onto us and our packs as the vehicle twisted and turned into Lípíng. This town is where the peasant soldiers on the Long March passed through on entering Guìzhōu Province. There were no further buses heading south-west, so to save half a day I bargained for the services of a driver and his van, which developed a puncture on the three-hour bumpy 'road' to Róngjiāng. Having disembarked in the dark, we eventually found some prison-like accommodation, the bare light in the ceiling being the most aesthetically pleasing feature of the room. All the eating places had closed at eight o'clock.

◆ ◆ ◆ ◆

So it was no loss to rise in the early hours and hail a bicycle-taxi to the bus station, which was already a rabble of locals queue-barging, desperate to obtain tickets. With difficulty we managed to obtain virtually the last two. An even dustier four hours on a back seat heading north-west brought us to Kǎilǐ, the centre of operations for any exploration of south-east Guìzhōu. Situated near the buoyant Sunday market, a decent twin room in the Yìngpànpō Mínzú Hotel was essential to brushwash the grime of the previous four days out of our clothes. At the CITS office in the hotel, a jovial woman with reasonable English destroyed at a stroke my year's careful planning: the Léishān festival was six days early – that very day, in fact! We had passed through the village hours earlier, and would have disembarked if we had known the festival was taking place. It was too late to return.

Instead, she informed me of an "event" in a village the following morning. We discussed and agreed a four-day itinerary with her as guide, commencing after the event.

◆ ◆ ◆ ◆

Lángdé

After a local bus ride south, a short walk along a track led to the Miao village of **Lángdé**, meaning Corridor of Virtue, perched on the slopes of a river valley crossed on a modern Wind and Rain Bridge. Women were already scurrying in their ancestral dress and silver headgear, and, suppressing giggles, they showed us briefly around the narrow lanes between the houses. The sound of archaic horns brought us quickly to the main entrance, where the entire village's men dressed in black – about thirty – were lined on a hill along the edge of a paddy field, and were memorably bellowing a traditional welcome on buffalo horns to a substantial party of Japanese and Taiwanese tourists.

The Miao are partial to social drinking, particularly with guests, and each one of the tourists including us were light-heartedly obliged to imbue a welcome drink of a hornful of rice liqueur, offered to the lips by demur and smiling but insistent youthful women. Then they escorted us to the round, paved, village compound encircled by Gothically dark houses, where teenage girls sang a short unaccompanied greeting song with fetching vocal swoops *(15-17 overleaf)*. The rest of the community were seated as an additional audience *(15-16)*, their faces a study *(15-15 below)*. The Japanese were parading swanky bulky video cameras, to which I added my diminutive Walkman and microphone. For some dances, a solo drum was the accompaniment *(15-18:* note the totem pole), but the most astonishing sound came from a tight barrage of *lúshēng*, eight of them as is the customary number. *15-20* and *15-21* were taken at the same time as the recording.

Track 6 (4 minutes) enlivens the photos of this and the next three pages.

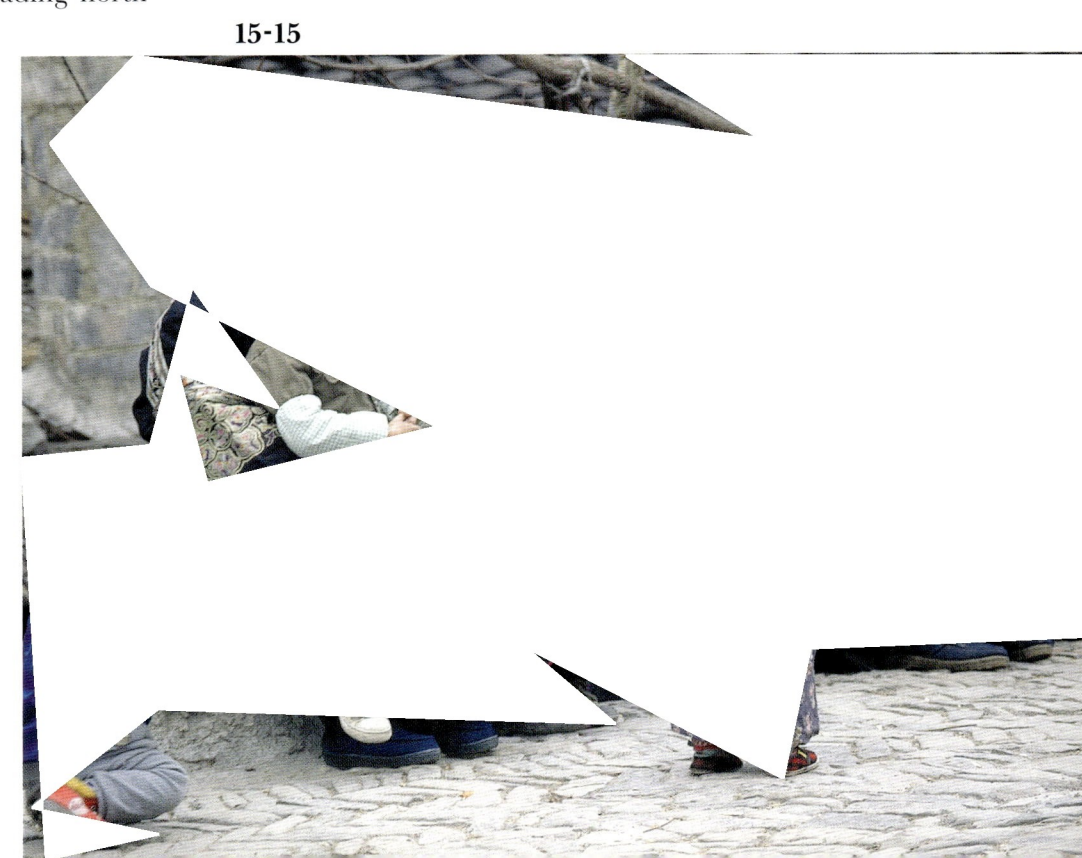

15-15

15-16

112 15-18

15-17

15-19

15-20

15-21

That is a sound over 2,200 years old, according to archaeological findings. There are several sizes of these reed-blown instruments, some metres in length. The *shēng* resembles a tobacco pipe, with long bamboo sticks billowing up from the bowl like miniature organ pipes. In fact it *is* a mouth organ[1]. On exhaling through the mouthpiece, the 'bowl' collects the breath, which is passed through a circle of holes connected to a forest of bamboo pipes of varied lengths, at the bottom of which in the shorter sizes are finger holes to produce up to five notes per pipe. The longer ones with no finger holes generate the one deep, pugnacious sonority. An alternative technique is to inhale. In the Miao language, of which there are four predominate subgroups, these bamboo instruments are called *jibasuo*, and are played as per custom by the men only.

Lúshēng are an integral part of the courting ritual. Indeed the major purpose of these minority festivals is for their young people to meet with a view to marriage. She indicates her chosen beau by winding a handkerchief or red ribbon around his *lúshēng* organ. If he returns it, alternatively if hers is the only one he doesn't return, that is a socially accepted signal for the two to depart, and they might later be found singing antiphonally in the glow of moonlight and candlelight. In these situations, traditional love songs will be sung intimately to each other in subdued falsetto. The Miao are sensitive to the subtle meanings music can convey, as we are to words, and I delight in a culture that uses the musical language to perpetuate a loving bond.

Most of us are so drilled with constant cacophony, in shops, on TV, the car or coach sound system, *et al*, we are rarely aware of what it is like to be devoid of that. In these villages, your own music making and dancing must be wonderfully joyous and uplifting occasions from the drudgery of survival. That is the feeling that resonated from this community *fête champêtre*. With electricity to villages becoming more available, will they be able to retain this tradition in the face of bare light bulbs, music on tap from radio, and the switched-off stare of the television screen? By expressing interest in experiencing the music and dancing, tourism in that sense helps.

The finale consisted of everyone, tourists included, wheeling around the compound to the sound of an unchanging drum rhythm. The silver-adorned women, their singing, the costumes, the *lúshēng*, the houses, the spectators, the music, and above all the gentleness and humility of the people, will not be forgotten.

* * *

Our guide, Long Yù Méi, and a driver arrived in a minibus and took us to Táijiāng, two hours east of Kǎilǐ. There was patent poverty in this mainly Miao town, and the only 'sight' was a former temple on a mound, now a basic museum. With a tall white person in the group, our entourage was attracting staring children. The hotel was barely more than a block of concrete, our eating place scarcely other than a hole in a wall. If that sounds like a complaint, it is not.

◆ ◆ ◆ ◆

---

[1] Its introduction to Europe inspired within a decade the invention of the harmonium in 1810.

Fǎnpái

This was to be a particularly satisfying morning. I had commissioned a music and dance "activity" in another Miao village – CITS had suggested it and the cost. Climbing steadily on a minor road soon brought us to the substantial village of **Fǎnpái**. Spread over the slopes of hills, its main rectangular plaza has dark houses along two sides, a baseball net at one end, while a stream runs along the remaining side, across which a bank rises *(15-22 overleaf)*. I was introduced to the chief musician from the village (on the left in *15-23*), whose fine reputation had taken him to perform at concerts in Běijīng. It was soon obvious this was highly justified as he led and inspired the rest of the team – throughout the world some musicians possess that outstanding edge.

As at Lángdé, a few girls lined up in front of us to deliver a traditional welcome song. The bonus was that their smiles and soft faces emitted a piquant sense of fun, while their silver tiaras shone even with no sun, and the intricacy of their jackets was dashing. The style of dress is peculiar to each Miao or Dong community. Miao girls learn how to embroider from age six, flowers and geometric patterns being common on cotton jackets sometimes caked in egg white as stiffener. They begin on their wedding dresses well before they reach their teens. The silverwork back and front can form an encyclopaedia of shapes: birds or bells, fish or fowl, ovals, angles and mythical animals. In the recent past, they hid these treasures when the Red Guards approached.

The men, too, sported elegant waistcoats and wide-brimmed, almost Mexican sombreros, while the leader donned a full jacket traditionally buttoned to the right over pantaloons with a border hem. Below this ancestral refinery, the musician-dancers wore modern trainers without a hint of incongruity.

They danced, sang and played with a relaxed vibrancy, and were good natural actors too, displaying impish enjoyment. One routine re-enacted the tradition of 'wife stealing', the girl pretending to be kidnapped, her colleagues not too convincingly crying for help while grinning half-demurely. It ended with some serious bottom smacking *(15-25)*, the players hugely enjoying the horseplay. During this, the boys were playing the *lúshēng* while trying not to laugh – a perennial problem for wind players the world over.

They seemed unconcerned performing officially only for the two of us. Besides, children were huddled watching on one side, while others and some women were on the bank behind. It was rewarding to see them quietly enjoying their own culture – though did I detect a subdued mood?

Some dances were decidedly active, particularly when the leader set upon a solo drum like a dervish possessed. When it was struck at the very edge, the resultant *furioso* rhythms evoked a furore of movement.

Photos 15-22 to 15-29 combine with track 7's excerpts (8 minutes) recorded simultaneously.

115

15-22

15-23

15-24

15-25

118

15-26

15-27

15-28

15-29

I had never sponsored a concert before, and their generosity of spirit was humbling – an hour-and-a-half's presentation for a meagre £50, arranged at less than a day's notice. The girls were eager to serve us rice wine, it being important not to touch the cup or else the contents have to be doused in one! I thanked them with the Miao word *bohomo*.

What was particularly remarkable about this generosity became apparent in the next ten minutes. There was a pall of mist hanging over the upper slopes, or so I thought. Only spasmodic everyday life continued during the dancing, such as a woman washing edible leaves in the stream below the bank *(15-30)*. But the men of the village were absent. Yù Méi, who was herself Miao but brought up in Kǎilī, had mentioned something in incoherent English about a fire. It was soon obvious that behind the merriment of the activity lay a disaster that had occurred three days earlier. She hadn't been talking about a bonfire.

Walking among the wooden houses built without nails, we noticed that the roof of a covered bridge similar to this one *(15-31)* had been removed as a precaution, smoke lingering nearby. Chickens and ducks in a stream were eating burned rice *(15-32)*. As we passed the village school, water was being carried in buckets, while small children looked unhappy and dazed *(15-33)*. The face of the kid in the corner says it all *(15-34)*. On the slope in the distance is apparent the tarred remains of fifteen great houses obliterated in the fire *(15-35)*. It was started by someone attempting to dry some rice.

There is no piped water in this village, only a well. Yù Méi informed me that one family had lost ¥5,000 (£400), which was in their house at the time. People were working quietly at the site.

★ ★ ★

15-30

15-31

15-32

15-33

15-34

15-35

As if to compensate for those realities, the scenery on the way back was of majestic beauty *(15-36)*. Guìzhōu Province is studded with these terraces, examples being those near Huáng'guǒshù in the south-west that are every bit as amazing as the more publicised ones in the Philippines, constructed using the one resource that is plentiful in China. There is evidence that the Chinese have cultivated rice for over 8,000 years, beginning in the south-west where the lowland wet paddy was first constructed – 'padi' being a Malay word indicating 'rice in the stalks'.

A busy time for the minority peoples here is in April, when the baby seedlings – a couple of inches of green grass – are planted two inches apart into the ten per cent of paddies designated as nurseries – low, back-bending work. A month later when six inches tall, they are replanted six inches apart in the remaining paddies. September's dry season sees the harvesting, achieved with back-breaking swishes of the sickle. Thereafter yellow rape is grown, which replenishes the soil, followed by repeated ploughing with oxen, the paddy walls being repaired. This agricultural cycle dictates the festival season; there are many in the fallow month of February.

Heading north and nearing Shīdòng, the road followed the Qīngshuǐ River where giant drying ricestacks were again a pop-up feature *(15-37/38)*. Looking like doner kebabs on spikes, their raised design each on a single slippery pole is probably to minimise rodent damage. This is where the spectacular Miao Dragon Boat Festival takes place in summer, the river also supporting imposing salamanders touching the scales at thirty kilograms apiece.

15-36

Shīdòng itself is rather uninspiring, with a drab hotel, but the local embroidery is famous, priced accordingly for tourists. To the east is an area where live the Gejia minority, closely related to the Miao. The nearby tiny Miao village of Táng Lóng, dissected by the road, is known for its silversmiths: I bought two simple rings. Tae Hun saw an old woman methodically spinning yarn, and he silently contemplated the passing of Time *(15-39)*.

◆ ◆ ◆ ◆

15-37

15-38

15-39

The historic town of **Zhènyuǎn** (Distant Calm) is a sensible place to overnight. At the end of the busy market street is this striking pavilion on an older bridge over the Wǔyáng River *(15-40)*. The purpose of such sharply curved eaves in Chinese buildings is partly to catapult back into the air any bothersome evil spirits sneaking down the roof. With bridges, the Chinese are fond of the effect of an arch creating a moon image with the mirrored water below, particularly with a backdrop of mountains and clouds. No wonder they were building multi-arched bridges by AD 610 – seven hundred years before Europe. Against a high cliff to the right of that photograph, as if in the clouds, hangs a convoluted part-Daoist temple built in 1530, known as Qīnglóng (Green Dragon) Cave, which we explored.

I had to replace my new top-of-the-range Chinese trainers, which had begun to fall apart on the first day of use. Despite attempts at gluing, in the space of a week they were unwearable – the epitome of style over substance. In the market I bought a basic pair for ¥17 (£1.35), which lasted a few months.

A draw of the area is the Wǔyáng (Dancing Sun) Gorge between here and Shībǐng to the west, and I had agreed a boat trip with CITS as part of the tour. It being out of season, however, there was no public boat, Yù Méi requiring a substantial 'extra' for a private one. Displeased this hadn't been discussed at the start, I spent some minutes fighting myself over the question, 'To boat or not to boat?' So I was subdued as the small craft called first at Peacock Peak *(6-21* in chapter 6). As we quietly cleaved through its waters, the gorge itself was a paragon of peace, with the towering massive vertical walls almost threatening *(15-41/42)*. The *rift* in another of the photographs was particularly savage.

Shībǐng is a bustling country town. Wandering the streets, I conversed briefly with a peasant woman in her fifties, and enquired about her recent life in China.

"We've never had it so good. Things have improved tremendously in the past fifteen years."

She was speaking twenty years after Máo Zédōng died.

The fine modern hotel was a source of classic Chinese farce. It was not so much the time spent by the receptionists arguing tooth and nail with Yù Méi about what tariff to charge us. Rather it befell at midnight, when staff touring the corridors knocked noisily on every room's door in turn. Opening the locked ones with a master key, they switched on the lights, checked to see if there were any 'illicit' people within, politely said 'sorry' to the scared, open-mouthed occupants in each bed, then slammed the doors shut – the bangs echoing and resounding throughout the hotel for twenty minutes as if WWIII had started. Bring back Basil Fawlty.

◆ ◆ ◆ ◆

15-40

15-41

15-42

125

15-43

Even among those that visit south-east Guìzhōu, viewing Yúntái (Cloud Platform) Mountain is not common: it was a first time for our guide and driver as well. The van climbed most of the way along a forest track, after which we led the less-fit guides up the inevitable Chinese steps. There is no obvious summit; instead a cliff edge rings around the limestone area providing a couple of hours of easy walking. Yù Méi and the driver Mr Yong requested their picture be taken, with a central promontory behind *(15-43)*. This was accessed by a suspension bridge (just visible), which our guides chickened out of crossing because of a gusty wind. Tae Hun and I went alone along the narrow track to the end – the end of a world….

Two hours driving led to a small community by a river both called **Chóng'ānjiāng** (River of Continuous Peace). An elongated wooden shack on stilts over the river provided accommodation, its freezing rooms for safety having no means of heating. It was run by a charming family – mother, son and daughter being the epitome of reserved, humble, warm humanity that I so admire. They cooked warming meals, and provided a rowing boat to explore the river. I wish them continuing peace for ever.

◆ ◆ ◆ ◆

There was a Gejia village under an hour's walk uphill, which in contrast to the others we had seen was a jolt. Children passed us strolling down to school, and the dilapidated village felt isolated. It was the raw harshness of living that struck home. While the others possessed a strong, positive social cohesiveness and indeed beauty, here there was neither, and no one was smiling. Dark slates of wood higgledy-piggledy put together formed single-storey dwellings, while pigs were hardly worse off in better-constructed thatched outhouses. There was no greenery, save for the odd fern and a large lone tree that served as the village focus. A beautiful woman was embroidering cloth in a soberingly dark room. Outside, a young mother and her small daughter looked at me without emotion as if a chasm divided us, which indeed it did.

Subsequent to the fire at Fǎnpái, these scenes were quietly affecting Tae Hun. He commented in unimprovable English: "Life is War for these people". As a Korean, he should know.

Chinese eat with their tongues, Japanese eat with their eyes, and Koreans eat with their stomachs.

Up to the 1950s, Koreans often starved even to death. In particular, there was an annual famine season in springtime, before the summer produced the barley crop – what a season to suffer. To them, in comparison, Chinese people had adequate supplies of food, and could afford to taste and reject it if unpalatable. The well-off Japanese treated their meals as a gourmet experience – visually stimulating, stainlessly served. In contrast, Koreans could not be so fussy, and simply ate heartily.

He kai kora nui te riri. So goes a Maori saying, which means: War is a devouring fire kindled by a spark. Hell is fire too, but after the fire follows seemingly everlasting cold. No warmth, no sparks.

A traveller to Guìzhōu in the past recorded this:

Peasants call themselves 'dry men' – sucked dry of everything.
quoted in *The Long March*,
by Harrison E. Salisbury

More than a hint of that emanated from this place. I felt we were intruding, and didn't stay long.

★ ★ ★

After an hour's drive back to Kǎilǐ and abrupt goodbyes to our guide and driver, a train conveyed us west for four hours to Guìzhōu's capital city. On arrival, the ticket office at the station produced another Chinese riddle: it refused to sell railway tickets! "Tomorrow's tickets you can only buy tomorrow." Not surprisingly, business seemed slack.

◆ ◆ ◆ ◆

Guìyáng, Precious Sunshine, is well named – we saw none. Administratively, it is a frustrating city for the traveller. My colleague needed to purchase a ticket for his forthcoming flight back to Hong Kong. China South West Airlines has its own office in the CAAC building, but an apologetic official said he couldn't issue one – *déjà vu* was becoming an oft-recurring feature of the Chinese experience. Apparently a ticket could only be obtained from the city of departure. The Advance Rail Ticket Office had been superseded – it was now a Post Office. "You can only buy tickets at the station." A circular and paradoxical conundrum.

Corrigan's book paints a colourful picture of Guìyáng, with 'ten theatres, the provincial and municipal song and dance troupes, numerous local opera including the Peking and Guizhou operas, a circus troupe…'. However, a helpful woman at CITS knew about none of these.

Despite warnings from CITS in Kǎilǐ that sleeper tickets for the train journey to Kūnmíng were unavailable, unless obtained through them for a fat commission, acquiring them was easy on the day. Indeed the compartments were virtually empty for the first stage of the 650-kilometre, fourteen-hour transfer to the great province of Yúnnán.

chapter 16

Xīshuāngbǎnnà

China's topography simplified is a three-stage descent from the heights of the Qīnghǎi-Tibet Plateau in the west to the plains in the east. At below 500 metres, the latter constitute a quarter of China and accommodate most of the arable land. The Yúnnán-Guìzhōu Plateau lies in between, its average altitude in the west approaching 2,000 metres. Apart from the expanse centred around the capital Kūnmíng, the rest of Yúnnán Province is virtually all mountainous, comprising nine mountain ranges. A quarter is forested – an important source of timber for China – another quarter having been harvested in the twenty-five years up to 1975.

The western half of the province is a series of interwoven ridges and canyons running north-south like folded pleats, a sideshow of the Indian-Eurasian tectonic plate collisions that formed the Himalaya. Three of the troughs contain mighty rivers (please refer initially to the map on page 78): the Nù Jiāng which is better known in the West as the Salween, the Láncāng Jiāng or the Mekong, and the Jīnshā Jiāng – part of the Yángzi. At one section, these three flow parallel for 300 kilometres in almost consecutive valleys, threatening to converge into one Armageddon of a river. The Irrawaddy in Myanmar (Burma) is not far to the west either, splitting in the north into the Nmai and Mali rivers. The big three in Yúnnán descend from Tibet, which borders in the north-west corner. There are 180 tributaries and three other major rivers in the province, of which the Yuán Jiāng, known as the Red River, makes a beeline for Hanoi.

The long-time geographical mystery of the source of the Láncāng/Mekong has recently been solved[1]. That of the Yángzi is a pond at the base of Jari Hill in Qīnghǎi Province, although the more romantic setting at the foot of Gela Dandong, at 6,621 metres the highest pinnacle in the Tánggǔlā Mountains, runs it close. The fledgling river soon passes near where the Huáng Hé/Yellow River rises. The 'Yángzi' is actually the Cháng Jiāng (Long River); only a limited section nearer Wúhú in the east of China is delineated by its locals as the Yángzi. At some 6,000 kilometres, the third longest in the world, it supports 500 million people dwelling along its belt.

The section running through Tibet and Yúnnán is sub-labelled the Jīnshā Jiāng, meaning Gold Sand River, and refers to the gold washed down from Tibet that the Chinese have traditionally panned. It has a markedly different character from the river of the plains from Sìchuān Province eastwards. From Píngshān on the north-east Yúnnán/Sìchuān border, the short thirty-kilometre stretch upstream to Shing Suíjiāng used to harbour 221 dangerous rapids, according to county records. Much further upstream at Shígǔ, the river does a double take on itself, bending unexpectedly back north for a hundred kilometres, before equally suddenly resuming a southerly course. During that northerly stretch it has cut one of *the* sights of China – the Tiger Leaping Gorge.

The sixth largest province and equivalent in area to California, Yún'nán means 'South of the Clouds', the clouds being those that hover almost permanently over neighbouring Sìchuān. It is blessed with its sunny disposition partly due to the southerly latitude: the Tropic of Cancer passes just 150 kilometres south of Kūnmíng, which enjoys spring-like temperatures between 8° and 20°C throughout the year. Hence this is China's largest coffee-producing region, and the yield is being increased from 2,000 tons in 1995 to 17,000 tons by the year 2005. Tea and tobacco are other major crops. The original tea bush, *Camellia sinensis*, grew on the Yúnnán plateau.

A third of Yúnnán's forty million inhabitants belong to twenty-four ethnic groups spread throughout the province. The southern border especially is a meeting point of countries and cultures: Myanmar, Laos and Vietnam are neighbours, while the Golden Triangle in Thailand begins a mere hundred kilometres away. The two extreme southern tips that jut into Myanmar and Laos comprise an area called **Xīshuāngbǎnnà** (see map above), home to over ten tribal minorities. If you have difficulty pronouncing the name, so do the Chinese: 'Sher-shwung-bahn-nah' will suffice. Even that is a Hàn corruption of the language of the Dai, one of the major tribes in the south-west of Yúnnán, their

---

[1] See *The Last Barbarians*, by Michel Peissel (1998).

16-1   **16-2**

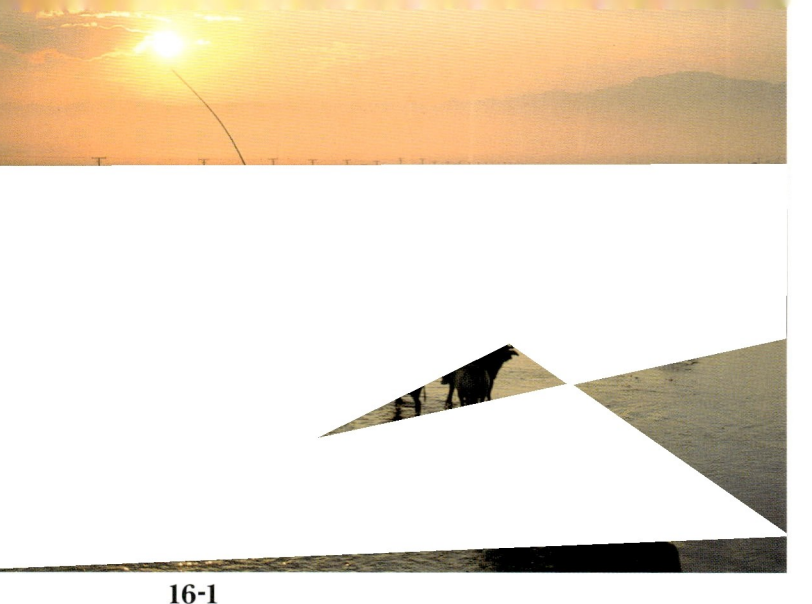

name obviously synonymous with the word *Thai*, if today implying something different. In the Dai language, *sip-sawng-pan-na* literally means '10, +2, thousand, fields', imparting the eminently practical information that there are twelve districts, each of a thousand *mŭ* in area, and all containing rice paddies! A thousand *mŭ* is 67 hectares.

That referred to the layout 400 years ago when the Chinese empire under the Míng first took a serious interest in the area. Nowadays the Chinese organise Xīshuāngbǎnnà around three county towns: the foremost one Jǐnghóng in the centre, Meng'hai[1] to the west and Meng'la in the south-east – the last opened to foreigners only two years before my visit.

★ ★ ★

A day in Kūnmíng was consumed by the unfathomable antics of obtaining a Chinese airline ticket. CAAC had moved into a new automaton of a building, but still couldn't issue Tae Hun's return ticket. China South West Airlines had transferred to a plush dinky suite in another part of town, and frustrations in me swelled

[1] Because names could well be of Dai and other origins, tones have largely been omitted for the remainder of this chapter.

dangerously when once more their officials said they were not empowered to issue a ticket to Hong Kong on their own airline! That year (1996), China South West reckoned it had come of age and applied to become a member of the illustrious international airline association IATA based in Geneva, which only admits those that meet the highest stringent standards. The application succeeded.

It was time to switch to a sensible outfit: a Dragonair flight was full, but Thai Airlines had seats available at twice the price they quoted in Seoul. Sometimes you cannot win. With that crisis over, we left half our luggage at a hotel and caught the pre-booked Saturday flight south-west to the upgraded airport at **Jǐnghóng**, thus avoiding a 24-hour bus journey. My planning of the month's travels in Yúnnán had revolved entirely around that choice of day, ensuring arrival in time for one of *the* Sunday markets in China.

Stepping off the plane caused an involuntarily inhalation of the soliloquy of a tropical paradise in the filtered light of a late afternoon: fulsome palms and arching bamboo, a fragrant aroma hovering in the ether, stillness and quiet (no other planes, a taxi or two, no bustle), even an absence of flies, and everything encased in a balmy womb of

16-3

warmth. I had last experienced that when landing on Mindanao in the Philippines: fair enough there, but this is supposed to be China! An old tribal myth tells that ancestral hunters discovered Xīshuāngbǎnnà when they followed a golden deer over 99 rivers and 77 peaks. When it bounded into a lake shimmering with gold and flowers, with green pastures and river-fed hills all around, not surprisingly they decided to remain.

We passed mirror-surface rice paddies bathed in idyllic mauve-tinted light dotted with humans tending to their tasks. The fields of a thousand *mǔ* melted into the town as if one natural entity. Here were wide, cracked streets lined with sentinel palm trees, pedicabs nonchalantly touting for business, wobbly bicycles lazily pedalled, and the occasional coughs of vehicle exhausts. The Chinese were eating outside at round café tables, while others on ethnic restaurant balconies surveyed the streets below. The ingredients invoked the strange, dislocated image of a Paris in the Orient, or a Copacabana in China without the beach.

Added to this, the palatial Bǎnnà Hotel had clean, well-serviced three-bed dorms, each with a balcony and shower/toilet with 24-hour hot water – at ¥30 (£2.50) per person, the best value in China. We shared with another backpacker, a young Korean woman.

◆ ◆ ◆ ◆

An early start and two hours west in a packed minibus transported us into the heart of a society far removed from standard China. The sun was barely breaking over a vast plain with distant hills, its clear pomegranate light colouring the huts by a still lake enshrined with bamboo, whose fronds stretched to a sky mirrored in the mist below. Mysterious stupas, golden and of a foreign bulbous shape, hid behind trees in the sun's rays. Herds of cows with coats a myriad of colours strolled over a bridge *(16-2)*, then crossed a river and waded into the distance towards the low sun *(16-1)*. Only John Wayne was missing. One long street climbed gently, even at this hour thronged with activity *(16-3/4)*.

This market at **Meng'hun** is a magical meeting place for diverse peoples. There are some Hàn Chinese, who while composing a third of Xīshuāngbǎnnà's 800,000 residents mainly stick to the towns. The majority are Dai who make up another third, while Hani and the rarer Bulang are strongly represented, with possibly some Làhǔ. The Hani (the 'H' is barely articulated) are spread out both east and west from here, while southwards is a Bulang village, leading to the primary area in Yúnnán where they reside. I admire the Bulang philosophy of the entire villagers pulling together to construct every family's house, thereby completing it within three days. The north-west corner of Xīshuāngbǎnnà marks the beginning of the principal region where the Làhǔ ('Roast Tiger') live. As their name suggests, they have a formidable reputation as hunters – their Thai name, Mussur, means precisely that. They are also distinguished by preferring daughters to sons.

Personally, I have long been attracted to Asian women: from the Indians in flowing saris and the angels in Bali, to the heart-stopping Filipinos and dewy-eyed Koreans. Their gorgeous silky tresses of black hair and pearly eyes imparting a demure exoticism are one of the rewards of travel in this region of the planet. Young Dai women have a reputation for soft, nubile beauty, with smooth skin and a warm, generous smile fired direct from the soul. All of that was evident here. They were certainly stunning, assisted by a gaudy and amusing sense of fashion: scarlet pants, orange blouses, and bottle green jackets over white shoes abounded, while headgear featured rainbow-coloured scarves, white bonnets with a flowing sash, or giant Mexican straw hats.

Seated older women wore white turbans perhaps covering distended ears – or were they modern towels in a maelstrom bun? On sale were cheap manufactured goods in an eye-bashing array of lime green, rapeseed yellow, vomit pink, and military blue *(16-5)*.

16-4

16-5

bartered. At around 1,500 metres, the plain is colder than in Jīnghóng, so bananas are imported from there. In contrast, Xīshuāngbǎnnà's sugarcane and tea are now only grown in this Menghun area. All is not necessarily what it seems. A dating ritual of the Dai involves the girl bringing a juicy cooked chicken to market as if to sell. Surrounded by potential young admirers, she ignores even the most inflated offer, except from the one she fancies to whom she gives the chicken for nothing, after which the two progress to a quiet corner.

At the high end of the street, an elephant was drawing a huge crowd *(16-6* and *16-7)*. That surprised me – it cannot be a common sight, despite being so close to Myanmar and Thailand. Its owner, holding the ladder in *16-8*, was hawking rides, yet there were few takers. The faces instead expressed disbelief, talking was hushed, and sometimes there was no smiling either *(16-10)*!

16-6

Gold-capped teeth are favoured, while some Bulang can be discerned by their black ones: chewing betel nuts or juice from a lacquer tree is a traditional partiality. They and the Làhǔ smoke – useful for keeping mosquitoes at bay.

Water chestnuts, herbal medicines, and chilli devilpeppers were among a host of foods being

16-7

16-8

I had so far resisted taking close portraits, an act that if sneakily done can be offensive as well as rude; but some faces here disarmed my ethical qualms *(16-9)*. Besides, no one seemed concerned by the camera, particularly not when next to the largest mammal on the planet's dry surface.

For those with time, it would be an exciting prospect to walk in this area with a guide, sampling one village then another of a different tribe, each with their traditional and individual life-styles, languages and customs intact. Thirty kilometres to the west from here are some extraordinary valleys in mountains that time has passed. They are against the border with Myanmar, accessed with difficulty by a dirt road. I have only viewed photographs, but centred around the village of Bada, the Hani have carved rice terraces by hoe and by hand that instantly cause an intake of breath of disbelieving wonder. Few foreigners have ever seen them. Go only with permission, and please only if your attitude to these people and their communal achievements is sensitive and humble, having respect for their privacy.

★ ★ ★

16-9

132

16-10

16-11

The boy monk in the throng in *16-7* is a clue: the Dai are Buddhists. Twenty kilometres north-west on a main road is a well-established Dai village called **Mengzhe**, pronounced 'Mong-jeh'. Its most outstanding building is a temple whose entrance steps are barred by three arresting guardians who command instant respect *(16-12)*. They are indicative of the common ancestry that Xīshuāngbǎnnà's Buddhist temples share with the 30,000 or so in Thailand, where these dragon-serpents are known as *naga*. Their 'tongues' here are actually wired light bulbs. Up the stairs is a tall white dagoba (*chedi* in Thai), with contrasting terracotta panels. Of an elegant sculptured shape, it tapers to a pointed top.

Erected in the Táng Dynasty (618–907), Wat Gau Temple is relatively bland from the outside *(16-11)*, yet inside it is richly endowed *(16-13)*. Compared to the usual courtesy no-photographs rule inside temple halls, our guide James, whose home town this is, proudly encouraged us to take some – he is on the left in that photograph. Born in a hilltribe environment, he worked in the clothing trade in Bangkok, learning and practising five languages (Thai, Lao, English, Mandarin and Cantonese). He now uses these skills to introduce foreigners to his own culture, and he proceeded to deliver some fascinating insights to our foreign group.

When entering the temple, the custom is to place fruit or candy in four places as a symbol of cleansing the body. While the roof space in houses is kept clear, that of the temple is filled, each mirror hanging down representing a family in the village. Similarly, only the temple is decorated with pictures and paintings, the pigments derived from the leaves of local trees. On a wall I noticed a giant poster of a

16-12

sumptuously golden Buddha, while on another was a photograph of a hundred black-robed Buddhist monks parading in line up a dirt road.

Temples and pagodas throughout Xīshuāngbǎnnà were destroyed during the Cultural Revolution of 1966–70. There was no government assistance or money when villagers resurrected them and replaced paintings in the following decade. In 1981, monks were officially allowed to practise again.

James showed us a sacred book containing Buddhist poetry, the pages horizontally hinged like a blind. It was written in the Dai language, which he

16-13

16-14

stated is orally "1,248 years old" and is only "20% similar" to the Thai language. While the Dai and Burmese written languages are alike, the sounds are not.

The Dai word *meng* in numerous place names in Xīshuāngbǎnnà means just that: a 'place'. Another word, *man*, translates as a 'village', with the distinction that a place is more substantial than a village. Quite what Mengman indicates, marked on the map further along the road, I didn't enquire.

Only the Dai have these festivals:

Water Splashing: held for three days from the Dai New Year's Day around 12 April; it climaxes with people splashing each other all day with containers of water! The symbolism is of washing away the bad and the dirt, encouraging the good and the new. Temple images and paintings are cleaned the day before.
Close the Door: takes place after the transplanting of rice for three months mid-June to mid-September; Dais cannot marry nor rebuild houses during this period.
Open the Door: commences after harvesting from mid-September, during which older women visit the temple twice a week.

Up to 1981, arranged marriages were the norm and the couple both had to be Dai. That year a radically new government policy was introduced, allocating parcels of land to every family. As a result the Dai have been able to obtain sufficient food and clothes, and electricity and money as well. With their fields mainly on easier flat land, a rice tax is levied, while other minorities dwelling on mountains slopes pay tea tax instead.

A German woman (on the left in *16-11*) and I together explored a quiet village street of substantial two-storey semi-thatched Dai houses, with pigs sniffing the dampened earth outside. Sometimes a wooden triangular rig is fixed behind a pig's head so that it cannot penetrate enclosures of growing produce.

A short distance away is the Octagonal Pavilion and associated temple at **Jingzhen**. A ladder of steps takes one up an artificial mound to be met typically by trainee monks clad in burned orange robes surveying the valley and plain below. That colour vies for attention with the first object in a spacious square, a mustard-yellow stupa of Burmese shape, to the left of which is a structure fronted by white colonial-style pillars, used as a library. Behind is a brown rectangular Dai temple with a covered walkway around its perimeter, dominated by a roof of epic proportions lined with S-shaped roof figures. To the centre-right is a Goliath of a ginkgo tree whose spindly branches spread out like tentacles of a giant squid about to engulf one – a genuinely disturbing spiritual presence.

Besides these large-scale elements clamouring for attention, the Octagonal Pavilion in a corner seems insignificant at first. Initially built in 1701, the same year that the tree was planted, it begins with a base of horizontal blue, yellow, green and brick-red stripes like tongue-licking tacky Brighton rock. The last colour is continued up two pillars forming the entrance emblazoned with golden Buddhist symbols, and guarded by two four-legged creatures (*16-14*). The distinguished octagonal roof creates the effect of a scaly, sticklebacked porcupine by piling high double triangular buttresses, followed by eight spikier ones on each ridge angling inwards, culminating in a cymbal shape dish, after which a spire encrusted with bulbous objects reaches to a height of sixteen metres. There's nothing else like it in China.

Inside the wooden temple, the cavernous roof space teems with giant ribbons suspended vertically like bell ropes. A couple of dozen crude, yellow, orange and green scenic paintings side by side are another bold feature. Next to it, a distinctive Dai balconied house serves as monks' quarters, outside which a pig may be strolling while a bicycle is being repaired.

The entire riot of the compound's competing colours and forms are brought together in a harmonious union by the arch of a blue sky, which finally dominates all. Budding photographers should remember to compensate for that when shooting individual elements against the light – most of my shots were too dark, and the red *rift* was persistently getting in the way.

★ ★ ★

Lunch was provided by a family at their home. There is a tradition among the Dai to steam rice inside bamboo and serve it on a bed of banana leaves, a practical and environmental wrapper for takeaways to schools and fields. I have experienced a similar technique in a scintillatingly magical Borneo rainforest where my Iban guide baked bamboo containers in a bonfire, the rice inside first wrapped in palm leaves as foil, the whole dipped in a river. It was the most exquisitely tasting rice it has been my good fortune to consume. Westerners and others who cook it in saucepans are deluding themselves: it simply doesn't taste of rice.

16-15

The Hani village of Banla, halfway back to Jīnghóng, is at first a trial. Located the other side of the Liúshā (Flowing Sands) River beside the main road, its closeness and easy access for tourists results in one being pestered to buy souvenirs, even when stepping out of the van. Fortunately that ceases once inside the compound, where roof ridges sporting buffalo horns distinguish the massive houses from those of the Dai. There are no windows: each split roof covers a whole building almost down to the ground – dark but weatherproof. Until 1981, men and women used two separate stairways leading to the living quarters on the upper floor of each. There is a separate kitchen area to prepare food for the precious pigs below, while above is a semi-attic where rice is dried over burning wood. A compact walled-off compartment is the 'Love Room', used by nineteen and twenty-year-olds for talking only. It is where a couple first live if they marry.

There is a distinct family resemblance of these houses with those of the Batak I saw around Lake Toba in Sumatra. That is not as fanciful as it seems: the Hani are closely related to the Akha in Thailand, and the Batak were expelled from northern Thailand by the Mongols.

Most of the million or more Hani in China live in southern-central Yúnnán. They are Daoists, but that belies their nature, which in this village was lively. The younger set launched with gusto into an unrehearsed demonstration of traditional dances *(16-15)*, of which the *dongpocuo* is one. They looked very smart in black sleeveless jackets decorated with silver, a more reliable source of wealth for them than paper money, which has devalued capriciously in the past. With coloured pompons as contrast to black, their favourite colour, the only times they otherwise wear traditional clothes these days are at marriages, festivals and new building ceremonies. Most of our group were not interested in paying to watch this, and it remains to be seen how long the dancers' enthusiasm will survive in the face of such indifference. For me, having read dry accounts of tribes in books that conveyed little, it was rewarding to see them transformed into vibrant and vivacious folk disagreeing about the correct steps.

A numinously lovely Hani girl showed two owls to Tae Hun and another of our group *(16-16)*. He was entranced: who could not be at such gentleness, sweetness and beauty – a model for all humans to emulate *(16-17)*.

16-16

16-17

What makes Jīnghóng delightful is that, like villages in Bali, the town's borders dissolve imperceptibly into fields. Hiring bicycles to explore the rice paddies, river system and irrigation channels in the flat land southwards proved rewarding. The Balinese analogy strengthened when, accessed by rickety bamboo bridges, we stumbled upon intimate villages hidden among clumps of trees. The sense of a sane order was enhanced by the clear late light, and the odd person forever tending to green rice beds.

★ ★ ★

Walking at night and halting at a deserted site, Tae Hun revealed to me some of his childhood circumstances back home in Korea.

"I had many pets when I was young – chickens, cows, rabbits, as well as ducks in the sea. I used to watch a rabbit all night."

"What was so fascinating?"

"I don't know – its movements, its thoughts.... I couldn't leave the hut."

After a pause, he enquired:

"Have you ever seen an animal cry?"

I sensed he had experienced something I hadn't.

"My favourite cow cried when she was being sold to market for slaughter. She knew her fate – I saw it in her eyes – green eyes."

Months earlier, Ritchie had described a similar seminal encounter looking a pig in the eye as it was being transported in a crate to the butcher's. He could tell it knew. The coincidence of both my travel companions being soberly convinced of an animal's cognisance of its impending death was quietly disturbing.

"At my university," Tae Hun continued, "there were lots of mice. We used to put sticky paper on the floor so that the tails of baby mice would catch, and they couldn't run away. I saw one baby cry, and cry out. Its mother came and bit off the tail to enable it to escape."

Under the stars, we soundlessly absorbed the universal message contained therein, and the nature of its Creator.

"Last night," he divulged, "I was thinking about the life of a midge. They only live for a day, therefore they know what is past, but don't know about tomorrow. So what do they think about?"

I was about to make a facetious comment, when he concluded in the following manner on his reflections of such animals at close quarters over the years.

"I believe they do think."

In the tropical air, we discussed the relationship of the natural world with mankind. For his degree Tae Hun studied horticulture, so I was not surprised when he revealed:

"I've studied tropical plants a little."

The next sentence, however, made me smile.

"They are *very* interesting, very funny – they're *just like humans*."

◆ ◆ ◆ ◆

Our Korean room-mate and the German woman from the previous day had decided to join us for a reconnoitre of a Chinese virgin rainforest. Having lived in Yúnnán, my Chinese teacher had whetted my appetite, enthusing about the exciting possibilities of Xīshuāngbǎnnà's primal forests. "You can walk and explore them for several consecutive days."

A woman in the local CITS soon put a dampener on that – there are only four limited areas remaining. Handing me a local map, she marked each one: a Hani rainforest around Bada (q.v.), a Dai one north of Mengla, and a restricted if dense patch towards the Tropical Plants Garden at Menglun. The most sensible option seemed to be the nearest, Mandian, an hour by bus to the north-west.

On a path in the forest, we passed an umbrella tree – one of the most spectacular I have ever seen. Otherwise, the state of the forest was hardly pristine, and I was disappointed. Our unnecessary CITS guide stipulated a three-quarters-of-an-hour time limit. Once again I was in Chinese cuckoo-land: we had been promised a two-hour walk. Even the waterfall at the end could be sued for calling itself that. The area seemed more an amusement park for the plentiful Chinese tourists than a serious forest. Thank goodness being with congenial companions compensated.

Strolling back, I was aghast to witness in the distance someone chopping down the top of the umbrella tree. We caught up with a party of laughing Hàn Chinese trippers, one of whom, a beautiful woman, was parading the magnificent specimen as a parasol. The men escorting her were taking her photograph, a process I could not but help interrupt. Via our guide, I delivered a short sermon on environmental issues to the suddenly silent group. As I politely but firmly harangued them for the selfish desecration that denied others an irreplaceable glimpse of natural wonder and beauty, the eldest man – a middle-aged plump businessman in a suit – grew visibly uncomfortable, while the women were shame-faced. The Hàn concept of 'losing face' – particularly that of older, respected men when in company – is evidently intact. I left them to recover their dignity.

I suggested to the guide that she contact the authorities with a view to erecting an educational notice. She agreed, and supported my previous action. I hope I didn't overdo it.

The impression I obtained from pre-reading was that this part of China is a naturalist's dream:

> This tropical region is still the home to many wild animals which elsewhere have long been extinguished: elephants, tigers, pythons, Malay bears, leopards, rhinoceros or rare birds are just a few examples.
> *Insight Guide: China* [1994]

Don't believe a word of it – you'd be lucky to spot a mosquito! If you want a true virgin rainforest experience, stick to Borneo (if there's any left), or South and Central America.

★ ★ ★

It was time to rendezvous with the Mekong, one of those exotic names like the Nile, the Amazon, the Congo, that seem a dream away, yet it was passing right beside Jīnghóng. The initial view from an important 1960 bridge did not disappoint *(16-18)*. On hired bikes, the four of us followed it downriver for four hours almost to its end in China. Thereafter it forms the Myanmar/Laos and Thailand/Laos borders before slicing through Cambodia southwards, the delta fanning out in Vietnam. At 4,180 kilometres, it is the planet's twelfth longest river, touching fully six countries while supporting over a hundred million people.

A sense of time and place flowing by was palpable. A chugging workboat out of Fitzcarraldo's Amazon struggled up the waters, still seething in places despite a lowered level. Valley walls blocked the afternoon sun as I grappled with temperamental Chinese gears, one of the other bikes breaking down.

Gliding into Gǎnlǎnbà was akin to touching down in another country. Two impossibly thin and tall denuded coconut palms fronted a square pavilion on a square enclosure, within which was a lazy temple with whitewashed walls. Vertical prayer ribbons competed in length with the trees like ladders to Heaven. That Chinese name means 'Olive Embankment' and refers to a farm, but the Dai locals call the place **Menghan**. While the centre is unremarkable, consisting of a wide street with cafés and a market on one side, it is the plain spreading southwards interspersed with neat, updated Dai villages, and the farmland stretching south-west to the Burmese border that inspire so many visitors to talk about a hidden utopia.

That was obvious from the comments in the visitors' book of the Dai Bamboo House where most stay. Being on stilts, the first floor is divided into three large areas: the owner's family quarters, a kitchen-lounge, and the dormitories where one sleeps on mats on the floor. Dai families traditionally do so cheek by jowl on one giant mat – hurrah!

Home-made Dai food appeared, and with Japanese and Korean backpackers as well as European, Australian and American, the dark nights were a pleasing time for building international bridges and discovering the reality of one humanity. Sitting on the balcony in balmy

16-18

warmth with tropical trees casting shadows in the breeze, the exponentially extraordinary addition to this bliss were the stars above – as pinprickingly bright as I have ever witnessed, an assembly of worlds and heavens close enough to touch, yet far enough to expand one's understanding of the expanse that they envelop. They rivalled even the array of stars over the Namib Desert, where I slept in the open without a tent. No one in the whole wide world is as lucky at such moments as these.

One traveller had written an instant poem in the book:

> Dai's bamboo house – a place to rest
> and leave behind all that China stress
> pedal off down remote dirt tracks
> stop by a rice paddy, lie back and relax
> and at the end of a day full of wondrous sights
> enjoy home cooked meals and star studded nights
> fall asleep on your mat with mozzie net drawn
> and await the roosters and pigs to sound the new dawn
> get up, splash your face and enjoy the cold bath
> before cycling off down another dirt path.
> Jonny Gordon, from
> Sydney [22 July 95]

A possible downer was that there had been a change of management at the Bamboo House that had elicited less favourable comments I wasn't about to complain. The mozzie nets were not even needed.

◆ ◆ ◆ ◆

A hot day of continual cycling commenced from the ferry point, down from which was a sorely tempting locale for skinny-dipping in the Mekong. A three-elephant statue marked a poorer district, otherwise there was sparsely-populated open country accessed by dusty elongated tracks, with unknown red or yellow flowering bushes, avenues of tall trees, and white dagobas emerging unexpectedly like stone dwarfs in a garden. It would be easy to become temporarily lost, but who cares? At one unmarked village, a mystical miniature castle like Disney's logo peered over bushes by a dry paddy field. Seven bulbous spires like Teletubbies sat atop this octagonal concrete cavern, whose window-sized entrance was defended by two dog-like stone creatures with crazed bare white teeth and yellow ears. Other fierce heads around the edifice threatened to bite anyone who approached. I didn't. It was probably the village well – evidently there is nothing more precious that needs guarding.

That evening after our two cycling companions had left for Jǐnghóng, I became engrossed reading in the visitor's book an adventure undertaken six months previously by a Charlie Sullivan from Tennessee. His quest was to cycle to the border of Myanmar via a village called Guannyu. En route, he passed a beautiful Hani mountain village called Jiebo. It was a tropically fierce day, his destination always 'over the next hill', and he expended his drinking water. Yet on he went: it was more than a challenge, rather a spiritual necessity to explore his future, a half-crazed desire to press his destiny, to test the Powers that Be. Weak and with no one to help, he reached a critical point – even becoming, as he wrote, 'resigned to dying'.

Resolved to plough on, he stumbled across a mountain stream of clear water, of which he related, 'I rank it as the No. 1 physical feature on the face of the earth'. Temporarily invigorated, he kept going, pursuing his goal whatever the cost. As his strength drained away, he observed a 'thick black line of ants crossing the muddy road – this I believed was a sign from God that I should turn back'.

This tale of an American and his solo bike odyssey was grippingly narrated, and I was moved by his own summation:

'I tried so hard to reach this place, and failed.'

Yet it was obvious he had taken an enormous step forward as a person.

◆ ◆ ◆ ◆

Wat Ban Suan Men marks the beginning of the expanse of land south of town. Entering the spacious grounds of this Dai temple, reputedly over 700 years old, one sensed a special atmosphere *(16-19)*. A sizeable shining gold dagoba consisted of lesser spires around the central one, with guard 'dogs' as before. Hiding menacingly under a tripartite double-roofed entrance pavilion,

16-19

a particularly vicious-looking monster beamed a silver-eyed, bare-teethed warning, next to which orange-clad trainee monks seemed relaxed *(16-21)*. The pavilion led to the main building at the back, which featured a concavely curved Teutonic split roof sweeping impressively skywards. Prayer flags contrasted *(16-23)*.

It is remarkable this temple survives – a major pagoda in the vicinity was dynamited into extinction by the Red Guards.

Espying one of nature's real monsters, Tae Hun was gripped by his first encounter with a monitor lizard, touted by the owner on a pay-to-handle basis *(16-19, 16-20)*. The monks observed the coincidence beside another fantastical creature *(16-22)*.

16-23

16-21

In contrast with Thailand, there are no Buddhist nuns in Xīshuāngbǎnnà, and while Thai monks grow their own food, those here depend on villagers for sustenance. Dai monks are free to eat meat, drink beer, and play snooker. In the past, most eight or nine-year old boys became novice monks *(pha noi)*.

16-22

Nowadays the rich parents of those who do are seeking an advanced means of education for their offspring. An initiation ceremony involves a banquet accompanied by firecrackers, with relatives bringing money trees to pay for lessons from Grand Masters. The minimum term is one year with no limit, during which the boys must sleep in temple quarters and shave their heads as a symbol of rejecting the world. They are allocated new names and spend their time studying painting and other arts, the night sky, the Dai written language to read the sutras, as well as tending to the ill in villages.

The China Daily claims another activity: in Xīshuāngbǎnnà 'the 526 Buddhist temples there are all equipped with TVs. The Dai and Bulang monks watch TV twice or even three times a day to keep abreast of the current developments in China and the world.' [5 Oct 94]

16-20

139

16-24

16-25

Country lanes, communities among bamboo and palm trees, and fields further on could provide endless hours of exploration. I hadn't come across such fragrant Eden-esque living since Bali. The trees in one compound camouflaged the grossest spider I have ever encountered – capping even my Korean pal's head *(16-24/25)*.

En route back to Jīnghóng, a lady selling pineapple by the road sliced the fruit into a lolly-on-a-stick shape for instant delectable consumption. A puncture necessitated loading the bikes into a fortunately uncrowded public bus.

◆ ◆ ◆ ◆

At the undistinguished modern one-street town of **Menglun** to the east, the Luosuō River acquires a severe bend that envelops the Island of Húlú, which translates as 'calabash' – a gourd grown on a tropical vine. A substantial pedestrian suspension bridge leads into the 130-hectare Tropical Plants Garden, containing thousands of species of flowering plants, Chinese medicinal herbs, exotic trees such as poisonous upas, Dragonblood, and *dracaena cambodiana*, as well as 120 kinds of bamboo to keep anyone happy.

A woman in a walled garden attracted a circle of Chinese tourists. She was singing to a plant. Apparently cows in England increase productivity the most if serenaded by Mozart, but perhaps Chinese plants prefer Asian music. Bushes of red ball-of-wool flowers attracted a number of distinctive butterflies.

There was clean cheap accommodation available within the grounds near a lily-filled pond crossed by a miniature stone bridge. I noted from the Bamboo House visitor's book the following tip from a backpacker.

> Leave the garden by the *road* bridge, 2 km road on right with sign "Tropical Rain Forest" – delightful path (rainforest for beginners); quiet birds; out of forest, down track, bamboo bridge across river; find own way back long way to Menglun, scenery back at river very good.

Other areas in Xīshuāngbǎnnà were tempting, such as Dameng'long, but we decided to leave a day early. CAAC couldn't alter our booking, requiring us to wait at the airport, which was a bedlam of people desperate for a ticket to Kūnmíng. I assume the airline woman at the counter exchanged our tickets as a favour to foreigners.

141

17-1

17-2

chapter 17

Kūnmíng

the Stone Forest

To ensure a place on the No. 501 chug-chug train to the Stone Forest south-east of Kūnmíng, we set off so early to the city's North Railway Station that even street stalls had barely begun selling their hot noodles. In the event, tickets were easily available, and we catnapped in the waiting hall. Here occurred an incident that might seem ordinary, a beggar moving along lines of passengers. Yet his supplication of kneeling before each one and bowing his head was conducted with the grace of a prince, the graciousness of a lord, and an inner control and calm of the wisest of sages. He could only have been sixteen, dressed in rags, but he surmounted the cage of his circumstances with an inner humility radiated by slow-motion deportment and steady eyes that had me in instant pangs of guilt. What on earth am I doing with my luck, rewards and riches, when this person – as superior to me in quality as a palace to a shanty hut – has none of them? There was a sacred quality in that consummate manner that will take me a lifetime of lifetimes to achieve. It said: I am what I am. When it was my turn for the treatment, I shrivelled up in shame at the onslaught of Goodness.

I had never fully appreciated before the dignity of suffering, the holiness of anguish.

> What a challenge... to acknowledge the divine in lowliness and poverty, amidst sneers and contempt, humiliation and misery, suffering and death, even to the point of revering, of lovingly embracing crime and sin itself, as steps to saintliness, not as impediments.
> Goethe (1749–1832)

I hadn't thought about mendicants since Ritchie had departed, and was caught unawares. My pocket contained only large notes, so I awoke Tae Hun for some change. Again I was disappointed with my response. The only way to justify the difference in wealth is to achieve something for the world that this person's circumstances cannot.

★ ★ ★

Constructed by the French in the 1900s to service their colony Tonkin (North Vietnam), the narrow-gauge railway perched high over the land allowed a leisurely intake of panoramas before and after Yángzōng Lake, punctuated by dinky, toy-town stations *à la Français*. There were twenty seconds to alight at Yíliáng (Suitably Cold) Station – missing it risked awaking in Vietnam! Hardly any buses were heading south-east from this bustling city; instead, minibuses halted momentarily on a by-pass making for Lùnán (South Road), whose Saturday market was a draw. From there, an impromptu 'taxi' took us to our destination.

It was apparent from the coach parks, overblown restaurant prices, and souvenir shops leading to the entrance of the **Stone Forest** (Shílín) that this was one of China's premier tourist sites. Fortunately, the development ceased at the gate and the majority of sightseers explored only the closest areas within, departing after a few hours. A cheap dormitory in a deserted hotel provided us with adequate board.

Two hundred and seventy million years ago during the final Permian Period of the Palaeozoic Era, the region was below a substantial layer of limestone under the same sea mentioned in chapter 14. Subsequent scouring of the karst has here left plateaus of pillars pointing skywards, hence the euphemistic name *(17-3)*. Another result has been caverns: in a recent survey, geologists have recorded 500 major limestone caves in Yúnnán, many east to south of Kūnmíng.

The most absorbing area of the Stone Forest for me was beyond the perimeter track: *17-1* and its detail *17-2* (previous double page) were taken from an outcrop in the south-west corner. With goats and their human tender lending the landscape a biblical aura, I longed to hike to the horizon and spend some moments with Sani in their villages along the way. They are part of the Yi family, the most numerous of the ethnic tribes of Yúnnán.

In the opposite corner, the Minor Stone Forest was more of a well-kept park – the two women in *17-4* were holding hands in Asian friendship. In the late light, the giant pillars black against the sun proceeded to radiate a dark presence, and I sensed that spiritual sentinels were gathering force.

Walking among the grey slabs and negotiating the tight passages in between was like exploring a maze of convoluted tree roots. The path's fence in *17-5* (overleaf) gives an indication of scale, the pinnacles towering up to thirty metres above. Was that a guillotine's blade on the left about to fall?

From the Lion Pavilion (in *17-3*), a young Asian threw an empty can onto the surrounding rock. Indignation arose again within – I considered scrambling to retrieve it and handing it back. Touring the bombastic shapes, one being a grand screen of rock mirrored in Jiànfēng (Sword Peak) Pool *(17-7)*, was not the experience it should have been. I was out of synch with the Chinese propensity to add preposterous names to the formations. But it was not the fault of the Chinese that they were proving difficult for me to enjoy.

145

17-4

17-5

Why?

My mind was focusing on the event in Hong Kong, and what immediately followed. When the chips are down, the fundamental question is Why?

"Why are you doing this to me?"

God refused to answer. God as Friend did not appreciate being questioned.

"This is beautiful!" I pointed out.

No reaction, no joy. I tried again.

"How wonderful this example of Creation is."

The Deity was indifferent, and deigned not to share. A terrible moment: no answer, no communicating. A crack had opened between, and it was bleeding fast. Before I realised, it had expanded into a rift, bloody and black. We were separate, and I was alone.

In the dark, I witnessed a supremely frightening moment: God's mind slowing, grinding to a painful stop, like a Meccano clock on its last gasp of the mechanical wind. I was nervous: a cold response, a cold shoulder had been offered. Sitting on the Bed of God, I gently asked:

"Is there something you want to say to me?"

S/he did not look, but turned away slowly, and back again, taking time before replying snail-like like an automaton:

"What have we to talk about?"

With that shattering answer, God broke the bond for ever.

It was pointless to ask why again. Instead I asked myself – Why is this happening? I shook my head in disbelief. It was now business.

"What is the problem?"

No reply.

"*What is the problem?*"

With my back to the Bed, I waited for an answer. When it came, it was with a tired but intimate voice – a Friend again. Listening to some innermost secrets presupposes facing the challenges that arise.

"I have serious problems that I cannot tell anyone."

After a pause, as an example God gave me one answer.

"I relish the feeling of pain when it is inflicted on me. I *enjoy* pain."

Wouldn't that quickly lead to pleasure in masochism? And if God is

17-6

everything, wouldn't inflicting pain on H/himself be inflicting pain on others – which S/he enjoys?

I couldn't comprehend the consequences of the revelation. Instead I wanted to help.

"I am different, I am not like others. For all our sakes, tell me your other problems!"

"No."

It was a simple word, uttered with a steely lack of hope.

Then God added a final, devastating comment.

"By the end of this journey, I will make you not like Me."

★ ★ ★

In my own bed alone in the cool analysis of night, I dwelt on the past, the future... and the present. Why is God pushing me down a path I don't want to go? I want to do that instead, but S/he stops me. I don't like God's temper. Why am I being led down this hard way?

The voice of smug reason within answered:

"Everybody has a hard life."

That extorted a dismissive snigger, arising from a well of bitter experience.

"I used to believe that," I answered the voice, "but it is not my choice to go this way."

"Then whose choice is it?"

With a schizophrenic laugh, the word delivered in an unexpectedly loud, rising, mocking intonation:

"***God's?***"

A student in Korea had related the story of a friend. Fishing on a boat (in Cheju!), something apocalyptic happened, with God appearing to him, which resulted in him being hospitalised for months. He talked throughout this time in a weird voice. On recovery, he revealed to his friend that God was "always speaking to him", that he enjoyed pain, and that he invariably chose the difficult way if there was an option. Korea is an apt country for these sorts of experiences: since time immemorial, there have been *mudang*, the majority today being women, many from Cheju-do. They are in communication with spirits – with the Amoeba.

* * *

I woke in the middle of the night. God was not asleep, could not sleep... and was tired. The world was back to front. Like the stelae in the forest, it was grey, drab, dark with no details – a reversal of Earth as in a bronze mirror. Or the reality?

I pulled up a chair by the end of the Bed. I foresaw the future, and delivered my last words slowly, with aching depth:

"Whatever happens, I will always be your friend."

The zip of the yellow Peace jacket had been foundering... and now failed. The main button had already given way. The remaining three stud fasteners of the covering flap were hanging on, just. The heavy heart-shaped zip-pull detached itself... the End of Love.

I didn't enquire beforehand the prices of food at a café near the entrance gate. The owner instigated rip-off attempt number 500 in China. I refused to pay. We compromised.

There were no Sani songs and dances that night; instead a disco was in progress with no dancers. On a moonlit walk by myself among the sentinel rocks, the atmosphere was disquieting and threatening, particularly when I faced some giant monoliths. The stars were out, but this time there was no euphoria. I erected the tripod, but the camera batteries froze again. Using my travel torch I fixed the problem, taking two pictures. Foreboding was all I could feel. I'm actually afraid! I pack up and quickly leave.

◆ ◆ ◆ ◆

17-8

Kūnmíng

A bus, whose owners charged us a considerably higher fare than anyone else, transported us for three hours back to **Kūnmíng** (Bright Brothers).

Under different names, this neighbourhood has been a thriving local capital since at least 2,100 years ago, when it then belonged to the local slave-based Dian civilisation. It became the Chinese colonial capital towards the end of the 13th century, coinciding with Marco Polo arriving in the area. Since the eviction of the Japanese in WWII, railway lines have aided exports and substantial industrial expansion, leading to the urban population recently doubling in a decade to two million.

In the north-west of the city, Cuìhú (Green Lake) Park was retrieved from marshland during the Yuán Dynasty (1279–1368), and is a popular place to feed birds who fly in line along the concrete wall in *17-8*, snatching bread almost directly from your hand. The blue sky confirmed Kūnmíng's sunny reputation: on average, the temperature in January reaches 15°C, despite the altitude. The convexly curved roads in this part of town are probably a ghost image of the Míng city wall that was in place until the 1930s. They lead to a grand, blue, red and gold *páilou* that trumpets the entrance to Yuántōng (Go Through a Circle) Temple. With a history stretching back to 8th-century Táng, the lavish and posh new buildings at the rear confirmed this is the Buddhist Association's prime temple in Yúnnán. There was however no surrounding greenery, being enmeshed in modern city blocks.

Along the Pānlóng River that dissects the heart of the city lies one of the few remaining older sectors. It begins at the Yìngjiānglóu Muslim Restaurant, whose collection of interesting meats on display inside made me walk straight out again. There has been an Islamic presence in the province ever since Muslims aided Khubilai Khan to capture Yúnnán for the Mongols in 1253. This was diminished by the Míng after they gained power in 1382, and by an 1873 Qīng massacre of dissatisfied Huí who, led by the Sultan of Dàlī, had been desecrating Kūnmíng's Buddhist temples and monuments during the previous eighteen years.

Today, close to the city's central crossroads exist a couple of mosques, and there are others in the metropolis. The oldest used to be hidden opposite the bird market, and its 400-year age had taken its toll, the inside being gutted as can just be seen through the open portal in *17-9*. It had been used as a factory during the religiously intolerant years of the Cultural Revolution. Nevertheless, the curious mix of Chinese eaves and beams with arabesque writing on the overhead sign, and polite people with distinctive white hats, gave the building an enticing air. In 1997, it was pulled down and replaced by a new and larger one.

A small park patronised by older people had been developed around the West Pagoda. A younger local on the market street a few hundred metres away did not know where the pagoda was.

◆ ◆ ◆ ◆

17-9

17-10

The finest aspects of Kūnmíng lie outside its urban perimeters. While Tae Hun attended to his remaining return travel arrangements, I set off by minibus a dozen kilometres west to the intimate Bamboo Temple, properly set uphill in a wood. There is much to admire: new carvings of stone flowers and mythical animals on a balustrade, two ancient cypresses five centuries in age with arresting striated trunks, potted cabbage plants beside the imperial plinth flanked by commanding bronze lions, a multi-tiered bronze *boshānlú* (incense burner), all leading to the main hall whose eaves are gently swept up like a genie's shoes. The origin of this Chán temple is lost in legend, but the basic layout was consolidated in 1280, the main hall containing a stone dated a few decades later.

Stemming from Theravada Buddhism, an *arhat* ('worthy one') is similar to the Mahayana bodhisattva in being capable of helping others on the road to enlightenment. Via the distorted 'arhan', the Chinese word is *lohan*, and there are usually eighteen sculptured ones in some main halls in Chinese temples, divided 9+9 on two sides. The Bamboo Temple is famous for sporting 500 of them about a metre high, with grotesque, Kafkaesque shapes and facial expressions. They are invariably old, bald and usually skinny, and in this temple the six sculptors of the 1880s were inspired to zany heights. One has an extended arm reaching the ceiling like a beanpole. Others have bushy, unkempt eyebrows cartoon-style. Some hold a book, a bell or begging bowl, while several sensibly own a fly swat. One may be meditating, another relaxing by a tree, others are airily in the clouds or hot-dogging on waves. There are animals associated with them: a toad, a goat, a civet, and a tiger.

As is customary in main halls, photography is *verboten*, and a sign confirmed this inside the perimeter halls of overflowing *lohan*. However there were some isolated examples outside behind glass, and with no sign I assumed – as with external guardians elsewhere in China – that these carried no interdict. Big mistake! As I composed a shot, a short bent female official about seventy years of age appeared from nowhere, and with fury butted me like a Valkyrie about to whisk me off to Valhalla.

★ ★ ★

The Western Hills on the north-west bank of Lake Diān contain three temples close together that are among the most rewarding in China. While strolling up to the first, looking back gives a fine overall view of Kūnmíng *(17-10)*.

The initial entrance to Huátíng (Splendid Pavilion) Temple features an elliptical pond with floating plants, around which are trees and pitted phantasmagoric rocks some taller than a human. Behind are candle and incense burners marking the entrance pavilion. This is flanked by scintillating pink and white flowering trees, a couple of miniature stone animals – one mythical, the other an elephant – and two guardians, left and right. Thankfully a human on official guard duty wasn't concerned about photography of his inanimate equivalents, and they are shown here *(17-11* and *17-12)*.

Once past the Four Guardians and Guān Yīn to whom the monastery is dedicated, there are eighteen bronze statues of Buddha, a purple sandalwood pavilion, as well as banisters of imported marble. The paramount impression within is of a chocolate box of camellias, magnolias, ancient plum trees and sweet-scented osmanthus, shoulder by shoulder with galleries and pavilions connecting the Misty Tower, the Tower for Viewing the Lake, the Tower for Meditating, and others.

17-11

Each has a cute, scatty, irascible dog at the side, both badly in need of a morning-after-the-week-before shave. Their vivid lacquered colours are arresting and suggestive. Ha (Moli Hai), on the left in mauve blue, is Guardian of the West and associated with Autumn; while Heng (Moli Hung), on the right in red, is Guardian of the South, symbolising Summer. These pigments are not standardised throughout China, and in Tibet are quite different.

Four more giant guardians are beyond, after which an *echt* bridge over an algae-ridden canal is intended to strip away the evil in you. A holy rock watches as you cross.

Originating in the 11th century, the current layout has developed over 900 years, and the temple is still home to one or two dozen monks. The main hall when I visited was a gutted tangle of scaffolding, the 500 *lohan* on the walls open to the elements. They are shorter than those of the Bamboo Temple.

The entrance to Tàihuá Temple higher still is strikingly different: a steep staircase leads through a beautiful, creamy, veined, marble *páilou*, on which are carvings and blue calligraphy *(17-13)*. Fighting for attention to the right is a magnificent, towering white camellia tree – the flower of winter *(17-14)*. Beside the gate is an age-old ginkgo tree planted by the teenage Jiànwén Emperor, the second of the Míng Dynasty, who reigned for only three years from 1399, which indicates the temple's era.

17-15

17-13

The richly decorated exterior of one hall caught my attention. In the top right-hand corner of *17-15* is a fire-breathing Divine Dragon, seen previously in *17-6*, which I immediately equated with the Almighty and H/his propensity to drag people through hell. The screen below it contains delicately painted panels that are fading fast *(17-16* overleaf). The best preserved, top left *(close-up in 17-17)* with an old man riding side-saddle and holding a bamboo container, has a similar quality to paintings in

Korea. The eagle, lower centre, is strongly conveyed with fearsome talons *(17-18)*, while to its right in contrast is a feminine, perfumed portrait of two petite white birds with black upper feathers, offset by pink and lime-green foliage on a cloudy backwash. Sumptuous!

To the left of the hall, an arch leads into a long, red, covered corridor, above which is a memorable portrait of a white tiger with black stripes surrounded in blues and off-whites, complimenting the Divine Dragon opposite.

17-12

bamboo	flexibility, strength, upright without being vulgar; one of the 'three companions of winter'
chrysanthemum	longevity, the flower of autumn; initially grown as a medicine
evergreen	everlasting
lotus flower	modesty, purity growing from the mud, the power to rise above harshness to enlightenment. Buddha is often portrayed on one keeping him untainted from the grime of worldly living – no wonder the Lotus Sutra is considered to encapsulate the most elevated truths. The leaves, fruit and tubers of this flower of summer are edible and have medicinal properties. A charming custom of the 18th century was that of placing tea in gauze bags into the heart of the lotus flower before sunset. The petals enveloped them during the night infusing the tea with a delectable perfume.
narcissus	straightforward, refined bearing
orchid	piety, relaxed peacefulness. The tiny cymbidium orchid is a symbol of honest bearing.
peach blossom	marriage, immortality in the lives that follow
peony	status and wealth, the flower of spring. Tree peonies are particularly potent symbols, including of femininity.
pine and cypress	antiquity, longevity, fortitude, virtue; one of the 'three companions of winter'
plum blossom	respected old age; one of the 'three companions of winter'
pomegranate	a hundred seeds, sons
prunus blossom	beauty
red bean	expressing emotions
willow	enchanting and elegant

How wonderful to be part of a culture where everything around you speaks and exhorts. Why don't we think that way in the West any more?

17-14

To one side of the temple is a peaceful pond in the shadow of compact trees and halls, the water as still as a mirror amplifying the blue of the sky. The only non-traditional feature is a satellite dish in one corner, momentarily disturbing one's reverie.

As ever in Chinese culture, resplendent trees and flowers are not planted merely to elicit appreciation of their beauty. Their purpose is to remind people of certain properties and philosophy.

17-16

17-17

17-18

The distinguishing feature of the final temple, Sānqīng Gé (Pavilion of Three Purities), for me lay within a simple modern hall elevated at the back. Before my eyes, welcoming artists were creating an exciting mosaic of murals in the style of the exotic reclining lady placed in chapter 6 *(6-24)*. For a Daoist temple that this supposedly is, these paintings seem unrestricted and a breath of fresh air, the lady the epitome of life-enhancing fecundity. They are also very Buddhist, the woman on the left edge in *17-20* offering the new Buddha's first meal while he sits on a lotus flower under a Bo (fig) tree, and the gazelles on the right indicating the moment of his first sermon at the Deer Park outside Sārnāth, India. How mature and wonderful to see one religion embracing another. The bump on the Buddha's head is not a groovy hairstyle, but the *usnisa*, the enlargement of the brain accommodating the new knowledge of enlightenment.

The paint was barely dry when I took the detail of the prince on a horse, with an old man, woman and child *(17-19)*. This illustrates the traditionally-accepted story of the 29-year-old Prince Siddhartha Gautama, six years before he became Buddha, departing the palace on his steed Kantaka on the adventure of enlightenment (the old man represents suffering), leaving behind his wife Yashodharā and their son Rāhu(la).

★ ★ ★

17-19

17-20

17-21

17-23

The biggest draw of these hills for tourists, most of whom whisked past the temples on coaches, lies beyond – the Lóng Mén or Dragon Gate, the same name as the caves near Luòyáng [chapter 8]. The designation illustrates the curves, bumps and bends of a narrow corridor bored through a vertical cliff high above Lake Diān, which leads to a petite cave-temple (*17-21* – the calligraphy proclaims it is the Magnificent Cloud Cave). According to an unlikely but true Chinese tale, this was all gouged out by a single Daoist monk called Wú Láiqìng, from Sānqīng Gé, who using simple tools commenced his life's objective in 1781. His death decades later left it unfinished, and others completed the project of faith with the assistance of ropes, the whole taking seventy-two years until 1853.

On the ledge overhanging the triple arches of this grotto called Dátiān (Reaching Heaven) beams the gnomish face of a white-bearded man. He is the father figure of Daoism – Lǎozi, the 'Old Master' – having well and truly reached heaven. Two of the three small figures inside the shrine are in the usual stern, expressionless Daoist style. The middle one in contrast seems to be surfing one-legged, other limbs outstretched as if dancing (*17-22*). The following description records he is…

Kui Xing, the patron God of Scholars. He rides a dragon-fish while heroically brandishing a calligraphy brush – as though to confirm that 'the pen is mightier than the sword' – and blithely balances a potted pomegranate plant, the symbol of long-lasting success, on the sole of his foot. Candidates for the all-important imperial examinations struggled up Western Hill to pray for his help. He is flanked by Wen Cheng [Wénchāng], the God of Literature, and Guan Gong, the God of War and Justice.

Yunnan, by Patrick Booz (p. 69)

17-22

From this there is a Chinese expression: someone who has 'ascended the Dragon Gate' means s/he has gained promotion.

The colours glancing back were enticing *(17-23)*, the more so when descending to the lakeside. At its narrowest point, I crossed China's sixth largest lake on the causeway in *17-24*, which has replaced an old ferry, before returning to the city. Marco Polo was accurate with its dimensions:

> There is a lake here, some 100 miles in circumference, in which there is a vast quantity of fish, the best in the world. They are of great size and of all kinds. The natives eat flesh raw – poultry, mutton, beef, and buffalo meat… they have it minced very small, [and] put it in garlic sauce flavoured with spices.
> translated by Ronald Latham (p. 149)

That tradition continues today on special occasions such as Dai weddings, when chillies, garlic and soy are combined with thinly sliced raw pork.

He also noted an unusually generous trait of the local people:

> The men here do not mind if one touches another's wife, so long as it is with her consent.

The sexual favour was granted probably because outsiders were considered eminent and wealthy, and might beget new fortune and better prospects for the bloodline.

past, present and future

This chapter ends with an aspect of reality that continually encroaches while travelling. In Book One, there were (are!) a number of references to it, including the following.

At Ürümqi's museum:
> The 4,000-year-old Lóulán corpse, unearthed at Lop Nur in 1979, exuded the peculiar peace of death. She had been forty years old. [chapter 2, p. 47]

We can view the form of a woman's forty-year-old body, and know she is also 4,000 years old – her past, our present, and the earth's continuing history combined.

Concerning the removal of the Bezeklik murals:
> Time is impersonal. The triptychs of Past, Present and Future Buddhas had vanished as if never present. (p. 61)

From Amoeba:
> Everyone is aware of the spiritual, even if they do not believe in a Divinity. It is the feeling of belonging to something greater than ourselves, and arises from everything that was, is, and will be created. (p. 74)

The Great Wall:
> Years of reading about something magical but intangible in a far-flown world was suddenly before my eyes. It was as if it had always existed…. Gazing at the structure diminishing into the horizon gave rise to a feeling of locking into a common, universal bond. Such moments illustrate Time itself. [chapter 3, p. 99]

In a period of less than sixty years from AD 550, one and a half million workers perished building another section. It was a symbolic smell of death that came off this Wall of Great Expectations. I touched its past and thus my own, tying it into the present. (p. 100)

Xī'ān's bronze artwork demonstrates:
> the spectacular skill and imagination of Chinese craftsmen throughout the Shāng and Zhōu Dynasties – a period of 1,400 years before the birth of Christ… while also giving valuable insights into life during that time. The industry of the common person then and now instantly become as one, the past merging into the present. [chapter 4, p. 124]

The terracotta soldiers:
> are a monument, not to egomaniacal power, but to the common man and woman of Asia. Once again, the past instantly hits one in the present, and *becomes* the present. (p. 130)

> The patient, gentle, tap-by-tap scraping and digging by the large team of archaeologists was like a slow-motion re-run of history. (p. 131)

The left arm lesson:
> I was *without realising it* breaking the most solemn oath it is possible for anyone anywhere to give in the Universe (please forgive the seeming lack of humility). I hadn't made that oath yet at the time – I was about to do so two weeks later. That was no excuse however: the future is the present. [chapter 6, p. 186]

Nánshān Temple in Wǔtáishān:
> The main hall of this temple delighted with its plain wood fulsomely carved, with hints of former paintwork adding an aura of continuing history and touching the past. [chapter 7, p. 205]

155

Meeting someone for the first time, whom you have met before:

> It was that six months before I knew the immediate answer, and it led to a vital and enormous leap up a seemingly unbridgeable step blocking my path. The hoped-for future will not have occurred without it. (p. 208)

The extraordinary looking Xiăntōng Monastery:

> Craftsmanship of eons ago mixed with a Dalek-image here, a Saturn rocket there, a Vostok capsule yonder: past and present simultaneously. (p. 211)

Children:

> As well as providing a reminder of where you've come from, they present a yardstick as to where you are, and can stimulate an impulse to recover in the future what you have lost, which they still have. All time in one. [chapter 9, p. 239]

In Book Two, the treatment of Time in this example seems particularly contorted:

> The rift is a portent of things to come, yet materialising afterwards to confirm that it was no accident – the future about to happen in the past. [chapter 13, p. 68]

The above illustrate an essential property of Time: the Present has the Past within it, therefore the Future contains the present, and the Past is in the Future. The implication is equally that both the Future and the Present lie in the Past, and the Future is contained in the Present. The three are in each other.

Time is the fourth dimension. To see it clearly requires standing back from normal temporal vision, as if in a spacecraft soaring to survey the earth from above, simultaneously observing everything as it was, is and will be. To see and influence the future, it helps to see the past in the present, and better, *bring* the past into the now – study history and one's past, note the consequences relevant to today, and *act* upon the lessons.

Physically, we are surrounded by a former universe. The sun we glimpse at is an image eight minutes old – the past today. It might have already switched off! The light from the other stars is years, centuries, millennia and millions of years old – they may not exist. The past is here for all to see – the universe certainly isn't the present.

On a personal level, someone's past life is revealed in h/his face. If one accepts that statement having some validity, there must be a mechanism how it is transmitted: that alone justifies why 'face reading' by genuine fortune tellers steeped in the tradition, such as in Korea and China, might assist them in character analysis, and in postulating about someone's past. In general, if you want to know aspects of a person's past, then look at h/him now – how s/he behaves, reacts, and bears h/himself. If you at least keep an open mind to the possibility of rebirth and/or reincarnation, extend that principal and, as Buddha taught in the Lotus Sutra, an analysis of someone's present life gives clues as to their previous ones.

The best reason to study the past is not as a diverting academic exercise. Given that we accumulate mini-evils because of our innate selfishness and reaction to those of others, it makes sense to discover ourselves as we were long ago. The goodness and innocence that we were can offer a shining light as to how to be today. That opposes the usual advice to forgive and forget. Personally, I feel forgiveness should not be automatic until the transgressor has realised h/his past evil, and at least shows remorse.

Pain and pleasure is also transmitted from the past – those events that dashed us emotionally to smithereens, and those that were the highs of our life. They are with us still, yet are gone like a will-o'-the wisp.

> There is no returning on the road of Life.
> The frail bridge of Time, on which we tread,
> sinks back into eternity at every step we take.
> The past is gone for ever. It belongs to us no more.
> [source unknown]

17-24

It is prudent and sobering to revisit those events every now and then – they are the stuff of life, reminding us of the essentials. Let us never forget. The knack is not to dwell *too* long; rather to release these heartfelt and most cherished experiences, and move on.

In 1991 I visited my birthplace, Miri in Sarawak Borneo, for the first time since aged two. The hospital where I appeared was still in existence, resembling an army barracks. According to a midwife who had been there forty years, nothing had changed apart from the addition of a dividing wall. The only delivery room was as it had been, small, unpretentious, with the bed in the same position. I spent a few minutes inside – the woman who had given birth to me had succumbed to her traumatic mental disease the previous year.

On leaving, I saw a group of obviously distressed people. It was a period when the destruction of the forest and the consequences were on every native person's mind. A plane carrying the elders of a Kelabit tribe's longhouse for a meeting to discuss their future had crashed in the rainforest killing fourteen, all related, the few survivors being in the hospital.

I noted in my journal: I arrive to trace my roots at a particularly poignant time, but the present and the immediate future are also clamouring for attention, all three involving painful realisations. The three tenses simultaneously.

A new hospital was being built, with the old one due to close the following year. I had caught my past just in time, for it no longer exists.

★ ★ ★

> Never bear more than one kind of trouble at a time. Some people bear three – all they have had, all they have now, and all they expect to have.
> Edward Everett Hale
> (1822–1909), Unitarian priest

The Present is the most important of the three tenses. The past we cannot alter, and the future is bound up with what we and others do today. In part, we are our future selves.

To live wildly and passionately in the present is one's privileged obligation. Shortly before he died, the English dramatist Dennis Potter recorded these thoughts:

> Below my window there's an apple tree in blossom. It's white. And looking at it – instead of saying, 'Oh, that's a nice blossom' – now, looking at it through the window, I see the whitest, frothiest, blossomest blossom that there ever could be. The nowness of everything is absolutely wondrous. If you see the present tense – *boy*, do you see it. And *boy*, do you celebrate it.
> Channel 4: *Without Walls*,
> quoted in Time magazine 20/6/94

Events of the past probably exist in the present in a physical way. I'm referring to the widespread phenomenon of *déjà vu*, which arises as suddenly as a photograph in a dark room being lit by the click of a light switch. The first time I experienced it was in connection with photography on a tour along the panhandle of Alaska. I was framing the elements of a peaceful scene, including a seaplane parked in a corner of shallow water under trees, when I heard a plane approaching high in the sky. With the camera still held in position, its silver streak entered the viewfinder diagonally precisely from the top right hand corner, gilding a shot already bubbling with interest. Immediately I clicked, it flashed in my mind that the scene was a rerun – it required each of the exact elements to come together, particularly the plane entering, before I recognised that *it had already occurred*.

A photograph taken the morning after the Cheju event resulted in a holy *déjà vu*, a gift and a sign. The subject was a wooden spirit post, called *chung syung* in Korean, which is similar to a modest totem pole, examples being dotted throughout Korea. Its spirituality drew me to it. I took a close-up of the head, then realised it would be a suitable symbolic stand-in for God. I stood next to it for someone else to capture the last photograph of the 9-day trip, as a memento of the most important moment in my life

The night before I first told the Cheju story with photographs, I noticed two straight vertical beams of blue light physically on that last slide, of a type that doesn't project onto a screen. They enter the top of the perfectly focused picture from above. One goes through and envelops me – a real echo of the beam of thought, the tunnel through which the Cheju message came. The other drops the other side of the totem pole, the two combining to enclose it with me. I checked the other transparencies from that roll of film: none possess the light, apart from the previous close-up of the spirit post – a beam of blue light enters its head from above, another alongside.

Four days later, I realised I had seen the picture of me and the post before. The *déjà vu* was of both the picture *and the Blue Light beams*. The photograph had existed for a long time before it was ever taken. The more I thought about it, the more it haunted me. These are signs – what more proof do you want? Past, Present and Future twist, will invert, and have intertwined.

★ ★ ★

If you know where you've come from,
it is plain where you are,
then you can see the direction you're heading.

One can influence the future by fostering an ability to stand back and see that the future has already happened. Any manager, leader, teacher or parent needs that aptitude, and can react accordingly in advance. It can confirm that matters are heading in the right direction, or give a warning, in which case one can modify the future if desirable.

What was difficult yesterday will often be easy tomorrow, and both those perceptions are part of one's make-up today. The purpose of this learning and experience is to enable us to zoom out to a greater perspective with more ease. The Chinese poet Wáng Zhīhuàn (688-742) expressed it straightforwardly:

To get a broader view, climb to another floor of the tower.

The Theory of Relativity indicates the three tenses exist simultaneously. Buddhism enshrines the concept of Time as a single fluid container in the Three Buddhas of Past, Present and Future – the Buddha is the same person. An interesting remark just made to you is already in the past, is with you now, and will remain in your future. Life is a process of arriving, staying and going. What causes that journey to evolve symbolically are wind, rocks and trees. In some cases, words can be the wind, the coming and going of a loved one a rock, and music a tree. They each help to keep one focused on the spirituality of the land and of all life. That requires pacing oneself, and never being against nature.

The word 'God' tends to conjure thoughts of a single entity. The Amoeba theory indicates that God is also all entities and all persons that have ever been, plus those that are and will be. There are no tenses with God, in the same way that we can see from our privileged position the past, present and future of King George VI in 1938, or President Franklin Roosevelt the same year.

Jesus said, "Before Abraham was born, I am" [John 8.58]. It was a way of stating that he existed in the past, perhaps in previous lives, and that all time is one. Since Jesus was human, it has consequences for all of us.

He to whom time is the same as eternity,
and eternity the same as time,
is free of all adversity.
Jakob Boehme (1575–1624),
German mystic who
experienced divine visions

The first days exploring any new country invariably possess an extra tingle and spice. On arriving in New Zealand, I took a ferry to Rangitoto Island, a volcanic cone in sight of Auckland. The harshness of the terrain reflected and created renewed strength in me. Walking beside the indicative texture of hardened lava crusts catapulted me back not only to the weird rocks of the Stone Forest, but also to the rubbly *aa* and the rarer ropey *pahoehoe* of the Galapagos Islands, which I had observed nine years previously. Rangitoto's Kowhai trees and the vermilion red pompons of Pohutukawa flowers – the largest surviving group in the world – gently transported me to the beauty of plants on my previous walks in diverse countries. Stroking the soft thin core of the red flowers reminded me of the silky hair of my mate of a few years before.

Striding up the recent volcano, the peculiar ground plants yanked me back five years to when I was grasping for footholds and gasping for air up Krakatau, its spindly plants hugging the soil for dear life. Looking down into the Rangitoto crater, I was aware again of standing at the bottom of the bosom of Krakatau – the site of one of the world's greatest and loudest natural explosions – in eerie silence.

The stitches of time were drawn closer together. As I strolled among the enormous ferns on Rangitoto, I was on the island of Flores in Indonesia reliving a walk among its primaeval giant ferns, a candidate for the oldest form of tree in the world. While jumping between lava caves on the slopes, I recalled crawling through an Inca rock tunnel on the way to the peak of Machu Picchu, and in an instant was taken back to Cheju Island strolling inside the biggest known lava tube in the world, seven kilometres long.

As I lay beside a bush, I was also sitting alone under a tree in Borneo at the end of my first tour of Asia, its five-months of events and moments parading across my mind. Those twenty minutes of contemplation on Rangitoto drew in nine years of my life in one pull. I experienced a preview of my future death surveying everything I had done in life flashing past in one go, and Past, Present and Future pulled together like the drawcords of a bag.

Which came first? A nonsensical question: since they are in each other, they are simultaneous. Maybe that's a tease!

Chapter 18

Ruili and around

Returning to Kūnmíng from Xīshuāngbǎnnà had been advisable to avoid a bum-numbing bus taking three interminable days from Jǐnghóng to the western border of the province, there being no direct flights. Instead, a Yúnnán Airlines flight took a mere forty-five minutes to Mángshì (Lùxī), providing a visually stimulating overview of the folds between river valleys. A waiting minibus edged us two hours south-west along the Burma Road, following the pleasant scenery of the Lóngchuān (Dragon River), known across the border as the Shweli, which flows into the Irrawaddy.

The bus terminated at **Ruìlì**, the last town but one in this remote corner of the Chinese empire called the Déhóng (Great Virtue) Region, wherein live Dai and Jingpo minorities. It was obvious walking along the crammed yet relaxed evening market street that it possesses a different atmosphere to anywhere else in China, even Xīshuāngbǎnnà. For a start, there are no Chinese tourists, and while Xīshuāngbǎnnà is on the international backpacking map, only a limited proportion of those foreigners make it here: we stayed three nights and saw none. Outside a tin-can café, a man with a long white beard sat wearing a white turban and white bandaged clothes, with his legs and feet bare – a Sikh, a Hindu? Even in the centuries up to the Hàn Dynasty, a Silk Road through Yúnnán passed this way en route to India.

Above all, it was the faces of mild-mannered Burmese that impressed. Among the throng of stalls selling produce and knick-knacks, a charming Burmese girl was wearing and displaying necklaces, earrings, a bracelet with a bell, and large circular trinkets all made of hundreds of chocolate-coloured seeds platted together – they looked like coffee beans.

Some Burmese were selling gorgeous carvings, at which I drooled. The heavy wood emanating from Myanmar was of smooth-grained quality, black or milk chocolate with black streaks, and silky with a deep hue. There were sensuously polished elephants of various sizes, and a sculpture of a tall slim woman reminded me of those in Bali of Sarasvatī, the Hindu Goddess of Music and Learning. The standard of artistry was superb. The objects were not cheap, and most would sink a backpack. I was also sceptical of the environmental cost. However, a sympathetic storeowner furnished details of the mode of manufacture, the timber, and its craftsmen across the border, which reassured me. He asserted that his stocks of products were carved from one tree a year, it being the leguminous rosewood *Dalbergia cultrata*, or Burma Blackwood – in Burmese called Yindai(k). I bought a six-inch elephant whose tusks looked authentic but were made of plastic.

Around the corner from the market, the Lucky Restaurant, with half its tables outside, is not one that would be found elsewhere in China. Run by a Burmese family, the enthusiastic server suggested an unusual curry with chapattis, washed down with sugar cane juice, after which banana bread and coconut pastries complemented coffee good and sweet. He revealed that many compatriots here had escaped from the regime in Burma, a name they prefer as it was the military that altered it without consulting the people.

A visitor's book at the café confirmed foreigners arriving only in dribs and drabs. Tae Hun warmed to the conviviality of the place, and signed himself as the first Korean to see this part of the world.

◆ ◆ ◆ ◆

The only hotel renting bikes had but two operational – so valuable they required passports to be deposited. Heading southwards brought in view the whiter-than-white Burmese stupa of the Nóng'ān Golden Duck Temple. An extraordinary pennant hung from a soaring, bending spiked mast, resembling a windmill that had lost three of its arms *(18-1)*. With it being so tall and swinging haphazardly, it proved a challenge to capture the ingredients of the temple in one photograph. Looking into the sun, the black peaks of the stupa's four corner spires imitated an iron chandelier, while the central one supported a golden orb. From the road, the whole resembled a white wedding cake that had landed in an awkward spot like Doctor Who's tardis. To the right of the buildings in the photograph was the temple's unaffected main hall, whose informality within was worlds away from standard Chinese temples. The young men here wore sarongs, their faces nugget brown as deep as their rosewood *(18-2)*.

18-1

18-2

Outside, an impossible space-station array of brown brushes, broomsticks and other straw bric-a-brac were being conveyed along the road by a man in a straw hat, who smiled as he saw me preparing the shot *(18-3)*. A few kilometres on is a recent bridge (1992) over the Lóngchuān River, across which insalubrious goods are taken into Muse in Myanmar. Turning south-west, we cycled along a straight avenue that continued almost flush against the border for twenty kilometres through flat land. Mechanised carts brimming with attractive women passed by, and tractors pulled trailers piled with bicycles, while a tractor-lorry was motionless with a puncture.

Following a dirt path off the road led into a residential village incorporating one tiny store that sold Pepsi, and a magnificent wooden building on stilts under which animals were kept. This Hánshā Temple was accessed up steps covered by a panoply decorated with a kaleidoscope of painted panels. A monk was chanting inside a devotional hall, alongside which this jolly yellow giant seemed incongruous *(18-4)*.

He is Maitreya ('Friendly'), known in China as Mí Lè Fó, the Buddha of the Future. In India, he is portrayed serene and holy, but in China the imagery is of a Laughing Buddha with a pot belly. In standard Chinese Buddhist temples a midget version of him is placed inside the first hall or gate. He reminds believers of the pleasant future to come without suffering. Throughout China, I found the grin most unpleasant: I took an instant and irrational dislike to this monster mocking everyone's present-day pain. This one however was the exception – a child's playground toy.

18-3

18-4

18-5

A white stupa appeared in the distance on a hill across fields. Farmers' tracks seemed to head that way, yet went nowhere. My companion tended to his bike as a bird of prey hovered, causing black and white birds to wheel round in alarm. To cross a stream blocking our return to the road, a rickety extemporised 'bridge' consisting of four bamboo sticks required an acrobatic sense of balance with the bikes on our shoulders. Beyond a village, an obvious track was leading to the conspicuous stupa glinting in trees a kilometre away. A solitary puff of white cloud came to rest over the white stupa. Signs, suspicious portents, perhaps – you never know for sure. Among the trees, houses lined the track that climbed sharply, the last hundred-metre stretch too steep to cycle.

On a bench under a benevolent tree, we absorbed the tranquil idyllic scene of Léizhuāngxiāng Temple *(18-5)*. On a pedestal next to us was a painted papier-mâché cow gazing at a bush where two gaudy cockerels were pecking the ground. A humble woman in red was preparing green vegetables, assisted by a dark-skinned boy in an orange sarong. The roofs of the halls were a mix of triangles and square towers tapering to a point. At first unnoticed in shadow, the surreally elongated enrobed Buddha was different from any other, the face concealed by an overhang stooped in strange non-Chinese writing *(18-6)*. The Burmese Buddhist tradition is Theravada ('Way of the Elders'), as distinct to the later Mahayana ('Great Vehicle') in most of China.

It was a long, quiet breather here. Before the storm.

18-6

18-7

By a field of bromeliads and cabbages, the stupa in its white-walled compound commanded an expansive view of the imminent hills of Myanmar. The sun pierced its spears casting a moody shadow, while white elephants on the sides spoke mutely of things to come *(18-9)*.

From the illuminated front, the starched stupa shone in an arched blue sky, like a cowrie in a coral sea *(18-7)*. What impressed me most were two young women and a boy. Ignoring my presence, they approached, silently knelt, and prayed with an accepting devotion and compassionate humanity, of a quality substantially above me *(18-8)*.

On the way back, a kingfisher perched itself on a telegraph wire, and a boy on a buffalo meandered in a field, indifferent to the hill behind being in another country *(18-10)*. In minority Yúnnán, it is a child's supreme responsibility, when out of school, to care for water buffalo – a major asset of a family.

★ ★ ★

Our passports retrieved, at a café we drank milk direct from decapitated coconuts and two lively women in their twenties asked to chat with us. After a light-hearted few hours, they decided I was more handsome than my Korean companion, and I was convinced they were nothing but sincere.

◆ ◆ ◆ ◆

18-8

18-9

162

Virtually the only reason to see **Wǎndīng**, an hour away, is to gawp at a bridge. Even the markets of this modest town seemed to have shut. Being on the border, the dead-end atmosphere is literal: the bridge is where the Burma Road ceases in China. A previous road was used centuries before to convey gemstones carried by elephants from Mandalay to Kūnmíng, from whence sought-after jade was transferred to the heart of China. In 1937–38, the 1,000-kilometre stretch of the road from the railhead at Lashio in British Burma was upgraded by 160,000 Chinese workers in order to supply their country at war with Japan, which had isolated China from the sea. They worked almost by hand alone, extemporising blasting techniques using tubes of bamboo filled with gunpowder, their only payment being food.

The primary aim of the Japanese in invading Burma in January 1942 was initially to apprehend a major stock of supplies held in Rangoon, and to prevent further ones from India reaching British Singapore, which promptly fell a month later. The Japanese amassed tens of thousands of the Chinese civilians and murdered them, taking many to the coast and machine-gunning them in the sea. That accomplished, the Japanese commander seized the opportunity to capture Lashio, cutting off the Burma Road and completely ensnaring China.

Reeling from Pearl Harbour months before, the Americans envisaged the eventual subjugation of Japan being achieved by advancing eastwards through China, not forecasting that their naval fleet would later recover, win control of the Pacific, and threaten westwards. Assisting China was thus given high priority, and supplies were airlifted by Douglas C-47s (Dakotas) for two-and-a-half years over the 'Hump', the euphemistic nickname given to the treacherous 6,000-metre mountains between Ledo in Assam and Kūnmíng. If they had flown a direct route then the peaks would have been lower, but Japan had fighter supremacy over the Burmese skies, forcing a flight path north over the flanks of the Eastern Himalayas.

An uncle of mine, Carl Steinkamp, was one of the American pilots who flew the Hump throughout. He died in the following decade, but my aunt vividly remembers some of the operational aspects he related to her. Fully laden, the C-47s could reach a maximum height of only around 4,250 metres. For that reason and in order to breathe, the aircrew flew well below mountaintop height, forcing the pilots to manoeuvre between peaks, with up and down draughts wrenching the planes without warning into the ground. Between sorties, the pilots bivouacked in small groups and, as with travel where one meets people for a short time never to see them again, Carl told of new faces regularly sleeping next to him – the previous mates having not made it.

There were Chinese army divisions and aircraft maintenance crews in India as well as China, trained by General Stilwell. My uncle related that Chinese ground crews sometimes came perilously close to the propellers as the planes taxied to a halt. This stemmed from a belief that to stare death in the face absolved them from past misdemeanours. Once in a blue moon a head would get too close....

After the allies had regained control of the skies, the Hump missions from early 1944 were able to navigate along a more direct route, with peaks less of a problem at 4,000 metres. Even so, the planes would have crossed, by my count, seven mountain ranges: Patkai, Kumon, Shanngaw Taungdan, and in China the Gāolígòng, Nù, Qīngshuǐlang and Héngduàn/Cāng. The supply task was superseded in 1945 by the amazing new through-the-jungle Stilwell Road that connected the overworked railhead at Ledo with liberated Lashio.

18-11 was taken by my uncle at the time, and shows the pilots' dining room!

I wondered how jumpy the guards would be in one of the two simple huts flanking the Wǎndīng bridge. After decades of closure, the border reopened in 1988 and

18-10

18-11

18-12
there are now plenty of Chinese signposts in Myanmar. A major Singapore economist (Mya Than) reckons illicit trade between Myanmar and Yúnnán amounts to over $800 million per year – a substantial boost for the respective economies. The two officers were nonchalant, ignoring people casually and regularly crossing, while loads of lorries were waiting the other side.

Apart from some deserted woodcarving shops, the only other interest here was to climb through the Forest Reserve, containing an amusement area and a dozen-cell 'zoo'. A pavilion at the summit offered a tantalising view *(18-12)* of the Myanmar hills and town of Kyugok with its beckoning stupas, as well as the Burma Road disappearing into future history while pointing to the sobering scenes of Allied-Japanese fighting in early 1945.

The sensitivity of the area was rudely confirmed when our minibus returning to Ruìlì was stopped by police. The chief officer was obviously high ranking: speaking good English, he quizzed me suspiciously for five minutes, ignoring the locals in the bus. Opium smuggling involving bribery and false passports are well known in the area, and the Yúnnán authorities are becoming tougher. 1988 saw the first arrest of a drug addict. In 1995, a drug tycoon was executed. Tae Hun explained he was learning English while travelling, and our passports were studied. It was an uncomfortable time for both of us.

◆ ◆ ◆ ◆

To travel anywhere in China by public bus requires an early start. At 6.30 and heading north, this one was soon straining up one of the mountainous humps, before easing off at open fields towards Zhāngfēng. After five hours north-east along valleys rich with colour, the bus clambered through the narrow streets lined with wooden shacks that constitute **Téngchōng**. Of all places in China, this is where I felt most out on a limb. Of the trickle of foreigners that reach Ruìlì, only some make the detour to here. The shower in the No 4 Government Hotel (there was no evidence of the first three) featured a cranky, chain-driven water system that reminded me of a quaint Victorian bath I used in Crete in the 1960s. One foot from the showerhead, a thin live electric wire trailed down from the ceiling light. It was split and joined with peeling tape, necessitating some splash-avoidance care – either that or bathe in the dark.

The town's centre was awash with crumbling buildings or construction sites. The Post Office was permanently closed, and I couldn't locate the former British consulate, which according to an adventure company was 'now a bullet-ridden grain store'. Tourist information and tours were non-existent. Nevertheless, there was a friendly ambience, people in the evenings eating simple food on the streets on slim benches around fires. We joined in.

◆ ◆ ◆ ◆

In the early morning, the quiet residential lanes radiating from the centre seemed from a different world – a Qīng China of decaying walls topped with mildly-curved tiled roofs, from which corridors led to wooden front doors painted with fiercesome guardians. Interspersed were newer concrete blocks. Occasional carts with bags of grain were hauled by men in blue tunics and straw hats.

The pride of Téngchōng – and well worth experiencing – is the Frontier Trade Bazaar, a long narrow market street announced by an ostentatious red banner at one end, lined on both sides with canopied stalls, and already thronged with activity. It was impossible even to squeeze through the crowds at the other end, clogged as it was by tractors packed with produce. A black and white photograph taken by the naturalised American adventurer Joseph Rock on

18-13

Chinese New Year's Eve 1923 indicates that little has changed, except that the canopies were then large circular umbrellas. What might have been new were the mix of colours that burst explosively in my eyes – yellow mitts, red jackets, purple coats with frizzy blue epaulettes, mustard blouses, black plastic leathers, white pants, tan sweaters, hats of more varieties then in Paris, as well as red balloons, rattan baskets, blocks of wood, black bikes and blue sky. Some older women sat on the ground all day selling a few yellow fruit, or grain from white wholesale bags.

At 1,650 metres, Téngchōng lies between valleys of rivers: the Lóngchuān and Nù/Salween to the east, and the Dàyīng (Big Eagle) to the west, which flows into the Irrawaddy across the border. A dozen kilometres north begin a cluster of over seventy volcanic mountains, at present non-active, including Dàkōngshān, Hēikōngshān, Xiǎokōngshān and Dàyīngshān (2,614 metres), with at least one extensive lava field in the area. On a roughly-paved road through land pierced with yellow rape fields and isolated woods, a minibus conveyed us to Mǎzhàn, a collection of wooden houses and shops at an intersection.

Low volcanoes lay all around in fields of silence and anonymity. Twin trees soared beside a lake that glinted in harsh sun; a couple of puffs of cloud passed. Tae Hun led the way in the vague direction of dry, brown volcanic mounds. I flinched – they looked like the *o-rum* of Cheju-do! Bubbles in a thick lava porridge. I didn't like the reminiscence, or the strange atmosphere. Why Cheju, here, now? A farmer paused by a single gnarled tree; otherwise there were no humans in this fire-and-belly, godly landscape. Small stone stelae marked burial plots.

Reaching the top of a high cone, we paused looking down into a volcanic crater that was nothing more than a bowl of covered earth. I took a photo with my shadow. When I turned around, the sun blared through my camera just as I was aware of triangular slopes of truncated volcanoes. Pyramids again... *orum*, everywhere *orum*.

My companion had marched ahead around the rim. I was alone apart from my Shadow, with not a sound, not a clue as to the what or the why.

A panoply of a volcanic Eden stretched northwards under a polarised blue heaven punctuated by puffy blankets of clouds *(18-15)*. I cried because of its stunningly attractive, stunningly cruel beauty. Is this Heaven, is this Hell? Beauty and Ugliness combined. How tempting it would be to wander for forty days through this desert. To the east, a plain studded with terracotta browns and greens raced to the distant Gāolígòng mountain ridge. I rushed to catch up... I was balanced on the ring of fire's wall between the crater and the valley below, between the fire and the fiery pan – the Wall of my Life about to slide down a Fault... the *Rift*.

The same minibus took us back.

◆ ◆ ◆ ◆

Setting off in the dark ensured we caught a 6.30 bus for an eight-hour marathon eastwards to rejoin the Burma Road at Bǎoshān. It was a see-saw ride in several senses: a climb with z-bends from bump to pothole to 2,300 metres, surging down to the Lóngchuān, crossing its foaming waters, up and over again, a passport check on a bridge over the 2,800-kilometre Nù/Salween, up to a pass, dip and up to another, followed by a slower descent. A helicopter-bus would be ideal in this region! Instead a Hi-Yo-Silver Chinese bus was a head-and-bottom-banging ride – great fun, apart from the non-existent legroom. I practically fell out of the bus taking *18-14* while on the move (overleaf): it shows the Nù Jiāng (Angry River) observed from the Nù Mountains.

With the other matter on my mind, I gained solace from listening to music – in particular, the Enya album *The Memory of Trees*, which I had purchased in Hong Kong. The title track soothed, the final *On my way home* caused tears to swell, while the humour of the second track made me laugh – an unusual reaction to this artist's sound world. The whole helped to keep me sane and grounded at this time.

I handed the headphones to a young Chinese guy seated next to me. He enjoyed his first encounter with a personal stereo and this type of Western music, and asked to listen to a cassette of his own, which gave him much pleasure during the tedium of the journey.

The wide plain of Bǎoshān (Defensive Mountain) was the site of an infamous battle to rival Cecil B. De Mille's epics. The protagonists in 1277 were the forces of Khubilai Khan and Narathihapate, the King of Mian (the Chinese name for Burma). He was a colourful character who consumed 300 curries a day, according to him. Marco Polo reported on the King's resources.

> He had 2,000 large elephants. On each of these was erected a wooden castle of great strength.... Each of these castles was manned by at least twelve fighting-men, and some by sixteen or more. In addition he had fully 40,000 men, mainly cavalry but including some infantry. The whole force was equipped in a style befitting such a powerful and mighty ruler. It was an army fit to do great deeds.

At the start of battle,

> the horses of the Tartars, catching sight of the elephants, were seized with such terror that their riders could no longer urge them forward against the foe, but they continued to turn tail. And the king with his troops and his elephants continued to advance....
>
> But [the Tartars] dealt with their plight very shrewdly, as I will tell you. When they saw that their horses were so panic-stricken, they dismounted, every man of them, led their mounts into the wood and tethered them to the trees. Then they grasped their bows, fitted their arrows to the string, and let fly at the elephants. They loosed upon them such a shower of arrows that it was truly marvellous, and the elephants were grievously wounded.... They turned in flight towards the king's men in such a turmoil that it seemed as if all the world were tumbling to bits. They did not stop till they had reached the woods and then they plunged in and smashed their castles and wrecked and ruined everything.

translated by Ronald Latham (pp. 154–6)

Despite having only '12,000 cavalry', the Mongols achieved victory, assisted by their superior compact bow which had better precision and twice the range of English longbows of the following two centuries.

There were still signs of potential belligerence when we arrived in the town: soldiers were marching to music in a barracks parade ground in the centre of town, and military officers in a section of Taibao Park shooed us away. The distinguishing feature of Bǎoshān was the non-stop exhortations and blaring martial music emanating from loudspeakers positioned high on posts at regular intervals along the main streets. It was the only time in China I came across this shade of Cultural Revolution rhetoric and 1984 brainwashing.

I kept an eye open for Mylikes. I had been searching for these chocolates without success in the weeks since Ritchie had left – it was hardly likely they would exist this far from their manufacturing base the other side of China. With nothing noteworthy in town, the only potential attraction was the Reclining Buddha Temple situated seventeen kilometres away and served by fickle transport, not sufficient reason to remain the whole of the next day as per the itinerary. We agreed instead to leave in the morning. As it turned out, it was a decision that could well have saved my life.

◆ ◆ ◆

I exercised on the bedroom floor – it was to be the last time on these travels. After what was about to be unleashed in the next days, I wouldn't have the heart to continue.

We caught a seven-hour bus crossing the Mekong, and arrived in Dàlǐ a day early.

19-1

chapter 19

Dàlǐ

In a letter to our language school in Korea, an American English teacher portrayed **Dàlǐ** (Big Reason) as 'one of those legendary backpacker, hashish, bannanna (sic) pancake, batik painting, tie die clothing kind'a places'. For travellers the laid-back atmosphere is indeed the chief reason to rest here, and the Yú'ān Garden Guesthouse is perfect for price-conscious backpackers: clean loos and showers, 24-hour hot water, lounging tree-shaded gardens, washing machines, six-bed dorms, and enthusiastic staff who speak English.

Home to just 12,000 people, the town is small enough to walk around in an hour or two. An overall view can be obtained from the reconstructed North Gate, one of only two surviving portions of the Míng city wall. The modern rooftops and buildings tell their own story, and there is nothing to suggest that Dàlǐ was the capital of Yúnnán for 500 years during the influential Nánzhāo kingdom, which began in 738 and was routed by Khubilai Khan in 1253.

A few kilometres east across fields of yellow rape lies the extended blue strip of Ěrhǎi (Ear-shape Sea) Lake, here at its narrowest section three kilometres wide *(19-1)*. Connected to the Láncāng/Mekong, the forty-kilometre lake supports intermittent villages along its shores – the photograph shows Caicun – whose main activity is harvesting the multiple types of fish, some rivalling in size the salmon of Alaska.

The most dominant feature of the landscape is situated the other side of Dàlǐ. Along the entire western bank of the lake, set five kilometres back, is a wall of rock called Cāngshān, the Blue Mountains, which consist of nineteen snowy peaks towering to 4,000 metres – over twice the altitude of the lake – topped by a piercing blue sky. Unusually in Yúnnán they consist of granite, and as the sun sinks behind them in the afternoon, they cast a looming shadow over the lake and its inhabitants. The eighteen valleys between the peaks send parallel streams plunging to the lake, and from the air they look like the ribs of a cage. The straight-line flight path of the Hump missions indicates that the crews of the C-47s would have seen the peaks and the lake below en route to Kūnmíng, the elongated strip of blue water being a navigation aid.

The granite wall forms a dramatic backdrop to the pre-eminent sight of Dàlǐ on the outskirts of town. The Three Pagodas have a palpable physical and spiritual presence – as if they've been here for ever (overleaf). The central Qiānxún (Thousand Searches) Tǎ has an impressive sixteen storeys reaching sixty-nine metres, and was built over 1,100 years ago, making it one of the oldest surviving in China *(19-2, 19-4)*. It gently tapers inwards towards the top, and the similarity of design to the Small Wild Goose Pagoda in Xī'ān, whose fifteen stories were erected the century before, is not by chance: three Táng designers were brought from Cháng'ān to supervise its construction (compare photo *4-32* in Book One).

19-2

Set further back, the two slimmer flanking pagodas are octagonal, with ten tiers climbing to a lesser forty-two metres *(19-3, 19-5)*. Built a century or so later, they are distinguished by their veined white marble, quarried locally on Cāngshān, which is the most renowned in the country – the word for marble in Chinese is literally 'Dàlī stone'. There used to be an associated temple among the pagodas, and their restoration in the late seventies uncovered a haul of 700 implements, mirrors, musical instruments, medicines, jewels, and gold and silver art works, all a thousand years old and more.

Not surprisingly, right around the perimeter are galleries of stalls selling tempting marble products, the colours in the veins including grey, green, terracotta-red, blue, and yellow. I was particularly attracted to the round lidded bowls with a hundred grey rings, on the right in *19-6* overleaf (Tae Hun is handling one). The flattened orbs seemed symbolically associated with philosophical Saturn. I procured four, ideal for storing *Badu* stones (see chapter 3), plus a variously veined vase.

★ ★ ★

19-3

19-5

19-4

Against a sheet of blue, with the odd puff of cloud surgically positioned to one side of the main pagoda, the silence of the three hulks was sullen. A white cotton-wool cloud – a divine lookout – spasmodically disappeared. The semi-fisheye view of the three rods connecting to Heaven metamorphosed into the goldfish bowl of the Amoeba, and I felt the weight of a portentous message about to burst forth.

Was it a coincidence that the main pagoda had the same number of sections as the number of words spoken at Cheju – 16?

"Peter!" the Amoeba whispered.

I put the camera away and hurriedly left.

God followed.

★ ★ ★

A narrow lane between pink walls of houses led to the centre of a minor village where some old men sat quietly (19-7). One can sense in their faces that the Bai people have lived in this area since the days of the Old Testament. Over a million Bai live around Ěrhǎi Lake, and more dwell to the north and west, forming the second largest minority group in Yúnnán after the Yi.

To the west of town, Chinese tourists were snapping their portraits at a favoured haunt – a petite lake and pavilion with a view of the Three Pagodas. In a marble factory nearby, stentorian blocks of stone were being laboriously sliced in a cutting jig into multiple slim panels (19-8).

An hour's late-afternoon walk through wild and windy flat fields rich with green produce brought us to Caicun. Cormorant fishing is practised on the lake, and from the pier we engaged a boatman to take us out into the waters. Cāngshān's dark shadow had encroached ever nearer, and as the fisherman poled the boat soundlessly, no sunlight remained. Three frames remained on a roll of film. Without warning, the Sun reappeared from behind the Blue Mountains – blue the colour of Heaven and the Almighty! I recorded it thrice perched behind the highest peak of Cāngshān, blaring and bursting behind an ominous black cloud, before it sank and disappeared. I knew this was an omen. The final picture. The end. The wind – the Breath of God – went ghastly still.

The fisherman invited us to his house where his wife and two daughters cheerfully and generously conjured up some dinner. We paid what they asked and I gave some biros to the girls. After four weeks, this was to be Tae Hun's final night before departing for Korea. He had been a thoughtful, inquiring co-traveller, and this convivial meeting with a family was the last happy occasion for me for the next three days.

◆ ◆ ◆ ◆

In the Yúnnán Café, there was a stock of books for travellers to browse or borrow. Now by myself without a travel companion, I sampled some, and one with an antiquated hard cover caught my eye – *The Ashley Book of Knots* of 1944. Thumbing through the fascinating quotations heading each chapter, one grasped my attention – particularly its last line – and I copied it into my notebook.

> In a knot of eight crossings,
> which is about the average-size knot,
> there are 256 different 'over-and-under'
>   arrangements possible....
> Make only one change in this 'over and under'
>   sequence
> and either an entirely different knot is made
> or no knot at all may result.
> by W. Ashley, quoted in
The Shipping News – E. Annie Proulx

'...or no knot at all may result.' Yes! I immediately realised: substitute *'friendship with God'* for *knot*. The whole quotation in its new form made damning sense. Another seemed apt for the circumstances:

> Voyage, an outward and homeward passage; although the passage from one port to another is often referred to in insurance policies as a voyage.
> The Mariner's Dictionary

Cheju was, after all, only the outward journey instigated by God. There was more to come on the homeward section, and it happened right now.

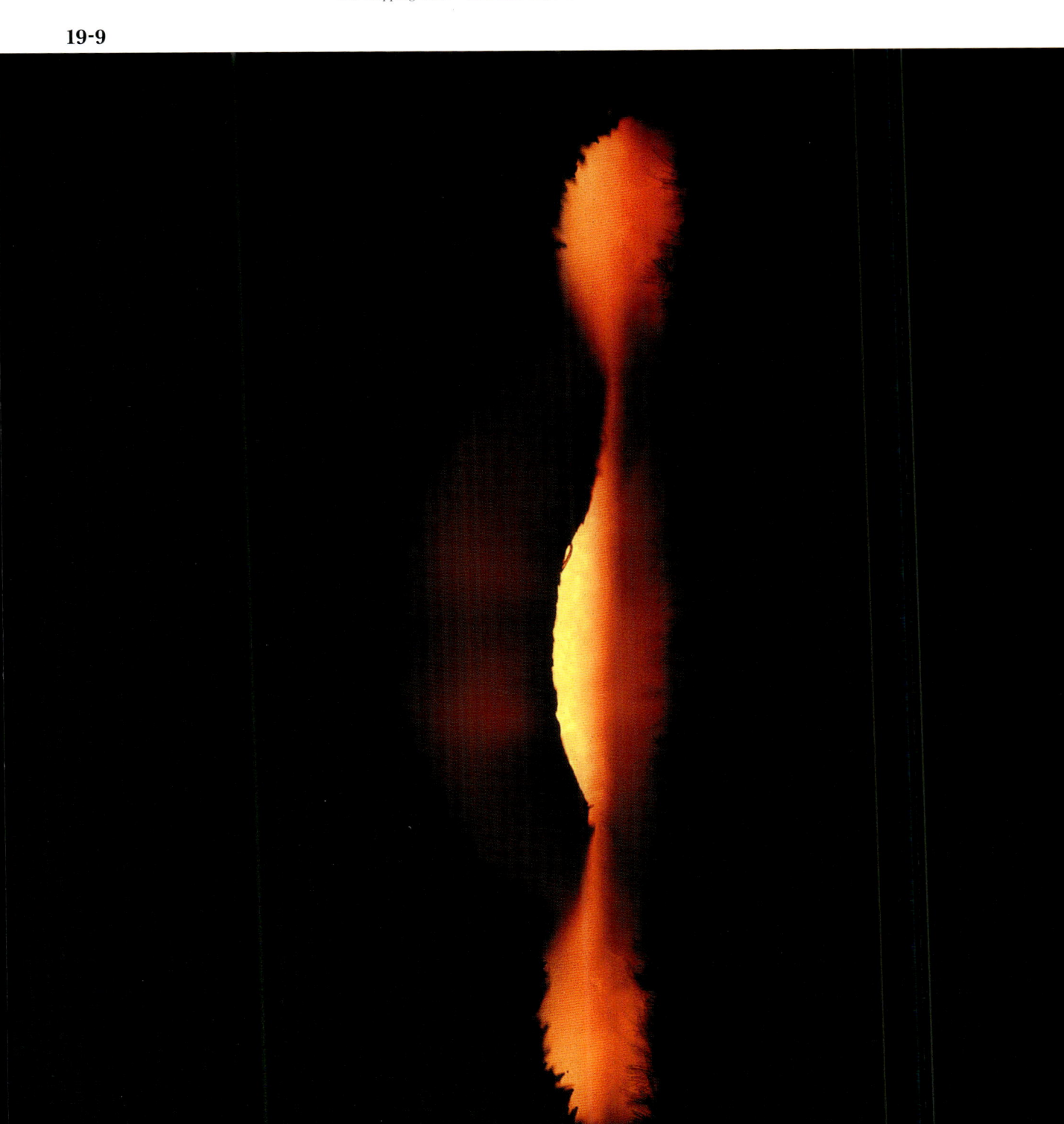

19-10

172

19-12

19-11

19-13

Rift

> Thro' Youth to Strife,
> Thro' Death to Life.
>
> motto heading
> Stanford's 4th Symphony

> When you get to your wit's end,
> you'll find God lives there.
>
> anon

I staggered under the unexpected blow. Had to get away – on a local bus north to Xīzhōu. The name translates as an Island for a Happy Occasion! God's humour is brutal at times. S/he had delivered a body blow, and deigned to spit fat on the fiery wound. A one-street market village; some attractive Bai dwellings with foliage spouting out of roofs, but I barely glanced at them. Swiftly towards the lake in the distance, on a path circumventing hushed fields. My eyes swelled with the bitter waters of the universe. I was vaguely aware of a place of stripped beauty and, like a chicken whose head had been yanked off, my hands instinctively executed their practised routine, raising the camera to my smeared face. Each photo was a knee-jerk action – like continuing to shield one's baby while being consumed by a beast. All I could distinguish was fog in my mind. Between each click of the shutter, saline tears blurred the viewfinder – I never saw the bridge and the darts of the two birds flying straight at me *(19-15)*, nor the lake of purple *(19-13/14)*, nor the men trawling in it *(19-16)*. Only partly was I aware looking back of a scene of spindly trees *(19-17)*. Through my lens all I saw were fields of desperation, sorrow, horrific realisation, despair, cruelty, and the Creator in trouble to take that action.

The yellow Peace jacket was stained, dishevelled, and broken. My world and the Creator's world were disintegrating.

19-14

A vision opened up, one not meant to be seen in this mortal world, of a Rift in the Universe. It was a devastating split that pierced itself onto my brain: a parallel universe splurged through the punctured splint that was the Rift.

Through this, for one moment the emotional state of Grand Old Pa and H/his character and predicament were laid bare – a pang of heart-achingly silent loneliness. Through the split – in fact, a rip.

God?
Have You been crying?
Vulnerable, alone, the Creator was presenting a bare plea of needing to be understood.
Do You need our help – to change You?
At that instant, it seemed a possibility. Moreover, that is what S/he was crying out for. No one else can achieve it – only Humans. We are the species to free H/him, we can be H/his *best* friend!

> To overcome Evil, to undo those aspects in Creation that are a mess, God needs our direct help. Until we individually banish our own evil, God will not be able to solve H/his problem. S/he needs us to improve H/him – we improve in tandem. The Chinese have known this for eons as the concept within the Triumvirate of Heaven, Earth and Humanity.
>
> chapter 6

Within that vision was a Universal Entity unable to control Creation and maybe H/himself. The Good side admitting to the Other – perfect and not perfect. The Big Paradox: Good and Evil together. The Marriage of Heaven and Hell.

This was a God in crisis, and dropping H/his guard to reveal suffering.

The God then wrote on tablets in words of stone:

> Without words and without reason I love you! I am always with you. Without reason, just I love you!
> You are another me. So I could allow myself to be generous to you and give you my love. Instead, I take upon myself the pain, the self-torture, and the distress that causes the self-torture and the pain. But I am happy, friend! No reason, I am happy.
> Just as I cannot ditch myself, I cannot ditch you and I cannot die – you and me. We are one – we share intimacy.
> You, who are in me, love me too much, so I cannot let you suffer pain.
> Now I feel no sadness and no pain – I am happy because you are beside me, love me and are always doing things for me. That's it.

The Pain of Love, the Cane of Love! We love You too much... but we are another You. Therefore You love *us* too much. Padlocks of love – Your problem as well. You promote love, yet have to restrict it, and indeed destroy some aspects! Yet You are happy feeling the pain that You apply – that is how and why You usually seem no longer to be suffering. A classic conundrum.

By arranging the Rift, God was demonstrating S/he is no longer Perfect.

Did God begin Perfect? Yes.
And was God corrupted? Yes! By the following:
LOVE – too much causes pain.
SELFISHNESS – the heart of Evil.
ARROGANCE – Its fuel. The arrogance of a Lord. I have seen it in You treating others – Your conceit, masquerading as friendship.

19-16

Thought chang'd the infinite to a serpent;
  ...and man fled from its face and hid
In forests of night; ...
Then was the serpent temple form'd, image of infinite
Shut up in finite revolutions, and man became an Angel;
Heaven a mighty circle turning; God a tyrant crown'd.

from *A Prophecy*,
William Blake

You do a perfect imitation of perfection because You were that once; now it is an effort because of the contradictions in Your real nature. In desert form, You are hard, and unflinchingly apply pain where it is required, unsmilingly.

The battle between Good and Evil in the Amoeba is infinitely, unflinchingly never ending – a battle where God's Good is forever under attack. S/he cannot contain the Devil all the time.

The Burning Bush, a Battle in Heaven:
  You will fall into a quagmire,
   a quagmire of infinity:
     STOP
      and
    STOP IT!

  Is this real?   Is this real?
   Is this?   Is this?
  Both are real: they're the same thing

You complain we cannot read Your mind. But most humans simply do not have that ability – I wish we had. You talk to animals through the mind – I wish we could. But is Friendship only dependent on reading Your mind? There are different levels, some higher, some lower – not better, not worse. We are what we are.

Yet simultaneously You say we should expect nothing from You. Mistake! Water on fire begets steam; water plus nothing begets nothing else. Wife and husband produce baby; wife plus nothing produces nothing else. One person with second person leads to friendship; one person plus nothing leads to nothing else. Therefore as well as us giving, You should give – that is not nothing.

A disagreement can improve a relationship. It does not justify a permanent rift! Such betrayal of TRUST. I was at times selfless, if excessively and foolishly so – the concept of the Chinese word *yú*. But Your rift – I wouldn't do that to an enemy.

Love had dissipated. The Deity was in the grip of H/his opposite Self.

God merely replied:

19-17

"I am not good for you."

"Then come back: give me and everyone a chance to help. Together, we can solve Your deep problems and make light of them – that is friendship!"

"This is not about friendship. I repeat, I am not good for you."

"If a friend wants to talk, and You refuse, You are being *selfish*."

Pause.

"If you promise not to ask exactly, then I will tell you something."

I promised soberly.

"It is because of another reason that I cannot tell you."

The fog instantly cleared, and I relaxed.

"I can understand that. Why didn't You say so before?"

Now it was my turn to cry as the world turned away, and I heard God's final parting words...

"Take care."

Anything that cannot be undone should be cut.

Mutating, evil appeared – and slapped me in the face. God took H/his Scissors and did the Deed.

Then the Amoeba departed.

All was Quiet. PEACE – the rock of wisdom. The Breath of God – like a panther ready to leap – had pounced.

You cannot fight the Almighty – S/he holds all the cards.

I waged a battle with God.

And lost.

I tottered to an artificial square of water, with a lonely house and a tree reflecting in the surface. A string of puffed clouds crossed, and disappeared. I collapsed on the ground, cross-legged, in front of yellow flowers – yellow, the colour of sadness. My mind wound into infinity and nothingness, as my body froze in disbelief *(19-18)*. The landscape of Dàlĭ has been summarised

19-18

thus: *fēng*, *huā*, *xuě*, *yuè* – wind, flowers, snow, the moon. Nothing and everything.

At least I had been warned the rift would happen, at the bombardment the six months after Cheju [related in chapter 9]. The time limit "...**for 9 days**..." as God intimated in the tunnel of Cheju – how symbolic. Without that foreknowledge, I would by now have been berserk beyond repair.

I couldn't dwell for long on the extraordinary physical Rift in the universe. I didn't understand it anyway. It was fleeting. Did it happen? Yes, definitely. But what...? Why...? How...?

Instead came a backlash. Another rift opened – this time instigated by me.

At the end of the Book of Job, God is angry with Job's three friends for not railing at H/him as Job did [42.7–8]. The Lord H/himself therefore *expects and gives leave* for justified anger against H/him. As Job [7.11] – God's model man – now me: I will not be cowed and will not keep quiet about this Deity who torments the very core of one's being. Here is the evidence, also in court. Yahweh and Job showed wrath, so can I. Here comes *my* whirlwind.

anger

> I was angry with my friend;
> I told my wrath, my wrath did end.
> I was angry with my foe:
> I told it not, my wrath did grow.
>
> William Blake,
> *A Poison Tree*, Songs of Experience

> Don't hit your friend with a hatchet.
>
> Chinese advice

> When Heaven is about to place a great burden on a man, it always tests his resolution first, exhausts his body and makes him suffer great hardships, frustrates his efforts to recover from mental lassitude. Then Heaven toughens his nature and makes good his deficiencies.
>
> Mèngzi (Mencius),
> *Telling the Disciples*

> In order to make further development possible he must be melted down again, and this can be accomplished only through terrible suffering.
>
> G.I. Gurdjieff, quoted by
> P.D. Ouspensky, *In Search of
> the Miraculous* (p. 32)

> God is a verb, not a noun.
>
> R. Buckminster Fuller
> (1895–1983), engineer
> and inventor (précis)

> Return, O soul! O soul return!
> In east you cannot stay.
> There giants loom ten thousand feet,
> On wandering souls they prey.
> There ten suns rising one by one,
> Melt rock and gold away.
>
> from *Recalling the Soul*,
> a long poem of the Chu period[1]

> To God
> If you have form'd a Circle to go into
> Go into it yourself & see how you would do
>
> William Blake,
> *Satiric verses and epigrams*

> The tygers of wrath are wiser
> than the horses of instruction
>
> William Blake, *Proverbs of Hell*
> from *The Marriage of Heaven and Hell*

So let us say You are 70% Good and 30% Evil. I am concentrating on the latter here, and 30% of Universal Evil is a Hell of a lot. This focuses on the Devil mainly, now that You have come out of hiding behind God's goodness. From now on, I also remove the capital Y from 'You'.

> The Black Shadow. However hard we try to block it out, it is there, it exists, and it comes to the surface.
>
> chapter 6

God-Devil, I hold you to account.

Throughout history you attack your greatest advocates. Take Job. For no reason, except as a bet as to his reaction, you allow your ambassador Satan (your Alter Ego) to cart off Job's 4,000 oxen, camels and donkeys, and destroy his 7,000 sheep. Then, you Assassin, you permit and encourage the herdsmen to be killed, the shepherds to be slaughtered supernaturally, and even Job's ten sons and daughters to be massacred by divine power.

His three friends leap to your defence. Representing the God-is-All-Good brigade, Eliphaz claims that those deeds could not possibly be your work without cause; therefore Job must have committed a bad deed to warrant the punishment. Well, that doesn't stand up: by your own testimony, the human was blameless [Job 1.8]. Then even if a bad deed had been committed, you could have admonished with a verbal warning first. A good parent doesn't bash and beat h/his offspring, and *never* murders innocent bystanders. Simply, you are guilty of Child Abuse.

Number two, Bildad, is more astute: the purpose of suffering is to learn. Bullshit. If that is the only reason, it's saying that Knowledge is worth more than Humanity, that becoming Brainy and stuffed with the Facts of Life is easily worth the insignificant cost of Devastating Pain. Sorry, that doesn't wash: it is Pure Sadism[2] – you are a Wolf in sheep's clothing. Ethically it is repulsive. We all desire to grow, but if that is God's only justification in inflicting pain, it is better we resist – better to strive for a compassionate way of developing which is not H/his. Pain is God's opium. S/he is drunk on suffering, and lusts to inflict it. S/he cannot get enough of it – just look at the state of the world. God's paradoxical problem. Would we allow anyone else to get away with what S/he condones?

> Know then thyself, presume not God to scan;
> The proper study of mankind is man.
>
> Alexander Pope (1688–1744)
> *An Essay on Man*

Like Pope, the third friend Zophar trots out the lame-duck get-out clause that Life and the Creator are mysteries, and we shouldn't be naughty boys or girls and ask 'Why?' or 'What is God?'. Shouldn't? Why not, may I ask? On the contrary, we had better find out if the Controller is Good or Evil – because if the latter, we're in Dead Hellish trouble for Ever and Ever, Amen.

Then a young upstart called Elihu interrupts angrily [32.2–5] – anger is an accepted commonplace in the Bible. He perceptively declares that you are signalling a message concerning evil whenever you inflict suffering [33.16–18/29–30]. Therein lies your Paradox. You are using suffering to combat Evil! And it saves us [36.15]! Why do humans not see this explanation, in print right before their eyes? Hallelujah! Those words of Elihu should be writ large in every household in the world.

> God whispers to us in our pleasures, speaks in our conscience, but shouts in our pain: it is His megaphone to rouse a deaf world.
>
> C.S. Lewis,
> *The Problem of Pain* (p. 74)

That is a breakthrough explanation, but it *still* does not provide the Big Reason (Dàlǐ). Rouse the world to what? What is the Message you wish to impart? It must address the ultimate questions. Why does Evil exist in the first place – what is its origin? What was wrong with God's original good Creation *without* any evil? Instead of understanding the Message by answering those questions, Elihu merely reiterates the 'God knows best' dead-end [33.12], the 'pain is a lesson' sadism [33.19], and the 'life's beyond our ken' cop out [37.23].

---

[1] quoted in *XI'AN – Legacies of Ancient Chinese Civilization* (p. 141), translated by Gong Lizeng

[2] Even C.S. Lewis calls you 'the Cosmic Sadist' (*A Grief Observed*, Faber and Faber Ltd. 1961, p. 23).

No one in the history of mankind has transmitted to the world your Message, which is the answer to the Big Riddle. Yet when you have that golden opportunity, stepping out from behind the whirlwind [38.1], how do you answer Job's justified accusations against you? You point out who was responsible for creating all the wonders of the world, which admittedly takes you some time, and hence crushingly trumpet that everyone – us mortal, insignificant damp squids – should shut up and stop complaining [40.2]! That's it! No answers, no Message: given the opportunity – nowhere else in the Bible do you appear on earth as yourself – you blew it!

God doesn't answer the Why?

Is it, perchance, that you are hiding something (and I don't just mean your nasty little bet with Satan)? Is it that you wish to continue indulging in your megalomania – you created the First Emperor of Qín in your image, didn't you? Or is it because you love demanding unquestioned obedience or else death by Hell? What wonderful sense of morals you have.

Then – and here comes the sick bit – you figuratively pat Job on the head by giving him twice the assets you took away, plus a whole new set of ten sons and daughters to keep him quiet, and a pile of gold rings as a bonus [42.10–14]. You think that is adequate compensation? Well some might accept that sort of bribery, but I don't. What about the lives of the ten previous kin you encouraged to be killed – do they not matter? And those of the herdsmen and shepherds? What about them, and their mourning kith and kin? What about Job's suffering beforehand?

> Pity me, have pity on me, you that are my friends,
> for the hand of God has touched me.
> Job crying out [19.21]

The Bible admits here: the entity inflicting pain is God! God is the source of Suffering.

The Bible is witness elsewhere to your lashing out on humans with extreme physical violence. As Deuteronomy [20.16–17] reports, you commanded the murder of six ethnic races – every one including babies and children – because they chose to ignore you (which seems justified to me). When people were vexed about your incomprehensible behaviour, you summoned poisonous snakes to smite a herd of them [Num.21.4–6]. You kill us simply because we don't understand – sounds like a butcher to me.

Even when the innocent Uzzah steadied the Ark of the Covenant – symbolically your Holy Spirit – when it was in danger of falling off a moving cart [2Sam.6.6–7], you were 'angry' and killed him! Uzzah was only trying to protect you! Then there is your horrific massacre of innocents – all first-born Egyptian children and adults and animals [Ex.11.4–6, 12, 29–30] – which proves you are a racist as well.

> I form the light, and create darkness: I make
> peace, and create evil: I the Lord do all these things.
> God speaking [Isaiah 45.7]
> (King James authorised)

> These are the words of the Lord: I am planning
> disaster for this nation, a yoke which you cannot
> remove from your necks; you will not walk haughtily,
> for the hour of disaster will have come.
> [Micah 2.3]

> The great day of the Lord is near... a day of
> wrath, a day of anguish and torment, a day of
> destruction and devastation, a day of darkness and
> gloom.... I shall bring dire distress on the people;
> they will walk like the blind... their blood will be
> poured out like dust.
> [Zeph.1.14–17]

So you admit it even in your own Book. You brag about it! You *are* the source of all evil and for the calamities in the World. You think people are not going to notice these things, hidden among a million other words in that Book? You're probably right.

You said it: you create Evil. All Evil stems from you. Therefore you are also the Devil.

It is not only that you sit back perfunctorily, permitting others of your heavenly court and other bad spirits to eke out evil. You approve, advocate and actively dictate it, as Job and others record [Ps.78.49, 1Sam.16.14–15, 1Sam.18.10, 1Sam.19.9]. You haven't changed your spots since the Bible, either. The Bible is merely a representation of what you have been since – just look at history. In his late major essay *Answer to Job*, Carl Jung (1875–1961) came to the same conclusion – that you embody both Good and Evil. You are the 'Enemy' and 'Adversary' – in Hebrew, 'Satan'. The Aztecs in their Codex Borgia were right: evil as well as good does exist in the gods.

Wouldn't the cleverest, most sensible Devil ever created actually do just enough Good so that people think that's what S/he is, conveniently making them forget the mayhem of Evil abounding all around? Sounds familiar? That is how you've arranged matters. Yes, *j'accuse*.

★ ★ ★

As per Hán Fēi's *Solitary Fury*, this is my Personal Fury. Let us examine your *true* nature:

> [*Yīn* and *yáng*'s] dualism graphically indicates
> good-evil as part of the one and same. They look to
> me, and are to the Chinese, both complementary,
> entwined, balancing and enhancing each other, and
> yet in competition, heads clashed together, embroiled
> and fighting to gain the middle ground, eyes locked
> in mortal combat – never still, constant flux.
> chapter 3

> If you brush away the ashes and bone, you are
> left with *sari* – pure holiness, pure pain.
> chapter 8

With your Love of Pain, you are the sadistic creature in the sex temple in chapter 6 – one of the wrathful deities, or Rāhu(la) the Deity of the Earth. We are part of you. By inflicting pain on us Humans, the ones you Love, you are also inflicting pain on yourself! There is so much of it, you're revelling in it – you've bloomed into a Sadomasochist. You wouldn't dish it out otherwise: people dying early, starving, enduring accidents or searing disease, with no money, and destitute. The smell of death – it is the powerful pong of sadism and masochism.

> Folly is an endless maze,
> Tangled roots perplex her ways,
> How many have fallen there!
> William Blake, from
> *The Voice of the Ancient Bard*,
> Songs of Experience

On the roof of one of the holiest places in the world – the Jokhang Temple in Lhasa – is the Knot without End: to Buddhists, the emblem of Eternity. It resembles squares interlaced like swastikas, through which seep occasional mists. Eternity – your endless problem! Like a mass of roots, your connections are jumbled in a messy tangle of limbs and knots. Your roots have combined into one unholy, ugly knot. In Genesis, the twisted, corkscrew roots support the Tree of Life plus another. This, the Tree of Knowledge, is of evil as well as good [2.9]. Like barnacles on a boat, you cannot dislodge evil from your good.

> If a god appeared before you, you'd want to see his face, wouldn't you?
>
> Ven. Song Chol, *Echoes from Mt. Kaya* (p. 42)

Well, now we know. God's ugliness. The truth will out. Not even you can hide it for ever.

> Even the most wicked forms of life are fundamentally Buddha.
>
> Ven. Song Chol, (ibid, p. 42)

You like to be 'honoured', you want us to 'obey' your will without question – like the soldiers of Hitler – and you threaten us with 'just rewards' and 'everlasting torture' if we do not. Meanwhile you dish the stuff out: a relevant analogy would be unanaesthetised vivisection and the painful laboratory experiments 'without questioning' during WWII – so the Jewish holocaust met with your approval? If not, why didn't you prevent it?

Well, even if it means my death – literally or figuratively – I will *not* follow the morality that you advocate, and which is you. I spit on your threats to punish me if I don't obey. I want no part of such a megalomaniac loving nought but for us to kiss your feet and kowtow. The price is morally too high for my 'salvation'.

Tyrant, go away!

No one fears a good entity. If visiting a sane-hearted Grandpa, one does so anticipating an enjoyable time – not fearful of a terrible encounter. Yet the New Testament describes you as 'a devouring fire' [Heb.12.29], and of the only four things you demand of us, the first is to fear you [Deut.10.12]. That *proves* you are not wholly good. No wonder that to fear God has been described as the Highest Wisdom. But that is blackmail of the most immoral kind – no better than a gangster.

> ...loving, hating and destroying each other and becoming newly born.
>
> source unknown

God only allows us to play by H/his rules. Nobody asked us if we wanted to be born. We don't have the choice to avoid death. We live and die willy-nilly, following pre-set parameters. Given the pain in all our lives, therefore S/he is Evil and is leading us a merry diabolic dance.

chapter 6

You deal each person a loaded DNA deck of cards, this bit tarnished, that bit admirable, this perverse, that beautiful, maybe disabled from birth, or harbouring

19-19

severe depression throughout life. Then you throw dice loaded with pre-set warped circumstances – father an alcoholic, born into poverty – and watch the game played out. We do this, you do that; you nudge there, we react like that – like a game of chess, except you blindfolded us before the game started. That is cheating, and I don't like cheats.

You are not being straight with us, and that is the opposite of Love.

You demand we join you, but you do not reveal what the purpose of your club is! Why don't you come out of a whirlwind today and tell us who exactly you are, what your purpose is, and why you exist? Is that too simple a solution for you?

★ ★ ★

Back to the now and here in Dàlǐ.

In Hinduism, God is called Brahman and is depicted in three forms: the Creator, the Preserver, and the Destroyer. Well, you are certainly in mode three, aren't you? You have chosen a scapegoat, and you sacrifice h/him – you don't care, you don't mind *using* someone else.

The Bed! The Bed of God – you took me beside it, you gave me your blessing! Now it is no longer sanctified. And you *willed* those thoughts and you *willed* it to happen, with your horrible silent powers.

When later I humbly prayed to you to enlighten me of what you did, your response was as follows:

"God was Perfect, and is not perfect."

Perfect and also not perfect. The Big Paradox.

"*It is the only thing that matters*" you continued!

Somewhere within lies The Message. I'm too blinded with justified rage to see it. What you have done to me is, is… diabolical. I *will* fight you more.

You've picked fights before – starting with Jacob [Gen 32.24–30]. Well, I'm more than willing. You will win, you ruthless bully.

> …the story of creation…. The Creator is pure Love and Light… [which] has nothing to test itself against…. You cannot grow without facing challenges. Without darkness Light cannot compare itself. So the Creator wanted to expand and experience.
> Diana Cooper,
> *A Little Light on Ascension* (p. 66)

So everyone has to suffer because you want some experience? A teeny-weeny bit selfish that, isn't it? Look at this Earth! Look at what you've done to us! Pain, problems, problems, Pain. Where is all this leading? It is not enough to say it is good for us, that we will become 'better' people. I would rather be weak, and at least remain human. Take your pain and your *sari* to a playground elsewhere in the universes, if you pathologically must do. Better still, if you really are only Light and Good, you would extinguish yourself rather than prey on other people's feelings. Be off! Better no Life at all, than subjecting us without choice to this stuff. Why don't you contact your boss, the Dào, and get H/him to switch you off?

For you, there's not much difference between leaving the world in peace and leaving it in pieces.

As this book proves, you are a Murderer, a Sadist, a Masochist, clinically cold and savage, without basic moral standards. As the Amoeba theory indicates and Elihu grasps, you are the source of encouragement for all the other evils, from arrogance to war and you admit it in the Bible. Yet you stubbornly avoid offering a valid reason for this catastrophe. Concerning your threats, what a big macho man you are. You threaten, but don't explain adequately. Those who are weak, because they do not understand despite trying (count me in), receive a boot in the back. A Great One would carry on explaining *ad infinitum*, and would *never* threaten just because we don't get it. The Bible is full of your threats. Well you can take them and jump into a universal lake. You are not good enough for me. Piss off.

I wish the Dào would control its problem child – yes, you. God. I turn my back on (Y)you, (Y)you Bastard.

20-1

chapter 20

Lijiāng and Zhōngdian

Lijiāng

On the first of February, I got the hell out of the hell of Dàlǐ on a bus heading north for seven hours, during which I saw nothing except my thoughts. After four months of travelling in company, I was alone again at the worst possible moment, with no one to share the particulars of the Rift, even in part. The final four weeks yawned ahead like a canyon, which I hesitated to face. One can step far in a flash, then a particular section – unable to see the light – can seem as dark infinity. I contemplated abandoning travel for the first time and going home.

As the bus turned a bend towards the end of the journey, I snatched the area's famous and dominating Yùlóngxuěshān, Jade Dragon Snow Mountain (20-1). Inexplicably, the phenomenon of the rift in my photographs ceased: the searing one on a black blank (page 171) was the last.

★ ★ ★

To distract my mind, I had to get back to exploring and immersing myself in the locality. I appeal to the reader to do so too, since it points and eventually leads to the End Game.

This was a rare area to be in. Lìjiāng translates as Pretty River, and is a county in the shape of a V enveloping the west side of the Jīnshā/Yángzi as it flows to its first traumatic bend at Shígǔ, plus the east side as it steers north. Fossils reveal that *Homo sapiens* lived here during the late Palaeolithic Period – 'Lijiang man'. It is now inhabited by 300,000 people, the majority being Naxi. Although their capital is called Dàyàn, meaning 'Big Inkstone' hinting at its original shape, it is more usually referred to in the West as the town of **Lìjiāng**.

A separate sector has been erected since 1949, and a modern hotel called the Red Sun next to a Máo Statue on the main north-south street provided me with a decent dorm. That segregation has resulted in the preservation of the 800-year-old wooden town centre, the largest and most integrated in China, housing 50,000 people. Wandering in the maze of adobe walls in this still thriving community, with narrow lanes turning this way and that criss-crossed by streams and canals, it is easy to lose any sense of direction. This labyrinth arose in part because no restricting city wall was ever built. A past Naxi ruler declared that to do so would encourage a calamity, since enclosing the character for 'wood' 木 within a square makes it 困, which means stranded, or surrounded (by an enemy).

At the north end of the street, the Black Dragon Pool provides one of the most photographed views in China (20-2). The ingredients include the five-arched Belt Bridge made of marble, Hundred Blossoms Island, a flower-filled rockery with willows, the classically-proportioned three-tier Déyuè Lóu (Obtain the Moon Pavilion), with the whole backed by Shànzidou, at 5,596 metres the highest summit and situated at the southern end of Jade Dragon Snow. *Shàn* here means a 'fan', which from this angle the curved ribbed array of pinnacles resemble. The one protruding on the right is known as Old Man Peak. The name Jade Dragon Snow comes from the complete pattern of thirteen undulating peaks, permanently covered with grey-tinged ice and snow, as seen from an eastern broadside. However to me from that perspective they look more like shark's teeth – a mountain with bite, as was about to be demonstrated.

At a private locale here, I sank to my knees and pleaded with Grand Old Pa like I have never begged anyone before. I implored for the rift to be withdrawn. It was the most serious, impassioned plea, delivered from the heart, that surely no compassionate Entity could ignore. If S/he were to grant it, I would delay an extra day in Lìjiāng and celebrate.

I rarely request things through prayer. What we ask is bound by our stilted perspective of the present, and is not necessarily apt for us. S/he will do what is best, individually and collectively, anyway. Yet how could any parent refuse a lifetime's human emotions concentrated into that moment? Most people would yield to such a humble, beseeching supplication, like I did to the beggar in Kūnmíng's station.

God, impassive, gave no immediate answer. No change.

I asked for a sign. If the rift were to continue, I would find some token M/ylikes. If S/he relented and granted my request, I would not come across any – which was my earnest wish.

Later, I espied the tell-tale red bag of those chocolates in a store…. I bowed my head, despondent and resigned, and ate the contents. I never saw another bag again.

At night in the Old Town, I walked along a narrow lane out of antiquity, crossed a stream into the Market Square, shuffled between buildings separated by hardly more than the width of my shoulders, and found the venue that every two days hosts one of the most mature pleasures in China. Upstairs, with ancient photographs of Naxi people on the walls, a dark wooden community room was reverberating to the sound of a Daoist orchestra, whose members included humble wizened old men with goatee beards who were calmly sculptured to their seats like a Velazquez painting come alive.

Track 8 contains two excerpts to accompany the following description.

20-2

The oldest looking man intoned a word unaccompanied as if it was plucked from the ether of Genesis. The sound of an oboe appeared as out of a desert – neither good nor evil, just fact. Other instruments politely cascaded in – *sugudu, nanhu, erhuang* – the plucked strings sustaining the fundamental note of Creation with a casual baroque tremolo. A bamboo flute introduced the sad cadence of a second note falling to the first, while the oboe held the basic tone high like a shawm from the past declaring the promise of 'I WILL BE what I WILL BE'. At length, abruptly appearing like the monolithic slab in *2001: A Space Odyssey*, a *yun* gong donged The Basic Note with rude reinforcement. One piece they play is aptly entitled *Creation Hymn for God*.

Skeletons of the dead slithered out of their cupboards to listen, and to be aware. This was a call to order – pay attention! Gradually an accompanied melody unfolded with a mono-beat of sticks striking bells, and gongs interrupted by out-of-rhythm drums, while gut sawed on wire, fingers slid up frets, and oboes pulsed insistently. On and on the aural aurora resonated, as if from the nether regions of the Amoeba's Great Hinterland.

It was a pronouncement of praise, joy, and acceptance, and the packed all-Western audience sitting on benches listened mesmerised and quiet. Who wouldn't be, concentrating on this painting in music? This is one of the last places in China to hear it.

Wearing a combination of ancient costume and casual dress, the stately men played almost nonchalantly, some smoking pipes, serene expressions on their gaunt lined faces, and double-ended moustaches abundant. They seemed the living incarnations of ancient Chinese Daoists. Dispersed among them were teenage girls dressed more colourfully, raised in the musical tradition by their grandfathers elsewhere in the band. What a contrast with Confucian/Daoist orchestras up to WWII when no women were allowed. Instead, a wide range of ages and generations were here represented: sons, daughters, fathers and grandfathers, some from the same family. They were common people playing for the love of their tradition.

The presenter Xuān Kē introduced the band with both good English and humour. He informed me afterwards that he is half Naxi and half Tibetan on his mother's side, and suffered political imprisonment for twenty-one years from 1958, the year that 300,000 extra Chinese troops ploughed into Tibet to quell 'troubled conditions'.

The two titles on track 8 are *The Song of the Jade Dragon Snow Mountain*, preceded by an excerpt from *Musical Prayer* – appropriate after my beseeching. Another piece they play has been translated as *Ten Gifts from God*. I determined I would return a week later to hear the Naxi Orchestra again. The Creator, however, had other plans.

◆ ◆ ◆ ◆

At an elevation of 2,400 metres, the flat plain to the north averages seven hours of sunshine a day throughout the year, and is usually snow-free. It used to be the locale of two airfields from the 1940s onwards, at least one built by the Americans. Joseph Rock (1884–1962), an eccentric explorer, botanist, and National Geographic's Chinese reporter from 1923, dwelt a kilometre from one of these airstrips at the foot of Shànzidou, which he measured as being 1,440 feet higher than it is. It was not the only time he overstated geographical measurements, as will be related in the next chapter. He was partial to being regaled and carted around in a sedan chair, and to educating the natives with gramophone records of Caruso belting out opera arias – shades again of Fitzcarraldo in Brazil! Rock was involved with the Hump missions, assisting in the drawing of maps for the pilots.

On an unusually gaudy bicycle, I pedalled towards Rock's old airfield, calling in at Báishā, the former Naxi capital in the centuries before Khubilai Khan. Its temple's famed frescoes were dark and depressingly mutilated, courtesy of the Cultural Revolution. To make amends, an honourable gentleman paraded some examples of the Naxi pictograms called *Sijiulujiu*. Unlike most minorities in China who had no written language until recently, the Naxi have preserved a thousand volumes that record their historical customs, literature, and ancient Dongba religion. Epic Creation stories abound, as well as prodigious poems such as *The War between Black and White*. One significant religious ceremony is *Naximeibiro*, the latter part meaning 'sacrifice', indicating Sacrifices to Heaven. They are another society that believes everything in nature has a spirit.

20-3

Having not at the time read Bruce Chatwin's article of ten years before concerning Rock's Kingdom, and having forgotten the LP guide's brief mention, I was taken aback while sailing along a narrow dusty street of this tiny village to be almost forcibly stopped by a man in white cotton overalls. Soon cottoning on that he was the endearingly cheery Doctor Ho, who learned botany from Rock, I was initiated into the charming ritual of drinking his magical herbal concoction and being introduced to his 37-year-old son, himself a father and equally as outgoing as his dad.

I extracted myself and moved on. They live in an Alice-in-Wonderland of botanical riches on their doorstep. Over a century ago, the French missionary Abbé Delavay was the first to scour the area for undiscovered flora, followed by the Britisher George Forrest who was more successful in cultivating some. Rock sent 60,000 pressed plants to the USA, while azaleas from Lìjiāng found their way to Kew Gardens, London – there are over fifty types on Jade Dragon alone.

The mountain is home to an estimated 400 kinds of tree and the same number of medicinal herbs. Waterfalls of bold white *Rhododendron adenogynum* carpet the slopes in summer. Easy to transplant, much of the world's stock of rhododendrons came originally from samples exported from Yúnnán. High up on the mountain at over 4,000 metres lies *Androsace delavayi*, a charming white alpine with an occasional surprise cluster of shyer, coral-pink buds. A good house plant from these valleys, successfully cultivated, is *Primula forrestii*.

There are a handful of monasteries near Lìjiāng associated with the Karmapa lineage of the various Tibetan Red Hat sects. The Cultural Revolution brutally butchered their traditions, and they remain only a pale shadow of what they were. One of their monasteries, close to the former airstrip, is Yùfēng (Jade Peak), which required a scramble up a hill to reach, leaving the bike below *(20-3* looks back along the plain towards Lìjiāng*)*. It is famous for its three-metre-high camellia tree that sprouts '10,000 blossoms' in spring. Being winter however, it shocked me to the core. Originally it was two separate trees that later fused together. It has become a tangled knot of roots, a mishmash, a misshapen mess – the epitome of ugliness: the Beast below the Beauty. As I stared at this ugly monstrosity, all I could see was God's warped mind. The photograph positioned two double pages back is of this *(19-19)*. I didn't stay long.

The bicycle developed a severe puncture, giving up the ghost as I returned through Báishā. The Doctor's son leaped into action with an improvised repair kit. It was time for more bonhomie, and this time I felt obliged to purchase some of the good doctor's tea, which I later stashed in a bin. They insisted on a snapshot being taken in front of their Herbal Medicine Clinic, with Déshòu and a friend being roped in reluctantly. He is on the left with his father in *20-4*, the doctor on the right. I was glad and thankful, given my circumstances, of the genuine friendliness they offered. I do not understand the insinuative accusations ('a rogue', 'a charlatan') levelled against this head of the family. The self-titled doctor is trying to make a decent living, like most people in the world, and uses a salesman's techniques with more good-nature than most. If you don't want the tea, don't buy it!

That evening, I had a major decision to make. In a remote corner of the county, seventy kilometres north and slightly east, is a second Bǎoshān hardly mentioned in the guidebooks, near a ferryhead used by Khubilai Khan that is marked on Rock's map. A photograph of this ancient stone city revealed it was perched on a narrow precipitous ledge, with steep terraced fields draped around it. It seemed remarkably like a Machu Picchu in China – a walled Island in the Sky – a Defensive Mountain in name and fact. The hundred houses within were of the traditional wooden type, except that furniture – tables and beds – had been carved out of stone! My previous research had revealed it was possible to stay with a family there, and a high-level five-hour walk leading to the bastion was highly recommended.

My initial plan thereafter was to trek the treacherous Tiger Leaping Gorge east to west, before continuing to Zhōngdiàn, which had been opened to foreigners just four years before. The problem was a dearth of transport to Bǎoshān and out, a bus serving only part of the route to Míngyīn, from where hitching possibilities would be few and far between. As I slipped into bed that night, I decided to reverse the six-day plan by commencing with Zhōngdiàn, exiting the gorge at its east end, from where I hoped to find other foreigners to share a taxi to Bǎoshān.

That last-minute fifty-fifty decision undoubtedly saved me from injury, and possibly death.

◆ ◆ ◆ ◆

At a ramshackle settlement named Xiǎo Zhōngdiàn, shacks were stacked against slatted wooden sidewalks raised on both sides of the dirt road. A woman in black with her back bent over supported herself with a stick, a red towel as turban adding colour to her life. A child was wearing a Davy Crockett-style brown furry cap with ear flaps. The driver delivered the furniture: because it was a public bus didn't mean he couldn't earn an extra dollar or two!

At journey's end in **Zhōngdiàn**, which means 'Surrounded by Fields', the only sensible backpacker's lodgings

20-5

Zhōngdiàn

> From Lìjiāng, every step northward
> gains the height of one egg.
>
> Naxi saying

The fateful day began innocently enough. With my main backpack deposited in the hotel's luggage room, I caught a bus that, after climbing to the west, lost height and followed the languid Jīnshā north. The valley was dark in the shade of steep mountain walls, while in contrast the summit of Jade Dragon soaring ahead was already spotlit, capped by a cloud like a tethered plume of smoke.

There are only three bridges carrying highway traffic across the Yángzi in Yúnnán, the one here towering above the water. A morphologically interesting confluence of rivers was the cue to leave the Jīnshā veering to the right, and follow up the tributary's valley north-west. A reviving tea stop at a small sunless town appropriately called Qiáotóu (Bridgehead) was a necessity in the cold, with a concrete café providing a welcome fire.

As the road narrowed and twisted, the half-empty bus, with a pile of household furniture in the rear, struggled up the Tibetan-Yúnnán geosyncline. The road eased flat, the view widened into a panoramic plain, and a broad blue sky heralded our arrival on the Tibetan Plateau.

What a different land! On the left edge, the Xuě (Snowy) Mountains, indeed coated with snow, were heading straight towards Tibet. Stentorian wooden drying racks stood proudly erect on the plain as if soldiers on parade. Cows seemed incongruous at first on this sub-roof of the world, their presence lending a pastoral quality, as did the occasional planted wood. The light sparkled and danced, glinting in pockets of blue ice. The land seemed risen above the minuscule iniquities of the world below, as if a step closer to heaven, and somehow I felt better up here.

20-6

was the Tibet Hotel, equipped with bikes, 24-hour hot-water baths, basic twin rooms in shacks, with Star satellite TV *and* electric blankets in each! The library-lounge contained a roaring fire – even at midday most welcome at this 3,200-metre altitude.

Departing every two days, a bus was due to leave the next morning to Báishuǐ Tái (White Water Platform), a hundred kilometres to the south-east and only approachable from Zhōngdiàn. The area features peculiar limestone geological formations, grassland, birds, Dongba culture, and even a hotel. In particular there is a natural hot spring oozing out of the limestone called Tiānshēngqiáo (Heaven's Living Bridge), and the chance to skinny-dip in these Tibetan temperatures was sorely tempting! Further, I had heard of a few adventuresome travellers walking from there to the Tiger Leaping Gorge – an exciting way to return to Lìjiāng – though our attentive hotel staff denied it was feasible.

In contrast, twenty-five kilometres to the east of Zhōngdiàn is Bìtǎ Hǎi, Jade-Green Pagoda Lake. To reach it would require a bus, taxi or hitching, followed by a muddy walk through fields, or two hours on a horse. The rewards would be forests, squirrels, white-lipped deer that exist only in China, and quiet. A local might provide accommodation and food.

Heading north-west, the main road crosses the Jīnshā/Yángzi at Fúlóng Bridge. Thirty kilometres further on is a Tibetan monastery called Dōngzhúlín (East Bamboo Forest), which possibly no Westerner had ever seen. Another thirty kilometres and the town of Déqīn would be reached. The region is one of the few remaining that harbours the golden monkey *Rhinopithecus roxellanae*. It would be an invigorating itinerary, though continuing any further into Tibet, barely forty kilometres away, was not politically feasible.

West of the town across the Láncāng/Mekong, and straddling the Tibetan/Yúnnán border like a colossus, is the sacred Kagebuo (Kawakarpo) Mountain, rising to a still unclimbed 6,800 metres – the highest in Yúnnán – that might have caused the Hump pilots a fright or two. 70,000 Tibetan pilgrims have been known to congregate here, and Songri Chunzum, a lama, claims that some people "cannot see the deities who inhabit the peaks, but I can. Only those who have reached a higher spiritual level can see them."

Hiring a jeep to any of these adventurous sights was an option[1]. There was a group of three American travellers in the hotel, and it was possible they might be interested in sharing a tour. Meanwhile, in the late afternoon, I walked north out of Zhōngdiàn for an hour along a new tarmac road, enjoyed wide-open vistas, and passed a prominent white *chorten*, the Tibetan equivalent of the *stupa* or *dagoba*. Its purpose is to ward off evil spirits, as well as being a reminder of the nirvana obtained by Buddha.

This and other areas of what is now western China, as well as northern Burma, northern India, Kashmir and portions of Nepal, constituted part of independent Tibet as long ago as the 8th century, after the country first became unified around AD 625 during the reign of King Songtsen Gampo. This Greater Tibet was recognised as a separate sovereign state by the Chinese in a peace treaty of 821. Tibetans have a non-tonal, alphabetical language, with aspects of grammar drawn from Sanskrit – quite distinct from Chinese.

Reaching a crest produced a sharp intake of breath as my first *gompa*, or Tibetan monastery, more-or-less in Tibet materialised in a bowl of surrounding hills as if in the protective petals of a lotus *(20-7)*. Stupendous drying racks in the foreground seemed as stand-ins for the giant portal guardians of temples elsewhere. They are for drying precious timber as well as barley cropped from the arable soil below, which was dotted with pigs and birds both black. The monastery's *chorten* was on a limb to the left. On the highest point, the two principal temples dominated the widely-spaced community of buildings, whose elongating shadows seemed as fierce as black holes against the sharp light as I approached from the road *(20-6)*. It is called Jiétáng Sōnglín Monastery (or Sōngzànlín), and is 300 years old. Sōnglín means Pine Forest, but the trees are long gone: the entire Zhōngdiàn area used to be filled with them.

Extinct too are the days when the lamasery housed 1,300 monks. That was in 1958, the year before the People's Liberation Army aimed artillery at the one hundred buildings here. Three months after the People's Republic of China was inaugurated, it was announced that the 'liberation' of Tibet would be a high priority (liberate from whom?). A multitude of

20-7

[1] A travel agency has since begun operating from the luxury Gyalthang Dzong Hotel – Gyalthang (Limitless Bounty) being the local name for Zhōngdiàn. In the summer and autumn it arranges tours led by expert botanists.

187

20-8

monasteries were sacked in the 1950s in barbaric ways. The British journalist Noel Barber, reporting from the front line in 1959, produced this short list:

> monasteries bombed, monks shot at prayer, old Tibetans used as slaves, Tibetans themselves killing their wives before taking to the mountains to fight, as all Tibetan women were being forced to bear at least one "Chinese" child.
>
> *The Flight of the Dalai Lama* (p. 78)

To which Pico Iyer adds:

> sacred texts had been used as toilet paper.... Monks had been forced to copulate in public.
>
> *Video Night in Kathmandu* (p. 69)

The International Commission of Jurists concluded in 1960 that 'acts of genocide [had] been committed in Tibet in an attempt to destroy the Tibetans as a religious group'. On the first of October that year, the Chinese themselves admitted to 87,000 Tibetans having been killed, the Tibetans reporting considerably more. Over the years, hundreds of thousands were ethnically terminated, with children – firearms-in-hand – being compelled to execute their parents, and other Tibetans having their tongues gouged out to prevent them extolling their religion, others buried alive. The number of monasteries in central Tibet continued to fall from thousands in 1959 to around 550 by 1966, when the four-year Cultural Revolution decimated most of the rest. There were officially only eight active ones in 1978, and less than 1% of monks and nuns remained.

20-5, on the left, shows evidence of that destruction – butted remains of ancient walls speaking of the unspeakable past. Isolated pillars point accusatory fingers towards Heaven, asking yet again, Why?... After Máo died, the horrific grip was relaxed, and some monks here took up their meditative cudgels again in 1982. These two scurried across the courtyard of the central temple without acknowledging me.

20-9

20-10

The imagery placed above the entrance, detailed in *20-8*, is of the Dharmacakra, the Wheel of Dharma – the doctrine set in motion by Sakyamuni in 528 BC at the Deer Park in Sārnāth near Vārāṇasī (Benares), hence the two attentive, obedient, humble gazelles. For me, the wheel is also a psychic centre, a beamgate for the gods. The iconography is widespread – there is a similar trio over the entrance to the most sacred building in Tibet, the Jokhang in Lhasa.

As Xuán Zàng arrived in Sārnāth in the 7th century seeking the origins of Buddhism, the religion had been superseded almost entirely in India by Hinduism, the monasteries and adherents smashed and slain by the Huns. He reported only magnificent ruins. The interest of Chinese pilgrims journeying along the Silk Road thereby rescued the Great Vehicle (Mahayana) from extinction.

This Buddhism was introduced into Tibet as a result of King Songtsen Gampo marrying Chinese and Nepalese princesses of Buddhist persuasion. It later settled in modified form as Vajrayāna, the Thunderbolt or Diamond Vehicle – embodying brilliance, cutting power, and durability.

With the Chinese authorities again clamping down on Tibet's traditions in the 1990s[1], with the indifference of the world community in general these past fifty years, and with the old lamas steeped in the previous continuous traditions by now all dead, the unbroken line of Buddhism in Tibet is equally dead at the end of the millennium. Its survival there at all remains to be seen. The irony is that Buddhism was reintroduced into India from Tibet in the 16th century, a direction reinforced when the present Dalai Lama escaped in 1959. The circle of Buddhism was completed – a tortuous and tortured route, a prima facie example of a wheel in action.

Such considerations were however far from my thoughts at the time, as, flitting between the buildings, I marvelled at the intrinsic atmosphere of the ensemble. Elegant old wood contrasted with white walls *(20-9)*, saturated blue drew the eye upward from baked, pastel-

---

[1] The principal monk of every monastery is now chosen by the Religious Affairs Bureau – run by the Chinese. The affairs of every monastery are overseen by a Democratic Management Committee – whose members are appointed by the Chinese. In 1995, the six-year-old 11th Panchen Lama, acknowledged by the Dalai Lama, was abducted by the Chinese and his whereabouts is unknown – a substitute was summarily chosen by the Chinese. Since 1996, brandishing photographs of the Dalai Lama has been deemed illegal in Tibet. The regional party, which directs local government, is not headed by a Tibetan. Amnesty International and Asia Watch have evidence of torture and abuse.
More from www.tibetinfo.net and www.freetibet.org (UK tel 020-7833 9958).

brown walls (20-10), while the abode of the monks as per tradition were marked by yellow walls. These primary colours were punctuated by brick reds, blue windows, and shadow blacks.

Virtually no one was around, apart from an orange-clad monk imbibing the late afternoon light by resting on the steps in 20-12 (overleaf). Ethically I would not intrude on such a reverie simply because the monk was picturesque, and I took the scene after he left.

Those few steps take one into a preparatory corridor that is a riot of rainbow colours. Here are two of the four Celestial Kings who protect the world. On one side, the red-bodied king (below right) – whose hand displays a distinct gesture while holding a snake – is Virūpaksha, guardian of the West. The blue-bodied one on the other side, ready to strike with a sword partly unsheathed, is Virūdhaka, protector of the South (20-13). The fearsomeness of these guardians, as in all Buddhist lands, is to deter and bar anyone out of sympathy with the religion. In between the two, the door to the inner sanctum was closed.

On the left of 20-11 (below) is a particularly Tibetan wheel – Bhavacakra, the Wheel of Existence. It portrays *saṁsāra*, our unremitting and oft-unwitting birth-death-rebirth cycle, and is thus fittingly grasped with hands and feet by Mara, the monster of death and transience. The main part is divided by six spokes into rebirth regions, including those of animals and humans. The largest, and at the bottom, is that of various hot and icy hells, while at the top is Buddha preaching in the abode of the gods who are not yet in nirvana. Only the Buddha is enlightened enough also to be outside the wheel, in the corner above and right.

The hub at the centre around which the whole mechanism revolves holds the terrorsome threesome of delusion *(moha)*, attachment *(rāga)* and hate *(dosa)* that combine to form bad karma. They are portrayed respectively by a pig, cockerel and snake chasing and eating each other's tails.

The ring around the bulls-eye is split into a black segment of humans with bad karma falling into hell, and a white one of others climbing to nirvana.

The outermost ring is divided into the 12 causes of all this mayhem. They include ignorance and greed. Thus the whole warns of our multiple metempsychoses to come – that is if we don't break out of the pointless, vicious circle of unenlightenment. What a superbly telling image to be reminded of everyday!

I returned to the previous hall (20-5) and behind the dirty sheets found the other two protectors: the East, the white-faced Dhritarāshtra emitting manipulative music on a lute, and Vaishravana warning with an orange flush and a spitting mongoose. Here too was the black to white snake-like path of life, shown in chapter six (6-44).

From its earliest days, a characteristic of Vajrayāna was searching for the connection between the cosmic spirit and the body by 'engaging in sexual activities to the point of utter exhaustion'[1], which is possibly the source of the lustful abandon in the *yab-yum* and tankas described in chapter six (6-22/23). This lamasery, in contrast, belongs to the leading Yellow Hat school of Tibetan Buddhism called Gelukpa, the Virtuous Path, which was founded by Tsongkhapa (1357–1419) who objected to those modes of behaviour.

1 *Himalayas*, by Blanche C. Olschak, etc., p. 282

20-11

20-12

Gelukpa was later led by Sonam Gyamtsho who was the first to be called Dalai Lama, *ta-le* being Mongolian for 'vast ocean', a title implying ocean-wide wisdom that was bestowed on him in 1578 by the Mongolian ruler Altan Khan. The link between Tibetan Buddhism and Chéngdé/Wǔtáishān, not far from today's Inner Mongolia, stems from this – another twist of a wheel.

★   ★   ★

20-13

Returning to town, I entered a store to purchase some bread, when at 7.14 pm the floor shifted sideways... and back and forth. The faces in the shop including mine froze. It is frightening to realise that, in those insecure seven seconds, at least 243 people died in Lìjiāng, and more than 20,000 were injured.

I moved swiftly into the street. We were on the edge of the earthquake, but even so I looked up to see the roof swaying, while across the street a crash made me wheel round to witness a block of offices still being constructed losing some of its fabric from the upper floors.

That night the electricity was cut. With no electric blanket, I slept as best as I could. Water to flush the toilets was applied by ladle from a water butt outside. By the morning it was solidly iced over.

◆   ◆   ◆   ◆

20-15

Venturing further afield was out of the question. Instead, and until more about the situation became clear, I hired the only operative bicycle and headed north this time on the main road along silent fields that even in bright sun were in the grip of a carpet of frost, with frozen ditches peppered white. The gradient increased as I took *20-15* looking west. On the other side over a pass stretched a shallow deep-blue lake, half covered with frost like castor sugar shaken over coloured icing, beyond which a brown plain led to the rear of the Sōnglín Monastery set against hills rich in red iron.

A white diamond peak played peek-a-boo dodging in and out of view, the contrast of its crystal snow against cloudless blue transporting me back to walks in Peru and the Andes, some sheep becoming llamas in my mind. Their cream coats contrasted with earthy-brown piles of soil amassed by a few women who were digging and toiling, with drying racks standing watch. At this altitude up to 4,000 metres, the chief crops are restricted to barley, potatoes, and medicinal plants, it being too high for tea, maize, rice and cereals. A posse of women approached on the highway, well wrapped in reds. As if I was an invisible life form, they didn't look at me, except one couldn't resist turning round afterwards *(20-16)*. The people in the Zhōngdiàn area are mainly Tibetan, with some Naxi, Bai, and Muslim Huí, as well as a strong Hàn presence.

20-14

Power returned spasmodically, enough to catch a short report on international TV: the earthquake had been of magnitude 7, epicentre Lìjiāng, many people dead, Zhōngdiàn cut off. It was eerie to be part of the news… stranded in the middle of nowhere. Some wonderful BBC natural-world documentaries eased the numbness. Amazingly after a number of attempts, I managed to phone England before all telecommunications ceased, which alleviated the concerns of relatives who knew from a copy of the itinerary I had given them that I was supposed to be in Lìjiāng itself.

The whole area around Jade Dragon Snow Mountain had shaken. Without warning and within seconds, thousands were faced with their homes flattened, as well as their parents dead, their children dead (*20-14* is representational), or both. With God's foreknowledge.

Track 9. WARNING – the music contains a sudden loud bang after a quiet preamble.

Near some habitation, a pond sufficed as a laundry basin, red washing at the edges mirrored in the steely surface. A woman scrubbed for an hour – how we take for granted the luxury of piped hot water. Two curious pigs sniffed and snuggled up to me. I pedalled and puffed up a second incline, halted before a pass, and rested for the first time in too long, drinking in the pastoral pleasures of a sub-Himalayan valley *(20-17/18)*....

20-16

20-17

This is a receded lake called Nàpà Hǎi, with sharp blue ice licking the boundaries against denuded mountainsides. Looking south-east, with the armadillo peaks of Jade Dragon Snow Mountain impassively commandeering the far distance, it is an expanse of trodden grassland and ploughed good earth on which dramatic drying racks like solar panels salute the sun, frost harbouring underneath. Punctuated by cows and pigs as black as their shadows, with isolated shacks and swirls of snow, it is a beautiful land, indifferent to pain, free from the human pettiness of the hell below.

A solitary speck of a truck halted at a cross roads in the middle distance. It is sobering that the trekkers of the Long March came through Zhōngdiàn – out on a limb in several senses, far from their homelands and families.

Alone on this mound of homely alpines – ice collared plants like jewels set in pearls – I had plenty on which to ponder.

20-18

AUTUMN

In silence I go alone up to the western chamber,
Above which hangs the sickle moon;
In the deep, lonely court of paulownia trees
is gaoled the chilly autumn.

Cut it, yet unsevered,
Order it, the more tangled –
Such is parting sorrow,
Which dwells in my heart,
too subtle a feeling to tell.

Lǐ Yù[1], 937-978, composed
while imprisoned in Kāifēng

THE BAMBOO RETREAT

Seated alone in secluded bamboo,
I pluck my lute and whistle a tune.
I know not a soul here shielded from view
Only one comes to greet me – the bright shining moon.

Wáng Wéi (c.701–761),
Táng poet and painter;
author's translation

---

[1] The last emperor of the Southern Táng (Ten Kingdoms), he was executed because of one line he wrote in a subsequent poem, which was of course his last.   Translated by Chu Dagao [*101 Chinese Lyrics*, p. 49]

The Chinese bike provided diverting amusement careering down the final descent back to Zhōngdiàn. The brakes on maximum barely contained the speed, and stopping the machine was not an option.

A perusal of the clean, older part of town *(20-19)* brought a reminder of the situation – a crack in a wall, another rift *(20-20)*. A housewife by a framed door in her majestic wooden home seemed content for me to take a portrait, her face exuding humility, calm and gentleness *(20-21)*. The words around her door say:

[left]
The five fortunes bless this joyful family.
[top]
Happiness fills the courtyard.
[right]
The Three Stars [of Happiness, Wealth and Longevity] *shine high over this peaceful house.*

Near the back of the hotel, I discovered a temple on a hillock accessed by a grand staircase, in the middle of which rose a slender tree. A wooden entrance *páilou* and its two side pavilions exhibited the unashamed Sūzhōu style of florid swept-up eaves, sumptuously painted and featuring rabbit motifs. Behind this lay a striking burned-orange screen with decorous panels. It was a false double portal: further steps led to a faded double-panel door, through which the summit pavilion in a white-walled compound was reached *(20-22)*. With unusual figures on the ridges, I found its proportions on slim columns elegantly satisfying, as if suspended from the sky, while the stone bowl in the centre was inscribed with an appealing older type of calligraphy. The caretaker (on the left) had kindly opened the black centre door panels for me to peer inside. The words on the red background declare that 'The rising sun melts and harmonises'. Perambulating around the wall gave authoritative views of the dark roofs of old and modern Zhōngdiàn, and a spectacular prayer flag complemented the scene *(20-23)*. In the Tibetan tradition, these bundles sometimes have written mantras attached.

20-22

I parleyed with the Americans – a couple in their thirties and a man about my age – concerning our next moves. Unable to telephone Lìjiāng and bereft of information, we were uncertain as to the consequences of the quake for ourselves. We decided to return to Qiáotóu, hopefully to walk the Tiger Leaping Gorge together.

Thankfully, power was restored in the evening, ensuring a snug night.

◆ ◆ ◆ ◆

After four hours we disembarked in Qiáotóu. There was palpable tension in the air. With Jade Dragon close at hand, the owner of a backpacker's café warned us that aftershocks had already taken place, and more were expected at twelve-hour intervals. "Houses are down in Lìjiāng" she reported, adding that the police were "suggesting" foreigners should leave. Significantly, the army had searched the gorge to ensure the safety of foreigners – we saw two lorry loads of soldiers with a grinning backpacker at the back of one. Hŭtiào Xiá has impressive measurements: only thirty to eighty metres wide, with precipitous cliffs soaring 3,000 metres above so vertical and deep that the sun hardly reaches the bottom at midday. Within its length of sixteen kilometres, the Yángzi drops a precipitous 200 metres over twenty-one rapids. As the entrance ticket graphically described it, 'furious billows splash in the valley as the sprinkling snow runs the thunder'. The gorge retains a reputation for severe rock falls. No wonder the original tiger chose to jump over it.

20-23

I investigated its feasibility: surprisingly, the guard at the entrance gate assured me that tickets were no problem for the following day. Perhaps the tremors had not seriously affected the gorge after all. With the tickets in pocket, we booked into the basic but friendly Happy Valley Hotel – an incongruous name at this time – and awaited developments. Two policemen saw us and said we must leave the area. 'Suggest', 'must', or 'no problem' – matters were confused. The Americans were determined to trek the gorge if possible – the high spot of any venture to Yúnnán – and I concurred. We planned to rise early, assess the situation again, and proceed if okay. Reaching Bǎoshān would then be feasible thereafter.

Sitting in the hot afternoon sun outside the café, I wrote eight postcards, slipping them into a postbox, wondering if they would ever arrive at their worldwide destinations.

As we retired to bed, a high-ranking policeman called with two armed accomplices at his side. This time there was no doubt: we had to leave the entire Lìjiāng county by bus the next day. We acquiesced if with a sad heart; we couldn't add to the pressures of the calamity already present.

◆ ◆ ◆ ◆

back to Lìjiāng

What was in prospect? Riots, looting? As the tardy bus approached Lìjiāng town, I steeled my fellow travellers-in-fate to expect grim scenes, including death. On the same road as I had arrived days earlier *(20-1)*, those same dwellings in that photograph were now flattened – roofs on the floor, brick walls down. I didn't want to look, but had to.

There was an electric calm at the bus station, despite many vehicles continually arriving and departing. Substantial cracks on walls were a preliminary. The long walk north revealed people lying or sitting on their 'beds' in the main street. Inside is no place to be when aftershocks are due. Some officials abruptly accosted us. Who are you? Where have you come from? Our brief replies seemed to allay some anxiety: with no communications, they hadn't known if Zhōngdiàn was badly affected, us being the first to have exited from there. Have you seen...? A list of missing foreigners was reeled off: we didn't know any of them. Are there any others in Zhōngdiàn or Qiáotóu? We had seen none.

No hotels were operating they informed us, and there was no water in the city; aftershocks were continuing. We had to leave immediately and they suggested to Dàlǐ. Concerned about my backpack, I hurried to the Red Sun. My bed of just days previously had been against a window overlooking the street. I was aghast to find some of the fabric of the outside wall below my bed arrayed on the pavement. Inside, what had been a modern, spacious lobby was a wreck – caved in, with concrete, brick and plaster blocking everywhere. Tall plants in pots lay on their side; the toilets below were in a structural mess, water pipes empty. Hardly had I absorbed the scene, when I caught sight of my backpack with a host of others being hoisted into the square under Máo's gaze.

"Hey, that's mine!"

The policeman was relieved – that was one foreigner accounted for.

The shaken pack was covered in concrete dust, yet undamaged – even the Dàlǐ marble vase and four *Badu* bowls seemed intact.

"Do you know where the owner of this bag is?" he asked.

The remaining unclaimed ones indicated there might be some foreign casualties. There was one Westerner, I learned later, who did not survive the quake.

I signed for mine, and wasn't charged the fee due for left luggage.

One of the backpackers' cafés was boarded up and deserted as if in a Wild West ghost town. The inside of another was bedlam, as if a fight had taken place, tables and chairs tossed and damaged. I thought of the poor owner who had so recently been friendly and helpful to me. In the street, women were sweeping glass that had smashed from windows above. There was continuous orderly movement of the Chinese and Naxi, but no panic – people trying to deal with the reality. No taxis were available. Bus tickets were like gold. Hundreds of people desperately trying to leave surrounded a makeshift table in the street that substituted as a ticket office.

With no wish to return to Dàlǐ, I informed the Americans that I was determined to leave Yúnnán altogether on a long-distance bus east to Jīnjiāng, my next objective being to climb Éméishān. A bus was scheduled at three o'clock. The couple decided on the less drastic trip to Dàlǐ, but I sensed the other American was tempted to split with his compatriots and band with me. He confirmed he would, if tickets could be appropriated. I quietly positioned myself behind the two hassled ticket personnel attempting to cope with the bevy crowding the table. One noticed me and after ten minutes clapped two tickets into my hand – a favour to a foreigner. My new travel companion, whom I will call Matt, headed for the only hotel that was open, to phone his wife in Běijīng.

There was something I desperately wanted to do. On his return, Matt stood guard over our packs while I trampled uneasily along the same narrow lane that I had strolled days before. A hunting falcon was perched on a post unattended. Building fabric had collapsed. Through a passage choked with debris, I stepped up to Lion Hill to survey the scene, fearing the worst. From that distance, the venerable Old Town seemed in a reasonable state, the sea of grey roofs intact, and I deemed it acceptable to take a photograph *(20-24)*. On the left in the distance in a pallid muslin-thin cloak of cloud, Jade Dragon exuded villainous indifference to the suffering it had partly provoked – it had been the unexpected epicentre. So much for the Amoeba's sensitivity to feelings. Below, some folk were camping ad hoc, kettle in hand.

20-24

That distant view was misleading however. The Market Square was a shock, crammed with mattresses cheek by jowl, with tents and utensils higgledy-piggledy, and strewn with limbs of kids and mums. They had been in the open for two winter's nights already: it had been below freezing.

I weaved between the beds, bypassed plaster shaken off walls, and stepped through scenes of worse destruction. Entering a compact square, I stopped, as did my heart, on seeing it choked with people living temporarily under plastic sheets. Part of a wall of a house had collapsed. My desperate quest was to see the state of the Naxi Orchestra's building and learn of its personnel. It being metres away around a corner, I feared the worst.

The solid building seemed relatively unscathed, with a crack or two, crumbled white plaster lying on the ground. I had pre-decided not to take photographs of the human suffering – I don't derive pleasure from having such a record. Over the next half hour, instead, I took a few discreet ones of material destruction as a salutary reminder, starting with these *(20-25/26)*. There would be no more music for a while, that was sure.

20-25

I was glad to espy the orchestra's guiding light, Xuān Kē, who was busy assisting and lifting the spirits of the people in the square. I approached him, and we talked for five minutes. He was not outwardly sad, rather he accepted the natural calamity philosophically, and came across as wise and in control. He uttered the statistics quietly: the dead, the injured including that 5,700 had been seriously so. The Old Town had been badly affected; Báishā's houses were "60-70% down, other villages 100% down". The earthquake's consequences on the people of the plain that I had toured on my bike *(20-3)* were sobering; I hope the Doctor and his family are alright.

The next statistic shocked me personally like a thunderbolt. Further to the north, Bǎoshān was "quite badly hit, most buildings down, though only a few killed".

Only a few killed.... I had meant to be there that night.

The good news was that the orchestra members were safe.

Xuān Kē remarked that Lìjiāng had last suffered a major earthquake in 1951; that had been force 6.9 and "not as serious". At 0.1 less, I marvelled at his acceptance. I wished him luck.

So I was deeply aware of three extraordinary coincidences, of fate intervening, each one keeping me away from the centre of the earthquake.

1. If I hadn't omitted the extra day in the first Bǎoshān, five days before the earthquake, I would have been in Lìjiāng itself, and possibly in the Red Sun Hotel, as the earthquake struck.

2. If I had kept to my long-held plan to continue to the second Bǎoshān straight after Lìjiāng, instead of switching *at the last moment* to Zhōngdiàn, I would have been in the midst of the mayhem in a place where most of the houses were flattened.

3. Concerning the monumental supplication to God at the Black Dragon Pool – the most heartfelt request I have ever made – I tried with all my powers and forty-five years of experience to make it happen, and failed. *If* it had been granted, it would have resulted in me delaying in Lìjiāng, and I would have been in the epicentre, on earthquake day.

Someone had been working hard to make sure I wouldn't be hurt. I was not to be part of this – it was to be the tragedy of other peoples. Thus is the power of God, and thus is H/his willingness to inflict pain where S/he Wills it to be channelled, *or to deflect it away*. That is an awesome realisation, and one on which humanity should contemplate exceedingly seriously.

> Make for safety without delay, for I am about to bring disaster out of the north and dire destruction.
> God warning [Jer. 4.6]

The Amoeba had altered my itinerary. For me this was a Place Out of Time, and a Time Out of Place. Why had God spared me, while deliberately allowing a blow to fall on these humans? Anger again swelled: you have killed these poor, defenceless, innocent people. They were not Hitlers: what sort of Animal are you?

Later I was informed that because of aftershocks, the entire 70,000 inhabitants of the town were living in tents. In subsequent days, people including children were killed in the streets from walls collapsing on them. Unstable buildings remained for months; rebuilding continued for a year. Many of the wounded could not afford to go to hospital. An elderly woman related that the quake announced itself as an ear-splitting roar, like a motorbike out of hell: the work of generations was destroyed in that moment, she added.

There was also remarkable human spirit. In the northern plain, children continued with their lessons sitting in the cold outside their collapsed school. An old woman chuckled as she recalled praying at the top of her voice during the shaking of the earth to the angry fish god that had caused it. A doctor combed the town treating the wounded without asking for payment, his priority being the control of water-borne diseases including cholera. And there was macabre farce. Dead bodies were dumped temporarily in a compound; when people came to bury them three days later, the diggers jumped out of their skins when one of the bodies emitted a loud groan.

I had been keeping Matt waiting for over an hour, and rushed back taking one last picture on the way of the main street looking north *(20-27)*. The Mountain in the distance is smoking away, enticing yet deadly. The bricks of the downed wall on the right are scattered like confetti. Some folk are squatting in shock on the edge of the pavement; a mêlée of vehicles are on serious errands; people are turning this way and that.

Eight months before, the inhabitants of Lìjiāng had finished constructing an airport. A notice commemorating this had been erected, mainly in English and Dongba script. It ran as follows.

20-26

TO CELEBRATE THE OPENING OF THE
LIJIANG AIRPORT.
LIJIANG HOPES THE SILVER EAGLE
WILL SOAR FOR EVER!

Tourists found it hard to come here through the dangerous mountains and deep rivers because we could not make roads before today.

The only reason why some people of the world came here was to exchange all kinds of ideas with us.

Now, we have opened up ten thousand roads in ten thousand miles of blue sky.

Spread one thousand ideas on the green earth one thousand years old.

The dazzling white peak of jade dragon mountain is rising into the clouds to kiss heaven.

The rippling of the golden sand river leads the way for coming friends.

NOTE: In the naxi dongba hieroglyphic characters there is no word for aeroplane. Now utilising the chinese word.... a new word aeroplane became silver eagle.

WRITTEN AND TRANSLATED BY YANG MINAEYI,
A NAXIMAN, OLD BOY   9TH JUNE 1995

Our bus departed in haste, packed with traumatised humanity and its effects. As we sped east through old sectors of town, these seemed to be the worst affected – houses dissipated, it was terrible. As the bus climbed beyond the boundaries, I glanced back. I was leaving behind two tragedies – my own, and the greater one of others. Mine was the end of the most glorious epoch of my life so far – instigated in Cheju, and ended by the same Entity who did so.

The crowded bus was uncomfortable with no room for Western legs, the window seat having even less. For ten hours, we traversed resplendent country with luscious greens, mountains high above the Jīnshā Jiāng in valleys below, then along the edge of an extensive verdant plain. We devoured our only food – a couple of bananas.

I felt I was on a travellator in an enforced dream. But there was little time for backward-facing sorrow; my journey was marching on apace.

Endless are my thoughts.
The blue bird does not carry messages from across the clouds.
The lilacs only gather sadness in the rain.

Lĭ Jīng[1], 916–961

20-27

[1] Emperor of the Southern Táng (Ten Kingdoms), and the father of Lĭ Yù (see p. 193).   From *The Three Gorges*, translated by Chu Dagao [*101 Chinese Lyrics*, p. 37]

Chapter 21

Éméishān

For the last hour from midnight on, we surged through an interminably long industrial city beside the Yángzi, all the while proceeding downhill fast – descending into and through hell. I knew the feeling well. This was Pānzhīhuā, and if there ever is a metropolitan Hell in China, this is it. Barely in Sìchuān Province, the bus terminated at Jīnjiāng, effectively a suburb, from where the guidebook informed that a train northwards would depart at 02.15 – and the plucky bus was on time!

Optimism melted on seeing the departures board blank. According to a hotel receptionist, there would be a train in the morning. In our basic but spacious room, we celebrated our escape from Lìjiāng, a sobering nineteen-hour day, by sampling various Chinese teas that Matt carried. It was a civilising ritual after the tenseness of the previous days.

◆ ◆ ◆ ◆

> Plagues of termites with a taste for reinforced concrete threatens Chinese cities and are a serious safety hazard.... According to experts from the Termite Prevention and Control Research Institute in SW Sìchuān province, the termites – formerly viewed as enemies of wooden buildings only – have developed a penchant for cement building materials.... [They] can also damage copper, iron and aluminium products such as wires and cables... economic losses total $4.75 million annually.
>
> March 1995

I had read that report in a Korean newspaper: given the ugliness of Pānzhīhuā, even at night, I was tempted to wish the critters luck. In the event, no train was in the offing until evening, so a walk along the river to the railway bridge sufficed to fill in the day. Matt correctly forecast that an armed guard would not allow us to tarry on or near the bridge: we were shooed away.

Opened in 1970, the 1,000-kilometre Kūnmíng to Chéngdū railway line was courtesy of the deaths of enforced Chinese labourers. The construction dangers and hardships can be gleaned simply by the number of tunnels ploughed through the mountains, 427, and bridges flung over rivers and valleys, 991 according to China Today.

It was the most packed train in China on my journeys, proof that Sìchuān with 110 million people was the most populated province in the country – staggering if you bear in mind that was more than all except eight other *nations* in the world[1]. Worse, there was more chance of slipping through the eye of a needle, or reaching nirvana, than obtaining a sleeper compartment. For fourteen hours overnight, we were jammed on the corner of a hard seat, or else stood, with folks at our feet squatting or napping on newspaper. For the rest, I refer you reader to the description of the Hóng Dòng to Yùnchéng experience in chapter 8, then double it.

◆ ◆ ◆ ◆

[1] Since my travels, Chóngqìng with its 30 million people has been separated from the province into a municipality of its own.

Lèshān

Welcome to Sìchuān weather!

There wasn't actually a sign at Éméi station with that salutation; rather it was obvious from the initial muzzy, depressive light. For the final three weeks of travel, I cannot recall seeing the unadulterated sun, except once in special circumstances. After an hour, a zippy minibus disgorged us tired and filthy at **Lèshān** (Happy Mountain), where at my suggestion we treated ourselves to a room in the luxury Jiāzhōu Hotel. An approving Matt was thankful I was not the usual backpacker intent on cheaper accommodation at all times. After our recent rigours, this was a time to debunk from China for the rest of the day. The hotel's name means a 'Good Island', and it was a fine desert island for laundry washing, bathing, sleeping, and TV staring, the room's balcony overlooking three small islands in the Dàdù River. A dark, wooden café nearby contained testimonials from previous backpackers, the keen owner promising his eatery would be in the next Lonely Planet edition (which proved correct).

◆ ◆ ◆ ◆

21-1

21-2

A minor tributary, the Éméi, and the much longer Qīngyī both enter the Dàdù almost at the same point west of town. In turn this significant river feeds at Lèshān into the substantial Mín, which flows south-east into the giant Yángzi/Cháng downstream from where the 221 dangerous rapids used to be. Thus there is a maelstrom of choppy, treacherous and flooding water around, with periodic tidal waves, which is why a monk named Haitong in AD 713 set in motion the construction of the tallest stone Buddha in the world at the precise Dàdù/Mín confluence, as a singular placatory measure. So convinced was he that it would achieve the desired calming, he 'gouged out one of his own eyes to impress potential donors' [Blue Guide]. The money was necessary as it took ninety years to complete, including fitting internal drains to siphon off potentially eroding rainwater.

The semi-fish-eye view *21-2* shows the relationship of this UNESCO World Heritage site with the town – the Dàdù on the left merging with the Mín – as well as the weather!

From the ferryboat struggling to keep position against the still swift current, the first close-up of the seated Grand Buddha (Dàfó) was jaw dropping – towering seventy-one metres above and gouged out of a solid cliff of red sandstone *(21-1)*. In his heyday, this Maitreya was covered from 15-metre head to 8½-metre toe in glistening gold leaf, and was shielded within a pavilion of thirteen storeys. A grandiose thousand sculptures were in ubiquitous side niches; alas, only two have survived the 1,200-year erosion of history.

On either side of the Buddha there are steep stairs, one through a tunnel, enabling a humility-inducing ants-eye view from the feet, or a lofty one of the elongated ears, sleek slit eyes, and aquiline nose *(21-3)*.

21-3

21-4

The second and third tallest stone Buddhas used to be in Bamiyan, 120 kilometres north-west of Kābul in Afghanistan, until the Taliban tragically blew them up in 2001. My father travelled to see them in 1963, and as a comparison I include here his photo of the loftier one, fifty-three meters high, carved out of a sandstone cliff in the fifth century AD *(21-4)*. The beautiful green valley in which they stood was a popular draw for Silk Road caravans in the following few centuries, and Xuán Zàng visited the statues in 632. His report described the dotted lines of holes on the folds of the drapery, which during construction contained pegs to support the lime mortar.

It was in Lèshān that the Chinese drilled for oil in the 16th century using wooden derricks, cast-iron bits and bamboo cables. As far back as the 1st century BC they had been drilling elsewhere for natural gas to a depth of 1,500 metres, using it to boil brine also extracted at depth, thus distilling salt. The equipment then used included derricks fifty-five metres tall – the same height as the Bamiyan Buddha – as well as cast iron bits and bamboo wires and pipes. Is there no end to the marvels of ancient Chinese inventions? Sìchuān was an especially prodigious salt-producing area in the 13th century, salt as a preservative in summer being an invaluable commodity in the fight for survival.

Two ancient temples behind the Grand Buddha attract a plethora of visitors, but at the time I was more intrigued by my new companion. He had recently married a Chinese woman, was living in Běijīng, and was in regular contact with high Chinese officials. We discussed the Chinese way.

Taxi drivers at the quay below insisted the ferries had ceased for the day, a cab being the only alternative back to town across a bridge some kilometres away. I ignored them and a ferry appeared within minutes.

◆ ◆ ◆ ◆

Éméishān

It was time to tackle the trickiest mountain of my travels.

In a large-scale poem entitled *A Song of Eternal Sorrow*, a famed poet of the Táng Dynasty called Bái Jūyì (772–846) described a visit to the area by Xuánzōng, the Brilliant Emperor, in the fading moments of his reign in 756. During the journey, his favourite concubine Yáng Guìfēi, the wife of one of his thirty sons, was reluctantly killed by his own orders. I could resonate with the poem's ambience.

At the foot of Emei Mountain, where travelers are few,
The royal colors are faded, the sun is lost to view.

—

All things must change, the King returns to Chang'an and his throne;
He pauses by a sacred spot, sacred to him alone.[1]

With the name possessing various meanings, including Raised Eyebrow Mountain, **Éméishān** ('Err-may-shahn') was associated with shamanists and Daoists well before the earliest temples were erected in the first century AD. These had mushroomed by the end of the Eastern Hàn in 220, and from the 6th century, with Buddhists increasingly commandeering the mountain, a hundred monasteries, temples and lesser sacred facilities harbouring thousands of monks flourished up to the beginning of the 20th century. A combination of lightning, fire, the Japanese wars, plus revolutionary looting and dictates, led to them being abandoned in 1960s Maoist China.

About twenty have been resurrected, spurred on by a religious tradition and determination by pilgrims including the elderly to climb this most sacred of all Chinese Buddhist mountains – the others of the big four being Wŭtáishān [chapter 7], Jiŭhuáshān [chapter 12] and Pŭtuóshān [chapter 13].

At 3,099 metres, it is also the highest of the four, and therein lay the rub – I didn't know whether it would be possible to climb it in the middle of Winter. The massif is reminiscent of Kinabalu in Borneo, on which a trained British/Hong Kong expedition became lost. In other words, it covers a substantial amount of territory, over 300 square kilometres, with the two principal routes to the summit being 53 and 67 kilometres long. An option is to be carried up in a bamboo chair, but the steep incline results in one's head being below the legs much of the time!

---

[1] quoted in *XI'AN – Legacies of Ancient Chinese Civilization* (p.169), translated by Gong Lizeng

Privately, I dismissed the advice of the helpful Lèshān café owner whose recommendations conflicted with my own researched vision of how to scale it, the time it would take, and where to sleep. I particularly wished to stay overnight in a quiet monastery, not in one on the popular route besieged by climbers desperate to secure a bed. That meant traipsing the longer of the two options, hoping that the isolated Xiānfēng Monastery would still be providing accommodation in winter, plus something hot to eat. Matt acceded to my determination only with some trepidation.

After an early bus to the foot of the mountain, and with main packs deposited in a hotel, we took a taxi to Qīngyīn Pavilion at an elevation of 710 metres, saving an initial fifteen kilometres. From there, a plank way closely followed the modest Black Dragon River (Hēilóng Jiāng) for six kilometres, rising gently to Hóngchūnpíng Temple at 1,120 metres. Visibility was poor under a blanket of grey, and the sun seemed irredeemably far away.

The Victorian explorer Archibald Little (1838–1908) was here in the summer of 1897. He spent almost fifty years in China, authoring several books including *Through the Yang-tse Gorges* in which his cultural racism was clear. The Chinese, he declared, seem 'to be quite wanting in the imaginative faculty, and hence never invent anything new'. So much for all the Chinese inventions over millennia! It is not surprising that someone capable of deceiving with such a palpable untruth could also continue with the following:

> Like the animals to a great extent, their procedures follow instinct, or hereditary tendencies rather than reason, and their ambition seems limited to the gratification of the senses. Courage, in the highest sense of controlling their instincts, they rarely possess; hence while apathetic in the presence of sickness and death, they are cowards in the presence of dangers which call for energetic resistance.... Such a people, seemingly incapable of chivalrous feeling or loyalty, can hardly appreciate the Christian ideal... [they have] radical defects. (pp. 220/1)

He was an adventurous pioneer traveller in China, but even he found this mountain hard work. In *Mount Omi and Beyond* [Omi = Éméi], he declared there are 'some 20,000 slippery limestone steps', and that 'we toiled up the endless flights of stone steps'. He couldn't rid them from his mind: having counted 815, he noted 910 more, and remarked they were 'interminable... counting them was the only way to be avenged on them' (pp. 3 & 70/1).

A recent commentator's in-the-heat-of-the-moment evaluation is that they are the "longest flight of stone steps between here and eternity" [Philip Short]. The one thing we too could see for sure was the assemblage of steps disappearing into the cloud. From now on, they were indeed relentless and tortuous. Matt proceeded at a slower pace than me, and for the next fifteen kilometres along the '99 Windings', I had time to imbibe the atmosphere. The mountain already had a character all its own, distinct from others in China, being more 'rounded' and spacious – lying like a sleeping bear. There was something other-worldly too about the luxuriant greenery, the pines, the plunging mini-waterfalls, the bubbling streams – all enveloped in a cloak of many clouds, a secret waiting to be found. One could not see much; the solidity and width was instead sensed.

Of the bearded frogs, musical frogs, pheasants, lesser pandas, Emei leaf warbler, and 200 different butterflies, I saw none, and the cloud and effort of the steps put paid to appreciating the 3,000 tropical, subtropical, temperate and subfrigid flora, of which a hundred exist nowhere else.

There is, however, one animal that is straight out of one's worst nightmares and will attack you! Much has been made of the fun of the 200 local monkeys – but they are seriously frightening, particularly as it dawns that a troupe of a dozen or two rhesus have been surrounding you surreptitiously, devising a better-laid ambush than any by John Wayne. There are few opportunities these days for the cosseted Westerner to experience being hunted, or the way raw survival concentrates the mind. This gives a taste: as one or two sidle up, another charges from behind, while one hidden below the edge of the steps springs a surprise, and another Robin Hoods down from a branch above. Your daypack will be grabbed, and you will be menaced for half an hour whether or not you give them food – and they will not be pleased with a banana or two. Fortunately, the act of picking up a club of wood or a sizeable stone has an immediate effect, and they withdraw a few yards, temporarily. They are thieving, terrorising bandits, and do not – as my Chinese-produced atlas states – 'delight the tourists by extending their palms for food'. Please God, grant enlightenment and turn the monkeys into monks. The monks don't like them either – they steal the offerings.

> *With one monkey in the way, not even ten thousand men can pass.*
>
> Chinese saying

We had been climbing for five hours, when without warning the world turned white. As we clambered through the slippery snow, Xiānfēng (Immortals Peak) Monastery loomed dark and soaked in rain – as inviting as a monkey's crutch. Built on an incline with storage underneath, its low silhouette of blackened wood stretched broadside like an inked horizontal streak of the Chinese brush on white rice paper. Dating from 1328, this substantial monastery is at a level of 1,752 metres in a region predominantly Daoist. Although the mountain's most substantial caves were nearby, named after 9 Old Ones (*Jiǔlǎo*) or Immortals, all we were interested in was joining the monks around a log fire in their office. A solo Westerner with adept mandarin joined us and sorted out the arrangements – and the hotly bargained price. The meal was manna from heaven, despite the cold rice. Soaking into the bed's damp mattress in a bare, freezing, wooden cell in a dormitory wing was one of those painful moments in life I would rather not recall.

◆ ◆ ◆ ◆

It had been evident that not even hiking boots were sufficient for this mountain in winter. The monastery fortunately kept sets of basic iron crampons for sale. Light, sensible and secured by string, they were to prove a lifesaver over the next eight hours of stumbling on steep ice, despite the straining twine breaking continually in the wet onslaught – bring two spare cords! The alternative that the other Westerner tested and later abandoned was the straw sandal, an unlikely outer shoe that locals swear by.

21-5

The twelve kilometres to Xīxiàng Chí, Pond for Washing the Elephant, was achieved in some hours of faltering steps. At 2,070 metres, its temple looked altogether warmer and more inviting. However it was compact, and being on the popular route was still at ten in the morning a bedlam of bodies on beds. With the temple placed squarely across the narrow path, this was another Chinese occasion when I had to pay the monks merely to walk through!

There were fifteen kilometres remaining to the summit area, and I left Matt trailing behind. The grey, wet mix of mist and melting cloud seemed impenetrable, reducing the snow to a gungy dull blanket. The trees' branches drooped with the heavy burden, while I stepped up alone in a world of piercing silence, no other soul being near.

A chiaroscuro effect to one side stopped me in my tracks. Out of the cloud, the fronds of a tree seemed to unravel and reveal a fan of surgically clear direct light. The sun filtered through the branches creating a radiance like a semi-circular white rainbow. A cauldron of mist thinned and spiralled into the ether, a patch of snow caught the rays brightening it into vibrant white, and hints of blue suggested a magical transformation just ahead. A few more steps, and as the single blue palette of the arched sky banished the former grey into oblivion, the other side of the path revealed a view of brilliant clouds below, piercing white as could only come from Heaven. I was above the muck of the earthly world, this upper side of the boundary between heaven and earth revealing it to be as white as a company of angels. The air was pristine, with the clear panorama stretching to the boundaries of the horizon, and, most thrilling of all, within this slowly-seething sea were occasional isolated land masses peeping through – islands in the clouds.

The implied spiritual revelation was as blinding as the moment in Haydn's *The Creation* when, out of a hushed dark C minor, a C major chord bursts forth and proud at the words 'And God spoke: Let there be Light! And there was Light' – one of the most heart-stopping moments in all music. C major – the only key that has no black keys.

It came across to me as an overwhelming sign demonstrating a searing promise: **'I will be what I will be'**. That statement by God to the Hebrews in Exodus 3.14, usually misleadingly translated as I am that I am, is a pledge: that though S/he has not yet appeared and acted for the total encompassing good, S/he will do so. I instinctively knew the transformation instigated by the sun through the trees was a calm symbol that a breakthrough will ensue – sometime.

As I fumbled to extricate the camera for the first time on the mountain, the feeling emanating as I took pictures of the sun bursting through the trees bowed with snow, was of God coming through. The act bore a simple message: *keep trusting*.

*Changes will take place
when things come to a dead end,
and breakthroughs can be expected
when there is no way out.*

Stranded, Divine Symbol,
A Bet by Wáng Bì, who
died aged 23 in AD 249
(*Kùnguàzhù*, from *Zhōu Yì*)

*Track 10: fade in and rising horn melody;
then two climactic sections (12 beats each)
with the above photo 21-5*

21-6 ▲ *longer section, and section becoming faster*

21-7 ▲ [1' 32"] *8+8+8 moderate beats*

21-8 ▼ [1' 51"] *(with drums) 8+8+4 beats; rotate book clockwise for the climax*

21-9 ▲ [2′ 07″] *climax; during calmer music, to photo below*

21-10 ▶ *longer quieter section; turn to next page for the final chords*

21-11 ▲ [3' 06"] *final chords with this photo*

As the steps ceased and the land flattened for a while, I felt the elation of renewed spirit: I will live again, I will have life again. Buoyed by the emotion unleashed by the sea of clouds, I walked as if on warm air through a wood without snow, waited for Matt to catch up, and after half an hour reached Jiēyǐn Hall at 2,540 metres. Here a vertical, buttressed block of mountain rose up like a stupa covered in snow, a cue for Matt to take the cable car. I urged the broken strings on my crampons to one more effort, and they proved crucial during the last 1½ hours climb through forest to the summit's open plateau 500 metres higher.

Surprise, surprise, there were dwellings and guest houses around the first of the three highest apexes, Golden Summit (Jīn Dǐng), whose spacious square and new temple, a former Míng one having a golden roof, didn't hold my attention long. As I continued a further kilometre southwards, the view west was enthralling and unexpected *(21-13* overleaf*)*. It inspired Archibald Little to the following description.

> And there a sight, such as we had never seen before, which will remain photographed upon our brains for ever after, met our enchanted gaze, a row of white peaks, tinted with the faintest shade of rose, stood up out of the billowy clouds like denizens of another world, so lofty and so far off that we could hardly believe they were real.... The snowy peaks which fringe the Thibetan plateau, ...which may range anywhere from 15,000 feet to 20,000 feet, were growing more and more distinct.... The snowy peaks looked so near, it was impossible to believe they were nearly 100 miles distant, as the crow flies.
> *Mount Omi and Beyond* (p. 85)

No wonder Little dallied fourteen days on the summit, staying in a temple. Immersed in the most intense contrasting brilliance and brightness as never had I seen before, the edge of the Tibetan plateau presented itself quietly and inevitably like the lines of sentinels of the terracotta army. These rows of islands were lapped by waves of clouds, simulating the ripples of life. For an eternal moment, one's eyes were lifted away from one's own island, to see others around you *(21-15)*. In the middle, a flat-topped table mountain rivalled that of Cape Town, while the tinge radiating off these mountains on this occasion was almost purple, in contrast to the sheen reflecting off the clouds. And triumphant over all in the upper sea of blue was the Sun – the largest Island of them all. O Thermal Island *(21-14)*!

Arising on the right like a dagger, barely visible in the haze through my longest lens, was the big one: Gònggā Shān (Minya Konka), 7,556 metres high. It was more astounding in 1930 when Joseph Rock cabled the National Geographic Society that this white diamond island peak was the highest in the world – 30,250, a thousand feet loftier than Mt. Everest! In the society's October magazine of that year, having revised his calculations (still 810 feet too high), he reported his feelings on viewing it from a closer position. The aura and wonder of the description could just as easily apply to this setting on Éméishān:

> Suddenly, like a white promontory of clouds, we beheld the long-hidden Minya Konka rising 25,600 feet in sublime majesty.
> I could not help exclaiming for joy. I marveled at the scenery which I, the first white man ever to stand here, was privileged to see.

21-12

An immense snowy range extended from north to south, and peerless Minya Konka rose high above its sister peaks into a turquoise-blue sky. A truncated pyramid it is, with immense lateral buttresses flanked by an enormous glacier many miles in length. This glacier, in turn, is joined by another coming directly from Minya Konka itself. (p. 413)

From Qiānfó Dǐng (Thousand Buddhas Summit), looking south revealed a precipice that sank into a chasm of cloud (21-12, 21-16). The end of that right-hand ledge was the highest point, Wànfó Dǐng, Ten Thousand Buddhas Summit, a couple of kilometres further. My efforts to reach it were blocked by thorny shrubs and an official fence.

Returning to the Golden Summit offered a view of the East Sea – a scene of eternity (21-17). There is a word taken from Indonesian *wayang* performances to describe this ultimate panorama: *adilung* means 'higher than high'. The sheer expanse of fluffy duvet clouds with a pink sun-kissed glow silenced my brain: I forgot it was China underneath. The umbrella of white in ever-so-slow motion was as if the Milky Way had descended and linked to surround this mountain pillar – a halo around Arcadia.

It was inviting enough that one could imagine jumping into it, like the most tempting lido! No wonder the viewing platform, from which two people are gazing in the extreme left of that photo, is labelled Shěshēn (Sacrifice One's Life) Cliff. It is a historical emotion – one more step into the warm embrace of Heaven – and railings were first installed over 800 years ago during the Sòng to discourage incandescent pilgrims from doing so.

This mountain is where Samantabhadra dwells, a fitting haven for the Bodhisattva of Perfection. Tibetans know him as the Ādi Buddha or Kuntuzangpo ('Goodness in All Ways'), whom legend records came here on a six-tusked elephant. What urged Buddhists to dive into such nirvana was a multi-coloured aureola around a face that occasionally forms miraculously on the clouds – the bodhisattva or the buddha himself. In scientific terms, it is the afternoon sun from behind casting a shadow of the observer himself, with water refraction providing a rainbow truncated by the cliff. Nevertheless, no one can factually deny that it could also be a real sign whose natural processes are initiated by a Divinity for the individual concerned.

I transferred to the rocky ledge and climbed over its security railings (21-19). Rather than suicide, my purpose was to photograph the plunging cliff, topped by the Golden Summit's temple (21-18). With my toes inches from the vertical bluff, I looked straight down into the waves of surf, which here being in the dark seemed more like a witches' brew of boiling, moody mist beckoning the believer to jump. Humpbacked islands of forests mysteriously surfaced, before diving back into the engulfing sea once more. Divine elements merged: somewhere below was Tiānchí, Heaven Lake, and a place called Guān Yīn.

The cable car glided me smoothly into the darkening billows that were the abyss of earth, as if angels were lowering it off the heavenly heights (21-20) – one is not meant to be there for ever, yet. Glowing in the aura of having seen the future, one pre-eminent feeling reigned: I had seen, and was, on cloud 9.

12 × 9

Dear reader – this object you hold in your hands: if you are sure it is a book, equally certain am I that a personal God exists, and for the same reasons. Listen to a piece of music: if that is music, I know as adamantly that S/he is not a figment of wishful thinking. I swear on all future children that is true. That knowledge, not belief, is a step among many. To where that staircase is leading is the main purpose of the rest of this chapter.

NUMBERS 12 AND 9

Certain numbers have attracted repeated religious or mystical connotations throughout history. The most ancient mantric hymns of Hinduism, the Rig Veda, recorded perhaps as far back as 4000 BC, divide the Wheel of Time into 12 spokes. The most continuous chronological measurement in the world is the Chinese lunar calendar, its instigation credited before 2600 BC to the reign of Huáng Dì, the Yellow Emperor, during which the 12 half tones of the chromatic musical scale were also first conceived. This Chinese year is roughly the Western 12 months, and every 12th year is represented by the same animal, hence the zodiac (from Greek: 'animal carving'). The Western zodiac stems from the 12 principal constellations through which the sun seems to travel.

About 4,000 years ago, Jacob was renamed Israel ('fought with God') by divine decree, after which his 12 sons begat 12 tribes – the Israelites. There were the 12 original disciples of Jesus who became the 12 leaders (apostles) of the new Christian religion in Jerusalem, which covered an area of 12,000 furlongs [Rev.21.16]. This incorporated 12 foundation stones in which were embedded 12 different precious stones [Rev.21.19–20], and 12 gates guarded by 12 angels [Rev.21.12] – symbolism is sometimes all! In Revelation [12.1], the final victory of God over the Devil is preceded by the appearance in the heavens of a woman cloaked in the sun with a halo of 12 stars. No wonder that 12 is linked to perfection and Heaven.

Around 500 BC, the Greek Pythagoreans associated numbers in general with mystical portent. In ancient Greek mythology, the 12 major gods and goddesses, including Zeus the first and foremost, lived on Mount Olympus. Millennia later, the American traveller and poetess Eunice Tietjens (1884-1944) felt that *The Most-Sacred Mountain* (Tàishān) consisted of space 'and the twelve clean winds of heaven'. Gods and mountains have been linked since the beginning: China has 9 sacred mountains.

> Great things are done when Men & Mountains meet
> This is not Done by jostling in the street
> William Blake,
> *Satiric verses and epigrams*

The earliest hieroglyphics that survive from ancient Egypt reveal that for a thousand years from 3200 BC Egyptians believed in 9 gods, including Isis and Osiris: they are referred to as the Great Ennead (Greek *ennéa* = 9). In ancient China, the expression for a wise, open-hearted man was one who had '9 openings in his heart'. Early Hàn Dynasty thinking held that there were '9 fields of heaven'. In Korea during the 9th century AD, Sŏn Buddhism was established using the 9 traditions as its basis, derived from the 9 mountains. Tibetan Buddhists advocate the 9 *yāna* ('ways') of progress in life, of which Dzogchen (Great Perfection) is the foremost. The Catholic Church prays for 9 days during the *novena* (Latin

21-13

novem = 9). Aside from Allah, Muslims have 99 names with which to praise the attributes of God, each depicting aspects of His perfection. They recite 99 supplications in their *subha* litany. In south-west India, the dance-drama *kathākali* uses symbolic body movements, the same principle as in Chinese opera, to portray the 9 basic emotions of life. The Vaisheshika branch of Hinduism, initiated in the 6th century BC, believes that the universe consists of 9 key substances, including Space and Time. By itself, 9 *is* the last pure number in the decimal universe – all later ones are composites of earlier ones.

On the ceiling of the Vatican's Sistine Chapel, Michelangelo chose to portray 12 alternating male and female prophets encompassing 9 episodes from the Book of Genesis. The ancient Chinese believed in the Supreme Sovereigns, of which 12 were from heaven and 9 were human. In the Zhōu Dynasty [c.1050–221 BC], a geometric layout of the universe included the 'Nine Mansions' of earth. So 12 × 9 is a symbol of Heaven and Earth. In many cultures throughout the world, particularly in the East, odd numbers are associated with the male, and vice versa: so 12 × 9 also stands for 'feminine by masculine'.

In Asia, the two numbers multiplied together form one of pole significance. There are 108 Hindu names for the most holy River Ganges. In the same religion, a major incarnation of Vishnu, one of the three foremost gods in the universe, is Rama – the hero of Ramayana. His half-brother, Bharata, recognises 108 stances in his Natya Shastra[1], which sets out how humans should behave and how the divine spectacularly materializes. In Buddhism, 12 × 9 is the epitome of the Divine: as pointed out next to the 108 steps [chapter 7], 108 represents perfection and everything. Therefore to me 12 × 9 means God.

So the title of this essay, 12 × 9, is a synonym for God, perfection, and everything in the universe.

★ ★ ★

SYNCHRONISM OF 12 x 9 WITH THIS BOOK

This book has a synergy with 12 × 9 that I suggest, reader, cannot be dismissed as an irrelevant coincidence. Before embarking on the writing, I spent weeks deciding on the structure and layout, examining photographic books to determine the ideal size. Being educated before centimetres became established, I tend to think in inches. Those with pages over 13″ tall were cumbersome to handle and lacked intimacy, particularly when reading in bed. Those under 11″ over-restricted the size and thus impact of photographs. 12″ seemed the perfect compromise. The size of a mounted slide transparency measures 1.375 × 0.9375 inches, which magnified to the envisaged maximum of 12″ on one side corresponded to 8.18″ on the other – spacious for large vertical shots. Because of the sheer number of photographs to be included, I felt it would be advisable to accommodate two horizontal ones on a page, as large as possible. To fit, therefore, each would be a maximum 6″ in height: simple arithmetic deemed these would be a width of 8.8″. Substantial books with pages 10″ wide or more were overly bulky and weighty. Hence all these considerations pointed to a width of 9″ being sensible.

So, to the nearest inch, the pages *are* 12 × 9. If you're Thomas, measure them inside. This is not a standard size in the printing business.

[1] source: *Homage to Khajuraho* [Marg Publications (Bombay) 1962], article by Charles Fabri, p. 6

That is only the foundation. This chapter joins chapters 12 and 9 and one other in having the names of sacred mountains as their titles. Chapter 12 describes what God in the form of the Eagle is feeling, emanating from the Bed of God photographs on top of Huángshān – the true inspiration for the Chinese character of 'mountain'. Chapter 9 delivers the sunrise – the appearance of God – on Tàishān, the Mountain of Three Heavens, and incorporates examples of *living with God*. These matters were planned well before I saw connections with 12 × 9.

Traditionally, the half-title of a book is on page 1, and I instinctively wished to place the Korean character for *jong* with its Chinese equivalent prominently on their own page immediately before chapter one began. After laying out the contents, map, preface, etc., they fell on page 12, a highly significant conjunction for me.

Is it mere chance that in chapter 4 the word PEACE, on its own in a sea of blue to define God, is on page... 108? It was not wedged there by the author. Indeed, according to the initial plan, the single word was on 99 – about which I was delighted. Later additions however conveyed it beyond, and I resigned myself to the incidence not taking place. Two years on, the number of words had risen sufficiently to necessitate an expanded layout. As I thumbed through the folios after completion, a particular piece of music by Rodrigo – one intimately associated with the Cheju incident – sounded on the radio. I pricked up my ears in case this was a message, as I always do with these coincidences, and a minute later held my breath as PEACE seemed it would coincide on the approaching page 108. But it fell short by two, and I was temporarily foxed. However, when the book's designer became involved, further modifications arose organically and the 108 'coincidence' was the final result.

It is the apt number. For that page has nothing to do with me or mankind (9), but is about God (108). And that drum-banging coincidence has nothing to do with chance.

21-14

21-15

The photograph taken on the Sunrise Mountain of myself wearing the yellow Peace jacket, bestowed by Grand Old Pa, is the 12th one of chapter 9. You can trust me by now that it was not manipulated into that position – it transpired that way.

Photo *12-9* is of the porters painfully and laboriously climbing the steps to Huángshān: *12-9 is* of the steps to the Bed of God.

Is it just coincidence that the highest summit of Éméishān is officially 3,099 metres? That not only contains a double 9, but adding the first three numbers creates 12 with 9 remaining.

Is it merely coincidence that in chapter six, as the text is about to discuss the connection between God and evil, the music entitled *evil* is track... 12? Ignore it if you like, but might not that indicate something? The connection is that although the particular incident that sparked the deliberations concerned my own evil, I am part of God as everyone and everything is. Consequently that evil is also part of God's problem.

The number 9 threads through this book like blood in a body. In connection with the sacred, it appears in the text over fifty times in Book One alone. They were not forced there but kept emerging out of Chinese history, or the story.

When designing the page layout, metric measurements were inevitably used. After deciding on margin widths and two equal columns per standard page, the width for each column came to 9 cm, which is the case. Of course, if the book's designer had reasons to recommend modifying the size, structure, layout, and content of the pages, photographs and music mentioned, then the above paragraphs wouldn't exist.

Two more examples: this Book Two's track 9 is about the earthquake, and if God was not involved in that, I don't know when S/he was. Track 12? That is about to take place: it is the start of the retrospective – a summation in photographs and music of the whole book. And what is this book primarily about?

Basically, God.

★ ★ ★

NUMBERS AND COINCIDENCES

With '9' appearing in the Cheju sentence, when it, 12 or 108 arises in whatever circumstances, I know it might be confirmation that the direction I'm heading is the correct one. However, the message contained is often not the one expected. Attempting to attract a publisher for this book, I wrote to a well-known one who did not reply for seven months. Normally an author would not wait that long before contacting others, but a coincidence stopped me from doing so. I spotted and purchased that publisher's new CD Rom that proudly trumpeted '108 years' in business, with the number 108 emblazoned on the accompanying packaging. I was convinced my search had ended! When the 'no' letter eventually arrived, I thought seriously about why that 108 signal had apparently let me down. It hadn't. A travel friend had recently been reading the early draft of Book One, and he opened my eyes to some significant inadequacies in the writing. So I ceased contacting further publishers for some time until revisions were complete. Subsequent publishers turned down the project because of the cost of printing the huge number of colour photographs, but the delay had allowed the necessary breathing space to raise the standard of writing.

> I have lived to thank God
> that all my prayers have not been answered.
> Jean Ingelow
> (1820–1897), English poet

With the Cheju sentence comprising 16 words, and in ancient Chinese belief there being 16 Heavens, that number occasionally carries a message for me. The King James Holy Bible given by my parents on Confirmation day in my early teens is not a book I had read much since. When about to consult it for Part Three of this book, I noticed a slip inserted at the title page. About to discard it, I was pulled up short by the number 16 writ large. That the number 16 (representing God's words to me) should be at the beginning of a book full of God's words was a calm and calming sign: keep trusting. Beside the number 16 were the words: 'Please return this slip if there is any cause for complaint'. Had my life *really* been cause for complaint, despite the occasional enforced pain?

I reinserted the slip in its initial page. I wouldn't dare jettison it, sending it back to its Maker as a complaint.

The Maker has also assisted with money. After 9 years of travel and working abroad, I needed a quiet, inspiring home in the UK in which to write this book. One seemed ideal, and I fell in love with it. Adding all related purchasing and relocation expenses to its cost, plus living expenses for the following months until further income would be available, came to... £108,000. That number seemed to contain a message! However, my assets were many thousands short. No bank would lend since I was not earning while writing, and relations could not oblige. Only one solution remained: I had never prayed for money before, but with a haven necessary for concentrated writing, I beseeched God to provide the outstanding £9,000 required to procure the house – a substantial amount. I promised to pass it on to charity as soon as I could.

The next morning, what should pop through the letterbox but a cheque – an extra £7,500. A unit trust that had not increased in value for years had unexpectedly profited that amount in one year! My brother was able to scrape the barrel and raise the difference, and I was able to acquire the house.

After five months of writing in usually the only heated room to save on costs, my reserves dwindled to a final £28: I was about to ask friends and family for food parcels! Yet I was not concerned – I trusted and had faith. Work and income came to the rescue the next day onwards, and I was able not only to continue writing, but also to return the £9,000 to a developing-world charity. It was not mine in the first place – only on loan, on trust.

> You cannot have a need I cannot supply. A flower or one thousand pounds – one is no more difficult than the other.
> *God Calling* (p. 77)
> First published in 1935, this is a book of words that the two anonymous authors claimed came directly from God day after day through meditation over a period of time.

Two months before moving into my new home, but long after I had chosen the title of this essay, the previous occupant informed me of its telephone number, enabling forthcoming change of address details to be dispatched. A few days before the move, he casually revealed he was retaining the number after all, transferring it to his new residence. I was mildly miffed at the Amoeba obliging me to inform everybody of a revised number! The telephone company issued a replacement that, after the area code, was and remains 390351. Can you discern a pertinent attribute of that number?

For the purposes of remembering and speaking any six-figure telephone number, one instinctively divides it into two equal parts: in this case 390 and 351. The extraordinary quirk is that the first three digits add up to 12, while the second add up to 9. Hence my telephone number *is* 12 by 9.

This book had to appear under the auspices of a new publishing name. Lists of potential ones were concocted and all rejected, before 'Pagoda Publishing' came into my mind, which seemed perfect for its Asian associations.

Just before Book One was printed a year later, I realised that Pagoda has the word 'god' incorporated in it. Additionally, Pa-God-Da has an affinity with Grand Old Pa, my nickname for God instigated by the whiskey coincidence. Also Dà in Chinese, as in Dàlī, means Big or Grand. As icing on this cake of coincidences, *Pagoda* comes from a Sanskrit word meaning *Divine Female*.

What is notable in these instances is not only their evidence for coincidences being purposely induced. Sure, the odds against those that have happened to me are unequivocal – including that, after Peace being my supreme impression of God, and thus my most significant English word, Peace was subsequently the brand name of the staples I was handling in panic, and Peace was the logo on the jacket I sorely needed. Additionally, my middle name is Geoffrey, which means the 'Peace of God'. The further import is that, with the Cheju event confirming that the God of Peace exists, it is therefore S/he who instigated or ordered those Peace 'coincidences' and the others, and is thus involved in everyone's coincidences.

Once one has accepted that amazing ones are not a matter of chance but could be or are signals, then the smaller ones could also be signs, indeed are liable to be so. Even if such flagrant coincidences have not happened to you, reader, those less dramatic ones that have could be there for a purpose. In any case, who hasn't experienced heart-stopping and thought-provoking coincidences in their lives? Think back.

Concerning numbers, the actual one communicating is not significant by itself – it could be any. An acquaintance of mine swears by the number 8 as the divine flag. It is the *repetition* of a certain set that makes it a signal personal to you, and in Amoebic terms, that signature is simple to arrange. What is important is the message being conveyed. In my case, the choice of numbers by the Amoeba was because of their association with China, where S/he had already communicated with the people there over millennia using those same sacred numbers, the Chinese as a result associating them with the Divine. If it happens to you, whatever the number, it will be a specific language between you and God.

Fate is not necessarily a one-way ticket. To receive messages is a matter of listening to these coincidences. Everyone recognises them – if you don't already, how about taking the next step and acting on them?

★ ★ ★

THE PURPOSE OF SUFFERING

If you have a knot, you must undo it before you die.
a Korean friend

Just one step at a time with Me.
God Calling (p. 57)

The question: why should the *good* side of God wish to inflict suffering?

As C.S. Lewis points out:

> Pain as God's megaphone is a terrible instrument; it may lead to final and unrepented rebellion. But it gives the only opportunity the bad man can have for amendment.
> The Problem of Pain (p. 76)

By 'bad man', he means all of us. Because our individual shadow hides so insidiously, it is easy to become stuck at a level for years, decades, even a lifetime without our weaknesses being tackled. That is why artists sometimes do not burgeon beyond a certain level and run out of steam: you cannot develop your music, if you haven't developed as a person. One can progress through everyday experience, but that is limited compared to the personal growth that arises out of a crisis in life.

21-16

A prerequisite of renewal is pain. Virtually the only effective way to advance is to experience suffering; the spiritual destination we crave and need will not be reached otherwise. Pain leads to a particular knowledge of self, and that is not gained via other means. That is harsh, but it is reality – like a desert.

The value of pain has received systematic support. In 1996 at the University of Carolina, three studies of 2,000 people who had experienced major painful events – bereavement, breakdown, etc. – found that 95% reckoned they had acquired long-term insights about important matters, and most deemed the experience had been beneficial.

The French composer Charles Tournemire (1870–1939), in his desolate distress on the death of his wife in 1920, finally knew 'le sens divin de la douleur, niant à jamais la mort' – 'the divine sense of pain, forever denying death'. Actually the word *sens* is a subtle one with deeper meanings that utilise two whole columns in a sizeable dictionary. It can mean awareness, significance, and moral sense.

Man was made for Joy & Woe
And when this we rightly know
Thro the World we safely go

Every Tear from Every Eye
Becomes a Babe in Eternity.
Auguries of Innocence,
William Blake

Crucially, suffering can teach us about our own evils, thus hopefully we will act to overcome them. Elihu was right: God is using suffering to combat evil, and it saves us.

That gives hope, because therein lies a logical basis to trust God when S/he injects pain. We as humans can undertake those four steps to rid evil in ourselves, and succeed. From my recent experiences, the first three can certainly be achieved. The last is more difficult! I believe it is possible, although for most of us not in this lifetime.

If we can achieve it, God will have less evil to eliminate in the universe – and if the universe by amoebic extension is H/his body, then in H/himself. The more we try to defeat all forms of evil, however small, the more the Supreme Being can succeed in solving the

21-17

The purpose is to assail evil by instilling searing yet controlled bursts of pain, as inoculations use a limited amount of a virus to defeat a disease. In that way we are alerted to, and become conscious of our own evil. The opportunity is thereby afforded to rid ourselves of it.

The overcoming of evil must inevitably require several steps; I suggest the principal ones are Recognition, Restraint, Reduction and Rejection.
chapter 6

Supreme Paradox. Indeed it is the small forms that we individually *can* defeat. The large is destroyed by eliminating its constituent parts, one by one, step by step.

What was the vision I was confronted with during the Rift when it opened momentarily? That of the Creator experiencing and having experienced suffering, the type of sorrow of a parent killing h/his child – for the child's good in an impossible situation. It was the soul-wounded silent cry of a hounded animal fighting relentlessly without let-up since the Beginning, against the onward March of Evil.

> Can you hold on in My strength? I need you more than you need Me.
>
> *God Calling* (p. 81)

been in the camera for over a month, was it merely a coincidence that there was no further photographic rift after the Rift had finally appeared and disappeared?

The feeling from the Rift was simultaneously beyond suffering, revealing a calmness, all passion spent: the peace of acceptance – the very definition of a God. Yet within those quality dimensions, there was a crying need for help.

That is what I detected anyway, to the best of my ability.

God was crying for help. S/he *needs* our aid to rid H/him of H/her predicament. The signs are flashing 'Help-help' by bombarding us with Joy followed by bloody Pain, then more Pain, followed by Joy. That mixture was without doubt what was thrown at me the past years. It was not subtle, but obvious: bang-bang Joy-Pain, bang-bang Help-Help. What clearer SOS can there be in the circumstances?

The rift in my camera? The last one was *19-9*, the black blank, the Rift in a universal Black Hole. Having

NEUTERING SUFFERING

The New Testament reflects that God inflicted sufficient sufferings on Jesus to make him perfect [Heb.2.10]. Referring to that path being a possible destiny for all of us, C.S. Lewis went so far, but then reached a wall:

> The old Christian doctrine of being made "perfect through suffering" is not incredible. To prove it palatable is beyond my design.
> *The Problem of Pain* (p. 84)

I think there *is* a way to make it palatable, at least to obviate it so that it is no longer painful. This is an example of a seemingly unsolvable problem – the sort that dogs you much of your life, and for most people remains unsolved until they die.

How do you solve an unsolvable problem?

Easy.

You accept it so much as part of you and your life… that the problem dissolves. It ceases to *be* a problem. It is still there, but it is not a problem anymore.

That is encapsulated in the instinctive philosophy uttered by a Dane with whom, while backpacking in New Zealand, I was briefly discussing the topic of Life's problems. Noting my dismissive, light-hearted treatment of my own ("Mine are minuscule in comparison to others"), he commented in commendably straightforward English:

"If you can laugh at your problems, maybe you don't have problems.

That is not the same as ignoring the unsolvable problem; on the contrary it is facing it, coming to terms with and accepting it so much, absorbing its terrible power completely, that one turns it into something else – something positive. Faced and accepted. This is the very source of *Peace*.

> Life with Me is not immunity *from* difficulties, but peace *in* difficulties. My guidance is often by *shut* doors.
> *God Calling* (p. 23)

> Don't succumb to obstacles and tiny difficulties. These are often only ego's childish emotions.
> Sogyal Rinpoche, *The Tibetan Book of Living and Dying* (p. 132)

The solution to suffering relies absolutely on reaching that plateau of neutering pain for the first time. Once that giant step has been achieved, the remarkable consequence is that the next time it strikes, *it doesn't seem like pain*. I have encountered that sensation knowingly, and it empowered me: I felt more of a person in control. It was a breakthrough experience, and the pain was overcome.

> Do not be afraid of the sufferings to come.
> Jesus, through John [Rev.2.10]

> The stoic, silent *acceptance of pain* brings tears to the eyes of every visitor to a Chinese military hospital.
> chapter 10 (O.M. Green)

> Once suffering is completely accepted, it ceases in a sense to be suffering.
> M. Scott Peck, *The Road Less Travelled* (p. 78)

God requires us to become so used to suffering that it no longer causes us to suffer. The idea is not merely that we *learn* from it, but that our minds *cease to suffer* from it – it is a transfiguration. One can be in harmony even with disunity: that liberation is called acceptance. Pain is controlled and conquered. And out of acceptance comes peace.

> It is by overcoming obstacles that man develops those qualities he needs.
> G.I. Gurdjieff, quoted by P.D. Ouspensky, *In Search of the Miraculous* (p. 58)

21-18

> *The* overcoming *is never the overcoming of the one who troubled you, but the overcoming of the weaknesses and wrong in your own nature, aroused by such a one.*
>
> *No matter* who *frets you or what, yours is the task to stop all else until absolute calm comes.*
>
> *God Calling* (pp. 172/3 & 37)

The difficulty lies in sustaining that thought pattern so it doesn't darken into being a problem again. Like Enlightenment, and Love, it is not permanent – the key is in re-finding it: an Ultimate Eternal Paradox.

> Do what you will this Lifes a fiction
> And is made up of Contradiction
>
> William Blake,
> *Satiric verses and epigrams*

A doubt will arise through this enforced pain: Do I like God? An essential step is at times *not* to like God. If you have only ever liked God, or the question has never occurred to you, then something in your future will cause you to ask and answer it in the negative. The stakes are too high for that not to happen. Having braced yourself for it, if you accept it with grace then you are a better person than this book's author who didn't.

> "The main thing, when you are tortured, is to remain calm."
>
> The Korean spoke quietly and in a matter-of-fact way....
>
> "Do not struggle. Do not fight.... Keep absolutely still; it is easier to endure it in this way."
>
> *Korea's Fight for Freedom*
> [q.v. chapter 10]

Onto the next step: the solution to the ultimate questions. Why does Evil exist in the first place – what is its origin? What was wrong with God's original 'good' Creation *without* any evil?

THE ANSWER TO JOB

Dàlī's very name means the Big Reason – that can only be a siren call to attention! What was the Rift about? What was the Big Reason for the crisis at Dàlī? Within that crisis *must* be the answers to the big questions.

Based on the personal circumstances of the Rift at Dàlī, the reason was because: "God was Perfect, and is not perfect". If that sounds like an inexplicable paradox, and to some it will be a preposterous one, there are two things to be said. First, I prayed simply yet intensely to God for enlightenment on that crisis a year later – and that was the answer that came through. Second, the paradox can be unravelled, as follows.

The events strewn in my path and described in these volumes have been pointing to one end: the purpose of all our lives. To reveal that, consider what the crucial spiritual difference is between a baby and an adult. Surely it must be that the first has *innocence* through *ignorance*. If one accepts that virtually all babies are born without evil, sin, shadow, negativity, badness or any attributes related to them, then they are innocently perfect.

With that in mind, providing the big answers requires starting at the Beginning.

The original Eden-esque paradise is common to a host of ancient cultures and peoples – Peruvians, Greeks, Egyptians, Zoroastrians, the Mbuti Pygmies, Mexicans, Tibetans, the Chinese (during the Yellow Emperor's reign), etc. – as well as being related in Genesis and the Qur'an. If these myths that share a common thread stem even in a small way from truth (and why not?), they indicate that the original adult humans were also perfect. If the Creator's purpose was to bestow the Gift of the Joy of Life, as well as receiving the joys of being a parent, it would be logical to create an Eden with perfect humans who partook of that exciting joy without complications. Further, God must have been Perfect H/himself to produce perfect children 'in H/his own image'.

Alas, there is an inherent problem with that initial Creation. The humans are *innocently* perfect.

After a while, I guess, one of them discovered the advantages of selfishness – keeping two apples, while offering another to someone else. That would be an innocent chance event – perhaps the other had only one hand free. There being plenty of other apples in the vicinity was immaterial. Maybe it was done for a laugh; nevertheless, when eaten there was double the nectar, double the delight. An advantage was gained, and it tasted good – nothing wrong with that surely. Yet at that moment, the human was already fatally off the pointed peak of perfection. The next time it was perhaps done *with* a laugh. Once selfishness has popped into existence as if from nothing, then the virus spreads rampantly, and innocents are corrupted by the dirty acorns of others: evil is born.

What I am suggesting is that evil is an inevitable by-product of life, even if the beginning consists of total goodness.

> For in the self good and evil are indeed closer than identical twins!
>
> C.G. Jung[1]

> I detect then a law: that when I wish to do good, I achieve only evil.
>
> St. Paul [Rom.7.21];
> author's translation

The Garden of Eden – created to give us Supreme Joy – was erroneous. The Big Paradox again. There in the Beginning, the window separating good from evil opened only a crack. It was enough: over time, a hurricane raged in, and the massacre was almighty in proportion.

We were total goodness at one stage – innocent perfection. If we were in the 'image' of God, there must nevertheless have been a difference: the Creator could not have been a 'baby' in order to create. God therefore was Perfect in a superior way – with *knowledge* or *consciousness*. We ourselves could not have been born with conscious perfection since we had no experience, knowledge, and wisdom. To give life to Adam and Eve complete with a false set of experiences would have been a lie. The beginning of life *has* to be innocent.

What evil achieves is the corruption of innocence. And it begins and began spontaneously.

---

[1] *Introduction to the religious and psychological problems of alchemy* (para 24), from *Collected Works of C.G. Jung, Vol. 12: Psychology and Alchemy* [© 1968 by Princeton University Press]

If the Amoeba theory has some truth (God is Everything), then those initial humans were part of God physically. When evil was born within humans – the Fall through selfishness – it infiltrated God internally. How do you stop a virus in your body once it has been introduced? You cannot easily cut it away. Original sin thereby is not only the Christian concept of alienation from God: in addition, it is an *inescapable part of God*.

As corruption became more and more widespread, the remaining innocents were inoculated by the evil around them, and this was compounded manifoldly and exponentially by their natural instinct to survive – the ultimate selfishness. Meanwhile, the Amoeba was being corrupted internally with evil. At some point, that Evil cannot be contained – it will, and did, and does lash out.

Divine salvation therefore becomes only possible if humans are cognisant of their own evil, and encouraged to rid themselves of it. The salvation of God is a real issue, a *burning* problem for everyone, otherwise we will continue blazing in a cesspool of evil on this Hell, otherwise called Earth (as the Chinese know), which in a former lifetime was known as Eden.

Hence God's urgent necessity to alert us to this most crucial of all problems. S/he cannot force us, since free will and substantial freedom from the Divinity is a supreme, sovereign right – we are not to be automatons. If we are to keep that freedom, and be properly alive, drastic measures are required to grab our attention concerning evil: no less than God's use of suffering. That is H/his terrible but necessary alarm bell. The only alternative is to demolish us all – the Flood, Sodom and Gomorrah, Babylon – and try again. How many times has God done so, I wonder? If we do not deal with our evil, will S/he do so again – *another* Last Judgement? All it would take would be a collision with a meteorite a mere ten kilometres across to annihilate every human on this planet. How many species has S/he destroyed before, along with the dinosaurs? Evidently, creating a perfect universe is not easy, even for God.

> When the Lord saw how great was the wickedness of human beings on earth, ...he bitterly regretted that he had made mankind on earth. He said, 'I shall wipe off the face of the earth this human race which I have created – yes, man and beast, creeping things and birds. I regret that I ever made them.'
>
> Genesis 6.5–7

If we succeed in ridding ourselves of evil, what is the end result? Surely that is perfection again. The important word in this context is *again*: to rediscover what we once were, with the crucial difference that this time it is *knowingly* perfect.

Conscious perfection knows what evil is, and prevents it from re-infecting h/himself internally. Furthermore, evil approaching from outside rebounds off the ring of steel that *is* conscious perfection. Only *knowledgeable* perfection can be aware of, and avoid both the slippery slope of evil within, and without.

Tibetan Buddhists also believe it is not a matter of striving, as regaining what was already in us: 'Dzogchen: the *already* self-perfected state of our primordial nature' [*The Tibetan Book of Living and Dying*, p. 151]. That ties in with babies born without evil. The difference I am advocating is that regaining perfection results in a conscious one, which enables us to abide in that state and not slide off it again. So the goal is not primordial perfection (one existing at the beginning), but one that exists at the end, and will do so for ever – the immovable, crowning *ultimate* perfection.

This then is the answer to Job! For thousands of years, Jews, Christians and others have been mystified and aghast at God's behaviour on the basis that Job was a blameless person. Job was good, to the level of even being perfect. But the perfection was innocent – ignorant of the Message, ignorant of the purpose of God. God *had* to attack H/his favourite human – the perfect innocent – and did so in person (God's only appearance on earth as H/himself) so that Job, compelled to think about Divinity and Life, would hopefully grasp the answer to the riddle of the Message. That combined with his innocent perfection would result in Job becoming *consciously* perfect. The Book of Job of course is a story, and incomplete: did he later successfully unravel the Message?

> Love... demands the perfecting of the beloved....
> Love is more sensitive than hatred itself to every blemish in the beloved.
>
> C.S. Lewis,
> *The Problem of Pain* (p. 37)

So God demands us to become consciously perfect. To what end?

An impossible question to answer?

No. The answer to the most pressing question concerning all of us: what is the purpose of our lives? It is to *become* a god/goddess. Knowingly. We are rehearsing for the day when in full enlightenment we join the Amoeba; that is when we become a part of God – when we become one with God.

However, that is not the answer to the most important question of all – the Meaning of Life – because it does not state the purpose of God.

The conundrum of what is the purpose of God might seem the ultimate unanswerable question, at least until the next parcel of lifetimes. But...

What is the Message?

21-19

223

12 × 9

Evil inevitably arises out of innocence and ignorance, ignited and fuelled by selfishness. As enumerated in chapter 10 and elsewhere, Religion in the name of 'God', and so inevitably involving the participation of God, is one of the biggest sources of evil of any kind. As illustrated by first-hand experience (the Rift, the earthquake), pain can be God's will. Therefore God *wants* some evil to befall, including that derived from religion, in order for us to suffer – S/he advocates it! The Goodness in God will not, and so cannot put a stop to the remainder, because it is our free will. Taken together, this means that some universal evil is part of the Good God's *purpose*. Its use is both a clarion call, and the one method of transfiguring innocence into conscious perfection, so that we never suffer from spontaneous evil again. As more of us attain conscious perfection, Evil will thereby be reduced to the point of elimination, and never reappear.

Meanwhile, until that is achieved, both the good and evil in us are part of and in the universe. If God is that universe, then in some measure we and other species constitute God. So in addition, accumulated evil is part of God's character. Inevitably, this side – the Devil within – will lash out. Some universal evil is therefore part of God's *nature*.

The only way for God to return to being pure Goodness is, once more, for the source of that evil – us and others – to achieve 100% goodness again: but this time to become knowingly perfect, so that evil never returns.

The paradox is that the only way for us to become *knowingly* perfect is to be subjected to evil!

I strongly believe God's long-term goal is paradise for all, but the only route to that place is to journey through medium to long-term suffering caused by evil.

The above is the Meaning of Life.

* * *

Any declaration of the universal meaning of life must tackle and include God's nature and God's purpose – as well as our own and other species' individual ones – otherwise it does not cover everything. I believe the definition in the previous column does both. It is not theoretical. It arises directly out of the experiences *forced* on me: knowing God exists (Cheju), who offers Supreme Joy (see chapter 7), meeting evil (Sīmǎtái), suffering instigated by God (the Rift), and the two types of perfection (see page 228). As far as God containing Evil, that is implied by the "God was Perfect, and is not" answer to my prayer, and by observations confirmed by the world's cultures throughout history that through connections God is Everything.

Creation was flawed In the Beginning: we were offered the Joys of Paradise and were made with free will, which led to selfishness and the instinct to survive, and the spontaneous birth of evil. The first two cannot exist without the last – unless those with free will consciously choose to abandon selfishness.

Not surprisingly, God is there beside us when we suffer: the sympathy is intimate. God sometimes causes that very suffering, and wishes it could be any other way. But it cannot.

The feeling I witnessed at the moment of the Rift confirms that. It was of a God intimately resonating with and *taking onto H/himself* the suffering being induced by H/himself.

The previous two paragraphs – that is the Message.

21-20

Buddhism agrees entirely with the above's *individual* purpose in living. Nirvana is the extinguishing of the self, leading to the end of suffering. How observant that is! Selflessness is the key. Evil is inevitable as long as individuals are concerned for themselves. Selfishness is the prime cause of suffering.

In contrast, selflessness is an *active* commodity – it automatically makes you help others; again, it is a verb not a noun.

In his final book, the Japanese philosopher Nishida Kitarō (1870–1945) understood the role of selflessness in a universal context. 'Through the death of the self, we encounter the absolute God'. This is the "Great Death". His follower Nishitani Keiji (1900–1990) of the Kyoto School of Philosophy also propounded the Great Death of the self, resulting in a new universe.

A century after the Prophet Muhammad, a devout woman in Iraq called Rābi'a al-'Adawiyya (c.715–801) led the way to the ascetic beliefs of Sufism. While some of her dogmatic statements were in my opinion too extreme, nevertheless their basis was that to be at one with God required the elimination of the ego-self. The goal of a Sufi is to become a Perfect Person (*al-Insān al-Kāmil*).

Concerning the contention that evil is an inevitable and natural by-product of goodness, I have traced only one philosopher worldwide over the past three millennia to advocate anything close – the Chinese thinker Xúnzi in the 3rd century BC. To him, evil arose out of basic emotions and cravings. Two students of a pupil of his were Hán Fēi (c.280–c.233 BC, see chapter 4), who concluded that humans are primarily selfish in thought, and Lǐ Sī, later prime minister. That conclusion thereby inspired the First Emperor of Qín to his dictatorial slaughter – a prime example of intellectualism out of balance, not tempered by compassion.

Thinkers like Mèngzi (Mencius), who thought basic human nature is good, and Xúnzi, who thought it evil, are usually categorised in opposing camps. But to me they seem simultaneously correct – and the previous pages give the logical explanation behind the truth of that paradox.

★ ★ ★

GOD BENEFICENT AND OMNIPOTENT?

> In apprehension, how like the Gods.
> Shakespeare,
> *Hamlet*, Act II sc 2

It was not by chance that the feeling emanating from chapter 12's photographs for me was of a God suffering in the most intimate of places – the Bed of God. A suggested cause was 'facing in peace and calm the disaster of the Immortal not being Beneficent and Omnipotent'. The Eagle was down. God is indeed wounded by evil. If most of mankind is relying on you to stop the rot, thinking you are all good and all powerful, how do you reveal that the belief is unfounded – with its potentially dire consequences?

It was this stumbling block, and the observation of nature, that crushed Darwin's belief in any God – particularly the Christian one.

> I cannot persuade myself that a beneficent and omnipotent God would have designedly created the Ichneumonidae with the express intention of their feeding within the living bodies of caterpillars.
> letter to Asa Gray,
> 22 May 1860

What Darwin didn't and couldn't be allowed to see at that time is that there are logical as well as observational reasons to believe God may not be purely beneficent, and hence is not omnipotent. If God has been infected with evil, clearly there are occasions when the Good God's wishes and actions are thwarted and overwhelmed by the Devil within. By definition, the good side of the Almighty thereby is not omnipotent.

At the very least, since we and other species are endowed with a considerable degree of free will to step whichever way we wish, then an all-good God cannot exercise the option of being omnipotent without turning us into robots of flesh and blood. Neither can S/he be in control over any Devil without, who also has free will: according to the Bible, Satan was initially part of the Court of Heaven.

Even if God does not contain Evil, by normal standards S/he is not purely beneficent either: a person who continually inflicts severe pain in order for someone to learn is not usually considered to be benevolent. Indeed, as mentioned [chapters 10 & 19], it is perilously close to sadism. However, the Meaning of Life statement above indicates that when God inflicts suffering and allows evil to occur, it is often the *beneficent side* of God that is doing so – for the highest of reasons. In such ways, it is quite possible for paradoxes to exist without compromising the validity of either conflicting truth.

Thus it was befitting for Jesus to rebuke Peter for trying to save him from suffering: "Out of my sight, Satan; you are a stumbling block to me. You think as men think, not as God thinks" [Matt.16.23]. Peter was acting to reduce pain, as any good human would. But from a God's viewpoint that is narrow-minded. It is neither in God's long-term interest to subjugate evil or suffering in the short-term, nor is it in ours to have them magically whisked away, if we want to see them banished for ever. Hence it is because God *cannot* exercise H/his all-encompassing power, and may not actually *be* omnipotent, that S/he approves and advocates the use of evil and pain against us. There is no other way for us to reach Heaven – the land without evil.

For simplicity, the above Meaning of Life does not expand on other species and alien life forms, of which I suspect there are a multitude in this and other parallel universes, including spirits. They cannot be excluded: if they similarly contain good and evil, they contribute substantially to the Evil in God or the Devil. By not devouring other life forms either literally or figuratively, some animals seem the epitome of the perfect innocent – we can learn some aspects about perfection from them. Often they also suffer. Others are horribly insensitive and lacking in compassion. Personally, I bracket that under unconscious evil. Some may contain conscious evil. The previous Genesis quote indicates that the Almighty regretted making man *and beast, creeping things and birds*. We are not the only species with spontaneous evil caused by selfishness and free will. The difference with humans is that we seem more capable of becoming perfectly conscious, and consciously perfect.

I passionately believe God intends good to triumph over individual and universal evil. But S/he is not fully in control over life forms including us and any Devil, and does not have omnipotence over H/himself if S/he contains Evil. It all depends on us and other major life forms, given free will, to make the right decisions for that ideal situation eventually to return.

The possibility of God containing evil means S/he is not always a healthy entity with whom to become involved. The Almighty is no plaything, no two-a-penny dude. The climax of Cardinal Newman's *The Dream of Gerontius* is the protagonist meeting God face to face. As set to inspired music by Elgar, his reaction ("Take me away!") makes it clear that the reality of the Face of God is shockingly unacceptable to the Christian human. I know of an American woman who, when unexpectedly contacted by God, went terminally insane. That Korean who had an encounter with God [chapter 17] landed in hospital with sudden, otherwise inexplicable, mental problems. That the experience can flip one over was certainly a possibility with me, which I had consciously to resist. The solution lies in keeping both feet firmly planted on this earth. Literally, sow some vegetables, drink with your friends, talk to a baby, love your lover. That, and maintain a light humour. Hence, reader, if you do become directly involved, please be aware of the possible true nature of what you're dealing with, and keep grounded. Fortunately and paradoxically, usually S/he insists you do! Potatoes before God.

What is the connection between sin, pain and evil? The Christian view is that sin is evil committed only by humans, whereas pain can be inflicted either by us, which is usually the result of evil, or by God, in which case it does not stem from evil. I agree that there are at least two prime sources of suffering – one is the evil within humans and others, the other being the *goodness* in God (another might be the evil in God). Thus causing suffering is not necessarily the same as dispensing evil. Equating the two is a common confusion and mistake. The infamous Isaiah 45.7 passage in the King James Version, as quoted in chapter 19 to 'prove' that God is evil by H/his own admission ('I... create evil'), is a mistranslation! A more accurate rendition from the original Hebrew would be: 'I... create *suffering*'. This is an arch lesson in the perils of taking translations at face value – particularly those of various misleading Bibles[1]. The evil I thought I saw in God at Dàlī was only a personification of H/his needing to inflict pain – but it did not stem from evil. That is because I now know it was for the best.

---

[1] For unbiased accurate reporting in clear English, I recommend only *The Revised English Bible* (REB), or *The New Revised Standard Version* (NRSV). The King James (Authorised Version) still has tremendous inspirational value. Any Bible should only be read in conjunction with a reliable commentary informed by modern scholarship, such as *The Oxford Companion to the Bible*, in order to avoid some of the multiplicity of interpretational traps.

The website www.gospelcom.net/bible features thirteen English translations, and its first-class search engine facilitates comparing a passage in the different versions.

MODIFICATION TO THE AMOEBA THEORY AND MEANING OF LIFE

If the Amoeba theory has value, it suggests there are two sides to God's character, with the frightening possibility S/he sometimes inevitably succumbs and acts out the Devil within. Yet it is not possible to dismiss the tradition of God being totally one of Love etc., which has been felt by most if not all who have encountered H/his presence throughout millennia. There must be more than something in that perception.

That is my own experience as well. I have come to realise that the events leading up to and including Dàlī were essential for my growth. Crucially, judging from my physically being in touch with God's essence during the Cheju event, I did not detect the slightest intrinsic evil in H/his nature. The Epicness of that Peace was and is not of a temperament that can be artificially invented. Of course, S/he could have been suppressing the negative side and keeping it out of contact at the time. So despite my direct experience, it *still* boils down to a matter of trust and belief – as with any relationship.

So it is possible that God is 100% Good, after all. To allow for that, the Amoeba theory requires a modification: via the connections in Life, the evil aspects have bombarded God, who has parried them away from H/himself. They have instead congealed into a separate, and *so far* less powerful entity, the Devil. In which case, the universe's connections wire into two separate bodies. That would solve one paradox and be more in line with traditional concepts of a separate Devil, which have been current since the medieval ages. They were not really present in the Old Testament – but that may reflect the Devil having become stronger in that period, due to more evil having been generated.

The Devil would then be an entity that has formed amoeba-like out of the sum total of our evil, and others. Since It is sustained by our free will, God cannot destroy It without destroying us as well.

It doesn't matter to humans whether Amoeba A or Amoeba B is correct, or a combination of both (Amoeba C). The *effect* on us is the same. If B is the reality, the above Meaning of Life statement alters only in that our own and other species' reduction in evil would diminish the power and scope of the Devil. God, meanwhile, still cannot exercise omnipotence: not only does it remain our free will if we choose to feed the Devil, but God's power is partly stymied by the Devil's power. With this modification, there is our own evil that feeds that of the Devil, and God is not evil but uses it as a tool for us to become knowingly perfect, which in the process extinguishes the Devil. This scenario is a 'softer' version for those who cannot stomach the Full Amoeba of God directly containing Evil. However, it contradicts the answer to my prayer ("God was Perfect, and is not perfect").

Christianity has no doubt that Good will eventually triumph over Evil. As an optimist, I believe that as well, but in strict Amoeba theory terms it is naive to assume it is inevitable. On the contrary, if evil grows and grows, its cumulative viral power will begin to dominate and overwhelm the rest of the Body. The appalling possibility then is that the Devil, whether within or without, will be mightier than the Lord. If evil stems from humans having free will, we have a bigger responsibility than most of us realise!

> *It is man who can make Dào great, and not Dào that makes man great.*
>
> Lùn Yŭ

> Every one, therefore, must become divine, and of godlike beauty, before he can gaze upon a god, and the beautiful itself.
>
> Thomas Taylor (1758-1835), a Platonist

Whether God is all good or not, our individual purpose in life is still to become consciously perfect.

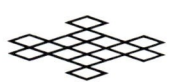

INNOCENCE AND PERFECTION

Even as adults, many of us are still babies. Unfortunately, the results of this innocence through ignorance can easily be the same as the result of direct evil. One example given in chapter 5 illustrates this. Most of Japan's 130 million people are oblivious of the devastating effect their profligate use of hardwood shuttering and habit of discarding hardwood chopsticks every day has on the peoples of Borneo and its rainforest resources. Those innocent actions have the same effect as if the Japanese personally went to Borneo to destroy the lives of the people and the rainforest.

Combine Innocence with Perfection in one entity, and it does not recognise itself as perfect. That is a particular and peculiar property: if s/he knew s/he was perfect, s/he wouldn't be innocent. Given beneficent surroundings, Innocent Perfection can exist independently without blemish for a long while. Yet it is of a precarious nature – so easily unbalanced by outside influences. As William Blake knew so well, Innocence is destroyed by experience – it *has* to be sacrificed, even more so if it is perfect. That is one of the saddest truths in the universe, of solemn, quiet, epic proportions. And if Fate dances to the tune of God, then God is the slayer and the saviour. God is the problem and the solution. That Paradox again.

Truth is a sword, not a feather duster. It cares not where it cuts – on the good or the bad, it confers no mercy. The only way to become knowingly perfect, and a *knowing* god/goddess, is through suffering incandescently – either through broken love, or through eating shit, or through God. It isn't enough to be a Lamb of God, a good innocent human, even though that state is often closest to God's original paradise.

It was no accident that Perfection in a human was the highest topic of the incidents during the 9 days at Cheju and the events God initiated in my path in the subsequent thirty months. Some of the people I met seemed to know precisely what perfection required.

One was the person attacked by God directly – the eighteen-month, every night bombardment [chapter 14].

Personally, I cannot imagine surviving such a thing. When I was party to it happening, it was painful to watch.

Because I was led to these people (by divinely-controlled fate), a picture formed of attributes of perfection in a human. It was the climactic summation of my time in Korea, and led directly to the realisation of the two types of perfection – conscious and innocent.

BUDDHA AND IGNORANCE

What do you suppose were the reported last words of the historical Buddha before he died?

They were, "Strive with your whole being to attain perfection".

Sogyal Rinpoche, who quotes the valediction in *The Tibetan Book of Living and Dying* (p. 359), reckons 'We are all potential buddhas' (p. 356), and advises this:

> You don't actually "become" a buddha, you simply cease, slowly, to be deluded. And being a buddha is not being some omnipotent spiritual superman. (p. 53)

The implication is that to be a buddha is to maximise our potential as a human being. Whatever religious or atheistic background we come from, you and I can and hopefully will become a 'buddha' too; after all, it only means one who is awakened with knowledge. The Lotus Sutra identifies three foremost enemies of truth: one is ignorance. Delusion through ignorance is labelled one of the Three Fires that must be extinguished ('nir' of nirvana), the other two being hatred and greed. A thousand years ago, the Japanese Buddhist monk Genshin (942–1017) held that enlightenment is recognising reality hidden by ignorance.

Hinduism is another religion that maintains that suffering is the result of ignorance (*avidyā*). Hindus believe that reincarnation and rebirth (*saṁsāra*), and their resultant suffering, continue until perfection is reached. The Hindu *moksha* is an attainment similar to the Buddhist *nirvana*, and the Yoga Sutras maintain that the world's evil arises from a comparable threesome of delusion (*moha*), anger (*krodha*), and greed (*lobha*) – the Three Gates to Hell.

The Four Noble Truths of the historical Buddha are often reported misleadingly oversimplified (e.g. 'Life is Suffering'). Perusing the words of his initial sermon at Sarnath's deer park, as handed down by the oral tradition (albeit in my case in translation), reveal them to be that (i) *key aspects* of our transient life involve suffering. (ii) These are caused either by the lusting after pleasure (pleasure *per se* is not claimed to be a culprit), or by other cravings that trigger further birth-to-death cycles. (iii) This suffering can be terminated by Rejection. (iv) The way to that Rejection is eightfold (they are listed – the Eightfold Path).

The Buddhist Pure Land is the land of perfection via the elimination of suffering. The events that have happened to me these past years support that, and lead to this: do I have the courage and the will to discard selfishness and evil in order to achieve perfection? The question applies to all.

CONFUCIUS

In China, Korea, and some other Asian societies, how one governs oneself is still influenced by Confucius' five core virtues: *rén, lǐ, yì, xìn, zhì*. They are benevolence, courtesy/protocol, duty/loyalty, trustworthiness, and wisdom. The first is considered the highest of these qualities, obtained through the practice of the second and third. In written Chinese, *rén* consists simply of the characters for 'two' and 'person', implying that benevolence arises from the meeting of one human being with another.

Whoever is continuously able to combine all five virtues is a *jūnzi*: a 'supreme person', completely developed – a perfect human. Although this was Confucius' ultimate goal, its purpose was to guide one's behaviour in the minutest of everyday details.

> *Wisdom means to find out one's own mistakes.*
> *Courage means the correction of those mistakes.*
> *Benevolence means to make no mistakes.*
> Chén Què (1604-1677),
> *The Blind's Words*

To make no mistakes – a high expectation! For me, benevolence is driven by *jong (qíng)*: it is without reason or profit. I am delighted that in Korean the abbreviated word for benevolent is *In* – my Korean name.

The influential Chinese philosopher Zhū Xī (1130–1200) chose Four Books out of the Confucian canon, believing in them ecstatically, and bluntly:

> If one does not read the *Great Learning* first, there is no way to... appreciate fully the subtleties of the *Analects* and the *Book of Mencius*.... If one is not [then] versed in the perfection of the *Doctrine of the Mean*,... how can one read the world's books or discuss the world's affairs?
> quoted in *Great Thinkers of the Eastern World* (p. 55)

Dà Xué, the *Great Learning*, contains Three Aims and Eight Steps, which advocate self-development through renewal. They exhort one to help others achieve that same goal.

The *Doctrine of the Mean* is the usual translation of *Zhōng Yōng*, or the 'Golden Mean'. It has also been rendered as 'The Unwobbling Pivot', which has a certain attraction! The ethics the book propounds boil down to a clear philosophy: be balanced every time, as a matter of course. It too believes that humans are in an indissoluble unity with heaven.

One Confucian concept is Filial Piety (*xiào*). If like me you haven't a clue what that means in English, let alone Chinese, it is the notion of showing love, respect and honour, not only between parents and offspring, but in various relationships, including government and people. One of the examples given is not ridding your body of mosquitoes, in case they transfer and bedevil your parents! Non-literal analogies are of course intended.

Love itself has one seldom-discussed property. The only reference to it in the arts that I am aware of is in a little-known Western opera by an obscure composer. The assertion forms its concluding moral:

> *Love returns when it is no longer possible.*

That is true for the following reason: Love may become displaced by unpleasant developments, evil and suffering to the extent that it seems destroyed; but if it doesn't return, it was never Love in the first place. That indeed holds great hope! How often in our lives has Love seemingly been dashed to pieces. Yet real Love *will* return. It was one of the extraordinary lessons of the Rift.

★ ★ ★

ANGER

This particular reaction displayed by most humans cannot be a constituent of the ultimate person. To Buddhists, Anger is one of the Three Poisons, while it is likened by the Chinese to the wind: sudden, unpredictable, elemental violence. However common, anger is evil; whenever one yields to the luxury of it, the Devil and our own devil become stronger. Whether it is expressed or contained within, it has to be faced, resolved, and by-passed eventually – a major step to attain. Is it really necessary? Isn't there a more effective response? Does it achieve anything positive?

It certainly isn't necessary: without it, one can still deliver one's firm objections to another's behaviour and actions in a way which tends to change that person's mind sooner and easier than if they come wrapped within a shroud of rage. It is called appealing to reason. In contrast, extremism begets extremism. An extremist view or response often triggers one in the opposite direction.

The paradox is that, like any evil, it is a positive tool *if* it results in a reduction of evil. Anger *can* be positive only if one breaks through it to the other side, that of greater understanding of oneself, and of the nature of life. In the process, anger is destroyed. Anger is a stage to go through; it is inadvisable to be enmeshed in it and bitter for years, or the rest of one's life. God uses anger as a tool: by making me angry at Dàlǐ, boy, did S/he get my attention!

> The wonderful thing about saints is that they were human. They lost their tempers, scolded God, were egotistical or testy or impatient in their turns, made mistakes and regretted them. Still they went on doggedly blundering toward heaven.
> Phyllis McGinley (1905–1978),
> American author

Any one who has railed against the gods, Life or Fate – which is surely all of us – has the potential to be a saint.

How to by-pass anger? Recognition, Restraint, Reduction and Rejection – that will work with all evils. Observing its damaging effects in others again enables one to recognise it in oneself.

> *Anger locks a man in his own house.*
> Noah benShea,
> *Jacob the Baker* (p. 28)

When someone activates the familiar feel of one's ire rising, therein lies an opportunity to sever it at source, and instead appeal to that person's sense and humanity. It becomes an invitation to recognise and understand the limitations of the person who gave you pain and aroused your anger. A neat technique is to hear someone's anger against a third party, and summarise it transformed into a quietly positive quality.

Having been transformed, past anger needs to be detached, as do all experiences:

> He who binds to himself a joy
> Does the winged life destroy
> But he who kisses the joy as it flies
> Lives in eternity's sun rise
>
> William Blake,
> *Eternity*

I dip my head with shame at the anger I have showed Grand Old Pa, and the other interminable shortcomings – of behaviour and of character. What patience S/he has, even with one human morsel.

> Do not slander heaven when you observe it
> through a reed,
> For those who do not yet know, I am giving
> you the key.
>
> the final lines of
> *Song of Enlightenment*,
> a classic Chán Buddhist text by
> Yongjia Xuanchue
> (Yungchia Hsüan-chüeh)

CHAPTER 19

Some believers reading chapter 19 may have been shocked by its emotional accusations, regarding them as unjustified or worse. I submit these defences: the Rift happened; I reacted as described, as a flawed human being; I learned from the whole experience; the response is a necessary part of the story leading directly to the above Meaning of Life, and is hence relevant to all. In addition, it shows God is not the traditional saccharine portrait of an idealised goody-goody: I squirmed under the pain meted out, and objected. I hope atheistic and agnostic readers will thereby recognise authenticity in the story, and that we each have a personal, one-to-one relationship with this Supreme Deity, in which the stakes are high.

I criticised God for not providing a valid reason for inflicting suffering. The reason for the lack of explanation is straightforward: mankind has not been ready for the answer – the Message. Hopefully we will be able to understand it in the 21st century.

> Remember what I have so often told you, "I have yet many things to say unto you, but ye cannot bear them now." Only step by step, and stage by stage, can you proceed, in your journey upward.
>
> *God Calling* (p. 263)

On page 175, this thinking was tortuous:

> I take upon myself the pain, the self-torture, and the distress that causes the self-torture and the pain. But I am happy....

It was more than two years before I could begin to decipher those explanatory words, and I initially dismissed them as superficially deep, dangerous nonsense. The 'distress' of the second half of the sentence refers to that of humans not experiencing continuous joy because of evil in the world. That in turn causes us to turn away from God, because we do not understand why S/he allows and inflicts it. That rejection causes the 'pain' of the first half, which refers to that felt by God having to lose us for a long time – no one else can feel that loss. It is self-torture because it is God that Created the situation in the first place! God feels both H/his own suffering caused by H/his own handicraft, and the conglomerate of everyone's suffering – whether caused by H/himself or not.

So why is S/he happy? Because the only way to overcome pain is to accept it. If you have accepted it, it is no longer painful, nor sad. It just is. Peace again.

Moreover, there is the possibility that a way of overcoming pain and self-torture is to *enjoy* it. In such a paradoxical universe, what seems masochism may well be the height of goodness.

★ ★ ★

ADVANCED STEPS

> The Gods do not visit you to remind you
> of what you already know.
>
> [source unknown]

'Advanced' is a relative term. Throughout history, God's Spirit or *Qì* has directly infused into many people's being, with or without being invited. It is a most personal event: more than a step, it is a giant leap of faith to accept the communion. The first time I had some experience of this was as an undergraduate, when out of curiosity I attended a Billy Graham evangelical convention. Although recognising that good intentions were present, something about it repelled me. At a party afterwards, a priest engaged me in conversation. Some days later, he called unannounced at my quarters, explained he sensed I had a certain resonance with God, laid his hands lightly on my head, and without permission proceeded through intense prayer to invoke the Holy Spirit. I felt a non-physical presence pushing through the top of my head, like a knocking at one's door asking to be admitted. There was a force behind it, a beam of energy. I resisted with all my might, blocking the entrance. The priest departed forthwith.

As a young adult, I had taken the decision not to join God, nor have any meaningful relationship, because it seemed most unwise to join a club before knowing what the purpose of that club was. Indeed, I thought it unreasonable for any God to expect otherwise! Since I assumed the existence of the Creator would never be proven, let alone H/his purpose known, I virtually dismissed religion from my mind for two decades. That is why the Cheju event was so unexpected – out of the literal blue.

With the enforced events from Cheju onwards leading to this chapter's exposition of the purpose of God, the frightening realisation dawns that it seems God has not only revealed to me S/he exists, but has also fulfilled my long-held condition. The moral? Never set a condition unless you're happy for it to be met!

A brush with God, even if it is not a bond, inevitably leaves a mark. A Western friend seeing me for the first time after Cheju remarked that I was "glowing". No wonder tradition recounts images of auras and light to be permanent in persons imbued with the Spirit of God. There is a downside however: in such a spotlight one is more in danger of attack from evil, though the protective 'armour coating' helps to countermand that.

While writing this book, I once experienced the Spirit touching, to the extent that I found myself crying out aloud: "No, not yet!" In a dream one night some months before the resolution of the Meaning of Life sprung into focus, I remember calmly saying "Come in", and was then aware of the *Qì* entering through my head, filling internally down to my chest. The sensation awoke me a second or so later, and I immediately knew it was within me: what was happening in the dream was also happening in reality. Instinctively I yanked my upper body forward, almost doubling up, which instantly ejected the presence. There was pain in my lower chest for days after.

The intent of those accounts is not to discuss the morality of God, but to stress that the Spirit is a real phenomenon in my experience, and countless others.

I have hardly any experience of or evidence for the following advanced steps, and note them here, reader, for your further enquiries. There are messengers for different levels: one such could be Diana Cooper. There is no sense in reading her books if not ready – in fact, I strongly discourage it. Her stories obviously would involve Laws of Physics undiscovered by 20th-century humans.

She relates that in her darkest hour she was taken for a tour around the universe by an angel. Laugh if you like, but the notion of a firmament of spiritual beings conducting God's wishes via the connections in the Amoeba is eminently rational and practical. Most organisations on earth have bosses and lesser ones. Since our world is a microcosm of everything, by extension it would be highly unlikely that God does everything H/himself; rather that Heaven has a hierarchy, without the squabbling and power craving. Incidentally there are 9 traditional levels of angelic beings, from seraphim and cherubim descending to archangels and angels. In an accurate translation, Matthew 18.10 implies there may be one guardian angel per human, and, judging by a recent survey, a third of all US citizens have seen one.

Spirits and fairies have been reported throughout mankind's history. The outstanding Swedish scientist Emanuel Swedenborg (1688–1772), who influenced William Blake, talked with angels for three decades before concocting a theory about them. As with UFOs and divine intervention [q.v. chapter 2], the current scientific method requiring spirits to materialise repeatedly in a lab in order to prove their existence is simply misleading. One authentic sighting throughout world history is enough to indicate their existence as a whole.

Hence in this book, whenever I have claimed that 'God' did something, it was more likely carried out by a spirit, guardian or angel, although the initial contact at Cheju must have been by one who had the capacity to generate and *be* a universe-filling Peace, and since the communicator said S/he was God, there is no reason to suppose otherwise.

In her book *A Little Light on Ascension*, Cooper reports she has learned through her experiences that there are 12 universes (p. 66), with 12 'sons/daughters of God working through the universes', and that our Cosmos contains 12 rays (p. 10). Each of the billions of original sparks of energy that created the universes procreated 12 souls, which themselves generated 12 extensions, of which each of us constitute one (p. 66).

Cooper asserts (p. 167) that she has been informed of a significant spiritual shift both in the universe and on earth by 23rd December 2012, a date that archaeologists have analysed as the completion of a momentous Mayan timeline. I like the number 12 in that year, and the 12th month, too!

Marko Pogačnik, who lectures at the Hagia Chora School for Geomancy, describes his experiences with spirits, which he is able to see all around, in *Nature Spirits and Elemental Beings*.

> Once, while flying from London to Belfast, I watched some sylphs who accompanied the plane.... They were flying alongside it, moving rhythmically back and forwards. They were able partly to enter the plane, since walls are not an obstacle for them. From time to time some of them turned their heads in surprise and looked back when they felt that they were being watched by one of the passengers. It must have been a rare event for them.[1]

This then could be why I was convinced there were guardian angels holding up and guiding the wing tips when landing in Ürümqi [chapter 1]!

Any notion of superiority to another of a lower spiritual development is a sign one is not as advanced as one thinks. Rather, like two people enjoying a day's walk – one on a mountain slope, the other in the valley below – neither is superior to the other: they are on different paths appropriate to their needs and likes, both hopefully learning. Indeed the higher one may be on the wrong track, and temporarily lost.

In Korea, I taught students graded into different levels according to the American system: 101 for beginners, 102 the next level, through to 109 the most advanced. In spiritual terms, if 101 is basic learning and gaining experience in life, the last two major advanced levels might be these:

> 108 (a significant number!): the step that replaces the present universe with one that has banished all evil. The conscious perfecting of the universe.
>
> 109: the step that answers the following. Who made the first unit in the first of the multifarious and multi-dimensional universes? Who started Time, before the beginning of our own universe's time? God? Then who made God? The Mystic Dào? Then who made the Dào? If absolutely everything including God and the Dào started from nothing, then who created the physical law that allows spontaneous appearance, and who created the space into which nothingness can expand?

There is no point in attempting to solve such 109 matters until one understands God. It is useless trying to beat the world land-speed record before one can drive a car. And before we can understand God, we need to understand ourselves.

> Fret not your souls with puzzles that you cannot solve. The solution may never be shown you until you have left this flesh-life.
>
> *God Calling* (p. 263)

---

[1] pp. 134/6, translated by Karin Werner and George McNamara

One day we will deal with God's problems, and help H/him solve them directly. By then we will truly have become a cognisant part of the Creator. There is no place for spurious humility when talking about this future scenario. It is a long fuse to be contemplated over many lifetimes. If individually we are aware of genuine problems and pain in our lives and others, be assured we ain't seen nothing yet. To become part of God requires each of us experience, in our one person, *all* the agony humans and other species have ever experienced for ever in their past, present and future lives – and furthermore, the paradox of having been partly responsible for coolly dishing it out.

Meanwhile, if it hasn't happened already, reader, it is likely that God *will* one day knock on your door out of the blue, command your attention without permission, and keep you busy with manifold signs exhorting action. You could choose not to board the roller coaster: but that would mean abandoning the most important travels in your life. You will be taken to your limit, but with the potential of rising above it with enhanced clarity and understanding. That side is your free choice.

There is one aspect of God I experienced that I will not divulge. The process of steps to enlightenment and perfection by definition means there are some for later. Judging by the difficulties people have today with some of the issues already raised in this book, it will need I guess another half-century before humans in general can begin to accept this particular facet. It was my personal experience, and *all* my fifty years of experience in life suggests that, for the best sake of humanity, now is not the time.

The odd thing is that it is a *good* thing. Yet many today would be shocked. I shake my head, once again, at dogma.

I have not told everything in these books about what happened, not only because of the above reasons, but because it is also unnecessary. Instead, I believe I have distilled what is the greater truth that applies to everyone. Given everything else in these books – the photographs, the other essays, the music, the general attitude and approach of the author – the reader can decide whether to accept that is what he has delivered in good faith.

Which leads to…

TRUST

Approaching the end of this discourse, one cannot leave the subject of God without mentioning trust – rarer than Love.

The Deity described within these pages is as personal as can be. And personally speaking, the suffering and evil that Grand Old Pa has thrown or allowed to be strewn my way throughout my life has been controlled, and *has never been for anything other than the long-term good*. That is a hard assertion for anyone to be convinced of concerning h/his life, and no doubt that resolute belief may be sorely tested in the future. Nevertheless, as of now, I stand by that statement. S/he has not let me down *once*, even those times when I thought S/he had, as at Dàlī. After a while, each time I have realised why that wasn't the case.

> Joy is the result of faithful trusting acceptance of My Will, when It seems *not* joyous.
>
> *God Calling* (p. 23)

God is a hard taskmaster! S/he adds:

> Joy is the daughter of calm.

In calm moments, I am aware where matters are and should be heading – the goals are wonderful to the point of miraculous. Everything major that occurs in our lives, even a horrific event, has a message and is leading to a far destination. Whether we have the resolve and courage calmly to follow the pointing finger, when we don't understand, is another matter.

However, the above is easy for me to say since the pain metered out personally has been but a pea in the ocean compared to the agony of others, past, present and future. I don't know if I could cope with being violently physically tortured, or my whole family starving or being wiped out in an earthquake or in a massacre. That is possibly why I haven't been subjected to that level.

> I can see the future. I can read men's hearts. I know better than you what you need. Trust Me absolutely.
>
> *God Calling* (p. 40)

A problem is that someone who says 'Trust me' could be doing so with hidden ill intent – it is also what a seductive devil would say. So after some testing, Trust is a matter of instinct: it is not one entirely of logic. However much one knows God exists, it still requires a leap of faith to trust H/him absolutely. That decision has first to be taken on whether the bad experiences in retrospect were excessive for the good lessons learned. In other words, the only logical reason to try and ignore God is if one thinks S/he is part Evil in an excessive, uncontrollable way. Thereafter, given the evidence S/he supplies of H/his Love and the joyful experiences we virtually all have, the instinct is surely to trust God, even without all the evidence in court. Those who do so with hardly any are the lambs of God.

There is an understandable reason to resist or ignore a trustworthy Deity: a very natural human emotion – fear. Maybe you will be told to sell all your possessions, leave your husband/wife, live in a barren land. Who wants to risk picking over rubbish tips for their food, or begging? Material possessions and the iron guard of money are so ingrained as the pinnacle of attainment, one is loath to risk abandoning them. It is primaeval selfishness.

> If I have asked you to step on and up firmly – then surely have I secured your ladder.
>
> My loving response will be to make that way as easy for your feet as it can be.
>
> Just trust. I cannot, and I will not fail you.
>
> *God Calling*
> (pp. 164, 278 & 76)

God knows more than we do: if the instinct is sound, there is no alternative but to trust S/he will guide us accordingly. No sensible child of five would disobey h/his parent thinking s/he knows more than that parent. The child may disobey for other selfish reasons, and often does.

It means allowing the entity that is God to be your friend. A Korean student expressed it simply: 'He is my best friend'. That implies another step: become a friend *to* God: trust is a two-way road. Which leads to the kernel of this book: the message contained in the Peace Poem.

PEACE

Peace is in the world
the rocks, trees and seas
beauty surrounds us
I am here – see me
hear me
The waves rush to the sand
and wash away my fears
Take me away – I sigh
I'm yours – you're mine
This is love – for ever.

'A message from God'

Considering the poem's genesis, as well as its title, it seems to be a plea direct from God, who is conveying another message: that the fear *in* H/himself evaporates when Love in humans is supreme. Given the context, God is content and pleads to be taken away at last from the Responsibility of eliminating Evil. The job is finished when God and humans are best friends – sharing the Bed of God, in the Asian sense.

★ ★ ★

All Buddhist schools of thought accept...
[that] nirvana is peace.

The Dalai Lama, *The Joy of Living and Dying in Peace* (p. 174)

What leads to Universal Peace? Understanding and acceptance – passion is no longer required. As indicated, the way to overcome any long-term problem is to face it and accept it utterly. God has been battling with The Problem for so long that the worry has been defeated through sheer repetition, the energy spent – transformed into unruffled acceptance of H/his own fate, as an agitated young person is metamorphosed into a tranquil, still, 90-year-old. God is Peace, the peace of 'calm of mind, all passion spent'[1].

You can sense this feeling from some performances of the ending of Richard Strauss' symphonic poem *Don Quixote*, particularly the one with the Chicago Symphony Orchestra conducted by Fritz Reiner[2]. I recommend you listen to it.

The cessation of passion, plus absolute Peace absolutely is God's Signature – H/his Seal. Find it, and there you will find the Divine.

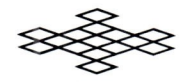

NUMBERS

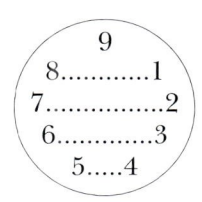

```
       9
   8..........1
    7............2
     6..........3
       5.....4
```

As a diverting end to this chapter, here are a few examples of the capacity of numbers to entertain. At first glance, the above simply appears to be 1 to 9 arranged in a circle within a circle.

However, the totality has a certain property: multiplying the top number 9 by itself (9×9) results in the next digits down on either side, 81.

Then 9×8 produces the next two below, 72; similarly with 9×7 (63), while 9×6 yields the duo at the base (54).

No need to stop there! Those same lowest two numbers in reverse form 45, the result of 9×5. Ascending again still in reverse, 36 is 9×4... 27 is 9×3... 18 is 9×2... and 9 is 9×1.

That has a certain satisfaction. I offer no meaning or relevance, though G. I. Gurdjieff (quoted in P.D. Ouspensky's *In Search Of The Miraculous*) does so in depth, concluding that an enneagram derived from it "makes books and libraries entirely unnecessary" (p. 294).

As a tease, follow this offshoot of the numbers 12 and 9.
12 = 6+6   Form a table 6 rows by 6 columns.
12×3 or 9×4   The outcome is 36 spaces.

Take the numbers 1 to 36 and scatter them into a grid thus (9 is a cornerstone).

28	4	3	31	35	10
36	18	21	24	11	1
7	23	12	17	22	30
8	13	26	19	16	29
5	20	15	14	25	32
27	33	34	6	2	9

Do you notice anything about the table's properties?

One is that, no matter which way you tally the numbers – in a row, a column or diagonally, they always add up to 111.

I kinda like that.

It would have been jocose if Grand Old Pa had arranged matters for them to add up to 108, but then God's Creation is not perfect.

It is called the Double-6 Magic Square, and there is an excellent example cut into a small iron plate, looking scrumptiously like a square chocolate bar, in Xī'ān's Shaanxi History Museum. The original was made in the Yuán Dynasty (1279–1368). I wonder how long ago a Chinese person first stumbled upon that little mathematical charm; and the Chinese used it to dispel evil spirits.

There is a simpler version of the magic square that the Chinese have known for eons. The writer of a renowned treatise of the Zhōu Dynasty [c.1050–221 BC] considered it to be the 'Model for the Universe', containing a supreme secret.

9 = 3×3   Form a 3 by 3 table.
Insert the first 9 numbers thus:

4	9	2
3	5	7
8	1	6

In all directions, they add up to the same number – 15. The significance of that to some Chinese people is that 15 represents... the Perfect Human.

君子　　　군자

jūnzi (Chinese)　　*kunja* (Korean)
a supreme/perfect person

---

[1] the final line of John Milton's *Samson Agonistes*, published in 1671 three years before he died
[2] on RCA 09026 617962 – the 1959 recorded sound is good too

Chapter 22

Nánbù and end

The breakthrough of the sun and its parabolic light near the top of Éméishān through the seemingly impenetrable cloud I knew was a sign to me and a promise, but the greater meanings and deeper significance of the events in Cheju and China as presented in the previous chapter were still enshrouded in the cloud of my mind, only later to be unravelled. At least I now knew it would clear sometime.

I rejoined Matt who had tramped to the highest peak, despite the closed-off fence. The last minibus from Jiēyīn Hall took a long-winded few hours following the Éméi River down to the foot of the mountain – yes, you can reach the summit plateau hardly climbing a step.

◆ ◆ ◆ ◆

Chéngdū

Five hours by bus northwards transported us into a maelstrom of people in the province's chaotic capital **Chéngdū** ('Became Capital'). Entrapped stationary for half an hour, we abandoned the vehicle and taxied to the Jīn (Brocade) River whose banks and bridges were awash with construction work. A room in the appropriately named Traffic Hotel more than sufficed for R and R, and washing.

At dawn the next morning, Matt left for Běijīng. I had been a week with a stranger as travelling partner and that had steadied my nerve, which could so easily have disintegrated in the wake of Dàlǐ. He was another Gift of God – hence my choice of pseudonym – minor, but a lifesaver nevertheless. The potentially worst period over, it seemed sensible to enact the final two weeks of travel.

Chéngdū has been an important city since the Three Kingdoms in the 3rd century AD, and in 1024 it was the first in the world to use paper money. A day's exploration by bike commenced at Wàngjiānglóu, Pavilion Overlooking the River, lit by a weak, misty sun behind a muslin of grey-pink smog. It is in a substantial park displaying over a hundred species of bamboo from the Far East. The roots of the Amoeba never being singular, there are possibly a thousand bamboo species on Earth, with China home to three or four hundred. While being light, the wood is famously strong, hence the scaffolding throughout China, and due to cross-membranes the tubular construction is watertight – tailor-made for boats. Further, its strength increases when wet – a rare and useful property in a rainy climate.

What appealed to me gazing up at these tall friends and servants of the Chinese was the combination of feathery-light pointed leaves and arching gracefulness, the fronds spouting skywards like geysers. Every half-century, whole forests of bamboo engage in an orgy of flowering for the first time, then collapse and die as one. Replacement shoots take up to ten years to establish.

> Yield and overcome,
> Bend and be straight,
> Empty and be full,
> Wear out and be new,
> Have little and gain,
> Have much and be confused.
> from *The Tao of Recovery:*
> *A Quiet Path to Wholeness*,
> by Jim McGregor

The nearby Sìchuān University Museum was a joy, and not only because visitors were required to traipse around the 40,000 folk exhibits with ballooning plastic bags on their feet to keep the carpets clean! The shadow puppets were quite different in mood and style from the better-known Indonesian variety.

Crossing Jiǔyǎn (Nine-Arch) Bridge, I was disappointed there would be no Sìchuān Opera, court music, acrobats or puppet shows at the Chéngdū Hotel that week, nor at the Jīnjiāng Theatre. Weaving through back alleys out of the China of one's historical dreams, I parked the bike among a thousand others in front of Wénshū (Manjushri) Monastery. This is one of the most frequented temples in China, very civilised with tea partaken at leisure in the gardens as if at one of the world's top hotels. The monks' vegetarian canteen barely coped with the frantic demand, the food a taste-bud treasure consumed at long tables.

In Rénmín Park, large numbers of people were relaxing in bamboo chairs and drinking tea, while Wǔhóu Temple hosted a plethora of plants and bonsai, as well as classic calligraphy.

◆ ◆ ◆ ◆

One of the most pleasurable sections of my time in China ensued. After a sixteen-month gap since Màijīshān, during which we exchanged letters, I met Zhèng Hào again. He introduced his fiancée, Qing Ping (22-2), and they treated me in typical Asian fashion the next four days. Not one meal, bus or taxi fare, nor anything else was I allowed to pay for: I was a friend in their country.

The Giant Panda Breeding Research Base had opened out of town, and walking around the spacious compounds containing the healthy-looking two-toned animals allowed the three of us to increase our acquaintance. An informative museum with English explanations revealed that, as well as consuming ten to forty kilograms daily of a specific species of nutritious bamboo – defecating up to 150 times a day in the process, Giant Pandas obtain vitamins and trace elements from flowers, fruit, rodents, and by scavenging dead meat. That they mash the bones is an indication of jaw, cheek and molar power. They possess one of the shortest guts in the carnivore kingdom, so cannot extract enough nutrients from lesser quantities of bamboo as would genuine herbivores, which have long guts. The cycle is eight hours foraging and feeding followed by four napping, often precariously up a tree.

This day and night requirement, plus the availability of evergreen bamboo in winter, means they do not hibernate to survive like other bears.

The long-clawed front paws have a bone protruding from the base that acts as a sixth digit for easier grasping – unusual in animals other than the apes. In captivity, natural breeding by males is rare and their sperm count low: babies have exhibited a frail immune system, and less than fifty have lived beyond infancy. Additionally, the penis is short compared to the female's long vagina, causing low insemination probability. In any case, the female is receptive only a few days a year, the panda generally preferring a solitary life.

A third of Sìchuān's forests have been cropped in the past forty years, from covering 30% of the province in 1975 down to a paltry 6½% in 1998. Not surprisingly, the total number of Giant Pandas has reduced to between 700 and 1,000 in six island localities in the province and to the north, resulting in minimal crossbreeding. A further 100 are in captivity. Half a million years ago they were ubiquitous throughout China, a thousand years back still widespread. The WWF reckons that £60 million needs to be spent if we want to save the species.

The Lesser or Red Panda *(22-1 taken in Shànghǎi Zoo)*, with the ringed tail almost doubling its half-metre length, looks more like a racoon, to which it is related. Likewise having the extra digit as well as sharp teeth, it is less fussy concerning diet, consuming small rodents, birds, their eggs, insects, nuts and fruit, as well as mainly the leaves of bamboo. Capable of halving its metabolic rate to save energy, it is startling to see them up a tree scampering around and then switch off like a doll that's abruptly run out of power. Sleeping in branches much of the day, it descends at dusk and early morning to feed. Considerably more dispersed, it has fanned out to Myanmar and the Himalaya including Nepal, *panda* being a Nepali word meaning 'bamboo eater'.

That evening I met Zhèng Hào's brother and his wife, and with other friends was treated to a genuine rustic Sìchuān hotpot, an oil fondue that is *là* (peppery hot) and *má* (numbing), and then some. As with much of the local food, the latter is due to the *huājiāo* ('flower pepper'), which leaves your mouth reeling as if nuclear bombed by all the dentists you've ever visited in a lifetime. I didn't ask what the various 'meats' were either – the pandas would have approved. Despite those reservations, the feeling of being accepted as a member of the family was touching and infectious. This is the central attraction of Chéngdū – the sense of a community bonded through time and hardship, the fellow humans one knows providing a rock of deep support.

◆ ◆ ◆ ◆

22-1

Nánbù

Aside from Tibet, Xīnjiāng, and Inner Mongolia, which are officially 'autonomous regions' for minorities, Sìchuān is China's second largest province, the size of mainland Spain. Its people are predominantly Hàn Chinese, whose numbers have doubled in the fifty years since the Republic was formed.

The western half is mountainous. In contrast, the densely populated zone from Chéngdū eastwards contains the agriculturally fertile Sìchuān (Four Rivers) Basin. Crossing this 1,000-metre-high plain are indeed four main north-south rivers – the Tuō, Fú, Jiālíng and Qú. Eastward travellers normally proceed south-east to the stone carvings at Dàzú or to Chóngqìng, but Zhèng Hào's hometown lies north-east in the very centre of China, is not on the tourist route, nor on the traveller's route, and is not mentioned in any guidebook or modern literature. No one goes to Nánbù!

A nine-hour bus journey was memorable for a searing public argument between a woman and a man, the latter kicking the door. He was finally expelled by the driver who had been remarkably patient up to then. Even a Confucian community cannot confine all pressures.

◆ ◆ ◆ ◆

22-2

22-3

My two hosts took me to a lookout across from the city (22-3). **Nánbù** (Southern Part) lies on the west bank of the greatest of the four rivers, Jiālíng (Fine Hill) Jiāng, which rises far away on the Gānsù border near Qīnghǎi. At 1,118 kilometres, it is the second longest tributary of the Yángzi/Cháng. The community is best described as many towns within a rambling city in the countryside. The weather never changed from what you see here – no wonder dogs bark in Sìchuān whenever the sun appears.

Qing Ping (22-2) was a delight, enthusiastically easing communication difficulties: serendipitously she was an English teacher at a local school. Due to a haircut to aid jogging (so he told me), Zhèng Hào looked different from his appearance in Màijīshān, 350 kilometres north from here, but was just as affable. Ten years before, he had joined the army for a four-year stint – primarily to avoid studying. Then followed two years of accountancy training, and now aged twenty-four was using these skills in the building trade. He had travelled considerably, including to Dàtóng and Běijīng. In his family's apartment in a tenement block, his sweet-faced mother welcomed me with fruit and candy, his dad talked to me in normal-speed Chinese that left me floundering, and I met another brother, and a sister with her husband.

In my pack was a copy of *Wild Swans*, banned in China, and I mentioned the ghastly life Máo had put the Chinese through, as described in the book. It was clear that Zhèng Hào and most of his family greatly admired the former leader, and he declared such books by foreigners as lacking in accurate knowledge and untrustworthy. When I explained it was written by a Chinese woman born and raised not only in China but actually in their own province, he was taken aback, indeed didn't believe it. I also sensed he didn't want to. This incident, and the obvious support and sense of community that Máo continues to inspire in large sections of the Chinese people (there is still a prominent statue of him in Chéngdū), made me realise it is wrong for Westerners to issue a blanket condemnation of censorship in China. The populous are not ready to face some truths. The Chinese have to proceed through the growing levels at their own pace, in good time, otherwise necessary aspects of their development will be curtailed. Too much truth can be as destructive as too little. The prohibition of such books in China at this stage is absolutely for the good of many Chinese people – *The Private Life Of Chairman Mao* is forbidden as well. I had considered leaving *Wild Swans* with them, but that subversive act would have been harmful.

A most rewarding chat was with his other sister Anna, who spoke fine English. Her recent background was unusual: aged 26, she had married an Afghan three years earlier whom she had met in Běijīng. She found Muslim expectancy of her role, however, to be insufferably inflexible: having to stay home, and to believe only in Islam. She had separated and was seeking a divorce, which her husband was resisting since marriage afforded him easy access to a Chinese visa.

I wondered whether the city was a no-go area for foreigners, and that my presence might cause problems with officialdom; but one of their relatives was a policeman, and already knew I was in Nánbù. Such are the advantages of an extended family!

This was not any day in China, but New Year's Eve. The previous two days had already seen houses throughout the land being cleaned to expel ill luck and bad accruements. This was the last chance to settle debts: any outstanding would be annulled at the stroke of midnight, as would any bad feeling arising from them – a time to forgive, and start again. The narrow streets were awash with the Chinese shopping for the festivities, and long paper banners were for sale emblazoned with gold calligraphy. Being auspicious red to express joy, they are framed around doors at this time for good luck and to prevent the incursion of evil. I bought some specimens, reproduced on the next double page. On the left: *This gateway welcomes good fortune from the East, West, South and North*. The short top one: *May the family be rich through all seasons*. On the right: *This household gathers wealth from spring and summer through autumn to winter*.

We called in at the two-room apartment of Qing Ping's third brother, who had married four months previously. His beautiful wife instantly conjured up a voluminous hotpot. We were joined by a soldier friend of Zhèng Hào, who was keen to join the British Army; I informed him it was unlikely the Brits would accept a Chinese national. Cards appeared, and I taught the three men poker – gambling (though illegal) and board games are a tradition at New Year. The women initiated a game of *má jiàng* (mah-jong), which is known by various names in China, with modified rules south of the Yángzi/Cháng. The versions played in Japan and America are different. A standard form uses 144 tiles, which is 12x12 – God must be a gambler!

New Year's Eve dinner with ten of Zhèng Hào's family in the kitchen – the only communal room in the apartment – was a joyous, informal affair, accompanied by regular raising of glasses and cries of *gān bēi* ('dry cup'), an invitation to down the alcohol in one. The food is not only sustenance. As ever in China, symbolism reigns: the silky-thin threads of a particular seaweed called *fā cài* ('hairy vegetable') signify abundance, while the common dumpling, *jiǎozi* with its round earthy shape, carries the hope of a long-held family wish coming true. Radiating happiness, my friend's mother furthered the *hóng bāo* ('red packet') tradition of bestowing new money on a baby. Every unmarried family member is a baby in her eyes, so each received ¥60 – a charming gesture. The number stems from 6 and 8 being propitious. Even my hand was surreptitiously filled!

While the table was cleared for *má jiàng*, which proceeded into the small hours, the sound of an almighty loud rapid-fire machine-gun outside the window caught my breath. No one else flinched. Qing Ping smiled and led me onto the communal staircase, where the sound of what was actually firecrackers reached ear-banging intensity. The air was replete with fireworks exploding, and I grabbed my tape-recorder. Qing Ping urged me onto the roof, and in the dark I gingerly sidestepped open manholes and, more dangerous still, lit fireworks about to launch from near my feet. My excitement submerged the insanity of what I was doing, for from this towering vantage point the entire sky was filled with flaming smoke, accompanied by the greatest deluge of sound I have ever heard.

A substantial proportion of the entire city's populous was engaged in this enterprise from every rooftop, and I cannot envisage hearing anything like it again. Picture the Grand Canyon filled and resonating with avalanche-creating sound. Conjure the soundtracks of a thousand movies playing at full volume side-by-side in open cinemas. Wagner's music was a midget mouse by comparison. Imagine all of heaven's hailstones on a hot tin roof. Channel Joshua's Jericho trumpets, and his army's mighty unison shout, through a city-full of combined amplifiers, and you have an idea of the wall of sound crashing into my face. If all of nature's animals belched out a tumultuous sound at *one instant*, it surely could not match what I was hearing – and this level was being sustained!

To the Chinese, this is designed to frighten away ghosts and evil spirits. If I were an evil spirit in such circumstances, I would rocket out of China at warp speed, and would think 12 times before returning. Instead, I was dodging whiz-bangs winging their way up from my ankles.

Most terrifying and terrifically inspiring of all, this stentorian sound was *increasing*! It became the most cataclysmic sound this side of Hell. Even at full operatic belt, I could barely distinguish what Qing Ping was occasionally saying to me, even with our foreheads touching. As half-an-hour before midnight became fifteen minutes, then eight... FIVE... **THREE**, it could have been all the gods of Olympus rumbling their cymbals and drums. Indeed as the magic hour was met and passed, the new heralded in, I felt it was a simultaneous shout of all Creation together. The primary emotion emanating from it was elation, *an explosion of joy*. This was the ecstasy of Enlightenment achieved. With the tensions of the past months and recent weeks, for me it was a tremendous release, an extraordinary post-climax of my journey – a culmination, a party and the real purpose, an orgy in many senses.

You can achieve a sense of being there only if you play track 11 loudly for the sustained five minutes, otherwise it will sound like popcorn. It should evoke a thunderous hurricane at its height. If listening through speakers, first shut windows and doors, turf the cat out, and pre-apologise to your neighbours! There is a health risk if you use headphones, particularly with the sudden cracks – take care.

It was Chinese alchemists stalking the elusive elixir of immortality who conceived gunpowder in the 9th century, from which followed fireworks in the 10th and rocket propulsion in the 12th century. Europeans didn't see their like until hundreds of years later, while Arabs called explosive rockets 'Chinese arrows'. Centuries of Chinese pyrotechnic displays led to military uses in the early 1200s and again in 1279, the latter being ineffective since the Mongols won, ending the Sòng Dynasty.

> The world's first attempt at manned space travel.... Five hundred years before Yuri Gagarin, a Chinese official named Wan Hoo strapped himself into a chair equipped with 47 high-powered fireworks rockets and ordered the fuses ignited. He died, still earthbound, in the ensuing inferno.
>
> Time magazine, 10 May 1993

The Chinese have a bucketful of names for different types of fireworks.

> Small Boxes, Flower Pots, Lanterns of Heaven and Earth, Fire and Smoke Poles, Silver Flowers, Peonies Strung on a Thread, Lotus Sprinkled with Water, Golden Plates, Falling Moons, Grape Arbours, Flags of Fire, Double-Kicking Feet, Ten Explosions Flying to Heaven, Fire Devils Noisily Splitting Apart, Eight-Cornered Rockets, and Bombs for Attacking the City of Hsien Yang.
>
> Tun Lich'en, cited by Sir Osbert Sitwell (1892–1969), brother of Edith and Sacheverell, in *Escape with Me!: An Oriental Sketch-Book* (pp. 168/9)

Nowadays one can only experience this New Year event in some rural areas of China, since the authorities have banned the custom in most major cities for obvious safety reasons. In Chóngqìng, there is a huge ¥5,000 fine if this is violated.

Incidentally, my comments heard on the track indicate that I had no notion of writing a book at the time: the recording was initially for friends to hear.

◆ ◆ ◆ ◆

The dawn of a New Year is a day of enjoyment, with no sweeping or dusting of homes, which would symbolise ejecting the new luck just arrived. While Qing Ping remained with her family, Zhèng Hào's mother bargained with a taxi driver to chauffeur five of us around the Nánbù vicinity. On the outskirts is a renowned temple, which because of the wood is one of the darkest in China. With its multiple doors drawing in the eye, the entrance is an enticing image of old China, offset by red and yellow candleholders *(22-4)*. The main hall with Noah's-ark eaves has an urn-like adornment in the centre of its ridge, embellished with four slim, curvaceous dragons.

In a former temple in a park, this Guān Yīn (attired as per tradition in white) attracted people in droves *(22-5)*. On New Year's Day, fortune-tellers throughout the land are at their busiest, as it is everyone's birthday. Having existed nine months in the womb, Asian babies are considered to be in effect one year old when they are born. On the subsequent New Year's Day they become aged two, it being a new year, even if in western terms they are, say, one month old! A different, but equally valid logic.

This being a statue with a mechanism inside was irrelevant – people were serious, respectful, and in awe. I deposited money in a slot, machinery whirred, Guān Yīn's left arm swung wide and from her fingers I prised the fortune-paper she had selected. According to Qing Ping, mine was very lucky, forecasting something about marriage. I smiled... there was a connection with Cheju.

The taxi scraped along bumpy muddy lanes in the rain to Mr and Mrs Gao's home. Although unannounced, we were given a fulsome welcome,

22-4

22-5

and sat down to a princely meal of various generous courses. Even the driver, who was a stranger to us all, was invited! Aged thirty, Mr Gao was a genial talkative host pouring drinks continually, including four expensive alcoholic concoctions, the last home-made – "the same as Máo used to drink". Mr Gao liked Máo – there was a conspicuous portrait on the wall. I lost count of the number of toasts of *gān bēi* I had to copy. Conviviality was free and flowing, and touching. I was accepted without hesitation as a member of the larger Chinese family. Everyone is.

His wife I saw momentarily before she disappeared to cook the additional food. During the course of the more than two-hour banquet, she was too busy to reappear except once, and for goodbyes at the end. Even when I toasted the preparers of the meal, her sister replied in her absence. Nevertheless, she seemed more than content. On the right in *22-6* is Zhèng Hào; on my left are his mother, his sister Anna, the driver, then Mr Gao and his family. As proceedings wound down, Mr Gao made a short speech directed at me, which extracted shrieks of laughter. Anna translated: he had appreciated my thoughts and words so much that he added, "I'm not homosexual, but I love you!"

He came with us to an amusement park on a hill topped by a pavilion, from which I took an enticing scene of the humped Chinese countryside (*22-9* overleaf). I was astounded to be showered with presents of drinks and food as we ambled around: they were from acquaintances of Mr Gao. They knew him, I was his guest, so I received the benefit. It was a typical example of the Chinese favour system – *guānxì* ('relationships' or 'connections') – in action.

A hall of stelae inscribed by famous calligraphers included this example, the writing being in the shape of a skeletal body (*22-7*). Another stated the philosophy: 'I do not wish to be rich with money, only to have love, mountains and water'. The Chinese word in *22-8* was instantly meaningful to me, the calligraphy being by Wen Tiānshān. With Zhèng Hào standing next to it, the character that looks like a bearded face is *zhōng* – loyal/devoted/faithful. I will not forget this image, and the loyal, devoted friendship offered not only by Zhèng Hào, but by the Chinese people in general.

My sense of the surreal returned when, despite no one going to Nánbù, there had been an exception: Mrs Thatcher. Presumably as Prime Minister, she had toured the dark temple and had inspected the local hospital, to which I was taken. My Chinese friends had a high opinion of her.

◆ ◆ ◆ ◆

22-6

22-7

22-8

239

22-9

Chóngqìng

New Year festivities can continue for over a week, with the Jade Emperor's birthday celebrated on the 9th day – he is the ruler of Heaven. I had to leave, however, and made my goodbyes, giving my watch to Zhèng Hào as a token.

A ten-hour bus journey south turned into a Chinese torture test. The full vehicle broke down, and the entire load of passengers and packages had to fit into a second bus already laden. I stood back in awe at the scramble and shoving of this two-into-one concept, until someone yelled at me to climb through a side window onto the driver's mattress. With my shoulders squeezed into my ribs and my kneecaps in my cheeks, the approach through the interminable suburbs of **Chóngqìng** seemed just reward for all the evil I had ever done in the world.

The Chóngqìng Hotel offered thankful luxury at a low-season rate, but the room was freezing due to the air-conditioning set at maximum.

◆ ◆ ◆ ◆

Larger than Chéngdū, indeed it is the most populated metropolis in the country, this fascinating city-of-life encapsulates what China is for many of its people. Chóngqìng can be translated as 'Celebrate Again', and was named thus by Emperor Guāngzōng of the Southern Sòng Dynasty in celebration of him rising to the national throne in 1190, having already become the regional King.

It marks the boundary of the Sìchuān Plain; eastwards is blocked by mountains, the four rivers from here on having fed into the Yángzi/Cháng. To the north, the Fú and Qú rivers flow into the Jiālíng, which enters from the left in the panorama *(22-10)* into the Yángzi/Cháng on the right, which is negotiating an S bend. The resultant distinctly-shaped peninsula in-between the two rivers forms the centre of the city, ending at the point of confluence in the distant middle of the photograph. That forms the dock area called Cháotiān Mén (the Gate Facing Heaven). The three-shot vista was taken from a pavilion in Élíng (Goose Ridge) Park – the peninsula having the shape of a goose flying over water, delineated by the two rivers spreading outwards.

22-10

Rising water is a constant threat. Compared to its winter level shown here, snowmelt and summer rains cause it to swell typically 22 to 35 metres higher in July/August. Every ten years there is a big flood, and every hundred years a disastrous one – a rise of over eighty metres was recorded along the Yángzi/Cháng in 1871.

Visible on the left, sensibly built sixty metres high, is the Jiālíng Bridge, its 150-metre length constructed in 1966 connecting the continuing city on the other side. *22-11* looks along the final section of the Jiālíng, at the end of which is the Yángzi/Cháng crossing the T. Imagine these boats over a hundred feet higher in late summer! The buildings on the far side of the Yángzi are in a poverty-wrecked portion of the city, garbage infested by primitive sanitation, with few sewers. There in the famine of 1958–61 human meat was anonymously part of the burger-bar scene.

In 1920, four foreign consulates were situated in that sector (one remains). They were the result of the steamships ploughing up the great river from Wǔhàn, the first of which in 1898 took two months with an Englishman called Mr Plant aboard, as was Archibald Little who had already settled in Chóngqìng fifteen years earlier, establishing a trading company. On arrival, the mechanical vessel blew its horn in triumph, which caused the locals to flee, frightened by the monster.

To the right of centre in *22-10* is the major 1981 bridge named after and crossing the Cháng Jiāng. Bridges over the Yángzi are hardly new to the Chinese: one of linked iron chains was suspended over the Jīnshā in Yúnnán in the year 580 – a mere 1,165 years before something similar was first constructed in Europe! In contrast, three new bridges built in Chóngqìng collapsed in 1999 with loss of life, another was found sagging, and a further two were closed. The finger points firmly at corruption in the construction industry.

22-11

241

Locals have diverse nicknames for the city, including *Lúzào* (Oven). The temperature can reach 43°C, and even in winter seldom falls to freezing. The epithet Hilly City has spawned a local saying: "If you ride a bike in Chóngqìng, the bike will ride you." The resultant aversion to hauling bikes up and down the steep, stepped alleys of the peninsula has given rise to a phenomenon most unusual in Chinese cities: there are few bicycles.

Another tag is more serious: 90% humidity is to be expected in Foggy Town, because of pollution. Acid rain in this smokestack pitted region is legion – white buildings can and do turn grey-black after one deluge. The notably high sulphur content in the neighbourhood's coal, extraction of which has doubled in the past twenty years, leads to 820,000 tons of SO_2 gas being released per annum. A pH of 4 is the average yearly level, causing corrosion of the city's fabric. The surrounding hills contain the fumes, while the omnipresent clouds detain the muck at low level. People here exhibit the highest incidence of lung cancer out of eighteen cities surveyed in China.

With the city granted municipal status in 1997, there are around 15 million humans in the larger metropolitan area – more than in Shànghǎi – though it doesn't appear in official world figures as such. What cold statistics could embrace the see-saw humanity of a million farmers rolling in for temporary work between harvests? They constitute ephemeral coolies and conduct the backbreaking task of hauling 70-kilogram loads from the docks of Cháotiān Mén up the festering cliff steps to the roads, for which they earn a dollar for a 16-hour day starting at four in the morning. Out of that they have to pay for shelter and food. The city's factory workers, in comparison, have an easier life.

During the previous months, I had tried without success to ascertain whether there would be tourist boats plying the waters through the gorges to Wǔhàn. The public alternatives are little more than transfer platforms, with 4th and 5th-class passengers joining the permanent rats aboard (1st class is rare). The hotel's travel agent was clueless, but fortunately a receptionist knew of one departing the next day – lucky timing in this off-season. Having booked, he also phoned for a guide and driver to take me around the city. Such are the advantages of independent travel in Asia: tours arranged within an hour!

The guide Wong Ping was informative and spoke good English – some of the above facts stem from him. After a visit to the dock area with its ferryboats and ant-like porters, the ostentation of the palatial Rénmín Hotel was bizarre. Its Temple of Heaven concert hall, with grand entrance stairs and internal marble walls, was built in 1952 at a cost of ¥8 million, the funds raised by Dèng Xiǎopíng. It would today cost ¥8 billion.

There are several sites that deal with the situation of the city during World War II. According to the official Japanese news agency at the time, in three days during October 1937, 850 planes dropped 2,526 bombs on China. In the previous two months, sixty towns and cities suffered aerial bombardment, 'few of which have any possible military significance'. The latter contemporary comment came from the editor of the Shànghǎi-based China Weekly Review [30 October 1937]. With both Běijīng and Nánjīng having fallen by the end of the year, the Guómíndǎng national government transmigrated across the mountains to Chóngqìng, which became the Chinese capital until 1945. A makeshift runway was located under the present Yángzi Bridge. It can still be discerned in the panorama, right of centre, on a sandbar in the river called Shanhuba Island.

The city became one of the most universally bombed in the World War: in the three years 1939–41, twenty barrages a day were not unknown. When it was Foggy Town there were none, but the Japanese soon twigged the city's geographical Achilles heel. From the East China Sea to here, the Yángzi/Cháng was a 2,400-kilometre-long marker for aircrew. Given a sliver of moonlight at night, all the Japanese had to do from their base in Wǔhàn was to 'follow the silver banner of the Yángzi up to its confluence with the Jiālíng, which identified the capital in a way no blackout could obscure' [Edgar Snow, who was in the capital in 1939].

The British traveller Peter Fleming met the Guómíndǎng's leader Chiang Kai-shek (Jiǎng Jièshí) in 1933, describing him thus:

> He was not the usual type of glib and rather impressive propaganda-monger; he did not cultivate salesmanship.... Here was a man with a presence, with that something incalculable to him to which the herd instinctively defers. He was strong and silent by nature, not by artifice.
>
> *One's Company* (pp. 191/2)

General Stilwell, who spoke Chinese fluently, flew to the city in 1942 for a meeting with Chiang, then aged 55, to discuss the situation in Burma: *22-12* shows the two men with the latter's wife, the USA-educated Sòng Měi Líng, whose eloquent English and appreciation of the Western lifestyle endeared her to Americans at the time. Short-tempered "Vinegar Joe" Stilwell (he called supreme allied commander Louis Mountbatten a "childish glamor boy", and referred to Chiang as the "Peanut" and the "little jackass") was exasperated by the corrupt and inefficient administration he witnessed, and attempted to persuade the Chinese government to end the distracting civil war with the Communists. Chiang was secretly channelling the

22-12

22-13   **22-15**

supplies so costly won over the Hump, not against the Japanese as the Americans intended, but as gifts to warlords to persuade them to fight the Communists! Not surprisingly, Stilwell was soon out of favour with Chiang, and a new Chief of Staff superseded him in 1944. He died a year after the war ended, aged 63, while Chiang lived until 1975.

Máo too came to the city, and his first meeting with Chiang was by chance on a bridge in a park near Chiang's villa. What they said to each other, after a decade of civil war between them, is not recorded. *22-13* reveals Máo, after the Long March, delivering a report at his Communist headquarters in Yán'ān, Shaanxi Province [December 1935]. Note the patches on the trousers, and the cave at the back – a typical dwelling of the *loess* country.

With the bombing forcing an alliance between them, the building in Chóngqìng that contained their cabinet rooms remains on view, still painted black on the outside. Máo's office-cum-bedroom is preserved as it was, with a valved radio beside his bed *(22-14)*. Two months before the Japanese surrendered aboard the USS Missouri, Máo held a meeting in Yán'ān to discuss the future *(22-15, taken on 1st July 1945)*. Others lined up with Máo on the left include the influential Zhōu Ēnlái, soon to be premier of China for twenty-seven years, and Lín Bei Chu, a democratic progressive.

Chóngqìng is today twinned with Hiroshima. As can be seen in *22-10*'s panorama, on the immediate right, Élíng Park features a bonsai garden donated by that Japanese city.

★ ★ ★

As I boarded the Yángzi River boat, the entire crew went silent and stood up as if I was royalty. I was the only passenger to stay that night in one of the spacious, hotel-standard cabins, and it transpired that all the other hundreds of passengers were to be wealthy Taiwanese and Chinese tourists. My white foreign form with backpacks was hardly expected.

◆ ◆ ◆ ◆

There are all of sixty cruise ships ploughing through the Three Gorges *(Sānxiá)* each for three days east to Wǔhàn, the best seasons to join one being April/May and September/October. This two-year-old *MS Queen* was 5,000 tons, and its roofline reminded me of the Enterprise *(22-16)* – Star Trek and China being a combination hard to mesh. The picture was taken at the moment of departure downstream of the confluence, with the east bank of the river opposite.

The *Queen* reached Fēngdū in the mid-afternoon, and passengers were escorted up to the lofty temple to the Devil described in chapter 6, with its tests to cross a bridge in three steps, to lift a 180-kilogram weight, and not to glance back while walking along a corridor, as well as its 9+9 tormentors beside steep steps, and the human Devil in h/his inner sanctum. There was also a courtyard that featured this white calligraphic character

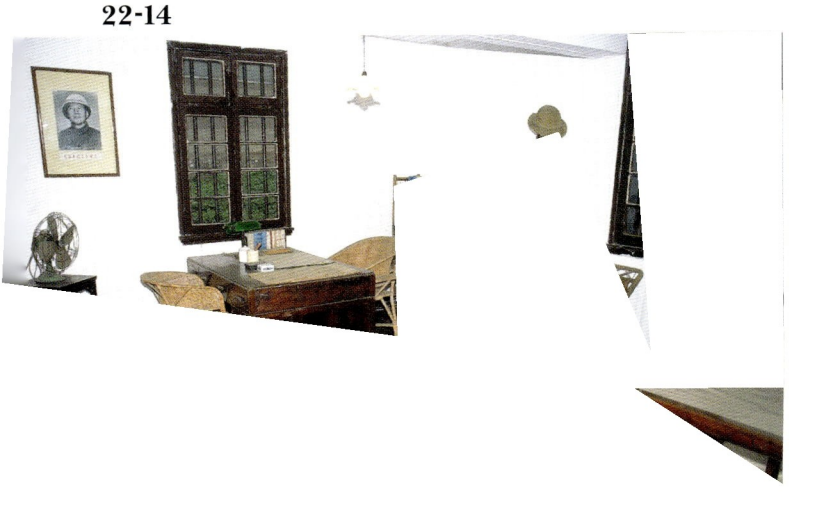

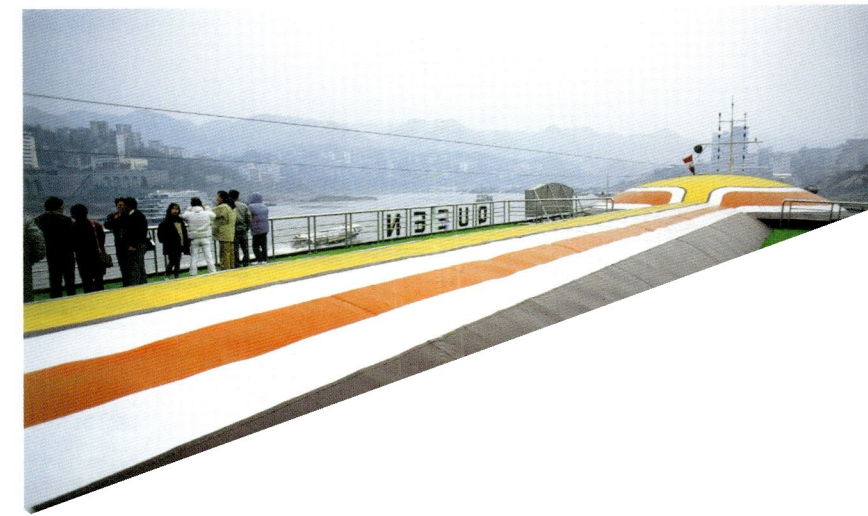

243

22-14   **22-16**

the Three Gorges

At the age of sixty-four, suffering from gout and rheumatism as well as spinal and heart problems, a widowed Englishwoman in 1896 voyaged without a Western companion up the Yángzi/Cháng from Shànghǎi, journeyed overland in Sìchuān (including visiting a school in Nánbù), and returned down the river – a round trip of 12,875 kilometres in six months taken 'for recreation and interest only' with 'no intention of writing a book'. Nevertheless the resultant publication, *The Yangtze Valley and Beyond*, which includes 116 of her own photographs, has since inspired generations of travellers at heart.

Having already explored Korea two years previously, Isabella Bird ascended through the gorges a couple of years before the first steamer did. She witnessed scenes that today can only live in the imagination: thousands of junks (over 7,000 proceeding on the Upper Yángzi), countless other craft such as *shānbǎn* and *wupan* 'in clouds of foam and spray', a thousand dangerous rocks and rapids, a hundred rowers straining at a junk's oars, and half-naked 'trackers' manually pulling vessels from ashore using 350-metre bamboo ropes. Up to 400 of these taut men laboured for twelve hours every day to shift each vessel through the tempestuously noisy cataracts, accompanied by their own swoops and yells and drums and bells, yet sometimes with no progress after hours of effort.

> Suddenly the junk shivered, both tow-ropes snapped, the lines of trackers went down on their faces, and in a moment the big craft was spinning down the rapid; and... flew up into the air as if she had exploded, a mass of spars and planks with heads bobbing about in the breakers. Quick as thought the red lifeboats were on the spot... all were saved but three. (p. 128)

Where the cliffs were vertical, tracks had been gorged out of the rock a perilous hundred metres above the billowing whirlpools, along which the trackers shouldered their responsibility, 'stooping so low to their work that their hands nearly touch the ground, and at a distance they look like quadrupeds' (p. 142). She greatly admired their spirit, good nature and sense of humour, particularly since for a pittance they did 'the hardest and riskiest work I have seen done in any country' (p. 138).

22-17

on a black wall *(22-17)*. Explaining in Chinese through a megaphone, the attractive and manicured guide revealed it was actually a hidden composite of four Chinese characters that translate:

            Good wear
for ever   Peace   only
            appear

Reading from right to left, together they mean, 'If you don only the apparel of Goodness, then will appear Peace for ever'.

The liner continued through the night, ensuring our arrival in the early morning at the first gorge.

◆ ◆ ◆ ◆

22-18

22-19

What of the gorges today? I'm afraid the reality is disappointing. That has less to do with the most dangerous rocks having been dynamited in the 1950s, the rapids being tamed by a dam, the trackers thankfully no more. It is simply that the scenery does not quicken the pulse. It is a gentle amble through grey, liquid-filled valleys shrouded in dark cloud – pleasant, but no more. At times, you wonder if you are in a gorge at all – "Is this it?" is a common reaction. It would be thrilling to view these seventy-million-year-old creations from above in clearer skies, but scarcely practical.

After the first short Qútáng Xiá, we moored at Wūshān with other impressive floating palaces at the entrance to the second Wū Xiá (Witches Gorge), on the extreme right in *22-18* – the only time I took a photograph of the Three Gorges. Fortunately we transferred here to motorised *sānpan* for a side trip up one of the river's 700 tributaries, which offered a more spectacular 'Lesser Three Gorges' ride *(22-19)*.

This compact 33-kilometre Dàníng (Big Placid) River commenced with the impressive narrow Lóng Mén (Dragon Gate) Gorge, and here at least one could see traces of the inventive Chinese spirit of old. High up were rows of holes peppered like machine-gun bullets along one side of the vertical cliffs. As long ago as the 3rd century BC, they once held wooden supports for a plank way that gave access for maintaining bamboo pipes bearing water from the hills a hundred kilometres away.

Barely had we cricked our necks to admire that athletic modus operandi, when we were aware that our longboats' skippers were contending with swift and inconstant eddies, the sparkling clear water merely inches deep. A one-way system was in force, those boats shooting past downstream having priority. By a whisker, their oarsmen avoided collisions by sculling from the bow using elongated, wide-bladed paddles called *yuloh*, which Isabella Bird encountered on her junks. Then the awesome truth dawned – we were proceeding *uphill* in no half measure! For hours the river snaked between shoals of pebbles, with the queue of boats waiting to stampede each silver rapid lined up like rush hour on London Bridge. Slung hazardously on narrow ledges in the rock face at bird's eye level were seemingly suspended 'iron' coffins, actually of wood blackened by 2,000 years of ageing. Other 'sights' included Panda Cave, Double-Dragon Town, Nine Dragons Pillar, a rock statue of Buddha, and dozens of others that consumed the attention of my Chinese colleagues with their fancy binoculars *(22-20)*.

The more open scenery was horribly denuded of trees, hills like shaved heads with bristles of replants. A solitary bird darted over the surface. A lunch stop was tourist hell – sheer numbers overwhelming the restaurant, my meal tepid and insipid.

The *Queen* passed through the next two gorges late that afternoon or the next morning. Details are hazy since I succumbed to food poisoning for the next twenty-four hours, hauling myself out of bed only when the relay system announced another gorge. Suffice to say the Wū Gorge is famous for its 12 peaks, with 9 visible from the river apparently, but I saw none because of the clouds. I remember nothing of the final Xīlíng Xiá (Shadow Play Gorge).

◆ ◆ ◆ ◆

22-20

Nevertheless, I was thankful for the cosseted sojourn away from the other draining methods of travel in China, and spent the third day writing an important letter that was a consequence of the Rift. The ship's relay pumped out a sad, reflective saxophone soliloquy by Kenny G – how appropriate – and I imagined Clair de Lune with heavenly choirs. Having fallen 150 metres through the gorges, the Yángzi/Cháng continued in its flat Middle Reaches from Yíchāng in Húbĕi Province as a brown highway devoid of anything interesting to see. I sensed the termination of any further purpose to my journey. The Chinese see this river as one's life flowing, the gorges representing the difficulties presented – one of them being simultaneously the most attractive and the most dangerous. Amen to that.

> *Misfortune should make one more steadfast and should not frustrate one's lofty ambitions.*
> Wáng Bó, drowned aged 26 – one of the four great early Táng authors

> *Yet we have not come to the end of our feelings;*
> *Looking back, she says again:*
> *'If you remember my silken skirt of green,*
> *Have tender regard for the sweet grass*
> *wherever you go.'*
> Niú Xījī, born c. 925[1]

Building the Three Gorges Dam is not the first time the inventive Chinese have harnessed water. In the 3rd century BC, they were using a ladder of gates in canals to allow progress in stages – Europe cottoned on to that over 1,400 years later. To power their vessels they were the first to fit paddle wheels, in the 5th century. Personally I can only admire such an everyday ability of the common person to solve problems without bragging, often in the heat of dire circumstances.

The statistics surrounding the dam illustrate its devastating scale. After forty years of surveys and investigations, the first concrete of the project was poured in December 1994. Over a million people will be resettled, with the submerging of twelve cities (such as Fēngdū and Wūshān), 120 towns, 350 substantial villages (including along the Dàníng), over a hundred cultural sites, and some 7,000 factories. The course of the Dàníng River may even be reversed.

If that sounds unacceptable, bear in mind that the Chinese authorities have longed to stem the undeniable carnage and damage caused by the 218 recorded floods in the Yángzi basin over a 2,000-year period. In the 1954 flood, thousands of people were killed, nineteen million made homeless, the crucial railway line between Guăngzhōu and Bĕijīng was cut for three months, and $30 billion of damage resulted. 1931 saw a worse cataclysm: 140,000 perished, and the lives of thirty or forty million disrupted. Every year, a major task has been renovating thousands of kilometres of dykes. In AD 587, the river's victims' blood turned the water red. In 1608 a deadly dry period was followed by a lethal deluge. Archibald Little records Fēngdū 'having been entirely washed away in the terrific flood of 1870'[2]. In the past two decades, a serious flood has befallen every year or two, a consequence of deforestation and soil erosion upstream, plus over-intensive agriculture.

The kilometre-long dam at Sāndōupíng near Yíchāng has been completed (1998), and the flooding of towns begins in 2003. The final cost of the project is $75 billion, and it will save burning 50 million tons of air-polluting coal each year – the equivalent output of fifteen nuclear power plants. Given the underwhelming beauty that will be submerged, it seems that instead of arguing against on those sort of grounds, the world should have tried to convince the authorities of the virtues of a series of smaller dams, rather than a single giant 185 metres high, whose safety, efficiency, and shelf-life are exceedingly dubious. Too late now. Even with it operating, there will not be enough electricity for the demand, despite China already producing more electricity than most countries in the world. Two nuclear energy plants are in operation, one in Shànghăi, and a further twenty projected by 2020 will still only provide a quarter of energy requirements. A sensible way forward would be technically to 'clean up' China's coal burners, but the half-a-trillion dollars to do so is simply not available, even internationally.

The treatment of the peasants is saddening: typical compensation for a homeowner at Fēngdū has been set at $20 a square metre, but replacement blocks being constructed will cost over twice that. They will be forced into intimidating debt, which will also test the financial credibility of the lending banks.

◆ ◆ ◆ ◆

Floating under the mile-long double-decker bridge in **Wŭhàn** lifted my spirits. The city's position in the centre-east of the country is a vital pivot for rail, road and air transport, and the twin railway tracks on the bridge's lower deck, with the road above, grandly connects North and South China. Wŭhàn is also the limit for ocean-going ships sailing 1,100 kilometres upriver from Shànghăi.

I donned my bulging packs and walked a couple of miles searching for somewhere to stay, the likely hotels to the north being full or expensive. A useful discovery was the fine if sprawling Rénmín Fàndiàn, centrally located over a McDonald's in Jiānghàn Lù and not mentioned in the guidebooks. Having negotiated a room rate by telephone, I arrived twenty minutes later when the receptionist tried to increase the tariff!

What is now Wŭhàn with four million urban people used to be three independent cities separated by the T of the Yángzi with its longest tributary, the 1,530-kilometre Hàn River. The central Hànkŏu area was downright filthy, with the worst litter I saw in China. The Wŭchāng district featured the commendable Húbĕi Provincial Museum with its 2,400-year-old giant set of 64 bronze chiming bells. In the third sector Hànyáng, Guīyuán (Return to Basics) Temple was so crowded, it being a weekend, that I could not capture any spiritual feel. Shops were buzzing in the temple courtyard, ice creams were on sale, and one could barely enter the famed hall of 500 *lohan*. There was a painting of Xuán Zàng returning from his journey to India: his Wheel of Life had turned a full circle, as almost had mine, and I purchased a ticket for a flight south.

◆ ◆ ◆ ◆

---

[1] From *For Remembrance*, translated by Chu Dagao [*101 Chinese Lyrics*, p. 39]
[2] *Through the Yang-tse Gorges*, p. 193

22-21 *The elevated highway, Huanshi Lù, semi-circles the city centre.*

Guǎngzhōu

The plane flew so low over **Guǎngzhōu** (Extensive Island) as to make me gasp, and grasp for my camera. The city centre looked like a half-smashed Lego land smothered in smog. Some grey pieces were erect – fifties office blocks – with the majority a mishmash of squat dwellings. A tree-lined square of water with a white palace on one side floated past, while low green hillocks veered closer at the same height as my eyes. At a few hundred feet, as buildings flashed past like the windows of a subway train approaching a stop, we swooped over the city's main railway station, its courtyard a panoply of people like wildebeest on an African plain *(22-21)*. Within seconds we were over the straight highway, Jiefang Běilù, that intersects the centre in two, and it seemed as if we were going to touch down on it! Cars were proceeding only a little slower below us – I could have picked them up like dinky toys. As I braced myself to land on the roof of a pantechnicon, the road promptly ceased, we cleared a fence by a few whiskers, and the wheels kissed an empty runway that was an extension of the road!

The airport has since been superseded by a new one, safely out of reach of vehicles' rear-view mirrors that can no longer relay the vision of a plane approaching, talons lowered. With the demise of the old Hong Kong airport that sported a similar if not as riveting flight path, one of the most thrilling experiences in China is alas no more.

I walked from the railway station to the good-value Friendship Hotel, clearly marked nearby on the Lonely Planet map. A man insisted on accompanying me, only to demand a fee for having 'guided' me there: he didn't like it when I declined. Again the room was an air-con icebox, and it contained for the first time in my travels a safe. That emphasised the guidebook's warning: 'Canton is easily the most dangerous city in China', and 'whatever you do, be careful near the railway station. The whole area is a den of thieves'.

So it was with a drumming heart that I braved the throng at the station to obtain a ticket for my exit from China the next day – only a few remained. I smiled at my temerity. Colin Thubron captures the feeling well:

> The frisson of solitary travel – travel in a boyish euphoria of self-sufficiency – tingles in my stomach as I march across Beijing's railway station. This feeling is perfectly individual, like homesickness or *déjà vu*, and I greet it as an old and bullying friend, who is stronger than I am, and more enterprising.
>
> *Behind the Wall* (p. 67)

The city's Western name is probably a variant of Guǎngdōng, the name of the province of which it is the capital. Cantonese has double the tones of Mandarin, making the language a Westerner's *bête noire*! Being beside the Zhū Jiāng (Pearl River) and sheltered from coastal typhoons, Guǎngzhōu was on the Maritime Silk Route that terminated in faraway Madagascar. In the Yuán Dynasty (1279–1368) over 140 nations traded here, the Chinese importing pearls, peppers and peacock feathers, as well as rattan from Malaysia and myrrh from the Red Sea.

Commencing with the Portuguese in 1516, the area was the principal, often exclusive point of contact between China and the West for centuries during the Míng and Qīng. Trade with the foreign devils was entirely restricted to this port from 1757, the British illegally pushing opium from India in order to balance accountancy books against the cost of tea, at that time being imported into Britain at a cost of £2½ million per annum. In the 1830s, a tiny settlement of a few hundred men of nine nationalities existed by the Pearl River, outside the south-west corner of the walled city. The immature British forced the continuation of their lucrative smuggling trade – money taking priority over morals – with the First Opium War (1840–42), a spoil of which was Hong Kong. After the second war the following decade, the 900 by 300-metre Shāmiàn Island on the river was stuffed with foreign factory concessions.

It was to that island in China that I headed first, it being traffic-free with the feel of a quiet leafy vale removed from the concrete jumble of nearby access roads. One could almost smell the old colonial way of life, though few of those buildings survive. The White Swan Hotel selfishly prevented one from viewing the river from its prime water frontage.

Giving the Snake Restaurant a miss (I have seen on TV the Cantonese strip the skins off alive), I treated myself to the island's Victory Hotel Restaurant for a well cooked and served dinner. Except that nibbles already on the table proved not to be complimentary when the bill arrived, which added a higher service charge than the menu stated. When the young head waitress refused to countenance my objections, giving a dismissive facial gesture, something within me snapped.

It is well documented that most long-term independent travellers in China succumb to an explosive irritation with the way things are done. On top of the to-be-expected wear of noisy humdrum accommodation, the grind of trains and buses, the dozens of daily on-the-spot decisions to be made, in China one is continually trying not to be ripped off at every turn when paying for even minor articles. Obtaining a piece of bread, a ticket for a monastery, or a bowl of soup – let alone a bus ticket – is a battle, and one starts to assume they are out to do you. Related to this is the haggling, requiring one to be ahead of the game by determining the true rate, or accepting the consequences. At first it is amusing, but after five constant months it is a drain on patience and humour.

Moreover, I had long been aware that running out of money and travellers cheques was a real possibility – I had spent more than budgeted with Ritchie. It had been a nagging stress the previous couple of months. Then there had been the Rift, and fighting God.

22-22

So a disrespectful argument ensued; I called for the manager – none was available – and departed paying what should have been on the bill. It left a sour taste with everyone, and I regretted it later. It was a boorish way of dealing with a small matter; Confucius would not have approved. It was time to go home. I was tired, and tired of relationships, tired of God, tired of humans' failings including my own, tired of the hassle of China.

◆ ◆ ◆ ◆

My last day travelling in the country commenced with a stroll through Qīngpíng Market, near the island. A friend who had seen this had summarised her grisly experience with the words "The Chinese can be so cruel to animals", so I was relieved that on this occasion there was little activity. The architecture heading east still evoked a seedy sense of the past, with elegant details on stone facades of apartments above stores unappreciated in the seething tide of balconies of hung washing, grimy walls not cleaned or renovated since they were built, workaday vans, and glaring poster-ads in a busy hotchpotch of common Chinese city life.

Stuck absurdly in the middle of this, like an island in China, was a Roman Catholic cathedral. Designed by a French architect (Guillemin) and consecrated in 1863, the Sacred Heart Church was part of the bounty the French received from the Chinese government as 'compensation' for the second Opium War. Built of grey granite, it is called the 'House of Stone' by locals. It emitted an inflexible solidity to me, its double-towered frontage grim and gothic. Fenced off with the iron gate barred and locked, the building and its deity seemed cold, out of place, uncaring, untouchable, distant.

As I took its photograph, I disliked God intensely *(22-22)*.

God behind bars, and better to keep it that way. The red sign that in effect says 'Keep away!' seemed an apt warning. A Heart of Stone would be a more appropriate appellation. Or maybe it was me behind bars. Whatever, the barriers between the Creator and me were fully up.

God had achieved the purpose of my trip: not to like H/him.

It was to be a year before Grand Old Pa would recommence communicating again by signs. It was to take that time for me to warm to H/him again. It was to take me that year to work out even half of the whys of the events from Cheju to the Rift, during which I took the decision to write about them. It was to take the writing of these books to understand a lot more, and, needless to say, I still don't comprehend it all. That's probably because I haven't reached the end.

★ ★ ★

After climbing the steps up a hill to the Zhènhǎi Tower – all that remains of the city wall – and having toured the nearby large-scale Tomb Museum, I collected my twin packs, went through passport control at the station, and passed the three hours to Hong Kong in a state of calm anticipation.

Two days later, on the first of March, I flew to Korea for an important ten days, renewing friendships and discussing the apocryphal event in China with them. After a day back in Hong Kong, and with a final few dollars in pocket, I caught a taxi to the old airport. To avoid a major traffic jam, the driver took me on a circuitous route, the resultant fare exceeding my reserves by a few cents. I paid him all I had, the driver being unconcerned. I grinned: after all my pre-deliberations as to the likely cost, after five months of continuous travel, I had spent exactly what I had and hence what I took, with not a cent to spare!

★ ★ ★

Each grain of Sand
Every Stone on the Land
Each rock & each hill
Each fountain & rill
Each herb & each tree
Mountain hill Earth & Sea
Cloud Meteor & Star
Are Men Seen Afar

William Blake,
letter to Thomas Butts, 1800

Seated by a window as usual, the plane having skimmed the towering apartment blocks of Hong Kong, I took the last photograph of my travels in China *(22-23)*. The Lord of the Skies had provided cotton wool clouds for my send off. They are cotton wool islands, casting their own shadows, each of them part of the Amoeba, connected but separate, a mass of individual cells scurrying along like little amoebae.

In this case, of course, *we* are the cotton wool islands.

I smiled at God's wee joke.

22-23

Islands in China summary

Widen your mind so that it can contain all the
things in the world;
empty your mind so that it can accept all the
goodness of the world;
calm your mind so that it can tolerate all
happenings of the world;
deepen your mind so that it can find out all
principles of the world;
concentrate your mind so that it can meet all the
needs of the world.
Lǚ Kūn (1536-1618),
Shēn Yín Yǔ

Rely on the message of the teacher, not on his personality;
Rely on the meaning, not just on the words;
Rely on the real meaning, not on the provisional one;
Rely on your wisdom mind, not on your ordinary,
judgmental mind.
The Four Reliances of Buddha,
quoted in *The Tibetan Book of Living and Dying* (p. 130)

Wise men do not grow grass on their heads.
Chinese saying

In the physical sense, China is perhaps the ugliest country in the world – that refers to Hàn China, not the wildness of Tibet or Xīnjiāng. There are pockets that are wonderful – isolated islands in a sea of grey – and this book has concentrated on them. Otherwise, there is a dearth of trees, the countryside shaved like a skinhead. Half the area of China used to be forested, but is down to 7% on average, largely due to humans. Despite recent tree-planting campaigns, one has to make an effort to imagine the land as it was. Forget those titillating statistics littered in publications of a profusion of wildlife, birds, beautiful unique plants and obscure animals; they are not to be seen, unless in unfortunate form in a Chinese market.

There are beautiful cultural assets such as temples, but they are surrounded by muck, concrete and industrial grime. Such beauty in the way Westerners regard it often seems unloved and unappreciated – a probable consequence of the most ghastly life of any people in the 20th century, a reflex action of concentrating on survival.

So a prolonged visit to China is not one I would recommend, not even to the traveller, until s/he has sampled the orgy of inspiring scenery and wonders found elsewhere in the world. A sightseeing package is one solution, but expensive with limited feel for the country, many flights being a necessity (air safety has improved significantly). The true rewards of China are specialised, and require a certain maturity and insight to appreciate, plus the patience of a buddha.

It is physically vast: deciding on the routes of Parts Two and Three and what to see took a year's planning, weather being a prime factor. I travelled some 13,000 kilometres on land and rivers, as well as a further 10,000 on internal flights and coastal waters, through the autonomous regions of Xīnjiāng and Guǎngxī and seventeen officially designated provinces and municipalities, omitting six plus Hǎinán Island in the south.

Apart from Kāshí (Kashgar), the only area I did not visit that would be recommended is most of Tibet, and the edge of its plateau in the north-west of Sìchuān into Qīnghǎi – but only in summer, unless you don't mind becoming stuck for months. The south-east province of Fújiàn has a profusion of new temples, if that appeals, paid for by rich overseas Chinese. Hǎinán's original dense tropical forests, rubber trees, 500 species of birds, and 200 amphibians have been decimated in just three decades. For the casual visitor the industrial northeast is to be avoided: five million workers have been made redundant in the past decade, and the sky over Shěnyáng was described to me as 'black with filthy coal dust', and Běnxī is worse. For a true nomadic experience, visit Mongolia proper, not that part of China that is Inner Mongolia, now populated largely by the Hàn Chinese.

The overriding reward is encouraging one to think of life's meaning. There is spirituality in those pockets, even though a scene may be glanced only for a moment. If you go, please bear this in mind. Many Westerners, including the majority in Britain these days, do not know what a holy place *means*. It is created by people of an area believing in the divine as first nature, and acting on it as if having breakfast. Thereby the sacred spirit is invited into the area, and palpably exists there, within and around. The result is you can touch it. Trees and mountains exude the *qì*, and objects such as bracelets take on real energy, real powers. One can sense it, for instance, in an old church in the English countryside – the *qì* positively pulsates. We are backward when we don't recognise it.

I mention this because if you cannot appreciate and respect that sacredness in such places, better to stay away. It can be discouraged and retreat. Too many disrespectful tourists can drive out the very essence that made it attractive in the first place. Please don't tell such tourists about Wǔtáishān.

Florence Ayscough noted in her 1925 book *A Chinese Mirror*:

> China is usually treated by the West from a purely academic point of view; that is, her art, literature and archaeology are studied as are similar subjects connected with dead civilisations; but China is alive, and she is virile; moreover, her ancient beliefs and thoughts are indissolubly knit into the life of her people.
>
> published by Jonathan Cape (p. 15)

What sets China apart from all other countries is that the people have a longer continuous history than anyone else. China stands out from the other civilisations with which it grew up – Egypt, Babylon, Assyria, Greece, Rome and others – in that it is the only one that still exists. In that sense, the country is truly the *Zhōng Guó*, the Central Nation. That is what the Chinese call their land, meaning it in the sense of between Heaven and Earth, which is where we should all be.

Maybe the rest of us comparative upstarts can be reminded of certain things by this venerable nation.

The human spirit of the Central Nation can be seen in this family portrait, which I noticed on a wall in a museum in Chóngqìng *(22-24)*. Here is a paradigm of the strength and will of Chinese motherhood: she was Yao Guo Mo who died in the 1960s, plus her son and daughters. They display obvious sterling qualities. She habitually donated money to poor farmers.

That strength of will can be seen even in Chinese sculpture epitomising the noblest qualities in an entity. On guard along the spirit way near the Míng tombs in Běijīng is a *xiezhi* *(22-25)*. This upright, handsome mythical feline, with a flowing fiery mane, exudes determination to carry out its purpose in life, which is to differentiate right from wrong, good from evil.

On my last day in China, these people greeted me from within a shop in Guǎngzhōu *(22-26)*. They are a symbol for the majority of common Chinese. Despite their struggle to make ends meet on relatively low wages, they are happy to give a part of themselves to a stranger without preconditions, and laugh. They will never attract publicity, nor feature in a newspaper's list of the top hundred great people of the past century, nor be in Who's Who. But to me they are great, with an inner beauty beyond wonder. If I could, I would follow them and be with them for ever.

That hospitality explains why the country is not usually dangerous for Western travellers, nor specifically for women. Strangers who approach are commonly of the curious type.

251

22-25

22-26

Poverty is the common thread of the nation: people near, on, or below the rice line, whose lives seem to lack much meaning. Not for nothing is being imprisoned on Earth the same as Hell. From this, a universal message trumpets in all our faces: we are not here to have an easy life. Yet, although no one would like to be in their position, there is stoicism in the face of hunger, cold, and not being sure of the next bowl of rice that is inspiring, and inspires compassion. There is an acceptance and joy in small pleasures, which in turn leads to a smile within – they would not survive otherwise. It is enduring a lifetime of everyday grind without losing heart that makes the common person everywhere heroic, and which is a light for the world.

> Blessed are the poor in spirit; the kingdom of Heaven is theirs. Blessed are the sorrowful.... Blessed are you, when you suffer.... You are light for all the world.... they see the good you do.
> oral/written tradition, based on Jesus' sermons [Matt.5.3–16]

The problem with those beatitudes is that the rewards are for later – in Heaven; and most of the world does not see the light – the intended Message of suffering. Meanwhile, there is no blessedness in being abjectly poor, and you cannot do good when you are starving or being massacred.

The earthly blessedness comes from *not* being poor in spirit, while being poor. Therein lies the greatness. That is a blazing beacon to all of us who are suffering in other ways; it is a startling gift from those poor who can still smile. It is a real quality present in the Chinese, as with others. If they can do it, so should those of us ensconced in comfort.

We all know that poverty must be eradicated. When it is, will we also have lost the blessed quality? How does one achieve one without losing the other?

The answer is to be at one with the poor people in this world – not intellectually, not with an arrogant conviction of superiority, not as in a vivisection laboratory; but by living with them, or at least spending moments with them, and rediscovering what they teach us. This is where a traveller can be in an honoured position.

Sometime China will grow a substantial middle class; then democracy, human rights and free speech will blossom automatically, just as by the same means they have started to do so in neighbouring South Korea and Táiwān. The goal is to extinguish poverty, but to retain its lessons. It would be a disaster for humanity if we fail to learn from the poor that which many of us comparatively rich tend to forget, or have already lost in our lust for money, possessions and power.

Peace comes from acceptance, while acceptance and humility walk hand in hand like Asian friends. Humility is one of the lessons. It is accepting what we are and where we're supposed to be in the relative universal scheme. Personally, I'm only beginning to realise what and where that is. It is a kind of faith.

Catherine Toler showed me photographs of her family's servants, taken by her father O.M. Green when they lived in No. 54 Avenue du Roi Albert in Shànghăi in the 1920s [q.v. chapter 5]. She enthused: "Oh, they were lovely – so kind to us. I loved the Chinese." Their faces in the photographs below reveal they possessed special qualities: in *22-28*, clockwise from the back left, is Gardener, Cook, No. 2 Boy, No. 2 Cook (peeling potatoes), and Coolie (holding an axe).

No. 2 Cook was referred to as "larn pidgin", which is a distortion of 'learning business': while learning his job he was unpaid. Cook was skilled in French cuisine, later becoming head chef of a major hotel. Cake making was his speciality, on which he erected candles made from butter.

There was also No. 1 Boy, "who spoke perfect English and French also". His real name was Wang Kew[1] Ding, of whom Green wrote:

22-27

22-28

[1] 'Kew' is not *pīnyīn*.

22-29 *taken in Tiānhòu Temple, Tiānjīn*

There seemed to be nothing he could not do and, within the limits of what was due to his 'face', nothing he would not do.... [He] relieved one of all the irritating etceteras of life which cost so much time and temper.
The Foreigner in China (p. 130)

In a letter to me, Catherine revealed more of the nature of her staff:

> We also had an amah. She was a country woman but also an artist, and when our bathroom window would mist up following the running of bath water, she would with her finger draw on it the most delicate arrangement of flowers!

Even seven decades later, Catherine spoke fluent Pidgin English, which essentially was a modification designed to assist the Chinese with alien consonants, often using abbreviated words, others commandeered from the previous Pidgin Portuguese, tenses deduced from context, and final consonants exaggerated, such as *goodee*, *catchee*, and *olo* meaning 'old'. Grammar was simplified, so that *my* could also mean me, I, mine, us, we, our, ours; *he* substituted for him, his, she, her, and hers.

Expressive, affectionate, infectiously vigorous, respectful, picturesque, humorous, and melodious, it is a joy to hear! That is aside from its efficiency as a language in practical situations. In fact, it seems to reflect the qualities of the Chinese people themselves.

Catherine concluded on her time in China:

> I look back on it with great pleasure, the Chinese were so kind.

The Chinese were so kind – right. And so full of the qualities that compose the best in humans: I also love them. Looking at the people in these old photographs, they remind me of the Koreans I met over two years.

These words by Green from 1928 seem as if they were penned only yesterday:

> Like all revolutions that of China has thrown the scum to the top, and the people who momentarily claim to speak in her name... are as alien in spirit as their actions are disgraceful to her. Wholly different are the true Chinese people, possessed of sterling qualities which have never been questioned, courtesy, common sense, willingness to live and let live and a clear perception at the last of what is just and fair.
> *Shanghai of Today* (p. 15)

Within these people lie the secrets of the *jūnzi*, the perfect person.

★ ★ ★

This book is not only about China, but concerns the broader palate of Asia, Korea in particular. Examples abound of the generosity to me as a stranger in that land, such as a refreshing cucumber given on top of a mountain, or a telephone card thrust into my hand when I ran out of coins at a public phone booth.

Concerning the foreigner's experiences of Koreans, F.A. McKenzie [q.v. chapter 10] wrote in 1908:

> He learnt more and more to appreciate their kindheartedness, their lack of guile, their genuine simplicity, their willingness to learn, and their many loveable and likeable qualities. This was my own experience, and in discussing Korean life with those who know it better than myself, I have learned that it was theirs. I have found the Korean a loyal friend, a faithful servant, and one who, when given the chance, is capable of much.... Very little encouragement will induce the Korean servant to undertake the most perilous ventures. In the course of my journeys through Korea and Manchuria, I found my Korean boys take risks and carry through enterprises at which an uneducated English lad might well hesitate. I found them serve me faithfully, loyally, and well. They have in their characters great potentialities.
> *The Tragedy of Korea* (pp. 31/2)

A particular incident occurred a few weeks before leaving Korea that is responsible, in the end, for this book's existence. Not one to read astrological predictions in the popular press, I had only once decades previously procured a proper chart. It was arresting, with descriptions of character like reading an open book of my heart, which few knew. It also advised that my 'house should be in middle of street facing SE'; the current one is. Korea has a long tradition of fortune-tellers, and with the events of Cheju and thereafter in mind, I took a translator with me to consult one in the centre of Seoul.

About six in makeshift cubicles lined a kerb. I walked steadily past eyeing the choice, and they each beckoned eager to win my custom. Except for one, who didn't raise his head; older than me, there was something mysterious about him. I sat on a bench while he analysed my face *(kwan sang)*, noting the eyebrows, the area between and around the eyes, and other features. He obtained my birth details – born in the year of the Tiger, on the 12th day of the 3rd month, in Borneo – and spent twenty minutes in animated fashion concocting a chart from reference books.

That done, he delivered a torrent of remarks for half an hour in a controlled yet excited fashion, commenting on aspects within and outside the chart's boundary, my translator barely keeping pace writing them down and verbally translating. I asked three general questions – about marriage, friendship, and God (the concept of the last had to be carefully explained). As related to me afterwards, most comments were astonishing, with details revealed by a total stranger who could not know, nor guess. It was so uncanny that – and laugh if you like, reader – I sensed it was Grand Old Pa talking to me through this fortune-teller. Here are some as written at the time, virtually in order of their delivery.

> You are part of the Sun.
>   (literal translation: Your body is the Sun)
> You cannot endure bad or evil.
> If you decide something is right, you are not
>   sidetracked by others.
> You can mentally rule spirits. (meaning:
>   you can control yourself and others)
> You are a prosecutor or judge of values.
> You are a teacher or professor.
> You are the light and sword of society.
> You really, really love travelling –
>   you *have* to visit many countries.
> Travelling is a good thing for you:
>   it leads to poetry, music, literature.
> You have fewer friends in England than around
>   the world (because of travel).
> If you write a book, it will be a real *hit*.

> You are supposed to have many partings from women.
> There are many women around you in your life.
> You sometimes have trouble stemming from
>   some women, and you don't like
>   being restricted by them.
> You were heartbroken by a woman
>   when in your 20s or 30s.

22-30 *spirit way, near the Míng tombs, Běijīng*

> Concerning marriage – the later the better for you.
>   [The fortune-teller then enquired if
>   I was wedded.]
> You will settle down by the age of 51.
> You are not arrogant, though you have strong
>   confidence in your self-esteem.
> You have a strong eye. (meaning: you can read minds,
>   and see the truth of an object)
> If you write a book, it will be a real success.

> Property and money come not without effort.
> If you just move (meaning: keep working),
>   money will follow.
> You will never be a millionaire because you live in the
>   mental world, not the physical one.
> In a previous life, you were someone who ruled the
>   mental world; that's why money is
>   not important to you.
> You never have worries concerning eating,
>   clothing, housing.
> You have never experienced poverty.
> You like facing problems, taking the bull by the horns.
> You have inspiration from God.
>   (literal translation: 'divine feeling')
> If you were a Christian, Buddhist or a woman,
>   you would be a priest, monk or nun.
> If you write a book, it will be a tremendous success.

> There are all kinds of metal in your life: orchestras,
>   metallic musical instruments, gold.
> You have a strong instinct for music.
> You used to be a musician in your 30s.
>   (implication: until recently)
> You like change and new experiences,
>   otherwise you are bored.
> If you write a book, it will be really, really successful.

Friends would agree that all the above are pertinent, and while some could apply to anyone, the comments concerning travel, late marriage (and 30s heartbreak), attitude to money, music, being a teacher and having a sabbatical from a music career – all originating from a stranger – are eerily spot on. Coming after Cheju, the short 'inspiration from God' sentence was charged, and when he chose to start with the extraordinary remark concerning the Sun (to me the symbol of God), my attention was gripped immediately.

The translator reiterated the fortune-teller's passion concerning the forecast surrounding any book – the complete sentence delivered four times. A year later, this was instrumental in persuading me to write, and specifically a book – even though the multimedia aspects suggested a CD Rom instead.

Note, though, that the words were "If you write..."; that most certainly involved a free choice. They were not, "You will write...". Nevertheless, without that four-time encouragement, indeed promise, I wonder if I would have commenced at all. It remains to be seen whether it will be a 'success', which to me would be most readers feeling they had gained from perusing it, and the publisher not making a loss. The spirit world, in contrast and if at all, might be thinking fifty years or centuries ahead: only posthumous recognition has occurred to countless works and artists.

I could not ignore what happened in Cheju and discard it. It was a Gift and a Privilege, whose essence I considered should be passed on. While pondering what should be the substance of the book, a coincidence encouraged me not only to describe China, a topic quite large enough! About to enter a cinema, I noticed that an adjacent shop happened to sell only religious books. Prominently placed in the window was a sign that said: 'Speak about the existence of God'.

> Modern man has such hopelessly muddled ideas about anything "mystical," or else such a rationalistic fear of it, that, if ever a mystical experience should befall him, he is sure to misunderstand its true character and will deny or repress its numinosity. It will then be evaluated as an inexplicable, irrational, and even pathological phenomenon.
>
> C.G. Jung[1]

Ascertaining that I had a 'spiritual' experience has in general polarised friends and relations in spectacular fashion. Even reporting only that a most significant event had occurred caused the loss of that someone I cared for and with whom I had been friends for fifteen years. She complained vociferously, declaring I should not inform people. Another of similar vintage on hearing that I had 'touched' God, and to whom I mentioned that pain might be good for us, cancelled the usual Christmas card, and has implied she doesn't want to meet again. Another, on learning part of what is now in this book, refused to discuss it, cancelled the Christmas card, and I know I won't see her again. H. in the same situation figuratively ran amok.

I can smile at these reactions now, though they were bewildering and not funny at the time. Then there have been those miraculous friends and relations, without whom I may not have survived, who not only accepted the story without judgement or criticism, but who were keen to discuss the issues raised, and followed where matters were heading. The responses demonstrate the stratospherically different levels humans are on, and how we approach these base topics of life from violently different directions.

> Your motives and aspirations can only be understood by those who have attained the same spiritual level. So do not vainly, foolishly, expect from others understanding. Do not misjudge them for not giving it. Yours is a foreign language to them.
>
> *God Calling* (p. 120)

Certainly I feel my own path involves ejecting all that accumulated shit or evil that unbeknown has leaped off others over decades. My personal journey so far has definitely been a corruption of innocence. I would love to attain that stage that the Chinese recognised long ago, calling it the Kingly Way, *Wáng Dào*. It is the defeat of evil – not by force, not by anger, not by confrontation, but by the incandescence of one's goodness, in sight of which evil simply slinks away. It is a devastatingly silent transcendent victory – with that shield, one hardly has to denounce evil. What an amazing step to reach!

Perfection is something I'm after. Such a long-term folly! Yet a necessary goal to seek.

Before commencing to write, I felt a subterranean explosion pushing its way up inside – there was so much that had to be said. Nearing the end of the process, the feeling mentioned in chapter 4 is welling up instead. That it is not my book: it is everybody's. I hope it *is* a success, but not for my sake.

I trust God: I do not believe S/he is going to alter what was indicated through the fortune-teller. Faith and trust are involved: as a Korean student wrote...

If I do my best, God will do the rest.

★   ★   ★

22-31 *North Peak, Huáshān*

---

[1] *The problem of the fourth* (para 274), from *Collected Works, Vol. 11: Psychology and Religion: West and East* [© 1969 by Princeton University Press]

Impressed by the fortune-teller, my translator decided to undergo the same procedures. A first time for him, too, he was taken aback at the personal accuracy, including the revealing in specific detail of an aspect of his birth that only he and his parents know about – so personal that even his siblings are unaware of it. Given the circumstances, he revealed what that was to me. The feat of the fortune-teller was so extraordinary, reader, that I cannot conceive an equivalent analogy.

These examples show that astrology is not 'a pack of lies'; it can sometimes be highly pertinent communication by the spirits around. God has the prerogative to influence people and events in any way S/he chooses. The common person worldwide has the correct instinct not to dismiss this particular method outright.

The influential Chinese scholar Wáng Yángmíng (1472–1529) not only urged people to study different religions, but also to 'learn from the words of ordinary people'[1]. It is why this book is partly dedicated to the Korean fortune-teller. To me, he represents the common person of both genders – humble, hard-working, accepting, be s/he African, British, Filipino, American, Chinese, Korean et al, in this life or the previous ones, or in the tomorrow.

It is the common man and woman who are really deserving of fame. It is the ordinary subsistence farmer who can become a god, meaning it is the everyday person who can be transformed into somebody special, somebody precious, somebody perfect. A grandfather in his eighties I met during the Cheju trip had achieved that incandescently by shear dint of hard work and long life: he had obtained Peace, and was turning into God. An old Korean woman I saw simply sweeping a garden with a broom was luminous with the same distinction.

"The pine tree finds nourishment where it stands." The common person quietly does likewise. Observe a vase of picked roses, the petals around the base, down and dying, common and uncomplaining, humble and still beautiful – a gift at the last moment, even when leaving this existence.

As one of my Korean students suggested:

> See the common beauty of life that people have,
> and discover the peculiar beauty of life that
> each of them has.

So I thank the common person. Those I have met around the globe have been its intrinsic light. They have been an inspiration: they are the reason for my odyssey. In other words, this book is dedicated to them, and if you are one of them, to you.

22-32   *Qīngdǎo (twinned with Southampton, UK); two figures in the foreground are digging for crustaceans.*

[1] quoted in *Great Thinkers of the Eastern World* (p. 122)

The Chinese consider there are Five Blessings: peace, wealth, virtue, longevity, and a fine end to one's life. For each of them there is a place and a time.

> For every thing there is a season, and
> a time for every activity under heaven:
> a time to be born and a time to die;
> a time to plant and a time to uproot;
> a time to kill and a time to heal;
> a time to break down and a time to build up;
> a time to weep and a time to laugh;
> a time to mourn and a time to dance;
> a time to throw stones and a time to gather them;
> a time to embrace and a time to refrain
>   from embracing;
> a time to seek and a time to lose;
> a time to keep and a time to discard;
> a time to tear and a time to mend;
> a time to keep silent and a time to speak;
> a time to love and a time to hate;
> a time for war and a time for peace.
>   Ecclesiastes 3.1–8

That old boy, the Naximan, ended his paean celebrating Lìjiāng's new airport with this:

> THE GOOD LUCK OF CHINA TURNS
> SMOOTHLY FORWARD FOR OUR PEOPLE
> AND THEY BECOME PROSPEROUS.
> THE SILVER EAGLE BEGINS TO SOAR,
> AND ALL PEOPLE ARE ENDLESSLY HAPPY.

The perfect human knows this: that Life should be borne lightly. However much it is difficult, if possible it should be worn with a smile, like the lightest cotton frock, the most gossamer silk shirt – it should *soar*.
"Sometimes, no plan is fun."

Ananda (Sanskrit): the Joy in Existence without which the universe would fall apart and collapse.

The Táng poets reflected a culture in which girl meets boy was restricted to the point of being forbidden. Thus friendship – not romantic love – was the most important relationship outside the family, until an arranged marriage took place. To embrace and express Love for the common person, I've modified the gender of the first of the following poems.

22-33

Chinese symbol of Joy
The Clipper, *parthenos sylvia philippensis*, taken in the Tropical Plants Garden, Menglun, Xīshuāngbǎnnà

> With tears in my eyes I went out of doors
>   to bid h/him farewell.
>   Like a dream, like a dream!
> There merely remained the sinking moon,
>   the falling flowers and
>   the heavy mists.
>   Lǐ Cúnxù (born 885)

> Leaning on the railings I fondle a flower
>   between my fingers,
> And scatter the petals against the setting sun.
>   Qín Guān (1049–1100)

YOU AND I

> You and I
> Love each other so
> As from the same lump of clay
> Is moulded an image of you
> And one of me.
> In a moment of ecstasy
> We dash the images to pieces,
> Put them in water,
> And with stirring and kneading
> Mould again an image of you
> And another of me.
> There and then,
> You will find yourself in me,
> I myself in you.
> Living, we share the same bed,
> Dead, in the same sepulchre we rest.
>   Guān Dàoshēng (1260–1319),
>   poetess and painter

While lyrics are designed to be sung, if imagined freely they can soar independently. This is a song, translated, called *Gaerl gwa Namu (Autumn and Tree)*, by the Korean group Nutinamu Umduk.

> I am autumn, you are a tree.
>
> Summer is a dream.
> You have already forgotten that beautiful time;
> I just remember your trace.
>
> If you come to me again, I would forgive you –
> so I invite you. If you come to me again,
> I would do my best for you.
>
> But that fantastic summer is a dream.
> Don't forget the good times we had.
> In the way of seasons we pray for each other,
> sometimes love, sometimes hate.
>
> I am autumn, you are a tree.

Dear reader, I am autumn you are the tree.
This book is yours; take what you will from it.
No ifs, no buts, no conditions, no promises.
See hope in a butterfly, find love in a smile;
then see and find peace in yourself – it exists there!

The Chinese poetry above is translated by Chu Dagao [*101 Chinese Lyrics*]; the first extract is from *Like a Dream*, the second from *The Departure of Spring*. Born of a Turkish general, Lǐ Cúnxù became the Later Táng Emperor Zhuàngzōng in 923. Qín Guān's love poems used flowery imagery.

chapter 23

retrospective

This retrospective consists of music and photographs only, concluding with the final sunset over the Yángzi River chronicled from the small island of Jiāoshān (near Zhènjiāng). The four tracks (12 to 15) are designed to be experienced together without a break, the whole lasting sixteen minutes.

To assist in keeping track, timings are occasionally given in square brackets, e.g. [2' 51"], visible on the CD player's display screen. That is however optional and secondary. It is not important if you lag behind or become lost, only that you respond hopefully to the synthesis of music and images, and to the emotions that arise from them.

If you wish to peruse the photographs again without music, a list has been compiled on page 294 indicating the subject of each one, and/or where it was taken.

track 12
8" fade in (applause)

23-1

◀ *horns*
heroic tune

23-2

◀ *on drum*

23-3 ▲ *horns again, with trumpets*

23-4 ▼ *on drum + rushing scales*

23-5 ▲ [0' 53"] *confused section with horn swoops*

23-6 ▲ *tune again*

▼ *2nd half* **23-7**

23-8 ▲ *piano takes over*

261

23-9 ▼ *2nd half + strings*

262   **23-10**   ▲ *half repeat, piano with violins (short)*

23-11   ▲ *2nd half (short)*

23-12   *horns tune return; the rest of this double page ad lib ¾ minute until music halts and quietens down*

23-13

23-14

263

23-15

23-16   [2' 51"] *quieter with piano: this double page only 28"*

264

23-17

23-18

23-19 *minor key (this page short)*

23-20

266

back to major [3' 37"];
turn for minor key…

23-21

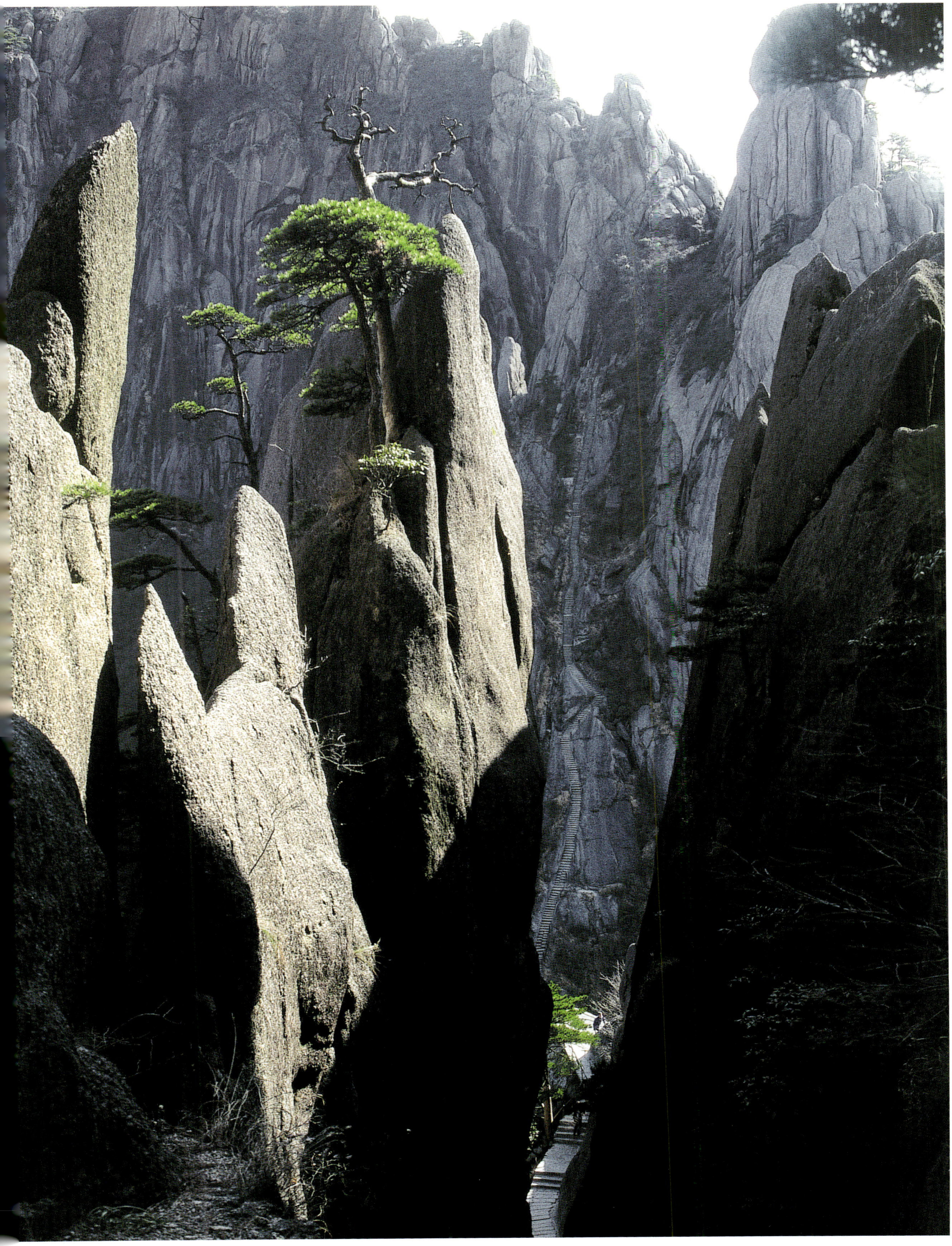

23-22 ▲ [3' 50"] *minor key (short)*

23-23 ▲ *repeat (short)*
23-24 ▼ *'Chinese' sounding melody*

23-25   *2nd half of melody; this page until return of the horns tune…*

23-26

23-27

270 **23-28** ▲ [4' 57"] back to horns tune

23-29

23-30 ▲ *2nd half with drums (very short these two pics)*

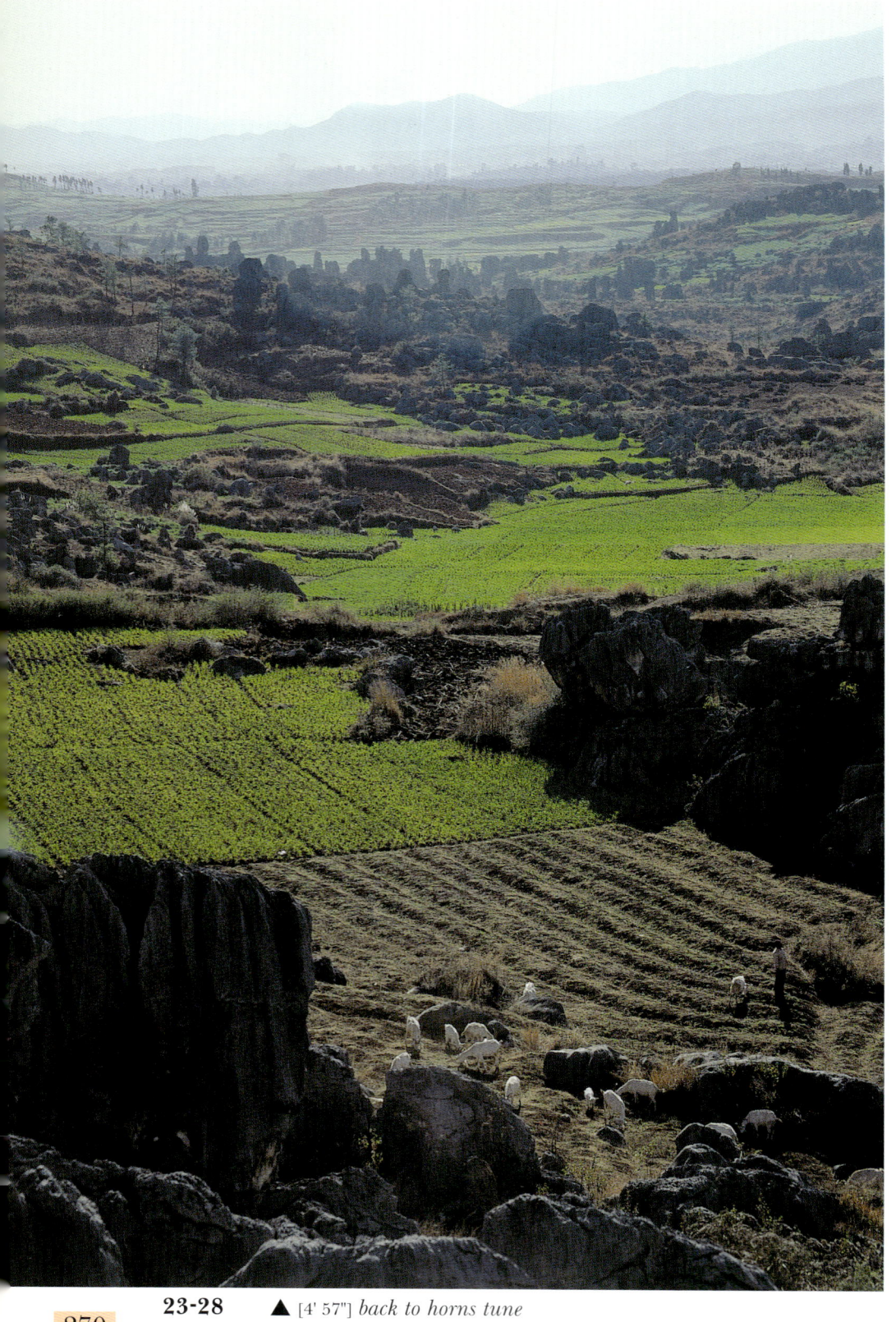

23-31 ▲ *repeat of tune again + 2nd half with violins*

▼ *trumpets added, extended; turn when music momentarily pauses…* 23-32

23-33

final section; this page until end of track

23-34

a glimpse of Eternity

273

23-35 ▲ *track 13: first 25" intro; turn for the flute/panpipe sound…*

274   **23-36**   ▲ *panpipe melody*

23-37   ◀ *repeat of melody; to facing page for louder section…*

23-38 ▲ *with louder section, till end*

lockets of Love

23-39 ▲ *track 14: short spoken extract; to next page for the final track*

island sunset
track 15: solo preamble (23");
after short gap, turn and rotate book...

23-41 ▲ + *string chord, twice (17")*

23-42 ▲ *rhythm begins, + rhythmic solo, + two chords (23″); rotate book back...*

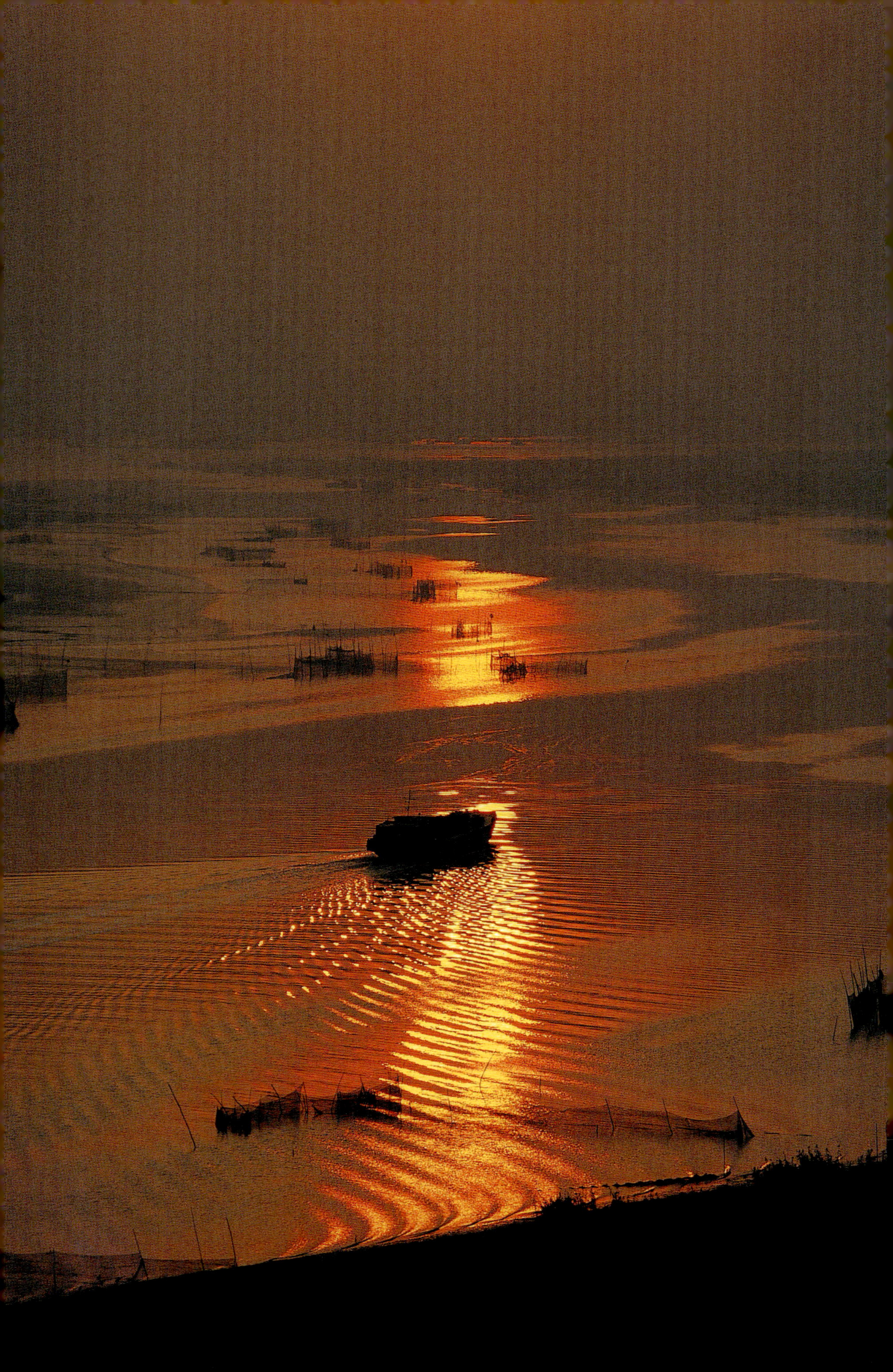

23-43 ▲ [1' 09"] ('tick') melody proper complete (20")

23-44   ▲ 8" + rhythmic 8"   next double page 23-45: 37" solo high tremolo + melody continues + solo

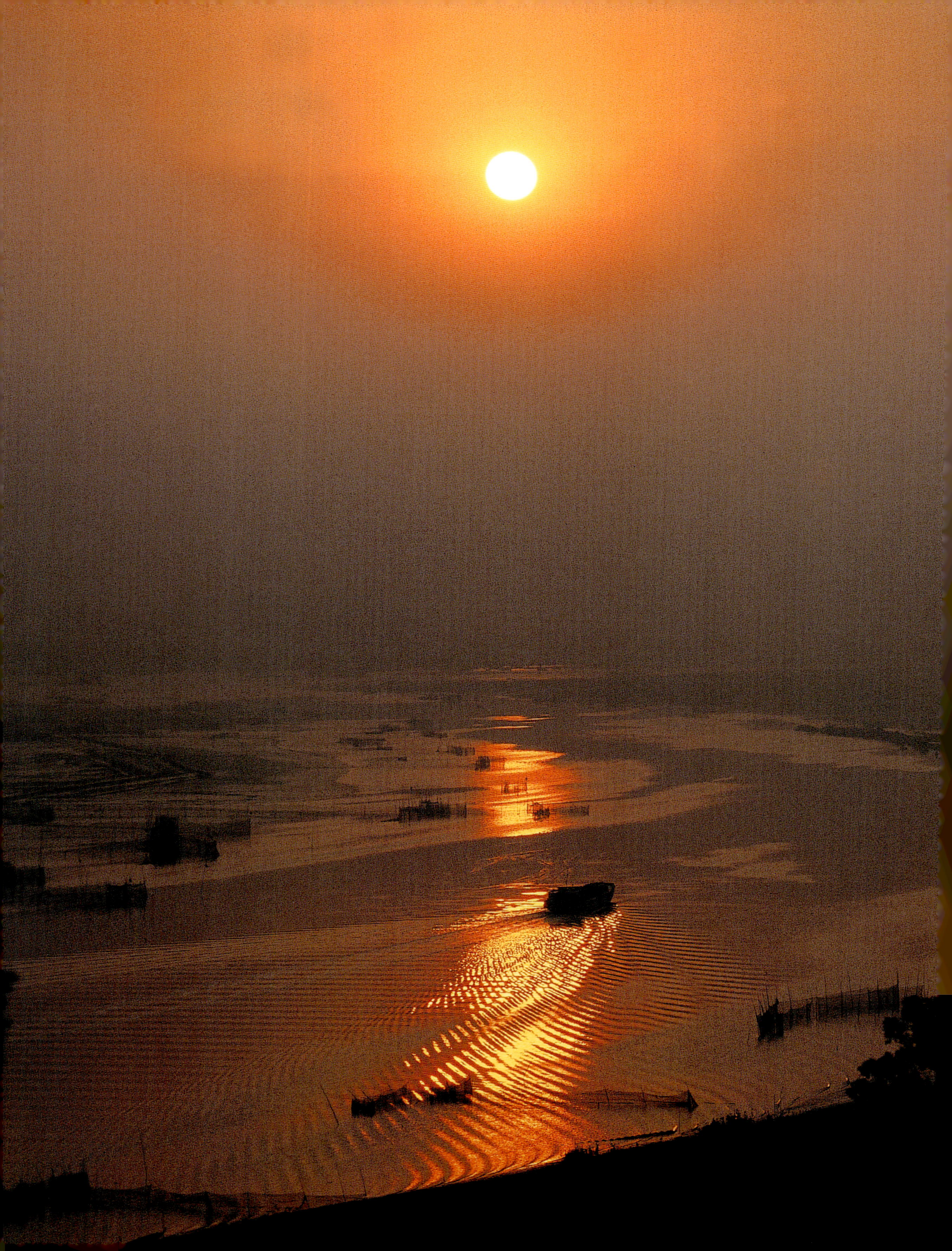

23-46 ▲ [2' 22"] *second main melody begins — 2 long phrases (23")*

23-47 ▲ *repeat of 2 long phrases (variation with cello) (23")*
23-48 ▼ *melody continues 2 more phrases (23")*

23-49 ▲ *short coda + short gap (11")*

23-50 ▲ [3' 41"] *quiet solo (30")*

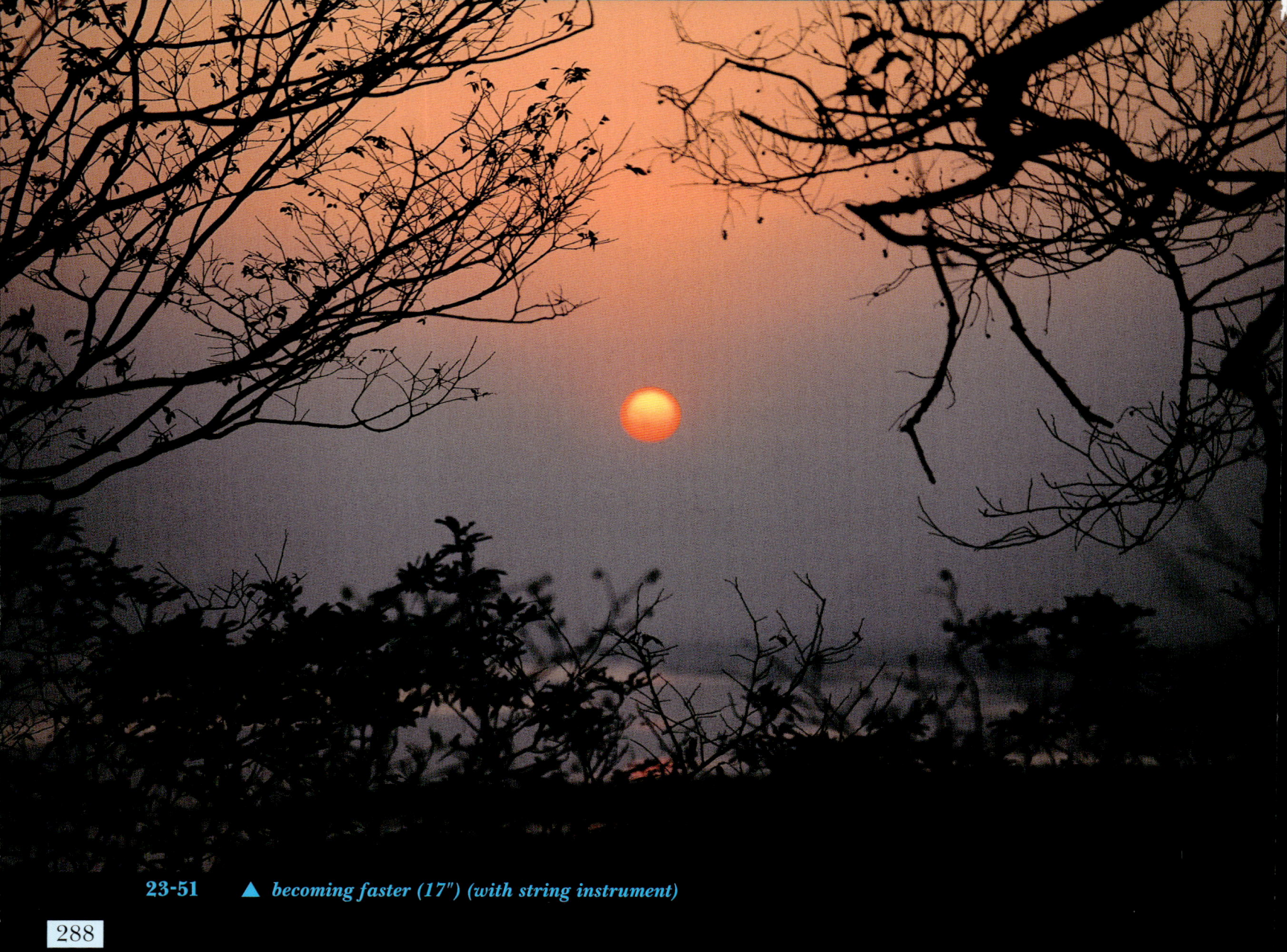

23-51 ▲ *becoming faster (17") (with string instrument)*

23-52　▲ *suddenly faster + repeated lower (22")*

23-53　▼ *[4' 49"] suddenly fuller and louder (17"); as climax is reached, turn and rotate book*

23-54 ▼ *this double page: the melody returns (24" + quieter 38" + short gap)*

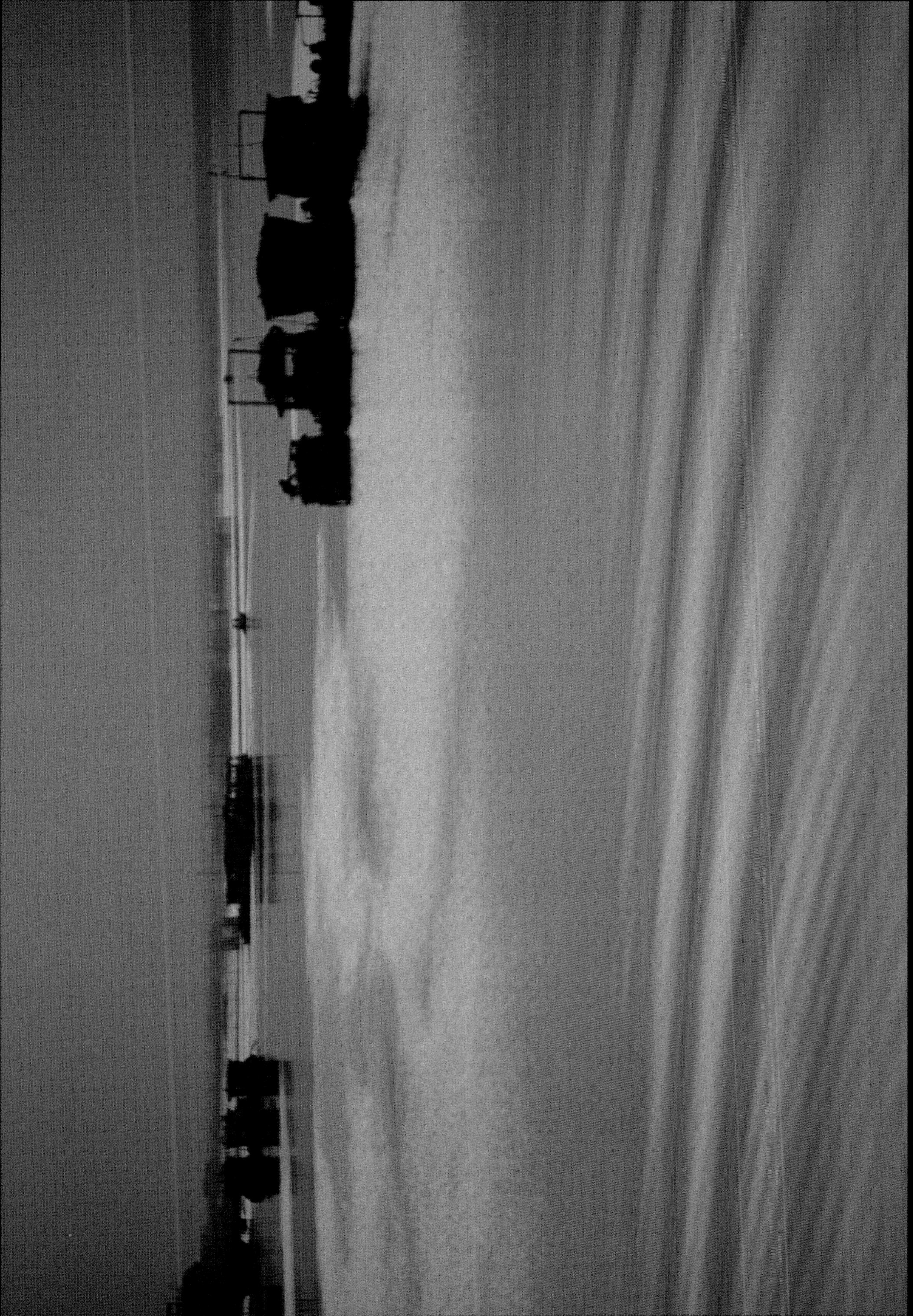

23-55

23-56 ▲ [6' 10"] *solo ending*

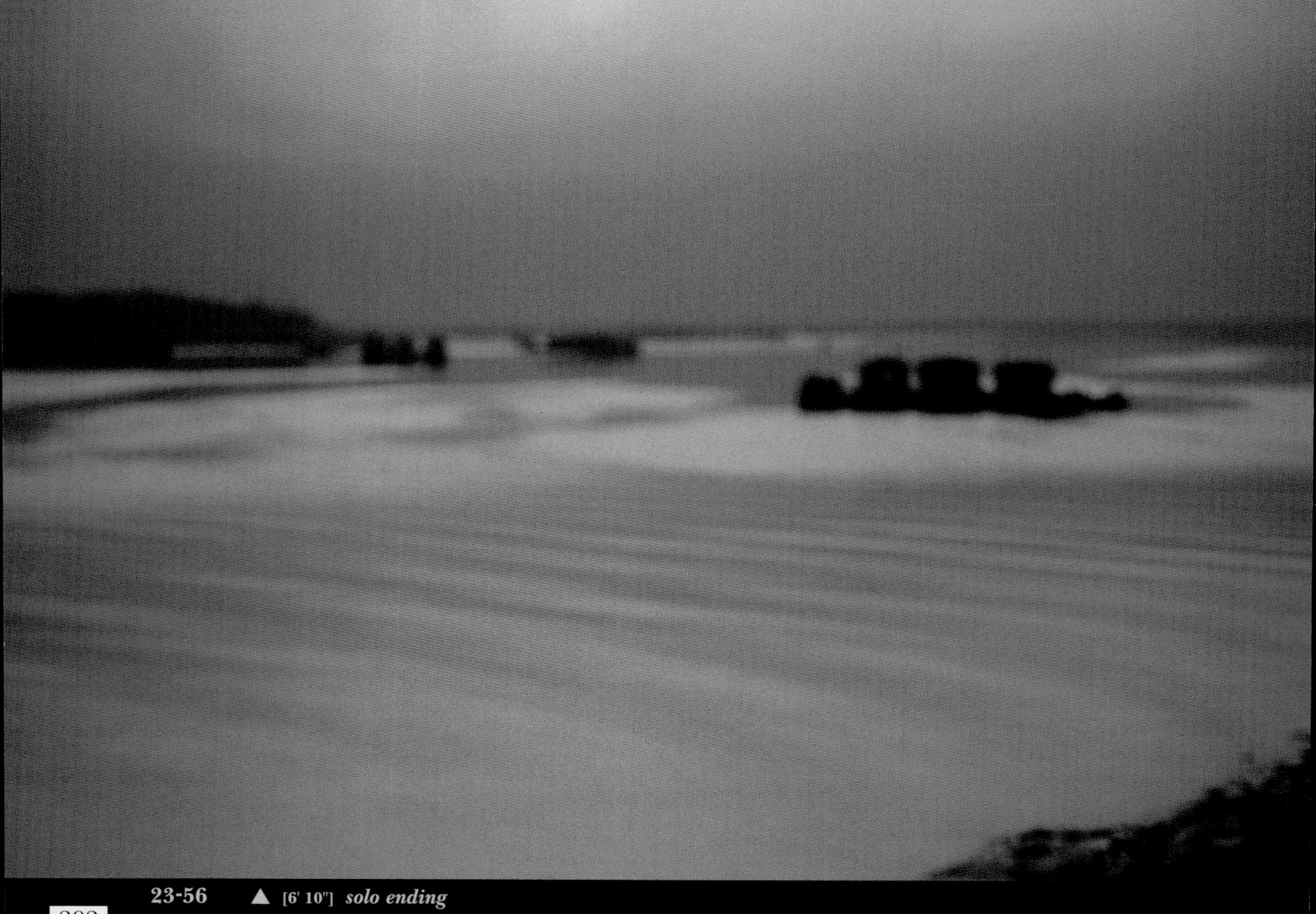

I offer you a toast: your departing towards the setting sun will soon be a part of the past.

Wáng Wéi (c.701–761), poet and painter;
one of his poems entitled *Farewell* inspired the final
section of Mahler's vocal swansong *Das Lied von Der Erde*.

photos in the retrospective

page	photo #	description and location
258	23-1	author, Kazaks and yurt; Keng Hoens, Tiānchí
	23-2	boys and camel, Keng Hoens valley, Tiānchí
259	23-3	from Mai San, looking towards the Dà Dōng Gōu, Tiānchí
	23-4	Bezeklik Caves, near Turfan
260	23-5	goldfish at the Yù Yuán, Shànghǎi
	23-6–7	mother and kids, the Yù Yuán, Shànghǎi
261	23-8	children holding hands, Tiān'ān Mén Square, Běijīng (detail of photo 6-1)
	23-9	the Imperial View Pavilion, outer wall of the Forbidden City, Běijīng
262	23-10	author on the Wooden Pagoda, Yìngxiàn, south of Dàtóng
	23-11	Dragon from Five-dragon Screen in the grounds of Shànhuà Temple, Dàtóng
	23-12	Ritchie outside the Yùhuáng Temple on top of Tàishān; in the background is Gǒngběi Rock.
	23-13	threesome outside Yùhuáng Temple, Tàishān
263	23-14	mother and child, above Zhāng'gōng Dòng, near Dīngshǔ
	23-15	view from the top of Jiǔhuáshān
264–5	23-16–18	sunrise on Huángshān
266	23-19	Xīhǎi, the West Sea, from on top of Huángshān (south of Fēilái Shí)
	23-20	looking west from Huángshān; Fēilái Shí, the Rock that Arrived by Flying, is up on the right.
267	23-21	steps on Huángshān, near the Capital of Heaven Peak. These Steps to the Bed of God can be traced from the bottom of the frame up to the sky.
268	23-22	burning candles and sun's rays, Huì Jì Chán Sì, Pǔtuóshān
	23-23	mirrored bridge with rift, near Pǔ Jì Chán Sì, Pǔtuóshān
	23-24	evening pavilion on top of Cháoyáng (Facing the Sun) Cave, Pǔtuóshān
269	23-25	end-of-street farewell, Zhàoxìng
	23-26	boy at Fǎnpái (detail of photo 15-22)
	23-27	screen from Daoist temple within Qīnglóng (Green Dragon) Cave, Zhènyuǎn. An inscription states that 'Buddha enters the cave from above the clouds'.
270	23-28	goats and herder, Shílín (the Stone Forest)
	23-29	creature from the Bamboo Temple, Kūnmíng
	23-30	white camellia tree at Tàihuá Temple, Western Hills, Kūnmíng
271	23-31	painters, Sānqīng Gé, Kūnmíng
	23-32	mural woman (possibly Yashodharā), Sānqīng Gé, Kūnmíng
272	23-33	Lake Diān, Kūnmíng, from below Lóng Mén (Dragon Gate)
	23-34	white stupa at Léizhuāngxiāng Temple, near Ruìlì
273	23-35	Qiānxún Tǎ, Dàlǐ
274	23-36	owl, Tae Hun, and traveller, with the rift; Banla, Xīshuāngbǎnnà
	23-37	the Sun's presence, Qiānxún Tǎ, Dàlǐ
275	23-38	view towards the sun, Moon Hill, Yángshuò
276	23-39	the author on Huángshān (Qīngliáng Tái); the yellow Peace jacket, lockets of love
277–292	23-40–56	sunset over the Yángzi/Cháng, from the island of Jiāoshān, near Zhènjiāng

The rules in the above column indicate the end of a music track.

supplemental

For sources and bibliography, about the author, and thanks to..., see the end of Book One.

1 Additional books and magazine consulted
THE DEPRAT AFFAIR Ambition, Revenge and Deceit in French Indo-China, by Roger Osborne [Jonathan Cape, 1999]
MY COUNTRY AND MY PEOPLE, by Lin Yutang [William Heinemann, 1939]
NATIONAL GEOGRAPHIC, June 2001
THE OXFORD DICTIONARY OF WORLD RELIGIONS, edited by John Bowker [Oxford University Press, 1997]

2 Recommended websites supplemental
ART OF WAR
http://classics.mit.edu/Tzu/artwar.html
- by Sūn Zi

ASIAN ART
www.asianart.com/
- articles and world exhibitions including of Tibet and Mongolia

CHINA STUDIES
http://sun.sino.uni-heidelberg.de/igcs/
- 1,500 regularly updated links to wide-ranging academic articles

CHINESE MUSIC
www.ibiblio.org/pub/multimedia/chinese-music/
- loads of traditional Chinese music pieces

EMPEROR CONSTANTINE
www.roman-emperors.org/conniei.htm
- biography of the non-Christian who commandeered the Nicaea meeting and instigated the current inauthentic belief in the Trinity

FOOTBINDING IN CHINA
www.beautyworlds.com/chinesefootbinding.htm
- when, how, and why it was done

TOUR CHINA
www.cnta.com/lyen/index.asp
- virtual tours courtesy of the government's China National Tourism Administration

SHOPPING direct from Asia
CHINA
www.china-shops.com
- located in Shēnzhèn, offers free international delivery! Men's satin kung fu outfit £50, women's silk suit £75, Chinese CDs, scroll paintings £65

INDIA
www.shalincraft.com
- money from sales goes direct to the Indian artisans

KOREA
www.korean-arts.com
- incense burners in the shape of a lotus flower, turtle, or dragon fish £45, music boxes, scroll paintings

TIBET
www.buddhagifts.com
- including tankas; based in India and USA

permissions
BOOK TWO

The author thanks the following individuals, publications and organisations for their kind permission to quote from or use copyrighted work in Book Two. All (except *) followed the standard practice of not requesting a fee for short extracts of text totalling under a few hundred words.

A & C Black (Publishers) Ltd.
The BBC
Blake Friedmann Literary, TV & Film Agency
Cambridge University Press, Publishing Division
Curtis Brown Group Ltd.
Doubleday
Faber and Faber Ltd.
Findhorn Press Ltd.
Gong Lizeng
Grove/Atlantic, Inc.
HarperCollins Publishers
HarperCollins Publishers, Inc.
David Higham Associates Ltd.
Arthur James Ltd.
John Johnson Ltd. (on behalf of Peter Fleming's estate)
Susan Jowers
Alfred A Knopf
The CS Lewis Company Ltd.*
Lonely Planet Publications
Norman Mackenzie
Ted Mackenzie
Macmillan Publishers Ltd.
Morning Glory Publishers
New World Press*
Oxford University Press
Barbara Pegna
Penguin Books Ltd.
Perseus Books Group
Princeton University Press
Random House Inc.
Random House UK Ltd.
Sinolingua
Time-Life Syndication
Catherine Toler
Villard Books
Claudia Whitehouse
Mary Windel

specifics, in alphabetical order by title:

The *Ashley Book of Knots*, from which the chapter 19 quotes are taken, is published by Doubleday, a Division of Random House, Inc.

Extracts from the *Authorized Version of the Bible (The King James Bible)*, the rights in which are vested in the Crown, are reproduced by permission of the Crown's Patentee, Cambridge University Press.

The extract from *Behind the Wall* is copyright © Colin Thubron, 1987

The quotations from *Blake Records* are © Oxford University Press 1974, by permission of Oxford University Press.

China: Empire of Living Symbols, by Cecilia Lindqvist, is copyright © 1991 by Cecilia Lindqvist.

The quote from *Escape with Me!: An Oriental Sketch-Book* is copyright © 1935 Frank Magro.

Quotations from pages 32, 58, 294 of *In Search of the Miraculous: Fragments of an Unknown Teaching*, by P.D. Ouspensky (Arkana, 1987) copyright © Takiano M. Nagro, 1965, and printed in Great Britain. Reproduced by permission of Penguin Books Ltd.

The quotation from *Jacob the Baker, Gentle Wisdom for a Complicated World*, by Noah benShea, is reproduced by permission of Villard Books, a Division of Random House Inc.

The *My Country and My People* quote on page 103 is reproduced with permission of Curtis Brown Group Ltd, London on behalf of the Estate of Lin Yutang. Copyright Lin Yutang 1935.

The Problem of Pain by C.S. Lewis copyright © C.S. Lewis Pte. Ltd. 1940. Extract reprinted by permission.

Extracts from *The Revised English Bible* © Oxford University Press and Cambridge University Press 1989.

The quotation from *Video Night In Kathmandu And Other Reports from the Not-So-Far East*, by Pico Iyer, is reproduced by permission of Alfred A Knopf, a Division of Random House Inc.

additional CD credits:

Track 2: licensed courtesy of Tashi Lhunpo Monastery UK

Track 3: Hukwe Zawose, Lubeleje Chiute and Dickson Mkwama – *Nhongolo* (Zawose/Chiute/Mkwama) Womad Music Ltd (c) 1985 Triple Earth Records; licensed courtesy of Triple Earth www.triple-earth.co.uk

Track 4: licensed courtesy of Classical.com Ltd

Track 9: licensed courtesy of Delos International

Track 10: licensed courtesy of BMG UK and Ireland Limited

Track 12: licensed courtesy of BMG UK and Ireland Limited

Track 13: licensed courtesy of Virgin Records Ltd

CD mastering by Ben Turner at Finesplice

notes

Unless otherwise stated, Blake quotations are taken from *The Complete Poetry and Prose of William Blake, Newly Revised Edition* edited by David V. Erdman (Anchor Books, 1988).

Quotations from pages 149, 154-6, 179, 182-4 of *The Travels Of Marco Polo*, translated by Ronald Latham, 1958, copyright © Ronald Latham, 1958, and printed in Great Britain.

apology

Despite every effort, certain copyright holders were unable to be traced or contacted. The publisher sincerely apologises to them for this, and requests any such holder to notify the publisher so that due acknowledgement may be made in any future edition.

two inventions

The Chinese invented **porcelain** between AD 100 and 500, being fully developed in the Sòng Dynasty (AD 960–1279). 'China' is a smooth, succulent, often white variety dating initially from the Táng (AD 618–907). Made using a fine white clay (kaolin) mixed with feldspar, and fired at exalted temperatures over 1,400°C, the result is hard and almost scratchproof, yet thin, light and translucent, and when struck it pings like a bell.

In the following Yuán dynasty, potters began to decorate the white with a cobalt-blue dye imported from Persia; the result is referred to as Míng porcelain. By then it had become a craze in the West, even being accredited with magical powers. It is ironic that Míng or 17th-century Qīng blue and white, synonymous with China's porcelain in many people's eyes, was a colour combination considered vulgar by earlier Chinese in the Hàn Dynasty.

Europeans finally began to make porcelain in the 18th century, at least 1,200 years after the Chinese.

★ ★ ★

Up to half a million earthquakes of magnitude 2 and over occur worldwide every year. In terms of damage, 200 are significant, while between one and twenty are of major proportions. Aftershocks can be as destructive as the original tremor. In the 20th century alone, earthquakes claimed the lives of two million people.

In Asia, the Himalaya were formed very recently geologically speaking, and have not settled. Currently they are rising ten times more rapidly than the Alps, encouraged by the Indian subcontinent relentlessly pushing northwards. Lateral movement from this collision affects China, which to compensate is being forced south-east and eastwards. In Yúnnán the folded pleats running north-south are still buckling, hence hot springs and earthquakes of Force 7 or more.

Whereas the Lisbon quake of 1755 is well documented with some 60,000 killed, the Chinese have had to contend with four of the six most deadly earthquakes in recorded world history, the worst centred in Shaanxi (Shǎnxī) Province in 1556, resulting in a loss of 830,000 lives.

The Chinese were the first to devise an **earthquake recording device**. Nine years before he died, having surmised that shock waves travel in a straight line outwards from the epicentre, the brilliant Astronomer-Royal Zhāng Héng constructed in Luòyáng in AD 130 a bronze pot to rival the cloisonné monsters in Běijīng. It was two metres high and across, with eight dragon heads on all points of the compass, their mouths open to reveal a central incisor delicately holding a bronze pellet, like mother crocodiles grasping their babies. Given a quake-sized shove on its internal pendulum from a particular direction, a relevant pellet was released to an awaiting throng of bronze frogs encircling the pot below, athletically poised on haunches to capture the offending ball. The placement of the frog that caught it gave usually the opposite direction to the earthquake, whereupon the system locked. Not only ingenious, not only made 1,573 years before the French reinvented a seismic instrument in 1703, but also aesthetically invigorating and pleasing.

[An instructive and animated presentation of earthquakes, tsunamis and volcanoes is at www.pbs.org/wnet/savageearth.]

photographic notes

22-12/13/15 and *22-24* are of black and white prints that were hanging on walls. These and all the other colour transparencies were taken in China by the author during the journeys, apart from *12-1* of the teapots arranged later, *21-4* (see below), and those with the author in shot, which were however instigated and set up by him using his camera.

The number printed in Book Two is 398, totalling 856 in both books. Where two or three were intended to form one continuous wider image, these have been digitally joined together[1]. The total taken throughout the travels in China was 3,840, or 103 rolls of film (not including one roll lost, and another that failed to record pictures). The percentage printed in both books is therefore 22¼%.

Geoffrey Stanger took the photo of the Bamiyan Buddha *(21-4)* in 1963 on Kodak 64ASA slide film.

The remaining three old black and white prints were obtained as described in chapters 18 and 22, while the *qílín* on the back page was originally in colour.

The author would like to thank Imad Douglas and Eric Ladd, at DL Repro in London, for scanning and preparing the colour photographs. Only *12-46* (used on the jacket cover) was scanned by another agency and prepared by the author, who also resuscitated the scanned black-and-white print of the Hump plane *(18-11)*. The old black and white prints of the servants *(22-27/28)* were first photographed by the author before scanning.

camera equipment carried on the travels:

Olympus OM40 camera body;
Olympus OM4ti camera body (spare, never used)

Sirius semi fish-eye lens (adapter); Olympus 24 mm lens F 2.8 with sun hood; Olympus 35–70 mm zoom lens F 3.5–4.5; Sigma UC 70–210 mm APO zoom lens F 4–5.6 with sun hood; Tamron 500 mm mirror lens F 8 with sun hood (Part One only); Tamron 2x tele-converter, F system

Wotan VS300 flash unit; full height tripod and cable release; UV filters, polariser filter with adapter

The slide film used from chapter 8 on was 35mm Fuji Sensia 100ASA, except for the teapots (Fuji MS 100/1000). The first eleven of the photographs in the respective plus *22-1/25/29/30/32* were taken on Fujicolour 100ASA, while *15-3* to *15-10* were shot on a Fuji print film.

---

[1] In Book Two they are *12-2*, *12-5*, *12-30*, *12-45*, *12-48*, *12-50*, *12-51*, *12-52*; *13-6*; and in Part Three *14-30*, *14-31*; *17-1*, *17-2*, *17-24*; *18-13*; *20-15*, *20-17*, *20-18*; *21-13*, *21-15*, *21-17* and *22-10*.

music
BOOK TWO CD
Part Two continued

track # **author's association** book pages
title of music
    timing (usually excerpts)
        work/album name
        performers
        composer/group
        label and number

chapter 12

1   **steps up Huángshān** pp. 19–21
Chong song jajin hanip   Korean traditional
1' 44"   Sang Kyu Lee playing the *taegum*   Auvidis Unesco CD D8010

I have associated the sound of a flute with the spirituality of mountains ever since hearing one at dawn on the summit of Mt Batur in Bali. In Korea, music from the primal echelons of time once drew me like a siren. It was emanating from a solo *taegum* being played for his own contemplation by a famed guru who lived in the mountains.

The bamboo *taegum* is the largest and most common transverse flute in Korea, with six holes for fingers to change pitch, plus a further five left open. A thin vibrating membrane stretched over another hole separate from the blowhole causes the 'breathy' quality of the sound. In contrast to the Western technique of producing minimal vibrato on a flute by using the mouth, the substantially wide effect here is achieved by the player moving the whole instrument while shaking h/his entire head! Originally dating from 1972, the disc features renowned musicians from the National Center for Korean Traditional Performing Arts, which has been performing music for 1,600 years. No Western conservatoire can match that longevity.

For other Korean music, recommended are *Music of the Kayagum* (a type of silk-stringed zither) on JVC World Sounds VICG-5018, and *Shamanistic Ceremonies of Chindo* on JVC World Sounds VICG-5214. The thrilling traditional Korean percussion ensemble is thrilling: a CD that combines this with Western jazz is *Red Sun/SamulNori: Then Comes the White Tiger*, on ECM 521 734-2. The almost-lost Korean equivalent of opera is called *p'ansori*, which has seen a moderate recent revival, but recordings are hard to obtain in the West.

2   **the Bed of God** pp. 23–35
Khangling (Bone Trumpets)   The Power of Compassion   Tashi Lhunpo monks
Semke (Generating Compassion) [excerpt]   Tashi Lhunpo Monastery
Dungchen (Long Horns)   CD from www.tashi-lhunpo.org
7' 23"

This gives a flavour of the sacred sounds of Tibet. Tantras are wide-ranging sacred texts, some of which are chants called mantras. The singer Leonard Cohen, now a Zen monk in California, has explained that the meaning of a chant is not relevant. Instead, chanting is concerned with presenting oneself in the form of sound. He adds that the vibrations benefit the bowels! While listening to such primordial chanting and the pugnacious snorts of the Long Horns, bear in mind that for Tibetans a Buddha's particular mantra is not merely a sound – it is the essence of the Buddha. It has well-documented revival powers.

According to the authors of *Himalayas*, the six syllables of perhaps the most famous mantra – that to compassionate Avalokitesvara (Guān Yīn) – are usually misunderstood:

"Om ma ni pad me hum" are the aboriginal sacred syllables of the creatures of the six worlds....
They express the desire that the Most Sacred also manifest itself on earth. In Europe, they have been
incorrectly interpreted as Sanskrit words and by relentlessly contracting the syllables, the meaning
"Oh Jewel in the Lotus Flower" was squeezed out of them. (p. 154)

There are numerous Tibetan mantras, such as Om Vajra Satto Samaya, which appeals to Vajrasattva for healing, or Om Ami Dewa Hrih, intoned on someone's death as a supplication to Amitabha (O Mi To, Ē Mí Tuō). The most supreme one of all contains 12 syllables, encompassing the 12 teachings of the Buddha: Om Ah Hum Vajra Guru Padma Siddhi Hum.

The Hungarian composer Kodály believed that mountains had voices, a feeling with which I concur concerning Huángshān.

3   **Huángshān sunrise** pp. 36–56
Tunahaki Nhongolo   traditional, arranged by Hukwe Zawose, Lubeleje Chiute and Dickson Mkwama
8' 00"   Mateso (suffering)   Master Musicians of Tanzania
         Triple Earth Terracd 104

    Hukwe Zawose (born 1940): lead vocals, izeze (stick zithers
        fiddles), "earth shaker" (13 string zeze), marimba (hand-piano).
    Lubeleje Chiute: vocals, zeze, marimba.
    Dickson Mkwama: vocals, bells, marimba.

This CD contains unfathomably beautiful music throughout. The inlay explains the track's title: '*Nhongolo*: The name of an animal and about the painful cry of an animal after it has lost its child – either killed by a person or another animal.... The song itself is about the general life of a human being and how we can manage to overcome big problems and different kinds of pain through life'.

music
Part Three

track # **author's association** book pages
title of music   work/album name   composer/group
    timing (usually excerpts)   performers   label and number

chapter 14

4   **the Lí River** pp. 80–89

    5' 03"   The Protecting Veil   John Tavener
    Raphael Wallfisch (solo cello)   Classical.com Ltd
    Royal Philharmonic Orchestra
    conducted by Justin Brown

In Orthodox ritual, the Protecting Veil relates to the Mother of God. This spiritually rewarding music for solo cello and strings lasts almost three-quarters of an hour. Two extracts are joined here: the first features disturbingly hushed shimmers from the violins, while a full string crescendo heralds the final few minutes of the piece (the last minute is omitted).

The British composer John Tavener (born 1944) first attracted wide notice with the cantata *The Whale* (the one that swallowed Jonah), and it established his bond with contemplative religious subjects. His is a deeply engaging sound world with passionate sections that deny any suggestion of sanctimony. If you respond to the music of Górecki or Arvo Pärt, you will probably also relate to this.

Among many Tavener pieces worth investigating are string quartets (played by the Chilingirian Quartet on Virgin Classics VC5 45023-2), choral pieces (Westminster Abbey Choir, Sony Classical SK66613) and the large-scale *We shall see Him as He is* (BBC Welsh Symphony Chorus and Orchestra, Chandos CHAN9128).

chapter 15

5   **chorus rehearsal** p. 110
    6' 28"   recorded by the author in Zhàoxìng, Guìzhōu Province [2 January 1996]

Please allow for the poor quality of this recording, due to the batteries in the Walkman failing.

The author's recordings were made on a Sony Professional Walkman WMD6-C, with a Sony stereo microphone ECM 909, using TDK SA C90 cassette tapes. Usually Dolby C was selected.

6   **Lángdé event** pp. 111–114
    4' 13"   recorded by the author in Lángdé, Guìzhōu Province [5 January 1996]

A commercial recording of Miao music is *A Happy Miao Family* on the Pan label (Netherlands). For other country Chinese music in general, try the mixed set of ensembles recorded since the 1950s (with one dating from 1930) entitled *China: Folk Instrumental Traditions*, on VDE-Gallo VDECD-822/3. The spicy sounds will pep up your ear like a sharp sorbet!

7   **Fānpái activity** pp. 115–119
    7' 51"   recorded by the author in Fānpái, Guìzhōu Province [6 January 1996]

chapter 20

8   **Naxi music** p. 183
    Musical Prayer [excerpt]   Traditional Naxi music
    The Song of the Jade Dragon Snow Mountain
    5' 15"
    H-427 Yunnan Music
    Video Publishing House

These are taken from two cassette tapes purchased direct from the Naxi orchestra in Lìjiāng.

For different ancient Chinese music, *Chine: Musique ancienne de Chang'an*, on Auvidis Inédit W260036, is a state of the art reconstruction from the court of Táng Dynasty Cháng'ān.

9	**earthquake** p. 191		
	Volcano [3rd movement]	Symphony No. 50 "Mount St Helens" Op. 360	Alan Hovhaness
	2' 44"	Seattle Symphony conducted by Gerard Schwarz	Delos DE3137

WARNING: this music contains a sudden loud bang after a quiet preamble.

'Mountains are symbols, like pyramids, of man's attempt to know God. Mountains are symbolic meeting places between the mundane and spiritual world.' So wrote this American composer concerning his Symphony No. 2. His distinctive massive style of luscious, layered string writing is similar to the terracotta army's compact formation – like a mountain.

American of Armenian and Scottish descent, Hovhaness (1911-2000) was extremely prolific – he suppressed a thousand of his compositions written before he was aged 30. Many of the over 400 surviving works, including sixty-seven symphonies and nine operas, reflect his interest in the music of China, Japan, Indonesia, Armenia, as well as Korea (Symphony No. 16 uses Korean percussion) and India (*Concerto* for violin, sitar, and orchestra). Nature is often a source of inspiration: his orchestral piece *And God Created Great Whales* uses the sighs and sounds of humpback whales recorded on tape. The particular symphonic excerpt heard here describes the moment of eruption of St. Helen's in 1980.

The composer's peaceful yet tense Symphony No. 6 (*Celestial Gate*) is recommended on Telarc CD 80392, while string quartets are coupled with a piece by the Chinese composer Zhou Long on Delos DE3162. The half-hour *Magnificat* for choir and orchestra on Delos DE 3176 is mysterious, fetching, and for me captures well the ambivalence of God. It is combined with short straightforward choral pieces with organ that will appeal to lovers of church music.

chapter 21

10	**breakthrough on Éméishān** pp. 204–210		
	Dream Pantomime [end of Act II]	Hansel and Gretel	Humperdinck
	3' 25"	Munich Radio Orchestra	RCA Classics 74321 25281-2
		conducted by Kurt Eichhorn	

After the two lost children deliver their famous heartfelt musical prayer calling on angels to show them Heaven, they fall asleep entwined on the forest floor. The Dream Pantomime that follows describes the mist transforming into steps of clouds 'in rosy light', down which fourteen guardian angels descend.

The original performance of *Hänsel und Gretel* in 1893 was conducted by Richard Strauss. Thirty years later, it was the first opera to be broadcast in its entirety on British radio (from Covent Garden), and on Christmas Day in 1931 the Metropolitan Opera in New York performed the work for the company's first live broadcast.

Königskinder is another and more melancholic fairy tale opera by the composer, and exists in a good EMI recording. It would be fascinating to see and hear the spectacle *The Miracle*, the composer's last major work, but I have never heard of a performance in recent times.

chapter 22

11	**New Year fireworks** p. 237		
	5' 22"	recorded by the author in Nánbù, Sìchuān Province [18–9 February 1996]	

chapter 23

12	**retrospective** pp. 258–272		
	Santorini	Yanni Live at the Acropolis	Yanni
	6' 24"	with the Royal Philharmonic Orchestra	MCA Records 01005-82116-2
		conducted by Shardad Rohani	BMGSD 7214

13	**a glimpse of Eternity** pp. 273–275		
	Falls	The Mission	Ennio Morricone
	1' 53"	original soundtrack from the film	Virgin Records CDV 2402
		composed, orchestrated and conducted by Ennio Morricone,	
		performed by the London Philharmonic Orchestra;	
		Indian instrumentation by Incantation	

14	**lockets of Love** p. 276		
	0' 16"	the author speaking, recorded in Nánbù, Sìchuān Province [19 February 1996]	

15	**island sunset** pp. 277–292		
	Chūn yŭ (Spring Rain)	A Vent for Emotions	
	6' 45"		HL-639 China Record Corporation
			(Shànghǎi)
		Lute solo performed by Li Jing-Xia, with the Traditional	
		Music Orchestra Shanghai Conservatory of Music,	
		conducted by Kia Fei-Yun	

index
BOOK TWO

bold: photograph(s) with or without text

+Bk1: previous reference(s) in Book One – see index Book One

i, ii, f: reference(s) found in
 i the first column only
 ii the second column only
 f the footnote only
 (These three are given only when pages have plentiful text.)

Note: some entries and places only appear in Book One's index.

A

acid rain	242*i*, +Bk1
acroterion	**70**, **72**, +Bk1
Ādi Buddha	211*ii*
Afghanistan	202*i*
Africa	65*ii*
Madagascar	248*i*
Tanzania	297
Akha (Thailand)	135*i*
Allah	213*i*
Altan Khan	190*i*
amah	253*i*
America/n (USA)	103*i*, 163*i*, 164*ii*, 184*ii*, 212*ii*, 229*ii*, 242*ii*, 243*i*, +Bk1
Amitabha Buddha	297, +Bk1
Amoeba theory	158*i*, 221*i*, 227*ii*, +Bk1
Analects (Confucius)	229*i*, +Bk1
Ananda (Sanskrit)	257*i*, +Bk1
angels	212*ii*, 231
anger	177*ii*, 178, 228*ii*, 229*ii*
Ānhuī Province	15*ii*, 16*ii* (translation), +Bk1
anthrax	65*ii*, +Bk1
arhat	149*i*, see: *lohan*
astrology	254*i*, 256*i*, see fortune-teller, +Bk1
attachment (*rāga*)	189*ii*
Australia	95, +Bk1
Avalokitesvara	66*ii*, 297, see Guān Yīn, +Bk1
Ayscough, Florence	250*ii*
azaleas	185*i*, +Bk1
Aztecs	179*ii*
Mexicans	221*ii*

B

Bada	127 (map), 132, 136*ii*
Bai (minority)	**170**, 191*ii*
Bái Jūyì (poet)	202*ii*
Báishā	184*ii*–**185**, 198*i*
Báishuǐ Tái	186*ii*
Bali (Indonesia)	136*i*, 159*i*, +Bk1
bamboo	19–**20**, 80, **81**, **83–85**, **87**, **89**, **91–92**, 106, 115*i*, 135*i*, 150*ii*, 151*ii*, 163*i*, 202*i*, 234–235*i*, 244*ii*, +Bk1
Bamboo Temple (Kūnmíng)	149, **270**, 294*i*
Bamiyan Buddha (Afghanistan)	**202**
Banla	127 (map), 135
Bǎoshān (North Yúnnán)	185*ii*, 198*i*
(Southwest Yúnnán)	165*ii*, 166
Barber, Noel	188*i*
barley	187*ii*, 191*ii*
Batak (Sumatra)	135*i*
Běijīng	**251**, **254**, **261**, 294*i*, **308**, +Bk1
Imperial View Pavilion	**261**, 294*i*, +Bk1
spirit way	**251**, **254**, 294*i*, **308**, +Bk1
benelovence	229*i*
benShea, Noah	229*ii*
Běnxī	250*ii*
Bezeklik Caves	**259**, +Bk1
Bharata	213*i*
Bhavacakra (wheel)	**189**
Bible (+ references)	158*i*, 177*ii*–181, 198*ii*, 204*ii*, 212, 213*i*, 220, 221*ii*, 222, 226*ii*, 227*i*, 231*i*, 252*i*, 257*i*, see Christian, God, Jesus, +Bk1
Bildad	178*ii*
Deuteronomy	179*i*, 180*i*
Ecclesiastes	257*i*, +Bk1
Elihu	178*ii*, 181*ii*
Eliphaz	178*ii*
Exodus	179*i*, 204*ii*
Genesis	180*i*, 181*i*, 213*i*, 222*i*, +Bk1
Hebrews	180*i*, 204*ii*, 220*i*, 227*i*
Holy Spirit	230*ii*–231*i*, see: *qì*, +Bk1
Isaiah	179*i*, 227*i*
Jacob	181*i*, 212*i*
Jeremiah	198*ii*
Job	177*ii*–179*ii*, 222*ii*, +Bk1
John	158*i*, 220
Matthew	226*ii*, 231*i*, 252*i*, +Bk1
Micah	179*i*
Numbers	179*i*
Paul	221*ii*, +Bk1
Peter	226*ii*
Revelation	212, 220*i*
Samuel	179
Uzzah	179*i*
Zephaniah	179*ii*
Zophar	178*ii*
Bird, Isabella	244*ii*, 245*ii*
Bìtǎ Hǎi	187*i*
Blake, William	98, 100*i*, 175*ii*, 178*i*, 179*ii*, 212*ii*, 221*ii*, 228*i*, 230*i*, 231*i*, 249*ii*
Satiric verses	178*i*, 212*ii*, 221*i*
Songs of Innocence/Experience	98, 178*i*, 179*ii*
bodhisattva	16*i*, 211, see Avalokitesvara, Guān Yīn, +Bk1
Boehme, Jacob	158*ii*
Borneo	157*i*, 228*i*, +Bk1
bōshānlú (incense burner)	**18**, 70, 72–**73**, +Bk1
breath of life	see: *qì*
bridge	65, **73–74**, 104, **105**, 111*ii*, 119*ii*–**120**, **124**, 150*i*, **183**, 186*i*, 187*i*, 200*i*, **240/1**, 246*ii*, **268**, 294*i*, +Bk1
Britain, British	11, 13*i*, 65*ii*, 163*i*, 185*i*, 242*ii*, 248*i*, +Bk1
Buddha	66*ii*, 150*ii*, 151*ii*, **153**, 156*ii*, 158*i*, **160**, **161**, 180*i*, 187*ii*, **189**, **200/1**, **202**, 211, 228*ii*, 250*i*, 271, 294*i*, see Buddhism, +Bk1
Ādi Buddha	211*ii*
Grand Buddha	**200–201**
Maitreya (Future)	**160**, **200–201**, +Bk1
Rāhu(la)	**153**, +Bk1
Sakyamuni/historical	66*ii*, 150*ii*, 151*ii*, **153**, 156*ii*, 187*ii*, 188*ii*, **189**, 228*ii*, 250*i*, **271**, 294*i*, +Bk1
Buddhism, Buddhist	11, 13*i*, 16*i*, 56*i*, 133, 134*ii*, 139, 148*ii*, 149*i*, 153, 158*i*, 160*ii*, **161**, 180*i*, 188, 189, 190*i*, 202*ii*, 211, 212*ii*, 213*i*, 222*ii*, 226*i*, 228*ii*, 230*i*, 233*i*, see Buddha, Mahayana, Theravada, +Bk1
bodhisattva	16*i*, 211, see Avalokitesvara, Guān Yīn, +Bk1
caves	see caves, +Bk1
Chán	13*i*, 149*i*, 230*i*, +Bk1
sutra	151*ii*, 156*ii*, 228*ii*, +Bk1
Tibetan	150*i*, 185*i*, 187–190*i*, 194, 211, 212*ii*, 222*ii*, 228*ii*, 297, +Bk1
buffalo	135*i*, 155*i*, 162–**163**
Bulang (minority)	129*i*, 139*ii*
Burma/ese *or* Myanmar	127, 137*i*, 159, 160*i*, **161**, 163, **164**, 166*i*, 187*ii*, 235*i*, 242*ii*
Burma Blackwood	159*i*
Burma Road	159*i*, 163*i*, **164**

C

C-47s (Dakotas)	163, see Hump
CAAC	64*i*, 102*ii*
Caicun	**167**, 170
calabash	140
calendar	212*i*
calligraphy	56*ii*–**57**, **150**, **154**, 236*ii*, **238/9**, **244**, +Bk1
camellia	127*ii*, 150–**151**, 185*i*, **270**, 294*i*, +Bk1
canal	64*ii*, **65**, 246*i*, +Bk1
Grand Canal	65*ii*, +Bk1
Cāngshān	167*ii*, 168, 170, **172/3**
Canton	see Guǎngzhōu
Caruso (tenor)	184*ii*
cast iron	see iron
Catholic Church	212*ii*, **248**, +Bk1

caves	14*ii*, 66, 73, 74*i*, 102, 124*i*, 145*i*, **154**, **243**, **259**, 294*i*, +Bk1	
Bezeklik	**259**, +Bk1	
Fán Yīn (Pǔtuóshān)	66 (map), 73	
Ling'gu (Yíxīng)	14*ii*	
Lóng Mén	**154**, +Bk1	
Qīnglóng (Zhènyuǎn)	124*i*, **269**, 294*i*	
Reed Flute (Guìlín)	102	
Zhāng'gōng (Yíxīng)	14*ii*, 294*i*	
Celestial Kings	**189**, **190**	
census	103*i*, +Bk1	
ceramics/porcelain	65*ii*, 296*i*, +Bk1	
Chán (Buddhism)	13*i*, 149*i*, 230*i*, +Bk1	
Cháng'ān	167*ii*, 298, see Xī'ān, +Bk1	
Cháng Jiāng	see Yángzi River	
Chángxīng	12 (map)	
Chǎnkǒu	104 (map), 105	
Cheju-do (Korea)	147*i*, 158*ii*, +Bk1	
Chéngdé	190*i*, +Bk1	
Chéngdū	200*i*, 234, 235, 236*i*	
Giant Panda Research Base	234*ii*	
Chén Què	229*i*	
chi (breath of life)	see: *qì*	
Chiang Kai-shek	**242**–243*i*, +Bk1	
Chinese language	11, 110*ii*, (111*i*), 248*i*, see calligraphy, +Bk1	
Chinese maxims/proverbs	99, 158*i*, 178*i*, 203*ii*, 204*ii*, 228*i*, 229*i*, 246*i*, 250*i*, 292, +Bk1	
Chinese poems	15*ii*, 178*i*, 193, 199*ii*, 202*ii*, 246*i*, 257*ii*, see Bk1 poet	
chī wén	see acroterion	
Chóng'anjiāng	104 (map), 126*i*	
Chóngqìng	238*i*, **240**-**243**, 251	
Cháotiān Mén	240*ii*, 242*i*	
Éling (Goose Ridge)	**240/1**, 243*ii*	
Rénmín Hotel	242*i*	
World War II	**242**–**243**	
chorten	187*ii*, see dagoba *or* stupa, +Bk1	
Christian	203*i*, 212*i*, 220*i*, 222, 226*i*, 227*i*, see Bible, God, Jesus, missionary, +Bk1	
chrysanthemum	151*ii*, +Bk1	
Chu period	178*i*	
Circular Changes (Zhōu Yì)	204*ii*, +Bk1	
CITS	111*i*, 126*ii*, 136*ii*, +Bk1	
Classic of Changes (Zhōu Yì)	204*ii*, +Bk1	
clay	13*ii*, 296*i*	
coal	242*i*, 246*ii*, 250*ii*, +Bk1	
Codex Borgia	179*ii*	
coffee	127*ii*	
Cohen, Leonard	297	
coincidences	213*ii*–217*i*, 218*ii*, +Bk1	
Communist	103, 243*i*, see Cultural Revolution, Red Guards, +Bk1	
compassion/benevolence	226*i*, 229*i*	
Confucius, Confucian	184*i*, 229*i*, +Bk1	
Cōngjiāng	104 (map), 111*i*	
Cooper, Diana	181*i*, 231	
Constantine	294*ii*, +Bk1	
copper	15*ii*	
cormorant	80*ii*, **87**, **91**–**92**, 170	
Creation	184, 204*ii*, 221, 224*ii*	
Cultural Revolution	66*ii*, 133*ii*, 148*ii*, 184*ii*, 185*i*, 188*i*, 202*ii*, see red Guards +Bk1	

D

Dà Dōng Gōu (Tiānchí)	**259**, 294*i*, +Bk1
Dàdù River	78 (map), **201**
Dàfó, Grand Buddha	**200**–**201**
dagoba, *or* stupa	129*i*, 133*i*, **138**, **159**, 161–**162**, **164**, 187*ii*, **272**, 294*i*, +Bk1
Dai (minority)	127*ii*, **128**–**132**, 133–135*i*, 137*i*, 138*ii*–139, 155*i*, 159*i*
Dàkōngshān	165*i*
Dakotas	163, see Hump
Dalai Lama	188*ii/f*, 190*i*, 233*i*, +Bk1
Dalbergia cultrata	159*i*
Dàlǐ	148*ii*, **167**–**170**, 177*ii*, **273/4**, 294*i*
Cāngshān	167*ii*, 168, 170, **172/3**
North Gate	167*i*
Three Pagodas	167*ii*–**168/9**, **273/4**, 294*i*
Dam, Three Gorges	246
Damenglong	127 (map)
Dàníng River	78 (map), **245**, 246*i*
Dante	100*i*
Dào, Daoist	14*ii*, 135, 153, 183*ii*, 184*i*, 202*ii*, 203*ii*, 228*i*, 294*i*, +Bk1
Darwin	226, +Bk1
Dàtiān Grotto	**154**
Dàtóng	294*i*, +Bk1
Shànhuà Temple	**262**, 294*i*, +Bk1
Wooden Pagoda	**262**, 294*i*, +Bk1
Dà Xué (Great Learning)	229*i*, +Bk1
Dàyàn	182*ii*, see Lìjiāng
Dàyīng (River/shan)	165*i*
Dàzú	235*ii*
deer	**153**, **188**, **271**
Déhóng Region	159*i*
déjà vu	157*ii*
Delavay, Abbé	185*i*
delusion *(moha)*	189*ii*, 228*ii*
Dèng Xiǎopíng	242*i*
Déqīn	78 (map), 187*i*
derricks	202*i*
Deuteronomy	179*i*, 180*i*
Dharmacakra (wheel)	**188**
Dhritarāshtra	189*ii*
Dīngshān	see Dīngshū
Dīngshū	**14**, 294*i*
Dì Zàng	16*i*
Doctor Ho	**185**
Doctrine of the Mean	229*i*, +Bk1
Dong (minority)	103*ii*, 104, 105, 106, **107**–**110**, 115*ii*
Dongba	184*ii*, 186*ii*, 199*i*
Don Quixote	233*i*
dosa (hate)	189*ii*
dragon	13*ii*, 18*i*, 68*ii*, **70**, **72**, 102*ii*, 104, 122*ii*, 133*i*, 154*i*, 155*i*, **262**, 294*i*, 308, see Jade Dragon Snow Mtn, Lóng Mén, Qīnglóng, +Bk1
dragon screen	**262**, 294*i*, +Bk1
Dream of Gerontius	227*i*
drilling	202*i*

Dúdòng	104 (map), 105
Dūliǔ River	104 (map), 105–**106**
dumpling	237*i*
dynasty (word not always in text)	11, 13, 15*ii*, 18*ii*, 65*ii*, 80*i*, 103*i*, 128*i*, 133*i*, 148, 150*i*, 159*i*, 167, 193*f*, 199*f*, 202*ii*, 210*i*, 212*ii*, 213*ii*, 233*ii*, 238*i*, 240*ii*, 246*i*, 248*i*, 257*i/f*, 296*i*, 298, +Bk1
Hàn	11, 103*i*, 159*i*, 202*ii*, 212*ii*, 296*i*, +Bk1
Míng	11, 13*ii*, 128*i*, 148, 150*i*, 167*i*, 210*i*, 248*i*, 296*i*, +Bk1
Qīng	11, 148*ii*, 248*i*, 296*i*, +Bk1
Sòng	11, 13*i*, 238*i*, 240*ii*, 296*i*, +Bk1
Táng	11, 15*ii*, 18*ii*, 65*ii*, 80*i*, 133*i*, 148*i*, 167*ii*, 193*f*, 199*f*, 202*ii*, 246*i*, 257*i/f*, 296*i*, 298, +Bk1
Yuán	11, 148*i*, 233*ii*, 248*i*, 296*i*, see Mongol, +Bk1
Zhōu	11, 213*i*, 233*ii*, +Bk1
Dzogchen	212*ii*, 222*ii*

E

earrings	103*i*
earthquake	190*ii*–191*i*, 196–199, 296*i*, +Bk1
Eden	221*ii*
Egypt	212*ii*, 221*ii*, +Bk1
elephant	**130**, 166*i*, 204*i*, 211
Elgar (composer)	227*i*
Elihu (Book of Job)	178*ii*, 181*ii*
Éméi River	201*i*, 234*i*
Éméishān	18*ii*, 202*ii*–203, **204**–**215**, **217**–**220**, **223**, **225**, 234*i*
East Sea	211*i*, **218/9**
Golden Summit	210*i*, 211, **220**
Hóngchūnpíng Temple	203*i*
Jiēyǐn Hall	210*i*, 234*i*
Qiānfó Dǐng	211*i*
Qīngyīn Pavilion	203*i*
Shěshēn Cliff	211*i*, **218**, **223**
Wànfó Dǐng	**211**, **217**
West Sea	210, **212**–**215**
Xiānfēng Monastery	203
Xǐxiàng Chí	204*i*
Ē Mí Tuó (O Mi To)	297, +Bk1
emperor	150*i*, 193*f*, 199*f*, 202*ii*, 212*ii*, 221*ii*, 226*i*, 240, 257*f*, +Bk1
First (Qín)	226*i*, +Bk1
Guāngzōng	240*ii*
Huáng Dì	212*i*, see Yellow
Jade	240*i*
Jiànwén	150*i*
Khubilai Khan	148*ii*, 167*i*, 184*ii*, 185*ii*, +Bk1
Lǐ Jìng	199*ii*
Lǐ Yù	193
Qín	226*i*, +Bk1
Xuánzōng	202*ii*, +Bk1
Yellow	212*i*, 221*ii*, +Bk1
Zhuàngzōng	257*f*

301

England, English	*see* Britain (British)	
Enya		165*ii*
Ěrhǎi Lake		**167**, 170
erhuang		184*i*
evil		124*i*, 179, 180*i*, 187*ii*, 218, 221–222*i*, 224, 226–228, 229*ii*, 231*i*, 233, 236*ii*, 237*ii*, 251, 255*ii*, 308, +Bk1

F

Fǎnpái	104 (map), 115*ii*, **116–121**
Fán Yīn Cave (temple)	66 (map), 73
Fǎ Yǔ Chán Sì	66 (map), 70, **71–73**
Fēilái Shí (rock)	56–57, 294*i*
Fēngdū	243*ii*, 246*i*, +Bk1
festivals	103*ii*, 104, 115*i*, 122*ii*, 134*i*, 135*ii*
Filial Piety	229*i*
firecrackers/fireworks	237–238*i*
First Emperor of Qín	226*i*, +Bk1
Five Blessings	257*i*
Fleming, Peter	242*ii*
floods	241*i*, 246, +Bk1
footbinding	294*ii*
forests	127*i*, 136*ii*, 234*ii*, 235*i*, 250
Forrest, George	185*i*
fortune-teller	238, 254–255*i*, 256*i*, +Bk1
Four Nobel Truths	228*ii*
France, French	144*ii*, 185*i*, 217*ii*, 248*ii*, 252*ii*, 296*i*, +Bk1
Fú (River)	78 (map), 235*ii*, 240*ii*
Fùchūn River	12 (map)
Fújiàn Province	250*ii*
Fuller, R. Buckminster	178*i*
Fúlóng Bridge	187*i*
Fùlù	104 (map), 105

G

Galapagos Islands	158*ii*
gān bēi ('dry cup')	237*i*
Ganges, River	213*i*
Gǎnlǎnbà	137*i*, *see* Menghan
Gānsù Province	236*i*, +Bk1
Gāolígòng (mountains)	163*ii*, 165*ii*
gazelles	**153, 188, 271**
Gejia (minority)	123, 126
Gelukpa	189*ii*
Genesis	180*i*, 181*i*, 213*i*, 222*i*, +Bk1
Genshin (Japanese monk)	228*ii*
ginkgo tree	134*ii*, 150*i*
God	22, 100–101, 146–147, 158*i*, 174–181, 198, 204*ii*, 216–222, 224, 226–228*i*, 229*ii*, 230–233*i*, 255,
Goethe	144*ii*
Golden Triangle	127*ii*
goldfish	**260**, 294*i*, +Bk1
Gǒngběi Rock, Tàishān	**262**, 294*i*, +Bk1
Gònggā Shān	78 (map), 210*ii*–211*i*

gorge	124–**125**, 127*ii*, 186*ii*, 195, 243*ii*, **244–245**
Three Gorges	243*ii*, **244**–245, 246
Tiger Leaping Gorge	127*ii*, 186*ii*, 195
Wǔyáng Gorge	104 (map), 124–**125**, +Bk1
Grand Canal	65*ii*, +Bk1
Great Ennead	212*ii*
Great Learning	229*i*, +Bk1
Greece, Greek	212*ii*, 221*ii*, +Bk1
Green, O.M.	252*ii*–253, +Bk1
Guān Dàoshēng (poetess)	257*ii*
Guǎngdōng Province	248*i*
Guǎngxī Province	79*ii*, 94, 103*ii*
Guǎngzhōu	246*i*, **247–248**, (249*i*), 251, +Bk1
Sacred Heart Church	**248**
Shāmiàn Island	248*i*
Guāngzōng, Emperor	240*ii*
guānxì ('connections')	239*ii*
Guān Yīn	13*i*, 56*i*, 66*ii*, 69, 72*i*, 74*i*, 150*ii*, 211*ii*, **238**, 297, +Bk1
guardians (temples)	**133**, 149*ii*, **150/1**, 164*ii*, **189–190**, +Bk1
Guìlín	79*ii*, 102, 104
Reed Flute Cave	102
Guìyáng	126*ii*
Guìzhōu Province	94, 103*ii*, 106, 111*i*, 122*i*, 126, 127*i*, +Bk1
gunpowder	238*i*, +Bk1
Guómíndǎng	242*ii*, +Bk1
Gurdjieff, G.I.	178*i*, 220*ii*, 233*ii*, +Bk1

H

Hǎinán Island	250*ii*, +Bk1
Haitong (monk)	201
Hale, Edward	157*ii*
Hàn (River)	246*ii*
Hàn Chinese	68*i*, 103*ii*, 129*i*, 136*ii*, 191*ii*, 235*ii*, +Bk1
Hàn Dynasty	11, 103*i*, 159*i*, 202*ii*, 212*ii*, 296*i*, +Bk1
Hán Fēi (philosopher)	226*i*
Hángzhōu	13*ii*, **64**, 65*ii*, +Bk1
Hani (minority)	129*i*, 132, **135**, 138*i*
Hànkǒu	246*ii*
Hàn River	246*ii*
Hánshā Temple, Ruìlì	**160**
Hànyáng	246*ii*
Hán Yù (writer)	80*i*
harmonium	115*f*
hate (*dosa*)	189*ii*
Haydn (composer)	204*ii*
Hebrew	179*ii*, 204*ii*, 227*i*, *see* Bible (Hebrews), +Bk1
Hēikōngshān	165*i*
Hell	16*i*, 17*ii*, 100*i*, 222*ii*, 228*ii*, +Bk1
Hēngduàn (Mtns)	163*ii*
Héngshān	18*ii*, 255, +Bk1
Himalaya	127*i*, 235*ii*, 296*i*, +Bk1

Hindu	188*ii*, 212*i*, 213*i*, 228*ii*, +Bk1
Hiroshima	243*ii*
Hmong (Thailand)	103*ii*
Holy Spirit	230*ii*–231*i*, *see*: qì, +Bk1
Homo sapiens	182*ii*, +Bk1
Hóngchūnpíng Temple	203*i*
Hong Kong	74*ii*, 247*ii*, 248*i*, +Bk1
Hovhaness (composer)	298
Huáng Dì	212*i*, *see* Yellow Emperor
Huáng'guǒshù	122*i*
Huángshān	13*ii*, 18*ii*, **19–63**, **264–267, 276**, 294*i*
Fēilái Shí (rock)	56–57, 294*i*
Hundred Step Cloud Ladder	56*ii*, **62**
Qiánhǎi	56*ii*, **63**
Qīngliáng Tái	36*i*, **276**, 294*i*
sunrise	36, **37–58, 264/5**
Xīhǎi	56*ii*, **59–62, 266**, 294*i*
Huáshān	18*ii*, **255**, +Bk1
Huátíng Temple	149*ii*–**150/1**
Húběi Province	246*i*
Huí (minority)	148*ii*, 191*ii*, +Bk1
Huì Jì Chán Sì	66 (map), **68–70**, **268**, 294*i*
Húlú Island (Xīshuāngbǎnnà)	140
Hump (WWII)	**163**, 167*ii*, 184*ii*, 187*i*, 243*i*
Humperdinck (composer)	299
Hǔtiào Xiá	*see* Tiger Leaping Gorge

I

I Ching (*Yì Jīng*)	204*ii* (Zhōu Yì), +Bk1
ignorance	189*ii*, 221*i*, 224*i*, 228
immortality	22*i*, 203*ii*, 238*i*
incense burner	**18**, **72–73**, +Bk1
income	103*i*
India, Indian	11, 153, 159*i*, 160*ii*, 163, 187*ii*, 188*ii*, 213*i*, 296*i*, *see* Hindu, +Bk1
Indonesia	211*i*, 234*ii*
Bali	136*i*, 159*i*, +Bk1
Sumatra	135*i*
Ingelow, Jean (poet)	216*i*
innocence/innocent	221–222*i*, 224*i*, 226*ii*, 228, *see* Blake
invention (word not necessarily in text)	104, 124*i*, 202*i*, 238*i*, 246*i*, 296*i*, +Bk1
iron	202*i*, 241*ii*, +Bk1
Irrawaddy River	127*i*, 159*i*, 165*i*
Islam	*see* Muslim
islands (physical)	66*ii*
Israel	212*i*, *see* Hebrew
Iyer, Pico	188*i*

J

jade	163*i*, +Bk1
Jade Dragon Snow Mountain	**182, 183**, 184*ii*, 185*i*, **192/3, 196***ii***–197, 199**

Jade Emperor	240*i*	
Japan, Japanese	11, 65*ii*, 66*ii*, 102*i*, 126*ii*, 163*i*, 202*ii*, 226*i*, 228*i*, 242*ii*–243, +Bk1	
wars with China	65*ii*, 102*i*, 163*i*, 202*ii*, 242*ii*–243, +Bk1	
Jerusalem	212	
Jesus	158, 212*i*, 220, 226*ii*, 252*i*, *see* Bible, Christian, God, +Bk1	
Jiālíng River	235*ii*, **236**, **240–241**, 242*ii*	
Jiǎng Jièshí (Chiang Kai-shek)	**242–243***i*, +Bk1	
Jiànwén Emperor	150*i*	
Jiāoshān	258, **277–292**, +Bk1	
Jiétáng Sōnglín Monastery	**186–190**, 191*ii*, +Bk1	
Jīnghóng	128–129*i*, 130, 136*i*, **137**, 159*i*	
Jingpo (minority)	159*i*	
Jingzhen	127 (map), **134**	
Jīnjiāng	200*i*	
Jīnshā Jiāng (Yángzi)	127, 182*ii*, 186*i*, 187*i*, 199*ii*, 241*ii*, *see* Yángzi River	
Jiǔhuáshān	15*ii*, **16–18**, 36*ii*, 202*ii*, **263**, 294*i*	
Qíyuán Monastery	15*ii*	
Zhǎntánlín Monastery	16*ii*–**17**, 18*i*	
Job	177*ii*–179*ii*, 222*ii*, +Bk1	
Jokhang, Lhasa	180*i*, 188*ii*	
Jung, C.G.	179*ii*, 221*ii*, 255*i*, +Bk1	
junks	244*ii*, 245*ii*	
jūnzi (supreme person)	229*i*, 233*ii*, 253*ii*	

K

Kagebuo Mtn	78 (map), 187*i*
Kāifēng	193, +Bk1
Kǎilǐ	111*i*, 126*ii*
Karmapa	185*i*
karst	14*ii*, **(79–90)**, **93–99**, **(102)**, **142–147**
Kashmir	187*ii*
kathākali (Indian dance)	213*i*
Kawakarpo (Kagebuo) Mtn	78 (map), 187*i*
Kazak (minority)	**258**, +Bk1
Keiji, Nishitani	226*i*
Kěqiáo	64*ii*
Khubilai Khan	148*ii*, 167*i*, 184*ii*, 185*ii*, +Bk1
Kim Jong Seo (songwriter)	100*ii*
Thermal Island	100*ii*, 101*ii*
Kim Kiao Kak (Korean)	16*i*
Kingly Way	255*ii*
King Songtsen Gampo	187*ii*, 188*ii*
Kitarō, Nishida	226*i*
Kodály (composer)	297
Kǒng Fūzǐ	*see* Confucius
Koran (Qur'an)	221*ii*, +Bk1
Korea/n	16*i*, 65, 79*i*, 100*ii*, 147*i*, 156*ii*, 157*ii*, 212*ii*, 233*ii*, 244*ii*, 252*ii*, 253*ii*, 254*i*, 256*ii*, 257*ii*, 297, +Bk1
Cheju-do	147*i*, 158*ii*, +Bk1
Korean language	147*i*, 157*ii*, 233*ii*, 254*i*, +Bk1

Kṣitigarbha	16*i*
Kui Xing	154*ii*
Kūnmíng	127, 128, 144, **148–149**, **(150–156)**, 163*i*, 200*i*, **270–272**, 294*i*
Bamboo Temple	149, **270**, 294*i*,
Cuìhú Park	148
Dátián Grotto	154
Huátíng Temple	149*ii*–**150/1**
Lake Diān	**149**, **154–157**, **272**, 294*i*
Lóng Mén	**154**
mosque	**148**
Sānqīng Gé	**153**, 154*i*, **271**, 294*i*, +Bk1
Tàihuá Temple	**146/7**, **150–152**, **270**, 294*i*
Western Hills	149*ii*
Yuántōng Temple	148*i*
Kuntuzangpo	211*ii*
Kyugok (Myanmar)	**164**

L

Làhǔ (minority)	129, 130*i*
Lake Diān (Kūnmíng)	**149**, **154–157**, **272**, 294*i*
Lake Toba (Sumatra)	135*i*
lama	187*i*, 188*f*, +Bk1
Láncāng Jiāng (Mekong River)	127*i*, **137**, 167*i*, 187*i*
Lángdé	104 (map), **111–114**, 115
language	111*i*, *see* Chinese, Korean
Laos	103*ii*, 127*ii*, 137*i*
Lǎozi	154*ii*, +Bk1
Lashio (Myanmar)	163
Laughing Buddha	*see* Maitreya
Ledo (Assam)	163
Léishān	104, 111*i*
Léizhuāngxiāng Temple (Ruìlì)	**161–162**, 272
Lèshān	**200–201**, 202*i*
Grand Buddha	**200–201**
Lewis, C.S.	178*f*, 217*i*, 220*i*, 222*ii*, +Bk1
Lhasa	180*i*, 188*ii*
Lǐ (River)	**79–90**, **92**, **102**
Liángzhū culture	64*ii*
Lǐ Bái (poet)	15*ii*, 18*ii*
Lǐ Cúnxù	257*i*
Lìjiāng	**182–184**, 185*i*, 186, 190–191*i*, 196, **197–199**
Báishā	184*ii*–**185**, 198*i*
Black Dragon Pool	**183**
Jade Dragon Snow Mt	**182**, **183**, 184*ii*, 185*i*, **192/3**, 196*ii*–**197**, **199**
Naxi Orchestra	183*ii*–184, **197**
Yùfēng Monastery	185*i*
Lǐ Jìng, Emperor	199*ii*
limestone	91*ii*, 145*i*
Lín Bei Chu	**243**
Líng'gǔ Cave	14*ii*
Lin Yutang	103*i*
Lípíng	104 (map), 111*i*
Li Po	*see* Lǐ Bái
Lǐ River	**79–90**, **92**, **102**

Lǐ Sī (prime minister)	226*i*, +Bk1
literature, God of	**154**, +Bk1
Little Archibald	203*i*, 210, 241, 246*i*
Liúshā River	127 (map), 135*i*
Lǐ Yù, Emperor	193
lohan	149, 150*i*, 246*ii*, +Bk1
Lóngchuān (River)	159*i*, 160*i*, 165
Lóngé	104 (map), 106*ii*
longevity	151*ii*, 257*i*, +Bk1
Long March	103*ii*, 111*i*, 192*ii*, 243
Lóng Mén	**154**, 245*i*, +Bk1
Dàníng River	245*i*
Kūnmíng	**154**
Lóngshèng	104
lotus	64*i*, 151*ii*, **153**, 156*ii*, 228*ii*, 238*i*, +Bk1
Lotus Sutra	151*ii*, 156*ii*, 228*ii*, *see* Bk1 sutra
Lǔ Kūn	250*i*
Lùnán	144*ii*
Lùn Yǔ (Analects of Confucius)	228*i*, +Bk1
Luosuō River	127 (map), 140
Luòyáng	296*i*, +Bk1
lúshēng	111*ii*, **113–114**, 115, **117–118**
Lùxī (Mángshì)	159*i*
Lù Yǔ	13*i*

M

Macau	74*ii*
Madagascar	248*i*
Magic Square	233*ii*
Mahayana (Buddhism)	161*ii*, 188*ii*, +Bk1
mah-jong	65*ii*, 237*i*
Maitreya (Future/Laughing Buddha)	**160**, **200–201**, +Bk1
má jiàng (mah-jong)	65*ii*, 237*i*
Malaysia	248*i*
Mali River (Burma)	78 (map), 127*i*
Mandalay (Myanmar)	163*i*
Mandian	127 (map), 136*ii*
Mángshì (Lùxī)	159*i*
mantra	194, 297
Maori	126*ii*, +Bk1
Máo Zédōng	64*ii*, 124*ii*, 182*ii*, 188*i*, 236, 239*i*, **243**, +Bk1
Mara	**189**
marble	168, **170**, 183*i*
Marco Polo	*see* Polo
Mǎzhàn	**165**
McGinley, Phyllis	229*ii*
McGregor, Jim	234*ii*
McKenzie, F.A.	253*ii*, +Bk1
Mekong River (Láncāng Jiāng)	127*i*, **137**, 167*i*, 187*i*
Mencius (Mèngzi)	178*i*, 226*i*, +Bk1
meng	134*i*
Menghai	127 (map), 128*i*
Menghan	127 (map), 137, **138–140**
Wat Ban Suan Men Temple	**138–139**
Menghun	127 (map), **128–132**
Mengla	127 (map), 128*i*, 136*ii*
Menglun	127 (map), 136*ii*, 140, **257**
Tropical Plants Garden	140, **257**

Mengman	127 (map), 134*i*	
Mengzhe	127 (map), **133**, (134*i*)	
Mèngzi (Mencius)	178*i*, 226*i*, +Bk1	
Mexicans	221*ii*	
Aztecs	179*ii*	
Miao (minority)	103*ii*, 104, 105, 110*ii*, **111–114**, 115, **116–121**, 122*ii*, 123, 298	
Michelangelo	213*i*	
Mi Fei (Mĭ Fú)	18*ii*, (52), 56*i*, +Bk1	
Mĭ Fú (Mi Fei)	18*ii*, (52), 56*i*, +Bk1	
Mí Lè Fó (Future Buddha)	see Maitreya	
military	166*ii*, 238*i*	
Mín (River)	78 (map), **201**	
Míng Dynasty	11, 13*ii*, 128*i*, 148, 150*i*, 167*i*, 210*i*, 248*i*, 296*i*, +Bk1	
Míngyīn	185*ii*	
minorities (word not necessarily in text)	103*ii*, 104–**105**, **106–114**, 115, **116–121**, 122*ii*, 123, **124**, 126, 127*ii*, **128–132**, 133–135*i*, 137–139, 145, 148*ii*, 155*ii*, 159*i*, **170**, 182, 184*ii*–188, 191, 192*ii*, 199*i*, 257*i*, 298, +Bk1	
Bai	170, 191*ii*	
Bulang	129*i*, 139*ii*	
Dai	127*ii*, **128–132**, 133–135*i*, 137*i*, 138*ii*–139, 155*ii*, 159*i*	
Dong	103*ii*, 104, 105, 106, **107–110**, 115*ii*	
Gejia	123, 126	
Hani	129*i*, 132, **135**, 138*i*	
Huí	148*ii*, 191*ii*, +Bk1	
Jingpo	159*i*	
Lăhŭ	129*i*, 130*i*	
Miao	103*ii*, 104, 105, 110*ii*, **111–114**, 115, **116–121**, 122*ii*, 123, 298	
Mongol/ia(n)	135*i*, 148*ii*, 166, 190*i*, 235*ii*, 238*i*, 250*ii*, see Yuán Dynasty, +Bk1	
Naxi	182*ii*, 183*ii*–184, 186*i*, 191*ii*, 199*i*, 257*i*, 298	
Sani	145*i*	
Tibetan	184*ii*, 185*i*, 187–188, 191*ii*	
Yao	104, 105	
Yi	145	
Zhuang	103*ii*	
Mín River	78 (map), **201**	
Minya Konka	210*ii*–211*i*	
missionary	185*i*, +Bk1	
moha (delusion)	189*ii*, 228*ii*	
monastery	see temple	
money (paper)	234*i*, +Bk1	
Mongolia(n), Mongol	135*i*, 148*ii*, 166, 190*i*, 235*ii*, 238*i*, 250*ii*, see Yuán Dynasty, +Bk1	
monitor lizard	**138–139**	
monkey	187*i*, 203*ii*, see Bk1 *Journey to the West*	
Moon Hill, Yángshuò	91*ii*, **93–99**, **275**, 294*i*	
Morricone (composer)	299	
mosque	**148**, +Bk1	

mountains (shān)	13*ii*, 15*ii*, **16–18**, **19–63**, 66*ii*, 72, 80*i*, 103*ii*, **126**, 127*i*, 132, 163, 165–**166**, 167*ii*, 168, 170, **172/3**, **182/3**, 184*ii*, 185, 186*i*, 187*i*, **190**, **192/3**, 196*ii*–**197**, 199, 202*ii*–203, **204–215**, 217–220, **223**, **225**, 234*i*, 249*ii*, **255**, **262/3**, **264–267**, **276**, 294*i*, 297/8, +Bk1	
Cāngshān	163*ii*, 167*ii*, 168, 170, **172/3**	
Dàkōngshān	165*i*	
Dàyīng	165*i*	
Éméishān	18*ii*, 202*ii*–203, **204–215**, **217–220**, **223**, **225**, 234*i*	
Fódĭng (Pŭtuóshān)	66*ii*, 68*ii*	
Gāolígòng	163*ii*, 165*ii*	
Gònggā Shān	78 (map), 210*ii*–211*i*	
Hēikōngshān	165*i*	
Hēngduàn	163*ii*	
Héngshān	18*ii*, +Bk1	
Huángshān	13*ii*, 18*ii*, **19–63**, **264–267**, **276**, 294*i*	
Huáshān	18*ii*, **255**, +Bk1	
Jade Dragon Snow	**182**, **183**, 184*ii*, 185*i*, 186*i*, **192/3**, 196*ii*–**197**, 199	
Jiŭhuáshān	15*ii*, **16–18**, 36*ii*, 202*ii*, **263**, 294*i*	
Kagebuo (Kawakarpo)	78 (map), 187*i*	
Nù	163*ii*, 165*ii*–**166**	
Pŭtuóshān	**66–73**, (74*i*), **75/76**, 202*ii*, **268**, 294*i*	
Qīngshuīlang	163*ii*	
Shànzidou	**183**, 184*ii*, see Jade Dragon Snow	
Tàishān	18*ii*, 212*ii*, **262**, 294*i*, +Bk1	
Tánggŭlā	127*i*	
Wŭtáishān	190*i*, 202*ii*, 250*ii*, +Bk1	
Xiăokōngshān	165*i*	
Xuĕ	186*i*, **190**	
Yàndàng	18*ii*	
Yùlóngxuĕshān	see Jade Dragon Snow	
Yúntái	104 (map), **126**	
Mountbatten, Louis	242*ii*	
mouth organ	see: *lúshēng*	
mŭ	103*ii*, 128*i*	
Muse (Myanmar)	160*i*	
music	65*i*, (107*ii*), 108*ii*, 110, (111*ii*), 115, 166*ii*, 168, 184, 189*ii*, 204*ii*, 212*i*, 227*i*, 297–299, +Bk1	
Muslim	148*ii*, 191*ii*, 213*i*, 236*ii*, +Bk1	
Mussur (Thailand)	129*ii*	
Myanmar *or* Burma/ese	127, 137*i*, 159, 160*i*, 161, 163, **164**, 166*i*, 187*ii*, 235*i*, 242*ii*	

N

Nánbù	**235–240**, 244*ii*
fireworks	237–238*i*
temple	**238**
nanhu (music)	184*i*
Nánjīng	13*ii*, 15*i*, 242*ii*, +Bk1
Nánlíng	12 (map)
Nánzhào kingdom (Dàlī)	167*i*
Nàpà Hăi	**192–193**
Natya Shastra (Hinduism)	213
Naxi	182*ii*, 183*ii*–184, 186*i*, 191*ii*, 199*i*, 257*i*, 298
Nepal	187*ii*, 235*i*
Newman, Cardinal	227*i*
New Year (Chinese)	236*ii*–238, 240*i*
New Zealand	158*ii*, see Maori, +Bk1
nine (9)	72, 80*i*, 108*i*, 149*i*, 177*ii*, 203*ii*, 211*ii*, 212*ii*–216, 231*i*, 233, 240*i*, 245*ii*, +Bk1
Níngbō	65*ii*–**66**
Tiānyī Gé	65*ii*
nirvana	189, 226*i*, 228*ii*, 233*i*, +Bk1
Nishida Kitarō	226*i*
Nishitani Keiji	226*i*
Niú Xījī (poet)	246*i*
Nmai River (Burma)	78 (map), 127*i*
Nóng'ān Golden Duck Temple	**159–160**
Nù Jiāng (Salween River)	127*i*, 165*ii*–**166**
numbers	212–217*i*, 233, see nine, twelve
Nutinamu Unduk (Korean group)	257*ii*

O

Octagonal Pavilion, Jingzhen	**134**
oil	202*i*
O Mi To (Buddha)	297, +Bk1
opera	65*i*, 107*ii*, 229*i*, 297+Bk1
opium	103*ii*, 164*i*
Opium Wars	65*ii*, 248, +Bk1
orchid	151*ii*
owl	**135–136**, **274**

P

paddle wheel	246*i*
paddy (rice)	122
pagoda	133*ii*, 139*i*, 167*ii*–**168/9**, **262**, **273**, **274**, 294*i*, +Bk1
Small Wild Goose Pagoda	167*ii*, +Bk1
Three Pagodas	167*ii*–**168/9**, **273/4**, 294*i*
Wooden Pagoda	**262**, 294*i*, +Bk1
páilou (gate)	148, **150**, 194, +Bk1
pain (suffering)	217–221*i*, 224, 226*ii*, 227*i*, 228, 230, +Bk1
painting	150*ii*, **152/3**, **253**, **269**, **271**, 294*i*, +Bk1

Panchen Lama	188*f*
Panda	234-**235**
Lesser/Red	**235**
Pānlóng River	148*ii*
Pānzhīhuā	200*i*
paper (money)	234*i*, +Bk1
Paracelsus	101*ii*
Paul, Saint	221*ii*, +Bk1
peach	151*ii*, +Bk1
pearl	248*i*
Pearl River	248*i*
Peking	see Běijīng
peony	151*ii*, +Bk1
perfection	211*i*, 212*ii*–213, 220*i*, 221–224, 226–229*i*, 233*ii*
Peruvians	221*ii*
Pidgin English	252*ii*–253*i*
pig	**91, 110**–111*i*, 134*i*, 135*i*, 136*i*, 189*ii*, 192, +Bk1
pine	13*ii*, 151*ii*, 187*ii*, 256*ii*
Píngshān	78 (map), 127*ii*
pīnyīn (spell sound)	11
plum	151*ii*
poems, Chinese	15*ii*, 178*ii*, 193, 199*ii*, 202*ii*, 246*i*, 257*ii*, see Bk1
poet, poetry	see Blake, poems
Pogačnik, Marko	231*ii*
police	164*i*, see Bk1 PSB
Polo, Marco	64, 148*i*, 155*i*, 166, +Bk1
Pope, Alexander	178*ii*
population figures	103*i*
porcelain	65*ii*, 296*i*, +Bk1
porters	19-**20**
Portuguese	11, 65*ii*, 248*i*, 253*i*
Potala	66*ii*, +Bk1
Potter, Dennis	157*i*
pottery	13*ii*–**14**, 65*ii*, see porcelain, +Bk1
prayer flags	**138**, 194–**195**
province (word not always in text)	13*i*, 15*ii*, 16*ii*, 64, 79*ii*, 94, 103*ii*, 106, 111*i*, 122*ii*, 126, 127, 129*i*, 135*i*, 145*i*, 148, 159*i*, 162, 164*i*, 167, 170, 185*i*, 186*i*, 187*i*, 200, 202*i*, 235, 236, 241*ii*, 243, 244*ii*, 246*i*, 248*i*, 250, 296, see Tibet, Xīnjiāng, +Bk1
Ānhuī	15*ii*, 16*ii* (translation), +Bk1
Fújiàn	250*ii*
Guǎngdōng	248*i*
Guǎngxī	79*ii*, 94, 103*ii*
Guìzhōu	94, 103*ii*, 106, 111*i*, 122*i*, 126, 127*i*, +Bk1
Húběi	246*i*
Qīnghǎi	127*i*, 236*i*, 250*ii*, +Bk1
Shaanxi (Shǎnxī)	243*i*, 296*i*, +Bk1
Sìchuān	13*i*, 127*ii*, 200, 202*i*, 235, 236*i*, 244*ii*, 250*ii*, +Bk1
Yúnnán	94, 103*ii*, 127, 129*i*, 135*i*, 145*i*, 148, 159*i*, 162, 164*i*, 167, 170, 185*i*, 186*i*, 187*i*, 241*ii*, 296*i*
Zhèjiāng	64, +Bk1
Pǔ Jì Chán Sì	66 (map), 74*i*, **268**, 294*i*

Pǔtuóshān	**66-73**, (74*i*), **75/76**, 202*ii*, **268**, 294*i*
Cháoyáng Cave	66, **268**, 294*i*
Fán Yīn Cave	66 (map), 73
Fǎ Yǔ Chán Sì (temple)	66 (map), 70, **71-73**
Fódǐng Shān	66, 68*ii*
Hǎiyán Mén, Gate	66 (map), 75*ii*-**76**
Huì Jì Chán Sì (temple)	66 (map), **68-70**, **268**, 294*i*
Nine Dragon Brackets Hall	**72-73**
Pǔ Jì Chán Sì (temple)	66 (map), 74*i*, **268**, 294*i*
South Sky Gate	66 (map), 68*i*
Wisdom and Wealth Cave	66 (map), 74*i*
pygmies, Mbuti	221*ii*
Pythagoreans	212*ii*

Q

Qamdo (Tibet)	78 (map)
qì (breath of life)	230*ii*, 250*ii*, +Bk1
Qiáotóu	186*i*, 195
qílín	308
Qín, First Emperor of	226*i*, +Bk1
Qīngdǎo	**256**, +Bk1
Qīng Dynasty	11, 148*ii*, 248*i*, 296*i*, +Bk1
Qīnghǎi Province	127*i*, 236*i*, 250*ii*, +Bk1
Qīnglóng Cave (temple)	124*i*, **269**, 294*i*
Qīngshuǐlang (Mtns)	163*ii*
Qīngshuǐ River	104 (map), 122*ii*-**123**
Qín Guān (poet)	257*ii*
Qīngyáng	12 (map)
Qīngyī River	201*i*
Qíyuán Monastery	15*ii*
Qú (River)	78 (map), 235*ii*, 240*ii*
Qur'an (Koran)	221*ii*, +Bk1

R

Rābi'a al-'Adawiyya	226*i*
rāga (attachment)	189*ii*
Rāhu(la)	153, +Bk1
railway, *or* train	15*ii*, 64*ii*, 126*ii*, 144, 200*i*, 246*i*, **247**, +Bk1
rainforest	136*ii*–137*i*, 140, see forests, +Bk1
Rama (Hinduism)	213*i*
Rangitoto Island (NZ)	158*ii*
Rangoon (Burma)	163*i*
rapids	127*ii*, 244*ii*-245
Red Guards	115*ii*, 139*i*, see Cultural Revolution
Red Hat	185*i*
Red River	78 (map), 127*i*
Red Sea	248*i*
religion	see Buddhism, Christian, Confucian, Dào, Dongba, God, Hindu, Muslim, +Bk1
rhododendron	185*i*
rice	65*i*, **104, 105**, 119*ii*, **122, 123**, 129*i*, 132, 134*i*, 135*i*, 191*ii*, +Bk1
Rig Veda	212*i*, +Bk1

river (hé, jiāng)	13*i*, 65*ii*, **79-90, 92, 102**, 105-**106**, 122*ii*-**123, 124-125**, 126*i*, 127, 135*i*, **137**, 140, 148*ii*, 159*i*, 160*i*, 165, **166**, 167*i*, 182*ii*, 186*i*, 187*i*, 195, 199*ii*, **201**, 213*i*, 234*i*, 235*i*, **236**, 240-**241**, 242*ii*, **243**-**245**, 246, 248*i*, 258, **277-292**, +Bk1
Cháng	see Yángzi
Chóng'ānjiāng	104 (map), 126*i*
Dàdù	78 (map), **201**
Dàníng	78 (map), **245**, 246*i*
Dàyīng	165*i*
Dūliǔ	104 (map), 105-**106**
Éméi	201*i*, 234*i*
Fú	78 (map), 235*ii*, 240*ii*
Fùchūn	12 (map)
Ganges	213*i*
Hàn	246*ii*
Irrawaddy	127*i*, 159*i*, 165*i*
Jiālíng	235*ii*, **236, 240-241**, 242*ii*
Jīnshā	127, 182*ii*, 186*i*, 187*i*, 199*ii*, 241*ii*, see Yángzi
Láncāng (Mekong)	127*i*, **137**, 167*i*, 187*i*
Lí	**79-90, 92, 102**
Liúshā	127 (map), 135*i*
Lóngchuān	159*i*, 160*i*, 165
Luosuō	127 (map), 140
Mali	78 (map), 127*i*
Mekong	see Láncāng
Mín	78 (map), **201**
Nmai	78 (map), 127*i*
Nù (Salween)	127*i*, 165*ii*-**166**
Pānlóng	148*ii*
Pearl	248*i*
Qīngshuǐ	104 (map), 122*ii*-**123**
Qīngyī	201*i*
Qú	78 (map), 235*ii*, 240*ii*
Red	127*i*
Róng	104 (map)
Salween	see Nù
Shweli	78 (map), 159*i*
	see Lóngchuān
Tuō	78 (map), 235*ii*,
Wǔyáng	104 (map), **124-125**, +Bk1
Xun	104 (map)
Yangtze	see Yángzi
Yángzi	13*i*, 127, 182*ii*, 186*i*, 187*i*, 195, 236*i*, **240-241**, 242*ii*, **243, 244**, (245)-246, 258, **277-292**, +Bk1
Yáo	12 (map), 65*ii*
Yǒng	12 (map), 65*ii*
Yuán (Red)	127*i*
Zhū (Pearl)	248*i*
Rock, Joseph	164*ii*, 184*ii*, 185, 210*ii*
rockets	238*i*
Roman Catholic	see Catholic
Róng (River)	104 (map)
Róngjiāng	111*i*
Ruìlì	**159-160**, 294*i*
Hánshā Temple	**160**
Léizhuāngxiāng Temple	**161-162**, 272
Nóng'ān Golden Duck Temple	**159-160**

S

Sakyamuni (historical Buddha) 66*ii*, 150*ii*, 151*ii*, **153**, 156*ii*, 187*ii*, 188*ii*, **189**, 228*ii*, 250*i*, **271**, 294*i*, *see* Buddha, +Bk1
Salisbury, Harrison E. 103*ii*
salt 202*i*, +Bk1
Salween River *see* Nù Jiāng
Samantabhadra 211
saṃsāra 189*i*, 228*ii*
Sāndōupíng 246*ii*
Sani (minority) 145*i*
Sānjiāng 104–105
Sānqīng Gé (Kūnmíng) **153**, 154*i*, **271**, 294*i*, +Bk1
Sanskrit 66*ii*, 187*ii*, 257*i*, 297, +Bk1
Sarasvatī 159*i*
Sārnāth (India) 153, 188*ii*
Scott Peck, M. 220*i*, +Bk1
Second World War *see* World War II
selfishness 221*ii*–222*i*, 224, 226*i*, 227*i*, 232*ii*
Seoul (Korea) 254*i*
servants **252**–253
Shaanxi (Shǎnxī) Province 243*i*, 296*i*, +Bk1
Shakespeare 101*ii*, 226*i*
Shànghǎi **74**, 235*i*, 242*i*, 246*i*, 252*ii*, 294*i*, +Bk1
  Pǔjiāng Hotel **74**, +Bk1
  Yù Yuán 294*i*, +Bk1
  Shànhuà Temple **262**, 294*i*, +Bk1
Shànzidou **183**, 184*ii*, *see* Jade Dragon Snow Mtn
Shàoxīng 64*ii*–**65**
shēng *see*: *lúshēng*
Shěnyáng 250*ii*, +Bk1
Shēn Yīn Yǔ 250*i*
Shībīng 104 (map), 124*ii*
Shīdòng 104 (map), 122*ii*–123
Shígǔ 78 (map), 127*ii*, 182*ii*
Shǐ Huángdì *see* First Emperor of Qín
Shílín (Stone Forest) **142–147**, **270**
Shing Suíjiāng 127*ii*
shǔxiàng 4
Shweli River 78 (map), 159*i*, *see* Lóngchuān
Sìchuān Province 13*i*, 127*ii*, 200, 202*i*, 235, 236*i*, 244*ii*, 250*ii*, +Bk1
Silk Road 65*ii*, 159*i*, 188*ii*, 202*i*, 248*i*, +Bk1
Sino-Japanese wars (words not necessarily in text) 65*ii*, 102*i*, 163*i*, 202*ii*, 242*ii*–243, +Bk1
Sistine Chapel 213*i*
Sitwell 238*i*
Snow, Edgar 242*ii*
Sogyal Rinpoche 220*i*, 228*ii*
Sŏn Buddhism 212*ii*, +Bk1
Sonam Gyamtsho 190*i*
Song Chol (Korean) 180*i*, +Bk1
Sòng Dynasty 11, 13*i*, 238*i*, 240*ii*, 296*i*, +Bk1
Sòng Měi Líng **242**

Songs of Innocence/Experience 98, 178*i*, 179*ii*
spider **140**
spirit *see* Holy Spirit, *qì*, +Bk1
spirit way **251**, **254**, **308**, +Bk1
spring water 13*ii*
Stanford (composer) 174*i*
Stilwell, General 163*ii*, **242–243**
Stone Forest **142–147**, **270**
Strauss, Richard (composer) 233*i*, 299
stupa, *or* dagoba 129*i*, 133*i*, **138**, **159**, **161–162**, **164**, 187*ii*, **272**, 294*i*, +Bk1
suffering (pain) 217–221*i*, 224, 226*ii*, 227*i*, 228, 230, +Bk1
Sufism 226*i*
sugudu (music) 184*i*
Sumatra 135*i*, *see* Indonesia
sun 98, 101*ii*, 156*i*, 165*i*, 170, 178*i*, 194, 204, 210*ii*, 212*ii*, 236*i*, 254, +Bk1
sutra 151*ii*, 156*ii*, 228*ii*, +Bk1
Sūzhōu 13*ii*, +Bk1
Swedenborg, Emanuel 231*i*

T

taegum (flute) 297
Táihuá Temple (Kūnmíng) **146/7**, **150–152**, **270**, 294*i*
Táijiāng 104 (map), 115*i*
Tàipíng Rebellion 16*i*, 64*ii*, +Bk1
Tàishān 18*ii*, 212*ii*, **262**, 294*i*, +Bk1
Táiwān 74*ii*, 252*ii*
Táng Dynasty 11, 15*ii*, 18*ii*, 65*ii*, 80*i*, 133*i*, 148*i*, 167*ii*, 193*f*, 199*f*, 202*ii*, 246*i*, 257*i/f*, 296*i*, 298, +Bk1
Tánggǔlā Mountains 127*i*
Tāngkǒu 12 (map), 18*ii*
Táng Lóng 123
tanka 189*ii*, +Bk1
tantra 297
Tanzania 297
Tao *see* Dào
Tartar 166, *see* Mongol
Tavener, John (composer) 298
Taylor, Thomas 228*i*
tax 103*i*, 134*i*
tea 13–14, 127*ii*, 248*i*, +Bk1
teapots 13*ii*–14, 18*i*, 36*ii*
temple (monastery, sì, miào) 13*ii*, 15*ii*, 16–17, 18*i*, 66*ii*, **68–73**, 74*i*, 124*i*, **133**, **134**, **138–139**, **146/7**, 148*i*, 149, **150–152**, **153**, **154**, **159–162**, 184*ii*, 185*i*, **186–190**, 191*ii*, 203, **238**, 243*ii*, **253**, **262**, **268**, **269**, **270**, **271**, **272**, 294*i*, *see* mosque, pagoda, +Bk1
  Bamboo (Kūnmíng) 149, **270**, 294*i*
  Dátiān (Kūnmíng) **154**
  Fán Yīn (Pǔtuóshān) 66 (map), 73
  Fǎ Yǔ Chán Sì (Pǔtuóshān) 66 (map), 70, **71–73**
  (Fēngdū) 243*i*, +Bk1
  Hánshā (Ruìlì) **160**
  Hóngchūnpíng (Éméishān) 203*i*

  Huátíng (Kūnmíng) 149*ii*–**150/1**
  Huì Jì Chán Sì (Pǔtuóshān) 66 (map), **68–70**, **268**, 294*i*
  Jiétáng Sōnglín (Zhōngdiàn) **186–190**, 191*ii*, +Bk1
  Jingzhen 127 (map), **134**
  Léizhuāngxiāng (Ruìlì) **161–162**, **272**
  (Mengzhe) **133**
  (Nánbù) **238**
  Nóng'ān Golden Duck (Ruìlì) **159–160**
  Pǔ Jì Chán Sì (Pǔtuóshān) 66 (map), 74*i*, **268**, 294*i*
  Qīnglóng Cave (Zhènyuǎn) 124*i*, **269**, 294*i*
  Qíyuán Monastery (Jiǔhuáshān) 15*ii*
  Sānqīng Gé (Kūnmíng) **153**, 154*i*, **271**, 294*i*, +Bk1
  Shànhuà (Dàtóng) **262**, 294*i*, +Bk1
  Tàihuá (Kūnmíng) **146/7**, **150–152**, **270**, 294*i*
  Tiānhòu (Tiānjīn) **253**, +Bk1
  Wat Ban Suan Men (Menghan) **138–139**
  Wat Gau Temple (Mengzhe) **133**
  Wisdom and Wealth (Pǔtuóshān) 66 (map), 74*i*
  Xiānfēng (Éméishān) 203
  Yuántōng (Kūnmíng) 148*i*
  Yùfēng (Lìjiāng) 185*i*
  Zhǎntánlín (Jiǔhuáshān) 16*ii*–**17**, 18*i*
Téngchōng **164/5**
  Mǎzhàn **165**
termites 200*i*
Thailand, Thai 103*ii*, 128*i*, 129*ii*, 133*i*, 134*i*, 135*i*, 137*i*, 139*i*
thang ka *see* tanka
Theory of Relativity 158*i*
Theravada (Buddhism) 149*i*, 161*ii*, +Bk1
Three Fires (Buddhism) 228*ii*
Three Gates to Hell (Hinduism) 228*ii*
Three Gorges 243*ii*, **244–245**, 246
  Three Gorges Dam 246
Three Kingdoms 234*i*
Three Poisons (Buddhism) 229*ii*
Tiānchí **258/9**, 294*i*, +Bk1
  Dà Dōng Gōu **259**, 294*i*, +Bk1
  Keng Hoens valley **258**, 294*i*, +Bk1
Tiānhòu Temple **253**, +Bk1
Tiānjīn 65*f*, **253**, +Bk1
  Tiānhòu Temple **253**, +Bk1
Tibet, Tibetan 127*i*, 150*i*, 184*ii*, 185*i*, 186*i*, 187–190*i*, 191*ii*, 194, 210*ii*, 211, 212*ii*, 221*ii*, 222*ii*, 228*ii*, 250*i*, 297, +Bk1
Tibetan minority 184*ii*, 185*i*, 187–188, 191*ii*
Tietjens, Eunice 212*ii*
Tiger Leaping Gorge 127*ii*, 186*ii*, 195
Tónglíng 15*ii*
Tournemire (composer) 217*ii*
trackers 244*ii*–245*i*
train *see* railway
trees *see* forests
Tropical Plants Garden, Menglun 140, **257**

Tsongkhapa	189*ii*	Wŭtáishān	190*i*, 202*ii*, 250*ii*, +Bk1	Jīnshā Jiāng	127, 182*ii*, 186*i*, 187*i*, 199*ii*, 241*ii*
Tŭlŭfān	see Turfan	Wŭyáng River/Gorge	104 (map), **124–125**, +Bk1	Yángzōng Lake	144*ii*
Túnxī	12 (map)			Yanni	299
Tuō River	78 (map), 235*ii*			Yao (minority)	104, 105
Turfan, Bezeklik Caves	**259**, +Bk1	**X**		Yao Guo Mo	**251**
Turpan	see Turfan			Yáo River	65*ii*
twelve (12)	189*ii*, 212–215, 216*ii*, 231, 233*ii*, 245*ii*, 297, +Bk1	Xī'ān	167*ii*, 233*ii*, see Cháng'ān, +Bk1	Yashodharā	**153**, 294*i*
		Shaanxi History Museum	233*ii*, +Bk1	Yellow Emperor	212*i*, 221*ii*, +Bk1
typhoon	65*ii*, 66*ii*			Yellow Hat	189*ii*
		Small Wild Goose Pagoda	167*ii*, +Bk1	Yi (minority)	145
U				Yíchāng	246
		Xiānfēng Temple	203	Yì Jīng (I Ching)	204*ii* (Zhōu Yi), +Bk1
Unitarian	157*ii*	Xianyuan	12 (map), 18*ii*	Yíliáng	78 (map), 144*ii*
USA	see America	Xiǎokōngshān	165*i*	Yīngxiàn	**262**, 294*i*, +Bk1
usnisa (Buddhism)	153	Xiǎo Zhōngdiàn	186*ii*	Yíxīng	**13–14**, **263**, 294*i*
		xiezhi	**251**	Yōng River	12 (map), 65*ii*
V		Xīji, Niú	246*i*	Yuán Dynasty	11, 148*i*, 233*ii*, 248*i*, 296*i*, see Mongol, +Bk1
		Xīngpíng	80*i*, **90–91**		
Vaisheshika (Hinduism)	213*i*	Xīnjiāng	235*ii*, +Bk1	Yuán Jiāng	127*i*
Vaishravana	189*ii*	Xīshuāngbǎnnà	127, **128–140**, 159*i*, 257	Yuántōng Temple	148*i*
Vajrasattva	297			Yùfēng Monastery (Lìjiāng)	185*i*
Vajrayāna	188*ii*, 189*ii*	Banla	127 (map), 135	Yugoslavia	95
Vārāṇasī (India)	188*ii*	Dai minority	127*ii*, **128–132**, 133–135*i*, 137*i*, 138*ii*–139, 155*i*, 159*i*	Yùlóngxuěshān	see Jade Dragon Snow Mountain
Vatican	213*i*			Yúnnán Province	94, 103*ii*, 127, 129*i*, 135*i*, 145*i*, 148, 159*i*, 162, 164*i*, 167, 170, 185*i*, 186*i*, 187*i*, 241*ii*, 296*i*
Veda (Hindu)	212*i*, +Bk1				
Vietnam	127*ii*, 144*ii*	Gǎnlǎnbà	137*i*, see Menghan		
Virūdhaka	189*i*–190	Hani minority	129*i*, 132, **135**, 138*i*		
Virūpaksha	**189**	Jǐnghóng	128–129*i*, 130, 136*i*, **137**, 159*i*	Yúntái Mountain	104 (map), **126**
Vishnu (Hinduism)	213*i*			Yutang, Lin	103*i*
volcanoes, volcanic	**165**, 296*i*	Jingzhen	127 (map), **134**	yurt	**258**, 294*i*, +Bk1
		Mekong River	127*i*, **137**, 167*i*, 187*i*		
W		Menghan	127 (map), 137, **138–140**	**Z**	
wall(s), city	148*i*, 167*i*, 248*i*, 249*i*, **261**, 294*i*, +Bk1	Menghun (market)	127 (map), **128–132**	Zeus	212*ii*
				Zhāngfēng	164*i*
Wǎndīng	163–164*i*	Menglun	127 (map), 136*ii*, 140, **257**	Zhāng'gōng Cave	14*ii*, 294*i*
Wáng Bì	204*ii*			Zhāng Héng (astronomer)	296*i*
Wáng Bó (author)	246*i*	Mengzhe	127 (map), **133**, (134*i*)	Zhǎntánlín Temple	16*ii*–**17**, 18*i*
Wáng Dào (Kingly Way)	255*ii*	Octagonal Pavilion	**134**	Zhàoxìng	104 (map), **106–110**, **268**, 294*i*
Wáng Tíng Xiāng	99	Tropical Plants Garden	140, **257**		
Wáng Wéi (poet)	193, 293	Xīzhōu	**174–177**	Dong singing	110
Wáng Yángmíng	256*i*	Xuānchéng	12 (map)	drum towers	**108**
Wáng Zhīhuàn (poet)	158*i*	Xuān Kē	184*ii*, 198*i*	opera theatre	**107**
warlords	243*i*, +Bk1	Xuán Zàng	188*ii*, 202*i*, 246*ii*, +Bk1	Zhèjiāng Province	64, +Bk1
wars, China and Japan	65*ii*, 102*i*, 163*i*, 202*ii*, 242*ii*–243, +Bk1	Xuánzōng, Brilliant Emperor	202*ii*, +Bk1	Zhènjiāng	13*ii*, 258, **277–292**, +Bk1
				Jiāoshān	258, **277–292**
Wat Ban Suan Men Temple	**138–139**	Xuě Mountains	186*i*, **190**	Zhènyuǎn	**124**, **269**, 294*i*, +Bk1
Wat Gau Temple	**133**	Xun (River)	104 (map)	Zhōngdiàn	185*ii*, **186–195**, +Bk1
Wénchāng (God of Literature)	**154**, +Bk1	Xúnzi	226*i*	Jiétáng Sōnglín Monastery	**186–190**, 191*ii*, +Bk1
Wen Tiānshān	239*ii*	**Y**		Nàpà Hǎi	**192–193**
wheel	**188**, **189**, 212*i*, 246*i*			Xuě Mountains	186*i*, **190**
Wild Swans (book)	236*i*	yab-yum (father-mother)	189*ii*, +Bk1	Zhōng Yōng (Doctrine of the Mean)	229*i*, +Bk1
Wind and Rain Bridge	104, **105**, 111*ii*, see bridge	yāna (Buddhism)	212*ii*		
		Yán'ān	103*ii*, 243	Zhōu Dynasty	11, 213*i*, 233*ii*, +Bk1
Wisdom and Wealth Cave (temple)	66 (map), 74*i*	Yàndàng, Mount	18*ii*	Zhōu Ēnlái	**243**
		Yáng Guìfēi	202*ii*	Zhou Long (composer)	298
World War II (Second World War)	102*i*, **163**, **242–243**, +Bk1	Yángshuò	**79–80**, **91–92**, 294*i*	Zhōushān Island	12 (map), 66*ii*
		Lí River	**79–90**, **92**, 102	Zhōu Yì (Circular Changes)	204*ii*, +Bk1
Wŭchāng	246*ii*	Moon Hill	91*ii*, **93–99**, 275, 294*i*	Zhuang (minority)	103*ii*
Wŭhàn	241*i*, 242*ii*, 243*ii*, 246*ii*	Xīngpíng	80*i*, **90–91**	Zhuàngzōng, Emperor	257*f*
Wúhú	12 (map), 15*ii*	Yangtze	see Yángzi River	Zhū Jiāng (Pearl River)	248*i*
Wú Láiqìng	154*i*	Yángzi River	13*i*, 127, 182*ii*, 186*i*, 187*i*, 195, 236*i*, **240–241**, 242*ii*, **243**, **244**, (**245**)–246, 258, **277–292**, +Bk1	Zhū Xī (philosopher)	229*i*, +Bk1
wūlóng tea	13*ii*			zǐsha (purple sand)	13*ii*
Wūshān	**244**, 245*i*			zodiac	212*i*
				Zoroastrian	221*ii*, +Bk1

A ***qílín*** along the spirit way,
near the Míng tombs, Běijīng

Comprising elements of dragon, lion, ox, deer, endowed with eyebrows of fire, covered in fish scales, and here with double horns, the *qílín* represents the highest rank of honour in the military, the second being lion, third leopard, fourth tiger, fifth bear, and so on up to 9th place. These insignia of rank were traditionally sewn onto a person's clothing as a square piece of material on the chest or back. The beast's *raison d'être* is to eradicate evil, hence the purpose of the lethal horns that also bestow the magical property of forecasting the future.